◆ ━━━━━━━ ◆

INTRODUCTION TO COLLECTIVE BEHAVIOR

David L. Miller
Western Illinois University

**WAVELAND
PRESS, INC.**
Prospect Heights, Illinois

To my son, Benjamin Rogers Miller,
his grandfather, Virgil Dalton Miller,
and his great grandfather, Archie Alvin Miller

For information about this book, write or call:

Waveland Press, Inc.
P.O. Box 400
Prospect Heights, Illinois 60070
(312) 634-0081

Copyright © 1985 by David L. Miller
1989 reissued by Waveland Press, Inc.

ISBN 0-88133-436-7

Printed in the United States of America

7   6   5   4   3   2   1

CONTENTS

PART

• 2 •

COLLECTIVE BEHAVIOR IN EVERYDAY LIFE 73

PART

· 3 ·

◆ FOREWORD ◆

The study of collective behavior and social movements began during the last half of the nineteenth century. It was part of an attempt to understand the sources, the development, and the consequences of the social and political revolutions of the preceding one hundred years. The ideas that developed between 1895 and 1925 dominated sociological thought about collective behavior and social movements for the next several decades.

Between 1962 and 1972 there were thousands of demonstrations, hundreds of riots, and dozens of social movements on college and university campuses and in the urban centers of the United States, Western Europe, and Japan. Although other decades may have included as many contentious gatherings and social movements, I doubt there has been another decade in which so many observers of such phenomena have had at least some training in the social and behavioral sciences. Such training may or may not have led some people to participate; but their observations—as participants, spectators, or researchers—led many to a subsequent examination and evaluation of the interpretations made by social and behavioral scientists about what they had seen and heard.

The more those interpretations were examined the less satisfactory they proved to be. Few people could accept the idea that participants in crowds, demonstrations, or riots became irrational and lost control of their behavior (contagion or transformation theories); nor could they accept the idea that aberrant psychological predispositions compelled participation in demonstrations, riots, or social movements (convergence or predisposition theories). In short, the claims of traditional social and behavioral scientists about the sources and consequences of collective behavior and social movements were not consistent with what witnesses had seen and heard. Nor were those claims supported by the extensive research that many social and behavioral scientists subsequently carried out in the late 1960s and early 1970s. Together these observations and research findings challenged the traditional characterizations and explanations of individual and collective behavior in crowds, demonstrations, disasters, social movements, and riots. The traditional views would no longer suffice.

The historian of science Thomas Kuhn argues that scientific revolutions are never accomplished by merely refuting the claims of earlier theoretical perspectives. It is not enough to merely demonstrate that those views are not supported by the evidence. Alternative perspectives must be set forth to explain all that earlier perspectives have explained and more. We have not yet witnessed an accomplished scientific revolution in the study of collective behavior and social movements because no comprehensive alternate perspective has yet been developed. But we have learned a great deal since 1960. Admittedly, we may have learned more about what does not occur and what does not explain than we have learned about what does occur and what does explain. But even this "negative" knowledge is useful if it debunks outdated stereotypes and warns of paths not promising to pursue. A great many fragments of new characterizations and partial explanations of collective behavior and social movements have been developed. In fact, this body of "negative" information and partial characterization and explanation has grown to such proportions that it has become virtually inaccessible to most professors, not to mention their students. A summary of this work has been sorely needed and is long overdue.

Fortunately for students and their professors, David Miller has now written an excellent introduction to the study of collective behavior and social movements. It reflects what transpired during and after the events of the 1960s and 1970s. He covers a very wide range of phenomena in an informed and interesting manner. Perhaps more important is how he introduces the reader to these phenomena.

There are no immaculate perceptions of collective behavior and social movements, nor of any of the other phenomena addressed in Miller's book. We perceive phenomena from the conceptual perspectives with which we have been introduced to these phenomena. These perspectives select and shape what we see and hear. To change the perspective from which one approaches a phenomenon is to change what one may learn. Many textbooks inform readers that there are several different perspectives from which to examine phenomena and that each has its advantages and limitations. Unfortunately, most textbooks then proceed to examine the phenomena from just *one* of these perspectives. Miller introduces students to the phenomena from several *different* perspectives, thereby increasing what they might perceive and understand about these phenomena.

The first perspective, social contagion, dates from the late nineteenth century. Two more perspectives, value-added and emergent norm, were developing around 1960 in response to the limitations of social contagion theory and guided a great deal of thinking about and research on collective behavior and social movements through the 1960s and 1970s. The fourth perspective, social behaviorism/interactionism,

is more recent and less well developed than the other three. Miller clearly prefers this fourth perspective and has made a number of important contributions to its development and application. Nonetheless, I believe he accurately summarizes all four perspectives, showing both the advantages and limitations of each through well-chosen examples.

I have found David Miller's book a very interesting and useful overview for several reasons: he commands a wide range of the scholarly literature; he has a talent for summarizing complex arguments in a clear, succinct manner. And, perhaps most important, he has observed as a researcher and as a participant many of the phenomena about which he writes. He has witnessed disaster; he has been on the picket line; he has observed street actions and riots; he has been at the barricades. I think these experiences combine with his academic knowledge in a way that will make his book as provocative and informative for beginning students as it will prove useful to their professors.

Clark McPhail
University of Illinois,
Urbana-Champaign

First and foremost, *Introduction to Collective Behavior* is written to be a genuine teaching text. It is not a single-perspective analysis of the field nor a book of readings. It is written with two parties in mind: the student and the teacher. For the student, there are frequent narratives and descriptions of collective behavior events designed to create an intuitive feel for the subject matter. Care was taken to use a lively writing style that does not sacrifice scholarly precision.

For the teacher, *Introduction to Collective Behavior* is sufficiently broad in scope that a course can be designed around the text with a minimum of additional readings. The mass hysteria, emergent norm, value-added, and social behavioral/interactionist (SBI) perspectives are used throughout the text. These four perspectives represent both the classic and contemporary traditions and offer widely divergent characterizations, observations, and conclusions about collective behavior. Additional paradigms, such as the resource mobilization approach to social movements, are introduced when relevant.

Features

A large number of collective behavior topics are covered ranging from rumor to social movements.

Individual topics are examined from the standpoint of the mass hysteria, emergent norm, value-added, and social behavioral/interactionist perspectives.

Narratives and descriptive accounts introduce each collective behavior topic. This material reduces the need for extensive outside readings.

Research methods are emphasized. Chapter 3 is devoted to methods of collective behavior research. In this chapter, students gain an appreciation of the problems involved in studying collective behavior, as well as solutions to these problems. In other chapters, the research methods used by McPhail and his colleagues in studying the origins and occurrence of assembling processes are discussed. Gamson's recent laboratory research is presented in the protest chapter.

An overview of mass hysteria studies is presented in Chapter 5. New approaches to the study of such unusual social events are also presented.

Disaster and riot research is examined from the individual, organizational, community, and societal levels of analysis.

Social movement chapters are included in which movements are examined from the standpoint of the four general theories as well as the resource mobilization perspective.

Versatility

Introduction to Collective Behavior offers a number of alternatives for course design. Some teachers prefer to teach collective behavior apart from social movements. The text offers an ample number of traditional collective behavior topics, such as rumor, mass hysteria, fads, disasters, and riots, from which a course can be built.

This text is also suitable for teaching social movements. For instance, Chapters 1, 2, 3, 4,

12, 13, 14, and 15 provide a sound social movement sequence. The first four chapters introduce students to collective behavior and social movements, general theories, research methods, and communication processes. Chapters 12, 13, 14, and 15 examine organizational, community, and societal responses to collective violence, the origins and dynamics of protest, and characterizations and explanations of social movements.

Acknowledgments

First, I would like to thank the following people for their thoughtful reviews of the manuscript: Rodger Bates, Lambuth College; Carl J. Couch, University of Iowa; Jerry M. Lewis, Kent State University; Reid Luhman, Eastern Kentucky University; Donald C. Reitzes, Georgia State University; and Howard Robboy, Trenton State College.

During the writing of this book, I have become keenly aware of my obligations to others. I am fortunate to have been taught by kind masters: Carl J. Couch introduced me to sociology and collective behavior as an undergraduate, and he continues to be one of my major sources of intellectual stimulation; Robert L. Stewart patiently taught me the ideas upon which the SBI framework is based; and Clark McPhail first took me and other students into the field to study collective behavior in a systematic fashion.

While writing this book, I was aided by three department chairs whose leadership provided a conducive environment for such efforts. Igolima T. D. Amachree provided much personal support in the early stages of the book. Richard T. Schaefer offered much advice and support during the production of this book. And Richard A. Mathers has contributed his warm friendship, help, and good humor throughout.

Many other colleagues have also provided their support and insight. In particular, John Wozniak, who read much of the manuscript as it was being written, offered almost daily encouragement. Kenneth J. Mietus provided a reliable sounding board for many of the ideas presented here and was particularly helpful with the chapters on social movements. Grant Bogue spent many hours in the darkroom preparing photographs for the book, and Diane Sandage kindly offered her proofreading skills when deadlines were near. I am also grateful to Carol A. Skiles, who put several of the chapters on word processor, and to my graduate assistants Pauline M. Brink and Herbert W. Bain, two sleuths who were always able to track down even the most obscure library material.

The staff of Wadsworth Publishing Company was of great assistance to me as well. In particular, the enthusiasm and encouragement of Sheryl Fullerton, the sociology editor, helped generate the momentum needed to turn a partially finished manuscript into a college textbook. The hard work and patience of Vicki Friedberg, the production editor, made the production of the book exciting and rewarding rather than burdensome.

Finally, I would like to acknowledge the great contributions provided by Kathleen "Kitty" Miller and our children, Benjamin, Catherine, and Christina. In the final analysis, my family provided the necessary personal support, encouragement, and welcome diversion that made the writing of this book possible. To you all, thank you.

INTRODUCTION: THEORY AND RESEARCH

CHAPTER 1

The Field of Collective Behavior

The field of collective behavior may have more diverse contents than any other field in sociology. All sorts of social phenomena have found their way into it. At present, the field contains things we encounter every day, such as rumors, fads, and crowds at concerts, theaters, shopping centers, and parties. Sometimes we are asked to circulate petitions, strike for better wages, or join other witnesses at the scene of an accident. We may take shelter with our family when tornado sirens sound or hurricane warnings are given. All these activities constitute collective behavior.

The field also contains events that most of us have experienced only vicariously through movies and television. For example, few Americans have firsthand experience with riots and revolutions. Most Americans experienced the rash of urban riots in the late 1960s only through video images of buildings burning and police brandishing nightsticks, shooting tear gas, and chasing people identified as "looters." Politicians describe revolutions in terms of military aid, human rights violations, and the spread of communism, but our notions of revolutions are also shaped by news stories of "death squads" and "rebel victories." The video image of revolution is one of armored personnel carriers on city streets or helicopters spraying the jungle with machine-gun fire.

The movies create dramatic images of collective behavior. Terrorized people stampede over one another in fleeing the monster that is destroying the city. Meddling citizens' groups keep tough police officers, like Clint Eastwood's Dirty Harry, from doing their jobs. The dregs of the town meet at the saloon and form a lynch mob. These cinematic images of panic flight, community action groups, and lynch mobs are often quite compelling, but few of us have enough firsthand experience with these events to judge their accuracy.

How did collective behavior come into being as a separate field of sociological study? To answer this question we must look at some Western history and the "new science" of sociology as set forth by the early writers.

The Idea of Collective Behavior

Two tremendous forces of social change were unleashed during the eighteenth century: the first was the *industrial revolution*, which was well underway in England by 1800, and the second was the *rise of popular democracy*, which culminated in the American and French revolutions. By 1850, the two Great Revolutions of industrialization and democracy had swept away the old order of Europe.

For several hundred years, the old order had rested on rigid distinctions of social status: nobleman, churchman, peasant, and serf. Each had a clear and traditionally defined role in society, and few people questioned or seriously challenged this arrangement. The old order also had a decidedly rural character. Land ownership was the surest and nearly the only source of wealth, power, and respectability. The nobility and the Church, of course, owned most of the land. Everyday life followed the relaxed rhythm of the seasons. Nearly everyone worked from sunup to sundown, planting in the spring, harvesting in the fall, and spending long winters isolated in small hamlets and villages scattered across Europe.

The industrial revolution changed all of this in a surprisingly short time. With the invention of the steam engine came factories, the ownership of which soon challenged ownership of land as a source of wealth. The nobility was threatened by a new social class composed of factory owners and merchants who sold the products of the factories.

Factories also changed the character and rhythm of social life. Peasants and serfs left the land and crowded into the cities to be near the factories. Ways of life suited to small communities quickly eroded under the fierce competition for jobs, food, and shelter in the cities. The pace of work was now set not by the seasons but by the erratic fluctuations of the marketplace. New factories also destroyed the influence of centuries-old guilds or protective associations for skilled workers. In the factories and mines, people adjusted as best they could to the nearly inhuman work pace and 16–18-hour workdays.

In the old order, most opposition to the nobility took the form of localized banditry, such as described in the legend of Robin Hood. Many of these primitive rebels did indeed seek to rob the rich and give to the poor, although the majority probably robbed the rich and poor alike. The nature of social conflict changed fundamentally as the industrial revolution pushed aside the isolation and provincialism of the rural way of life. Conflict over the necessities of everyday life began to be eclipsed by conflict over *ideas*. The masses began to hold political views, and these views began to count for something in the affairs of nations. Terms such as *radicalism*, *liberalism*, and *conservatism* arose to describe the development of conflicting political views.

In many respects, the American and French revolutions were the first to be fought in the name of clearly political ideals. Chief among these ideals was that of *democracy*. As conceived in these revolutions, democracy was more than simply the right to vote; it also included ideas such as the age of majority and the age of consent, which shattered the tyranny of the eldest male in family life. Democracy also embodied the ideal of public education. Education would now be enjoyed not only by the elite but by the masses as well. Further, public education was conceived as a practical education, suited to making people into productive workers, good soldiers, and intelligent voters.

In England, France, and America, most of these changes occurred within a single generation. The social order that had stood for centuries and had thrown off invasions of the Eastern hordes had now crumbled before the factory and the idea of democracy. The new order arrived with shocking suddenness and finality.

The Great Revolutions of industrialization and democracy produced a new age of intellectual activity in Western society. Advances occurred on all fronts in the physical and biological sciences. A new science of sociology was established that, from its beginning, sought to explain the causes and effects of the Great Revolutions. In the process, nearly all of the central concepts of modern sociology were set down—concepts such as society, community, social change, norms, anomie, class, status, party, property, power, prestige, formal organizations, authority, and alienation, to name a few. These concepts were made part of sociology and modern thought by such writers as Comte, Marx, Durkheim, Weber, Michels, Pareto, Veblin, and Spencer.

These writers usually discussed the origins and consequences of the Great Revolutions in deliberately cold and analytical terms. Their style of writing was often heavy and unattractive, and their lines of analysis frequently took them far from the immediately obvious. It is not surprising, then, that the writers' new scientific objectivity was taken as a lack of concern for the blood and fire of real-life conflicts by many readers who had witnessed them firsthand.

For at least one critic, this omission represented a fundamental error. Gustave LeBon (the father of collective behavior) dismissed the classic statements as "ill-observed fact" and "pure imagination" ([1895] 1960:48). For LeBon, the key to understanding the origins and consequences of the Great Revolutions was their *emotional component*. It was the intense emotions of widespread and mindless expectations, hero worship, hatred, and fear that eliminated the possibility of orderly social change and made precipitous and bloody revolution inevitable. This intense emotional atmosphere was created in the crowds that were a daily occurrence in the streets of the rapidly growing industrial centers of Europe and America. Change would remain unpredictable, disorderly, and bloody until the crowd was brought into check.

Diversity of the Field

LeBon's work did little to dissuade readers from taking the classic writers seriously, but it did sensitize them to the role played by the crowd and emotions in social change. About twenty years later, Robert Park and Ernest Burgess (1921) first used the term *collective behavior* in an introductory sociology text. They devoted a chapter to the discussion of social unrest, crowds, publics, sects, social contagion, mass movements, the crowd mind, propaganda, and fashion. Collective behavior was defined as the behavior of individuals under the influence of a collective impulse. This impulse was fundamentally different from the impulses that guided normal behavior; instead, it was a type of rapport, or hypnosis, that produced a loss of self-control and increased people's suggestibility.

For many years thereafter, the field served as a kind of dumping ground for a wide variety of social phenomena that at first glance seemed to reflect the operation of the collective impulse. Such phenomena displayed characteristics different from those expected of socialized individuals, formal organizations, and institutions. According to this thinking, socialized individuals are normally law abiding; therefore, lynch mobs and riots must be part of collective behavior. Formal organizations such as the military instill discipline in members; therefore, mutinies must be part of collective behavior. Institutions such as the male-dominated family meet fundamental human needs; therefore, women's suffrage and feminist movements must be collective behavior.

Those who suggested that lynch mobs, mutinies, and the suffrage movement belonged in the field of collective behavior usually had little interest in studying these topics. Collective behavior was also seen as a subarea within which fads, crazes, hysterias, and other odd events could be discussed and studied without imparting a sensationalistic and nonsensical taint to general sociology.

Definitions of the Field

Question: "What is collective behavior?"
Answer: "It depends on who you ask!"

Almost thirty years ago, Herbert Blumer (1957) began his survey of the field of collective behavior by noting that the field had not been charted effectively, which meant there was little agreement among scholars as to the full range of events that represented collective behavior. Further, there was no general, underlying theory to guide the study of collective behavior.

Since Blumer's survey of the field, the number of collective behavior studies has increased at least a hundredfold, and several new theoretical perspectives have been set forth. Still, Blumer's initial assessment of the field holds true. Scholars continue to debate the issue of which social phenomena properly constitute collective behavior, and no theoretical statement since Blumer's survey has provided the unifying conceptual framework he envisioned.

Introducing students to collective behavior would be a simple matter if it were possible to present a neat, concise definition of collective behavior. Likewise, understanding collective behavior would be much easier if a single, clearly stated theory encompassed the field. Few if any fields of sociology are so well set forth, but, comparatively, the field of collective behavior is unusually diverse in terms of the kinds of events studied and the nature of competing theories. At the outset, then, we will consider the various ways in which the field of collective behavior has been defined, including as aroused emotion, as adaptive response, and as response to social strain.

Collective Behavior as Aroused Emotion

The field's earliest and most longstanding tradition defines collective behavior as spontaneous social behavior directed by aroused and extreme emotion that distorts people's normal critical abilities and exaggerates their normal likes, dislikes, and loyalties (LeBon [1895] 1960; Park and Burgess 1921; Blumer 1939; Brown 1965; Klapp 1972; Lofland 1981). This definition is most easily applied to people's behavior within crowds.

It is often said that people do things in crowds that they would not do as individuals or in the company of their family and friends and it is certainly not difficult to illustrate this line of reasoning. Some crowds seem to distort people's critical abilities. About every four years, we witness political rallies at which people cheer approvingly as politicians rattle off one cliché after another. In some crowds, people seem to lose their usual inhibitions and caution. During Pentecostal revivals, for example, normally modest people quiver, shake, thrash about, and speak loudly in tongues. Almost every week, news broadcasts bring us segments in which unarmed crowds openly taunt armed police or soldiers. Other crowds seem to intensify people's hatreds. Within lynch mobs, otherwise law-abiding citizens inflict barbaric and bizarre atrocities on their victims. Finally, crowds seem to intensify people's attraction to certain objects and activities. The most obvious phases of fads and crazes generally involve crowds. Activities such as goldfish swallowing, phone booth stuffing, streaking, and various dances are carried out in crowds. Video arcades and contests to solve the Rubik's cube attract crowds of participants and spectators.

Defining collective behavior in terms of aroused emotion has appealed to generations of scholars. Doing so, however, assumes what McPhail (1971) terms a "monolithic" view of the crowd, which exaggerates the uniformity of emotional response and other behaviors among people in a crowd. On close examination, people in noisy and agitated crowds do not appear to be uniformly emotional. Videotapes of the anti-American crowds outside the United States Embassy in Tehran, Iran, after the taking of hostages in October of 1979, illustrate this point. Some in the crowd appeared to be so angry they were about to have seizures, yet others lethargically waved their protest signs and appeared to be engaged in casual conversation. Before they were expelled by Iranian authorities, American reporters noted that students and workers were being brought to the embassy on more or less fixed schedules for crowd duty. Construction workers stayed on the job at nearby buildings, and street vendors worked the edges of the crowd.

This example shows that emotional arousal is not uniform among crowd participants. Further, if we observe a crowd for a sufficient length of time, we see that the intensity of emotional display fluctuates greatly. Many specialists in collective behavior argue that the emotional impact of crowds is rarely sufficient to overcome people's usual psychological tendencies or the social influence of family and friends.

Defining collective behavior in terms of aroused emotion is intended to set collective behavior apart from social action that occurs within institutionalized relationships or formal organizations. Carl Couch (1968) points out that interaction between husband and wife, parent and child, or employer and employee can be as emotionally charged as any found in an agitated crowd. Whenever status is threatened, whenever people struggle to gain rights they feel are clearly theirs, and when high material risks are taken, emotions are likely to flare. The presence of aroused emotion in the crowd fails to set the crowd apart from other social relationships.

Defining collective behavior in terms of aroused emotion also tends to call attention away from the seemingly instrumental and adaptive aspects of collective behavior. During disasters, for example, survivors are quite likely to experience fright, grief, and shock. Still, as we shall see in later chapters, survivors are usually able to mount effective rescue and recovery efforts within minutes after disaster strikes. They gather information, discuss alternative lines of action, evaluate possible outcomes, and form definite plans and strategies. Similar planning also precedes such diverse events as sports rallies and protest marches.

Planning is part of social movements and revolutions as well.

A few specialists, such as Traugott (1978), suggest excluding these adaptive phenomena from the field of collective behavior. Whether anything is to be gained by this exclusion has been a subject of spirited debate, but in any event, there are other definitions of collective behavior that apply to both emotional and adaptive aspects of collective behavior.

Collective Behavior as Adaptive Response

A definition encompassing both emotional and adaptive phenomena conceptualizes collective behavior as emergent and transitory social behavior that is an adaptive response to new or ambiguous situations (Turner and Killian 1957; Lang and Lang 1961). This definition calls attention to collective responses to situations for which no preexisting rules or expectations (norms) apply. In this sense, collective behavior is adaptive and problem-solving behavior that involves people collectively defining problems, clarifying expectations for appropriate conduct, and entering new social relationships.

The conspicuous and rapid adoption of new products and activities is part of fads and crazes. Europe's seventeenth century was made more turbulent by recurring waves of large-scale speculation in tulips, tobacco, corn, chocolate, and other products introduced through new trade routes. South Seas island societies were disrupted by the unannounced and rapid introduction of modern technology during World War II. Types of social movements referred to as *cargo cults* were formed throughout the South Pacific as a response to this exposure to new objects, ideas, and people. The development and use of hallucinogenic drugs during the 1960s served as a focal point around which new networks of organized crime were established. Recent and localized efforts by groups of parents to limit or totally ban video arcades is one of the first negative responses to a new technology being packaged and marketed to appeal to children.

Crowds frequently confront unstructured and ambiguous situations. What others have attributed to the psychological deficiencies of the crowd, Turner and Killian (1972) attribute to the ambiguity and lack of structure in these situations. Police often describe celebrating crowds and crowds at scenes of accidents as unruly, but such crowds may seem unruly, in part, because large portions of the crowd are unaware of the intentions and commands of the police. Some in the crowd may be more attentive to the demands of family and friends who accompanied them to the event than to the demands of the police. Immediately following community-wide disasters, survivors generally form loosely structured groups and begin the task of rescue and recovery. Group efforts are often described as ineffective and makeshift when compared to the actions taken by authorities, but the actions of impromptu rescue crews may seem ineffective and makeshift because these groups lack the information needed to make more informed decisions. Also, many of these groups are based on newly formed and transitory relationships. People who rarely associate with one another in a direct, face-to-face manner are suddenly compelled by circumstance to work as a team. The banker, welfare mother, taxi driver, and schoolteacher must, for the moment, associate with one another in ways they might normally try to avoid. Members of rescue and recovery groups may well be torn between the immediate demands of their family and friends and the strong but implicit expectation that one should serve the community in the hour of need.

Collective responses are often made to situations in which traditional patterns of behavior are challenged. Court-ordered programs of desegregation or racial busing are usually a di-rect challenge to traditional race relations and ecological patterns. These directives often precipitate disorderly confrontations between police and crowds of civilians as well as locally instigated programs of resistance or accommodation.

In the instances discussed above, collective behavior is an active but transitory phase of larger processes of social change. The frisbee fad of the 1960s and, in all likelihood, the video games of the 1980s represent temporary phases of rapid introduction of products that later become permanent features of our material culture. Interpersonal relationships formed in rescue and recovery groups seldom endure once order is restored to community life. Social movements that advocate specific programs generally decline rapidly when governments put part or all of these programs into effect. Some types of collective behavior, such as the utopian communes of the 1800s and the hippie movement of the 1960s, represent unsuccessful experiments in social organization. Finally, some forms of collective behavior succeed in grand style. To paraphrase Carl Couch (1968), groups and ideas that seem odd today often form the social institutions of tomorrow.

Clearly, many aspects of collective behavior represent collective responses to new or ambiguous situations in which few guidelines for conduct exist. On the other hand, it must be noted that sometimes the collective behavior event itself may create or heighten the ambiguity. In April 1963, blacks began a series of marches in Birmingham, Alabama, to demand fair employment opportunities, the desegregation of public facilities, and equal voting rights. For the blacks, there was little new or ambiguous about the conditions they were protesting or the demands they were presenting. The marches, however, were certainly a new and ambiguous event from the standpoint of both white authorities and white citizens. The white response to these marches was violent. Birmingham police used dogs, firehoses, and mass arrests to halt the marches. Four black children died in church bombings, protest leader Medgar Evers was assassinated, and black and white civil rights workers were harassed, beaten, and a few were killed. This violent response sparked hundreds of sympathy civil rights demonstrations throughout the nation and voter registration drives throughout the South.

Another difficulty with the view that collective behavior is a response to new or ambiguous situations is that collective behavior response may involve traditional forms of association and the proposal of traditional solutions. Whites volunteered by the hundreds to assist blacks throughout the "Freedom Summer" of 1963. Many of these volunteers were not content with the role of civil rights worker. Blacks began to complain that these volunteers tended to seek out, in an abrasive manner, the traditional white roles of boss, planner, or strategist. This difficulty eventually led to the expulsion of many white volunteers from the black groups. The hippie communes were a new departure from the middle-class lifestyle of the 1950s. This break was not complete, however, because in many communes women continued to fill the traditional roles of cook and cleaner and remained sexually and emotionally subservient to men. Finally, the Moral Majority's proposal to turn fundamentalist Christian doctrine into government policy to solve current social ills is a theme that has been heard periodically in the United States since the 1700s.

Many types of collective behavior are adaptive responses to new and ambiguous situations that involve trying new relationships, definitions, and solutions. However, many instances of collective behavior represent responses to old and recurring problems and clearly defined opportunities, threats, groups, or objects. Collective behavior at times involves traditional relationships and traditional responses. A third definition of the field encompasses the novel as well as the traditional and recurring aspects of collective behavior.

Collective Behavior as Response to Social Strain

Breakdowns in social structure such as disasters, value conflicts, or deteriorating economic conditions quite logically seem to increase individual and, in turn, collective levels of anxiety, hostility, and desires to "set things right." The term *social strain* is conventionally used to refer to these breakdowns in social structure and their emotional accompaniments. Collective behavior can be defined as uninstitutionalized responses to social strain (Blumer 1939; Smelser 1962; Perry and Pugh 1978; Rose 1982). Collective behavior—be it panic, fads, wild celebrations, riots, religious revivals, or revolutionary social movements—represents mobilization because of social strain. All these instances of collective behavior are attempts to eliminate or otherwise cope with social strain.

The paradigm that social strain produces collective behavior is intuitively quite appealing, but it has not stood up well under close examination. In later chapters, we will review studies showing that the relationship between empirical measures of social strain and instances of collective behavior are not as strong or as clear-cut as this definition of the field suggests. Here it is sufficient to note that many collective behavior events occur without prior evidence of social strain. There are "issueless riots" (Marx 1970), and some fads appear to be more the results of clever advertising than an escape from serious concerns. Some social movements seem to function more for the personal gain of the leadership than to bring about social change or meet the needs of the membership (McCarthy and Zald 1973). Social strain, therefore, does not appear to be necessary for the occurrence of collective behavior.

Nor does it seem that social strain alone is sufficient to produce collective behavior. In the 1960s and early 1970s, many commentators attributed urban disorders to the disproportionate economic and social hardships experienced by blacks. Since about 1973, however, there have been few serious urban disorders involving blacks. This certainly does not indicate any marked improvement in the economic and social standing of blacks; in fact, the difference between the earned incomes of blacks and whites remains essentially the same as it was a decade earlier. Nationwide, current black unemployment is higher than it was during the riots, but our cities are no longer riot-torn.

The "social strain produces collective behavior" paradigm must be questioned at a more general level. Protest, social movements, and revolutions may, in the long run, improve the economic well-being and increase the liberties of participants. In the short run, however, they generally produce the opposite results. Gary Marx (1980) points out that strikes, boycotts, and civil disobedience may be the cause of social breakdown rather than the reverse. When the strike is finally settled or the hostilities of revolution cease, conditions of social breakdown are likely to be greater than when the strike or revolution began. Wages have been lost, factories and crops may have been destroyed, repressive laws may have been enacted, and domestic and international markets and sources of credit may have been lost. The relationship between social strain and the incidence of collective behavior is one of the field's major unresolved questions.

The No-Real-Difference Approach

Three general definitions of the field of collective behavior have been considered. Each speaks to longstanding concerns within the field and seeks to identify the characteristics that set collective behavior apart from "normal" social behavior. None, however, has withstood the critical probing of those who study collective behavior.

The failure to find a fully acceptable definition of collective behavior is, in part, due to the way in which the field developed. Recall that collective behavior initially served as a dumping ground for any and all social phenomena that at first glance seemed to reflect impulses different from those expected of socialized individuals, formal organizations, and institutions. It may well be that there is no characteristic common to all the phenomena traditionally identified with the field.

An implicit recognition of this possibility led some early scholars, notably Park and Blumer, to suggest that there is "no real difference" between collective behavior and other forms of social behavior. Park (1924:42), for example, once defined sociology as the "science of collective behavior." Blumer noted that in a broad sense collective behavior refers to the behavior of two or more people who are acting together. Milgram and Toch (1969:509) define the crowd simply as "people in sufficiently close proximity that the fact of aggregation comes to influence behavior." Defined in this manner, the term *crowd* applies equally well to shoppers passing through a grocery store, concert patrons waiting in line to buy tickets, or ranks of demonstrators charging police lines.

The most serious advocates of the no-real-difference approach to collective behavior include Couch (1968) and McPhail (1978). Couch views the crowd and collective behavior as no more or no less pathological and bizzare than other social systems. McPhail (1978:3) defines collective behavior as "what human beings are doing with and in relation to one another." The no-real-difference approach to collective behavior encourages more unified conceptual and analytical approaches across sociology's subject matter. It also encourages efforts to discover commonalities among phenomena seen as quite separate, such as the actions of corporate executives in response to the latest move of a competitor and a group protest to a court order. The no-real-difference approach gives insights into seemingly bizzare events such as hysterias, panics, and fads. It lessens the need to call upon novel explanations such as "crowd mentality" to account for many collective behavior phenomena (Marx 1980).

To suggest that there are no real or fundamental differences between collective behavior and other forms of social behavior does *not* mean that the field of collective behavior is unnecessary. Indeed, it is necessary precisely because many sociologists have been reluctant to study the crowd and other phenomena consigned to collective behavior.

Categories of Collective Behavior

Instead of trying to specify the true nature of collective behavior, Gary Marx (1980) avoids the definition dilemma by *cataloging* the phenomena that have come to constitute the field. He developed classification categories from a consideration of what people who identify with the field have already studied and a concern for what the field should encompass, given the existing though incomplete definitions of collective behavior. For Gary Marx, the field of collective behavior embodies six traditional and interrelated concerns.

Problems within Social Systems. First, there is an interest in social systems that are in a pronounced state of breakdown, strain, maladaption, crisis, or disruption. Much of the disaster and crisis research falls within this area. Quite clearly, this area also includes the study

of protest, political violence, rebellions and revolutions, most migrations, and many social movements.

Undifferentiated Groups. Second, there is an interest in newly emerged or undifferentiated groups. Undifferentiated groups refer to the mass and the public (Blumer 1939). Here the concern is with such issues as the methods and effects of mass advertising and the nature and operation of public opinion. Newly emerged groups include spectator crowds at the scenes of accidents and fires, people standing in line to purchase concert tickets, and some disaster response groups. Collective behavior research includes studies of crowd formation, behavior within waiting lines, crowd control, formation of rescue groups following a disaster, and bystander intervention in emergencies.

Communication Processes. Third, there is the interest in the processes inolved in the development and communication of collective images. This includes a concern for the development of symbols and ideologies of social movements and generalized or widespread images and beliefs of fear, dissatisfaction, exploitation, scapegoats, and hostility. Many of these concerns are reflected in the study of rumor.

Social Influence and Interaction. Fourth, there is an interest in direct, immediate, visual, and highly involving social influence and interaction. This includes the concern with audience reactions to speakers and decision making within the crowd. Concern with the relative effects of face-to-face versus mediated recruitment into groups of various sorts also falls within this area.

Group Emotion. Fifth, there is an interest in highly emotional states collectively experienced by groups. This includes panics, hysterias, collective visions, and extreme instances of suggestibility.

FIGURE 1.1   *The Field of Collective Behavior*

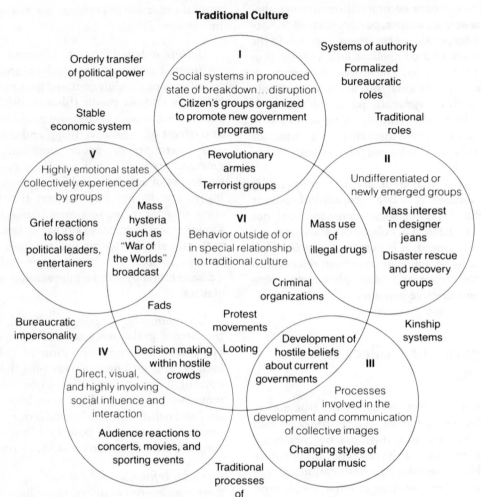

Traditional Culture

I
Social systems in pronouced
state of breakdown...disruption
Citizen's groups organized
to promote new government
programs

Orderly transfer
of political power

Systems of authority

Formalized
bureaucratic
roles

Stable
economic system

Traditional
roles

V
Highly emotional states
collectively experienced
by groups

Revolutionary
armies

Terrorist groups

II
Undifferentiated or
newly emerged groups

Grief reactions
to loss of
political leaders,
entertainers

Mass
hysteria
such as
"War of
the Worlds"
broadcast

VI
Behavior outside of or
in special relationship
to traditional culture

Mass use
of
illegal drugs

Mass interest
in designer
jeans

Disaster rescue
and recovery
groups

Criminal
organizations

Fads

Kinship
systems

Bureaucratic
impersonality

Protest
movements

Development of
hostile beliefs
about current
governments

IV
Direct, visual,
and highly involving
social influence and
interaction

Decision making
within hostile
crowds

Looting

III
Processes
involved in the
development and communication
of collective images

Audience reactions to
concerts, movies, and
sporting events

Changing styles of
popular music

Traditional
processes
of
instruction and socialization

Behavior outside of Traditional Culture.
Throughout the collective behavior literature, there is an interest in behavior outside of or in special relationship to traditional culture. This final category includes an interest in novel behavior such as fads or innovative behavior in disasters. Also standing outside traditional culture are collective and criminal acts such as looting, outbursts of vandalism, smuggling, and trading in illegal goods and services. Finally, there is behavior directed toward institutionalizing alternate forms of action. This includes the social movement to establish the juvenile justice system in the United States during the 1890s as well as the desegregation and civil rights movements of the 1960s.

This sixth category is very broad in terms of the range of events it encompasses. In addition, behavior outside of traditional culture also includes elements of the other five categories. That is, interest in social systems in a pronounced state of breakdown (first category) can include events outside a system's traditional culture, such as the emergence of new religions. Other events, such as reform movements, are in keeping with that culture and may even seek to reinforce dominant cultural themes. Figure 1.1 illustrates the relationship of these six categories to each other and to traditional culture.

Plan of the Book

Four general theories of collective behavior are presented in Chapter 2. A general theory sets forth a unified approach to a wide range of collective phenomena, from interaction within small crowds to major social movements. First, we will consider *social contagion*, or *mass hysteria* theory. (We will use these terms interchangably throughout the book.) This theory defines the field in terms of aroused emotion and originated with the writings of Gustave LeBon. In *The Crowd* ([1895] 1960), LeBon presented a very negative assessment of the role of crowds, popular democracy, and revolutions in national events. He laid the groundwork for a theoretical tradition that endured almost unchallenged for nearly fifty years. One must understand the social contagion perspective in order to appreciate the direction of most early work within the field.

Next, we will consider the *emergent norm* theory developed by Ralph Turner and Lewis Killian. This theory casts collective behavior as an adaptive response to novel or unique social conditions. This approach emphasizes the impact of norms, collective definitions, and social roles in the development of collective behavior and deemphasizes the role of aroused emotion.

Neil Smelser's *value-added* theory will then be considered. The value-added model is the most comprehensive of the approaches that view collective behavior as a response to stressful societal conditions. The value-added theory divides the field into collective episodes of crazes, panics, hostile outbursts, and value- and norm-oriented social movements.

Finally, we will consider the *social behavioral/interactionist (SBI)* perspective, which is the most developed of any no-real-difference approach to collective behavior. Many new and traditional concerns are examined from the standpoint of processes of crowd formation, behavior within crowds, and their dispersal. Taken together, these processes provide insight into how celebrations, civil disorders, disaster responses, and other collective behavior events develop. On a larger scale, these processes tell us a great deal about rallies, marches, and confrontations, which are important components of migrations, protests, social movements, and revolutions.

The four general theories presented in Chapter 2 will be our guides throughout the remainder of the text. In other chapters we will consider several theories that address a narrower range of concerns than the general theories. These "midrange" theories are more readily understood when introduced with specific subject matter. Davies' (1969) *J-curve theory of revolution*, for example, will be considered in chapters dealing with revolutionary social movements and political violence. Davies' theory is an alternative to Smelser's view of structural strain. Likewise, McCarthy and Zald's (1973) *resource mobilization* approach will be considered in chapters dealing with social movements. This approach is substantially different from the emergent norm and value-added orientations to social movements.

In Chapter 3 we present the problems and methods of collective behavior research. Three major problems have greatly influenced the character of this research and set it apart from research conducted in other areas of sociology. First, there is the problem of studying unanticipated events, such as reactions to disasters or the development of riots. Second, there is the problem of studying the crowd. Directly studying crowds is not an easy task, and most early discussions of crowd behavior are based on informed speculation. Only in the past fifteen years have researchers attempted to systematically observe, record, and otherwise analyze what people do in crowds. Finally, there is the problem of studying collective behavior under controlled conditions. Various moral, legal, and practical considerations limit the kinds of events that can be produced and manipulated for the purpose of studying collective behavior under controlled conditions. Simply put, one cannot yell "Fire!" in a crowded theater to study panic.

In Chapter 3 we also consider how the basic research methods of sociology have been adapted and applied to the study of collective behavior. We will consider methods such as the analysis and use of historical material, simple and participant observation, survey research, and experiments.

In the remaining chapters we present specific collective behavior topics, reflecting, as Gary Marx (1980) has observed, a concern for what has been studied and what should be studied, given the existing definitions of the field.

In Part 2 we will consider collective behavior in everyday life. These chapters concern events that most of us have encountered firsthand. In Chapter 4 we examine rumor and communication in collective behavior. At one time or another, all of us hear, pass along, and act on rumors about our community and neighbors. We will see how the information contained in rumors fits into our daily lives. In Chapters 5 and 6 we will explore the sometimes related matters of mass hysterias and UFOs. Mass hysterias include the aftermath of

the "War of the Worlds" radio broadcast of 1938, epidemics of mysterious rashes and fainting, and the periodic sighting of monsters such as Bigfoot. Nearly every week, people in the United States report seeing mysterious objects like flying saucers. To many people, mass hysterias and UFOs represent collective delusions and silliness. Still, a closer examination of these events reveals a great deal about what we take for granted in our social life. In Chapter 7 we examine *fads* and *fashion*. Nearly every aspect of social life is subject to fads and fashion. To some, fads and fashion represent people's mindless and often quite costly preoccupation with superficialities. To others, fads and fashion are fundamental ingredients in community life and social change.

In Part 3 we will consider collective behavior and threats to the social order. In Chapter 8 we examine migrations that result from natural catastrophes such as drought, as well as broken economies, race and ethnic hatred, and war. Throughout the world today, millions of people are homeless because of these conditions. Chapters 9 and 10 concern disasters. In Chapter 9 we will see how individuals cope with disaster. We will consider people's nonadaptive or "panic" responses, adaptive responses, and altruistic responses to disaster. In Chapter 10 we look at disaster from the standpoint of the many groups and organizations that work together to carry out rescue and recovery efforts. In Chapters 11 and 12 we examine riots. In Chapter 11 the question Who participates in riots? will be considered. In Chapter 12 we will look at how groups and organizations respond to riots. In Chapter 13 we consider protest—the means through which people with limited financial and organizational resources can influence the political process. Finally, we discuss social movements in Chapters 14 and 15. The conditions under which different types of social movements arise will be discussed in Chapter 14. In Chapter 15 we examine how demonstrations and marches are organized, and we will evaluate the recent *resource mobilization* explanation of social movements.

The subject matter of collective behavior spans a wide range of topics, from the silliness of fads to the deadly serious business of revolutions. Throughout this text, we provide examples that give an intuitive feel for collective behavior. Considerable attention has been given to the who, what, when, and where of the events in question. Though we present both early and current work in the field, each student should keep in mind that there is always room for additional insights, more studies, and new theories. In few areas of sociology is this more appropriate than in the study of collective behavior.

◆ CHAPTER 2 ◆

Theories of Collective Behavior

We will present and summarize four general theories of collective behavior in this chapter: social contagion theory, emergent norm theory, value-added theory, and the social behavioral/interactionist theory. We selected these theories from the larger body of existing collective behavior theories for several reasons. Each one speaks to collective behavior as it is most broadly conceived, including both short-lived crowd phenomena and the large-scale and enduring processes of social movements, while other theories address a narrower range of concerns within the field.

These theories reflect the four major efforts toward defining collective behavior that we discussed in the first chapter. Collective behavior as aroused emotion is the foundation of social contagion theory. Collective behavior as an adaptive response to new or ambiguous situations is central to the emergent norm position. Value-added theory is the most elaborate statement of the "social strain produces collective behavior" approach to the field. The social behavioral/interactionist theory is the most developed of the positions that assume no real difference exists between forces that produce collective behavior and other types of social phenomena.

In part through default and in part because of their merits, social contagion theory, emergent norm theory, and value-added theory could each, at one time or another, properly lay claim to being the dominant paradigm in the field of collective behavior. These three theories guided most debate and research until the early 1970s; then the field of collective behavior rapidly became more theoretically diverse, as interest peaked in the areas of protest, civil disorder, political violence, and social movements. Today, no introduction to collective behavior would be complete without consideration of more recent theories. Still, social contagion theory, emergent norm theory, and value-added theory remain as the stepping-stones over which recent collective behavior theory has progressed.

In this chapter effort has been made to present these four general theories in a straightforward summary fashion. Attention is given to laying out their origins, basic assumptions, and the ways in which they claim collective phenomena develop. No attempt has been made here to discuss the limitations or points of contention usually associated with these theories. (Having read the first chapter, however, one might anticipate some of the problems with these theories.) Instead, in later chapters, we will consider the limitations of these theories when applied to real situations. For example, we will discuss the limitations of the social contagion perspective throughout several chapters, including Chapter 5 ("Mass

Hysteria") and Chapter 6 ("UFOs"). We will discuss the limitations of the value-added perspective throughout several chapters, including Chapter 11 ("Individuals and Riots") and those dealing with social movements (Chapters 12–15).

Having a working familiarity with these four theories gives one a good grasp of the central themes within the intellectual tradition of collective behavior. Familiarity with these theories also provides an appreciation for the necessity of the other theoretical positions that will be encountered in later chapters.

The Social Contagion Perspective

On May 27, 1871, the heart of Paris was in flames. Thousands had already died in the six days of bloody, hand-to-hand fighting that had continued without pause through the districts, streets, and across the barricades of the city. These were the final hours of what Karl Marx came to describe as "the first modern revolution"—the Paris Commune of 1871. Parisians were not in revolt against an oppressive hereditary monarchy, as was the case in 1793. Rather, they were in revolt against the government of the National Assembly that had been popularly elected four months earlier. The National Assembly turned out to be composed primarily of conservatives and monarchists who, just three weeks after their election, began to vote measures that directly threatened the economic survival of the almost destitute Parisian working class. On March 10, 1871, the National Assembly transferred the seat of government from Paris to Versailles. On March 26, the Commune of Paris was established. The Paris Commune of 1871 was a self-proclaimed governing body of men and women who declared Paris to be a free, politically self-determined city. Similar communes were es-

tablished in the French cities of Lyons, Marseilles, Toulouse, LeCreusot, Saint-Etienne, and Narbonne.

Prominent among the Paris communards were socialists, anarchists, pacifists, humanitarians, and a few Marxists: the red banner of socialism hung over Paris. During the next ten weeks, the men and women of the Paris Commune of 1871 voted for a moratorium on payment of commercial bills and an agreement to transfer the operation and ownership of abandoned factories to workers; they also voted to lower salaries of public officials. The commune approved a law forbidding employers the right to deduct penalties from the wages of workers and declared a strict separation of church and state. During this time the commune also directed the construction of barricades throughout the streets of Paris.

On the afternoon of May 21, National Assembly armies entered Paris. This was the start of Bloody Week, in which fighting was house by house, barricade by barricade. During the fighting, communards burned many memorials of former governments, including the Royal Palace, the Tuileries Palace, the Hotel de Ville, and the home of the president of the National Assembly. These buildings were themselves architectural and historical treasures that contained countless art objects. Buildings housing important government and financial records were also destroyed. Hundreds of other buildings were set ablaze by the incendiary weapons used by the troops of the National Assembly. Communards executed at least one hundred prisoners, including the archbishop of Paris. Forces of the National Assembly, in turn, shot more than twenty thousand communards and Parisians. By the end of May, much of the beauty of Paris was destroyed, corpses still lay in the streets, and crowds of mourners gathered at mass graves.

Throughout this episode, there was an underlying sense that large-scale events were unfolding at an unusually rapid and dangerous pace.

Within weeks after the hasty election of the National Assembly and its transfer of government from Paris to Versailles, at least seven cities broke from the National Assembly and established themselves as independent communes. Over all this stood the crowd. The National Assembly in brief, noisy, and crowdlike deliberation began to pass edicts having tremendous economic and political impact before it had fully assessed and consolidated its base of power. The communes were led by men and women who usually had large followings in the crowds of urban workers but little political experience. The communes arrived at edicts by noisy debate and vote but little formal procedure.

Then there was the fighting and destruction. A year earlier, French men and women would have died to protect their national treasures from harm; now, these treasures were put to the torch because they were symbols of the old order. Discipline broke down among troops of the National Assembly as they used incendiaries against the barricades, seemingly mindless of the carnage and unnecessary property damage they might cause. Bands of soldiers brutally executed their countrymen in large numbers. Afterward, troops stripped and mutilated many of the corpses. It was as if a civilized people had, for a time, slipped back into the barbarism of a distant past.

Gustave LeBon

One eyewitness to these terrible days in Paris was the French scientist, physician, philosopher, militarist, writer, and world traveler Gustave LeBon (1841–1931). For LeBon these events were more than a national tragedy, they also demanded an explanation. Throughout the rest of his writing career, LeBon probed the workings of crowds, representative forms of government, and social movements. The ideas LeBon set forth, and their subsequent interpretation by others, came to constitute the *social*

contagion perspective within the field of collective behavior.

LeBon's most influential and widely acclaimed book was *The Crowd*, published in 1895. In very bold terms, LeBon states that all crowds exert a profound and inherently negative influence on people. He describes this influence as contagious or rapidly transmitted mental unity that emerges whenever people interact in a group—be it the National Assembly of 1871, a parliament, or a revolutionary crowd. For LeBon, contagious mental unity was the root cause of the horrors he witnessed in 1871. Those who followed in the tradition established by LeBon argue, however, that contagious mental unity emerges only in some crowds and under certain conditions. Nonetheless, throughout the social contagion literature, contagious mental unity is considered to be a powerful and mischievous force.

The Crowd and Its Effect on Individuals. By the end of the nineteenth century, terminology used by Darwin in his essays on biological evolution had been popularized into jargon embellishing most discussions of economics, politics, and society. LeBon uses this terminology throughout *The Crowd*. He states that the contagious mental unity of crowds reduces the mental capacity of enlightened and cultured people to the level of "those inferior forms of evolution" such as "women, savages, and children" (see box, p. 24).

LeBon's discussion of the effects of the crowd on individuals builds to the conclusion that the crowd transforms rational, law-abiding people into violent, irrational enemies of the state. This transformation begins with intensified emotion and behavior: people lose their sense of reserve and inhibitions to act; the tempo of their behavior is rapid. Accompanying this state of arousal is a shared willingness to follow suggestions, which LeBon describes as similar to the hypnotic trance. The crowd is unable to sustain focus and moves rapidly from one object or idea to another, but it does sustain a fearful degree of unanimity of mood and action. This contagious mental unity overcomes the individual's rational capabilities. People in the crowd do not reflect on outcomes of their action; perceptions are distorted, and feelings of power emerge that become the basis of attack on authorities. Without critical ability and powers of reflection, people within crowds are incapable of respect for social standards, conventions, and institutions. LeBon's crowd is amoral.

The Crowd and Its Effect on Society.   LeBon stated that Western society was entering an age of crowds. Henceforth, through the action of crowds, the masses would figure ominously in the destinies of nations. When LeBon wrote *The Crowd*, explosive population increases and massive rural-to-urban migrations had transformed the very character of social life within Western society. Prior to the eighteenth century, the hamlets and villages of the British Isles and the European continent seldom contained more than one hundred residents. The population of Rome at the birth of Christ was approximately 350,000, making it at that time the largest city in human history. Rome's population had declined dramatically in the third century A.D., and until 1700 no city in Europe had a population greater than 80,000—most populations were below 30,000. In 1801 London was probably the largest city in the world, with a population of 100,000. Judged by later standards, social life had been carried out for centuries by very small social groupings.

Prior to the eighteenth century, most inland hamlets and villages were totally isolated for weeks and months because of seasonal deterioration of roads and trails. Snow or mud made commercial overland travel impossible; casual travel was exhausting, usually dangerous, and infrequent. At the height of the Roman Empire, an official could travel from Rome to the British Isles in thirteen days. Seventeen hun-

dred years later, this journey still took thirteen days for British officials of state who traveled "post haste, sparing no expense."

These conditions changed dramatically following Telford and MacAdam's development of techniques for building relatively inexpensive, all-season roads in the 1730s. Telford and MacAdam produced the first major innovations in road-building technology since the Egyptian roads of 2000 B.C. During the last half of the eighteenth century, at least three times as many miles of roads were built in Europe and Britain as had been built during the Roman Empire. By the 1840s, railroads began to connect rapidly growing European population centers, and by the 1850s, the telegraph had connected England to the European continent. Within a hundred years, a degree of geographic mobility and interpersonal communication had been achieved that was unprecedented in human history. LeBon was correct in his claims that mass society had arrived. Because of increased geographic mobility and the capacity to communicate among themselves, larger portions of the rapidly growing populations of Europe were able to intrude on the political processes that once had been carried out only by elites.

For LeBon, the great civilizations of the past had been created by small intellectual aristocracies—the "rivalries of sovereigns" and "councils of princes" determined the courses of empires and nations. Decisions were made and policies established in the quiet halls, chapels, libraries, and gardens of nobles and high officials. The institutions and laws of these civilizations were the embodiment of the cumulative wisdom derived from the calm deliberations of intelligent and cultured men.

In contrast, the age of crowds would be a new Dark Ages, an era of barbarism wherein the crowd would assume the prerogatives and power of earlier sovereign classes. Central to this transition were criminal juries, electoral bodies, and parliamentary assemblies, which

LeBon characterizes as special types of crowds. Criminal juries had become part of the judicial operations that once had been the sole domain of magistrates appointed by the king. Juries of intellectuals delivered verdicts no different from those of tradesmen. Unlike a magistrate as judge, the jury displayed "suggestibility" and had only a "slight capacity for reasoning." Electoral crowds, invested with the power of electing people to office, had a pronounced absence of critical spirit and aptitude for reasoning. Voters responded best to flattery and fantastic promises. For LeBon, universal suffrage brought society's "inferior elements" into the political process. The work of parliaments was always inferior to that of isolated statesmen and specialists. The parliamentary assemblies of different nations produced strikingly similar debates, votes, and ill-conceived decisions. All parliaments had an unavoidable tendency to produce financial waste and to destroy individual liberty. For LeBon, juries, electorates, and parliaments had the power of tyrants and the wisdom of fools.

LeBon states that the workings of modern institutions could not be accounted for in terms of economic or political theory. He characterizes the theories of his day as mixtures of "ill-observed fact" and "pure imagination." Additionally, these theories were mischievous because they were readily transformed into the rallying cries of the crowds. Elaborate theories were unnecessary for LeBon, because the massive upheavals of the eighteenth and nineteenth centuries obviously resulted from distortions in people's judgment and action caused by contagious mental unity. In this sense, LeBon presents a single-factor explanation of Western history.

Although LeBon is quite definite in his descriptions of the effects of contagious mental unity, he remains quite vague when explaining how this mental unity emerged in crowds. For this reason, Robert K. Merton (1960) characterizes LeBon as a problem finder rather than a problem solver. Sigmund Freud, a contemporary and critic of LeBon, attempted to explain contagious mental unity as the result of crowd members' unconscious love of the crowd leader. This psychoanalytic explanation, set forth in *Group Psychology and the Analysis of the Ego* (Freud 1921), has had relatively little impact within the field of collective behavior, but other attempts to account for contagious mental unity are part of the social contagion perspective.

Herbert Blumer

In 1934, thirty-nine years after *The Crowd*, Herbert Blumer wrote an essay called "Outline of Collective Behavior" ([1934] 1969). Blumer's "Outline" is much less value laden than LeBon's *The Crowd*. For example, contagious mental unity is not described as similar to the mental processes of "inferior forms of evolution." Unlike *The Crowd*, Blumer's "Outline" is more suited to an objective classification and analysis of crowd-related phenomena. More so than LeBon, Blumer attempts to describe a social-psychological mechanism through which mental unity develops. He suggests that remarkable events create tensions that dispose people to behave like a crowd. Once underlying tensions are created, people move about in an aimless and random fashion, which Blumer calls *milling*.

According to Blumer, the milling process can transform human interaction in a fundamental way. He states that there is ordinarily a largely covert, interpretive phase to human interaction; that is, people respond to one another by interpreting the other's gestures and remarks, rehearsing or visualizing a possible response, and then conveying a response. This phase of interaction acts as a buffer, that is, lengthens the time between stimulus and response, thus allowing people to differentiate themselves from others by composing responses rather than mirroring, in a simple stimulus–response fashion, the other's action.

Finally, it is within the interpretive phase of interaction that rationality resides, where outcomes of action are envisioned, and where alternative lines of action are compared.

Under conditions of intense milling, the interpretive phase of the act is disrupted; in some situations, it may become so noisy that people cannot "hear themselves think." As the interpretive phase of interaction deteriorates, the buffer effect is lost and behavior becomes intense and rapid, differentiation becomes more difficult and people act alike, unanimity in mood and action prevails. Finally, with the interpretive phase of interaction gone, people become suggestible and irrational. Blumer describes this state as circular reaction, which is the "natural mechanism of collective behavior" (see Figure 2.1).

Blumer presents a classification of crowds based on focus and internal cohesiveness. *Acting crowds* develop a sense of goal (focus) and a plan of action to achieve the goal (cohesiveness). An example of the acting crowd is a throng of townspeople who assemble a brass band and hastily build a speaker's platform in anticipation of a surprise visit from their governor. An *expressive crowd* lacks a goal and is primarily just a setting for tension release, often through rhythmical action such as applause, dancing, or singing. An expressive crowd, for example, is an audience offering a standing ovation at the end of a concert.

Blumer states that aggregates of people dispersed over large geographic areas can, under conditions of social unrest, assume some of the characteristics of compact acting and expressive crowds. The *public* is an aggregate of people, often from the same social class, who are concerned with a specific issue. The public discusses ways to meet the issue, such as a community deciding on a school bond referendum. The *mass* is composed of anonymous individuals from many social strata; it is loosely organized, does not engage in discussion, and behaves in terms of each individual "seeking to

answer his own needs." Blumer cites the California gold rush of 1849 and other human migrations as examples of mass behavior. The widespread purchase of video games by all economic strata of American society would also fit within Blumer's definition of the mass.

While LeBon places great emphasis on the destructive effects of crowds, Blumer considers the manner in which collective behavior evolves into new forms of group and institutional conduct to be the greater concern. Within crowds, publics, and the mass appear new "expectations, values, conceptions of rights and obligations, tastes, and moods" upon which new social systems are founded. For LeBon, crowds marked the end of civilization; for Blumer, crowds played an important part in the development of new forms of social life.

Orrin E. Klapp: Tensions and Social Definitions

In 1972 Orrin E. Klapp published *Currents of Unrest: An Introduction to Collective Behavior.* In this work Klapp offers further comment on how socially induced tensions become transformed into social contagions and on what determines contagions' particular content. Generalized tensions arise from strains generated by relationships that are part of the larger social structure. Most generalized tensions for contemporary Americans derive from cultural values of work, achievement, and the trauma of adjusting to rapid and continuous change. Using a domino metaphor, Klapp argues that people became involved in social contagions when sufficiently sensitized or "tilted" by tensions. Social contagion episodes start when the weakest people buckle under to tension, which in turn may trigger social contagion among substantial portions of the "respectable rank and file" and lead finally to the bandwagon stage, in which almost everyone participates. Such episodes may act as "safety valves," because after the social contagion has run its

FIGURE 2.1   *Two Types of Human Interaction*

Interpretive Interaction. Normally, when people interact, they interpret the stimuli they receive from others. People assign meaning to these stimuli, construct a response, and consider possible outcomes. Blumer and others refer to this type of relationship as interpretive interaction. Interpretive interaction allows people to make differentiated responses to one another's actions.

Circular Reaction. The pushing and shoving, noise, and blocking of vision sometimes encountered in the crowd interferes with the interpretive phase of the act. Without such reflection, people begin to react to one another in a direct, rapid, and imitative fashion. Blumer refers to this relationship as circular reaction. Circular reaction produces intense, homogeneous, and impulsive behavior.

course, tensions are lower and people are much less responsive to the mood of others. When protest of the Vietnam War threatened the very fiber of American society, Klapp advocated that a national tension measurement and management agency be established.

According to Klapp, the content of social contagions depends on the defining process— only after meanings and beliefs are built up can contagion develop. Klapp cites the early organizational efforts and slogans of ecology groups as a "belief-building" prelude to mass hysteria. For Klapp, stark images and simple beliefs, often skillfully manipulated by leaders, exert hypnotic control over people's behavior during social contagions.

The preconceptions and questions many students bring to their first course in collective behavior derive largely from the social contagion perspective. The text they used in their introductory sociology course probably presented collective behavior from the standpoint of social contagion theory. This perspective has fostered many familiar phrases used to describe crowds. These phrases often compare the behavior of humans to that of animals: crowds can be led like "a flock of sheep"; crowds are likely to "stampede" in emergencies; crowds "roar" their approval or disapproval. Further, terms such as *mob psychology* and *crowd mentality* are used to describe the decisions and actions of groups with whom we disagree.

Finally, the social contagion perspective is also commonly referred to as the *mass hysteria* perspective of collective behavior. We will use both terms throughout the text. Let us now turn to other theories of collective behavior.

The Emergent Norm Perspective

One of the largest anti–Vietnam War rallies occurred in Washington, D.C. on the last weekend of October 1967. It was billed as the rally that would end the war. It didn't. However, for the nearly 250,000 people who attended, it was a memorable event.

During those three days, one was impressed by the pervasive concern of the protesters that this be a nonviolent protest. On Friday evening a clean-cut young man approached a group of less well groomed young people camped in the backyard of a Georgetown residence. He announced that he had a large supply of cherry bombs and said he would give them to the protesters if they would throw them at police and soldiers during Saturday's rally at the Lincoln Memorial. His proposal was initially greeted with derisive laughter and then with outright hostility. One protester pointed out how stupidly dangerous it would be to discharge fireworks around nervous and perhaps trigger-happy soldiers. The fellow with the cherry bombs left shortly after a young woman offered a rather vulgar plan for disposing of his explosives. Later, someone suggested that the cherry bombs were probably supplied by the FBI in an effort to discredit the protest.

Saturday's rally consisted of antiwar speeches throughout the morning, as protesters assembled around the reflecting pool between the Lincoln Memorial and the Washington Monument. At about 1:00 P.M., the march to the Pentagon started. By early evening large groups of protesters were sitting-in on the steps and parking malls of the Pentagon. Thousands of others were camped on the surrounding grounds. Sandwiches, coffee, milk, and soft drinks were being passed hand to hand throughout the crowd. This welcome food and drink seemed to appear from nowhere and added to the relaxed and festive atmosphere.

Troops made their first serious efforts to remove the crowds from the steps of the Pentagon at about 9:00 P.M. There was shouting, shoving, kicking, and the use of night sticks and gun butts as troops moved into the crowd sitting before them. This clamor ceased abruptly each time the television floodlights

Social Contagion Theory and Women: 1895–1972

LeBon stated that the contagious mental unity of crowds reduced the mental functioning of enlightened and cultured people to the level of "those inferior forms of evolution" such as "women, savages, and children." Perhaps it is inaccurate to attribute the sexual bias of later social contagion/mass hysteria studies entirely to LeBon; however, throughout the social contagion literature, it is assumed that women are very susceptible to hysterical outbursts:

"It will be remarked that among the special characteristics of crowds there are several—such as impulsiveness, irritability, incapacity to reason, the absence of judgement, and of the critical spirit, the exaggeration of the sentiments, and others besides—which are almost always observed in beings belonging to inferior forms of evolution—in women, savages, and children, for instance." (LeBon [1895] 1960:36)

"Naturally the more suggestible people accepted the story at face value. Of these only a small percentage reported physical symptoms from 'gassing,' presumably because of some personal motivation toward, or gratification from, such symptoms. It might be predicted from psychological and psychiatric literature, those who succumbed to the 'mental epidemic' were mostly women and were, on the average, below the general population in educational and economic level. This supports the above analysis and puts the 'phantom anesthetist' of Mattoon, in some aspects at least, into a familiar psychological pattern." (Johnson 1945: 234–235)

"The incident under study occurred in a southern clothing manufacturing plant. . . . Within about one week in the summer of 1962 sixty-two persons suffered what was purported to be insect bites and received some kind of medical treatment. . . . Almost all (54) of the victims were women. . . . A physician and an entomologist from the Communicable Disease Center in Atlanta visited the plant but could find no toxic element capable of causing these symptoms. . . . The only reasonable conclusion seemed to be that this was a phenomenon that was 'almost exclusively psychogenic in nature.'. . . We interviewed only women." (Kerckhoff, Back, and Miller 1965:388–392)

"A typical example of human milling leading to a stampede would be a fire in an auditorium. Perhaps a woman in the audience whispers audibly to her companion, 'Do you smell smoke?' Her companion answers, 'No. Do you think there is a fire?' The lady on the other side hears the word *fire* and looks alarmed, asking, 'Is there a fire?' The first two ladies now see her scared look and, being alarmed by it, look scared themselves. This frightens the third lady even more, and now all their scared looks are being observed by others in the audience. A little smoke or some triggering stimulus such as a raised voice can bring on a condition in which many people are scared . . . frightening each other by their own behavior more than by the signs of the external situation. Running could precipitate a stampede." (Klapp 1972: 44) came on. At one point, protesters standing in the rear of the crowd began to throw fruit, pop cans, and other trash at the soldiers. Protesters sitting at the feet of the soldiers turned back and shouted for the barrage to cease. One particularly loud voice shouted, "If you want action, come up here and sit in the first row. Otherwise, knock it off!" This comment was cheered by the protesters, and the chant "Peace now" went up. Nothing more was thrown at the soldiers.

Ralph H. Turner and Lewis M. Killian

The first edition of Ralph H. Turner and Lewis M. Killian's *Collective Behavior* was published in 1957. These authors present a view of collective behavior that departs greatly from the social contagion perspective. The *emergent norm* approach is based on the view that the impact of groups on individuals resembles *normative constraint* rather than contagious mental unity. Turner and Killian argue that total uniformity of mood and behavior within the crowd is seldom observed. Within crowds various motives for participation exist, diverse feelings are in evidence, and many types of behavior can be observed. For example, those gathered at a protest rally have a variety of motives for being there, in addition to protest. Some may be seeking excitement, sex, or drugs. Police and protest leaders are concerned with maintaining order, while FBI agents are concerned with national security, and those selling protest buttons, with making money. Seldom will all these people express the same feelings or act in unison. Turner and Killian refer to these features of the crowd as *differential expression*.

Behavior within the crowd is guided by "norming acts," such as nonvocal gestures and verbal statements, that establish parameters or norms for conduct. In the example above, protesters taunted and occasionally verbally abused soldiers and police, but this abuse was not extended to throwing cherry bombs or trash. Under a norm, people experience implicit and explicit social pressure to overtly conform to a particular line of behavior. Compliance with a norm is not a function of heightened suggestibility or emotional arousal. Unlike the emotion-charged settings described in contagion theory, Turner and Killian argue that compliance with norms occurs in quiet settings, such as funerals, as well as settings characterized by excitement and arousal.

Turner and Killian state that much crowd behavior is guided by traditional norms. Frequently, however, crowds confront novel or ambiguous situations, and hence the norms that guide behavior are *emergent*, new, and untried.

When people join together to rescue friends and neighbors after a community disaster, an ephemeral or temporary division of labor emerges. The emergent patterns of authority and lines of communication may be quite different from those extant prior to the disaster. Heavy equipment operators, for example, may find themselves in positions of authority, giving orders to bankers and city officials. Teenagers may become rescue workers and couriers of important information, performing tasks of greater responsibility than usual. To the casual observer, these arrangements may seem chaotic; however, Turner and Killian argue that they are an effective, normatively guided collective response to urgent situations.

Classification of Crowd Participants.   For Turner and Killian, collective behavior is basically social behavior, guided by both traditional and emergent norms. Even in crowded settings where excitement is high, people retain critical ability and a sense of personal identity, and they behave in terms of personal motives.

Turner and Killian use individual motives as a basis for a five-category classification of crowd participants. The classification categories reflect a decreasing level of personal identification with the events and issues that are part of any specific episode of collective behavior.

The first type of participant is the person who feels a strong personal commitment, or ego involvement, with the situation at hand. Consequently, the ego-involved participant is likely to demand or incite immediate action. In a disaster-struck community, ego involvement characterizes those whose family and property are in jeopardy. They are the first to initiate rescue efforts and may be the most active in organizing and directing rescue teams.

The second type of participant is motivated by a feeling of generalized concern. The concerned participant is typified by outsiders who converge on disaster-struck communities to assist in rescue and cleanup operations. Their families are safe—the concerned are simply being good neighbors. The concerned participant is unlikely to take the initiative but very likely to follow the lead of others and comply with emerging norms.

The third type of participant is the insecure. People may participate in collective action because doing so offers a sense of direction and identity. Adolescents, who are casting off the identity of the child and striving to achieve adult status, find temporary security in associating with other youth at rock concerts or within religious fellowships, cults, or protest groups. In the case of disasters, young people may derive a sense of importance to the community as they carry messages, clear rubble, or heft sandbags.

Curiosity is the fourth type of individual motivation considered by Turner and Killian. Rescue and reconstruction efforts are often hindered when large numbers of people converge on the disaster scene and survey the wreckage. Protesters are often outnumbered by spectators to the confrontation. Curiosity can be easily transformed. Spectators may cheer or jeer protesters and become involved in battles between police and demonstrators. Spectators at disasters may aid in rescue efforts or, perhaps, turn to looting.

The final category of motivation is ego detachment, often characterized by an exploitive attitude. Those who loot at disaster scenes do so because they can emotionally divorce themselves from the plight of others. Other forms of ego detachment are evidenced by such profiteers as those who sell fresh water and gasoline at exorbitant prices. But ego detachment need not entail an exploitive attitude. For example, professional rescue, medical, and media people must be able to face the threat of personal injury or confront scenes of horrendous suffering while maintaining a degree of emotional detachment in order to efficiently perform their jobs.

Individual Tendencies. For Turner and Killian, people retain a clear sense of personal motivation when participating in collective behavior. Some researchers have used people's statements of their attitudes and beliefs as measures of "individual tendencies" to participate in collective behavior. These measures of individual tendencies have been examined to determine whether, for example, people expressing negative attitudes toward police are more likely than others to riot. Ascribed statuses, such as sex and ethnicity, and achieved statuses, such as level of education and occupation, have been examined. Do workers of low occupational prestige, for example, engage in wildcat strikes and protest more often than workers in higher status occupations?

In 1971 Clark McPhail reviewed the volumes of riot participation studies conducted between 1965 and 1970. McPhail pointed out that at least 215 separate individual tendency variables had been examined in efforts to account for individuals' participation in riots. These variables included "attitude statements" regarding race relations and the political process in the United States. Other variables included "socioeconomic attributes," such as occupation and level of education, and "demographic attributes," such as age, sex, and length of residence in the city where the riot occurred. We will consider McPhail's review of the riot participation studies in later chapters; here it is sufficient to note that the riot participation studies constitute one of the largest bodies of research in the collective behavior literature. Though few of the riot participation studies explicitly acknowledge the emergent norm perspective and the point of view that the influence of the crowd does not supercede people's personal motives for action, they still proceed on the assumption that an examination of people's motives, attitudes, frustrations, and fears is the key to understanding riot participation.

Social Movements

For Turner and Killian, the boundaries of collective behavior range from individualistic behavior of limited duration, such as looting, to the social movement. They define a *social movement* as a collectivity acting with some continuity to promote or resist a change in the society of which it is a part. Membership is indefinite and shifting. The power and function of leadership within the movement are usually determined by the informal acknowledgment or acquiescence of members rather than by conventional and formal procedures for legitimizing authority.

External Processes of Social Movements. The external relations between a social movement and the larger society are an important factor in a movement's development. Every movement creates a public concern as to whether it is consistent with, irrelevant to, or contrary to existing values and power relationships within the society. Community reaction

will in part determine a movement's access to legitimate means for promoting its goals. Such reaction can range from amusement and token support to informal hindrances and violent suppression. Turner and Killian emphasize that there is a reciprocal relationship between community reaction and movement strategy, goals, and structure.

A consideration of the recent proliferation of religious cults in the United States illustrates this point. The emergence of Jesus movements in the late 1960s was seen by many commentators as a welcome departure from student activism and protest. Conservative spokesmen such as Paul Harvey and James Kilpatrick initially praised these movements as a voluntary repudiation of the moral permissiveness that characterizes youth culture. Public approval turned to skepticism, however, as the number of Jesus groups increased and their religious practices became more unorthodox. Established churches began to "fundamentalize" their practices in efforts to compete with emerging sects.

By 1981 the new sects included such variants of Eastern religions as the Krishna Consciousness, the Divine Light Mission, and the Rajneesh Neo-Sanyas International Commune. Within many sects, highly authoritarian structures and practices maintained strict control over members. Established churches now began to condemn the cults, and a general public concern emerged regarding the "brainwashing" techniques used by cults. Deprogramming groups were formed that actively opposed cults and, in some instances, technically kidnapped cult members in efforts to "save" them.

The Rajneesh Neo-Sanyas International Commune for all practical purposes bought the town of Antelope, Oregon, after bitter and costly legal battles over zoning regulations and ordinances (Buckwalter and Legler, 1983). The Internal Revenue Service has challenged the tax exempt status of many groups such as the

Reverend Sun Myung Moon's Unification Church. Faced with such opposition, cults have taken on characteristics of conflict groups using the courts, and in extreme instances (as with the People's Temple of the Disciples of Jesus Christ), the threat of armed conflict in dealing with those who oppose them.

Internal Processes of Social Movements. The internal processes of social movements are a second point of emphasis in Turner and Killian's approach. The character of social movements is shaped by the interplay among value orientations, power orientations, and participation orientations. A movement's value orientation is given expression in the movement's goals and ideology, which provide a simplified prescription for how adherents should look at other people and events. Turner and Killian define *ideology* as the tangible expression of some value or complex of values. A humanistic value, for example, led to the abolition movement and its goal of eliminating slavery as an institution, while values of racial superiority and purity led to the Nazi movement and efforts to exterminate non-Aryan groups. Ideologies construct an account of the past, a criticism of the present, and a prediction of the future, and they cast the movement's goals as ultimately consistent with the general welfare. Ideologies morally elevate the movement's constituency or potential constituency and create conspiratorial villains.

Changes in ideology alter a movement's goals and character. Initial successes by a loosely organized and emergent group will lead to a period of ideological elaboration and refinement in an effort to encompass divergent groups attracted to the growing movement. Ideology may be recast, for example, to include and describe the roles of women, educators, or businessmen within the movement. The ideology of a movement can also change in response to challenges from the established order. In the face of early charges that antinuclear groups were largely ignorant of the technology they opposed, many antinuclear groups have become compilers of information about nuclear and alternate energy systems. The fundamental point of Turner and Killian's discussion of value orientations is that ideologies evolve in response to events as well as to isolated intellectual and moral dialogues.

For Turner and Killian, the development and use of power becomes a central task of all social movements. Power orientations are necessary even if the movement is attempting little more than obtaining building or parade permits. The principal orientations in the exercise of power are persuasion, bargaining, and coercion. Persuasion is the attempt to manipulate target groups without the use of substantial rewards or punishments. Emergent groups may not have the power to use other tactics. Compliance with the movement's demands is encouraged by appeals to humanitarian ideals, fairness, the common good, or the target group's self-interest. Growing movements may establish control of some resource that target groups want. The movement's power orientations can then include bargaining or the exchange of value for concessions. Finally, power orientations can include nonviolent civil disobedience. Civil rights groups violated segregation laws; war protesters burned draft cards and then peacefully submitted to arrest in an effort to tie up the courts and generate sympathy for their cause. Groups such as the Weatherman faction of Students for a Democratic Society (SDS) utilized violent civil disorder during the late 1960s and early 1970s to press their demands. Finally, groups such as the Palestine Liberation Organization (PLO), the Red Brigade of Italy, and right-wing Salvadorian death squads turn to terrorism. Coercion is likely to emerge as a power orientation when movements are threatened or attacked by target groups. In some instances, persuasion and bargaining tactics are either impossible to implement or have already been tried without success.

People must obtain gratification from participating in social movements if they are to continue their support. Participation orientations may come to dominate a social movement. Value and power orientations are modified so that participation in the movement resolves the worries and personal problems of members. Participation orientations dominate millennial movements, which have a religious/mystical character centering on the prophecy of a catastrophic transformation of the world order: the movement's worldly tormentors will be punished and the movement or its leaders will rule. For Turner and Killian, millennial movements most likely occur among very oppressed people. Participation in the movement revolves around prayerful and festive preparation for the millennium. Millennial movements occurred frequently among the colonized people of New Guinea, Fiji, and other islands in the South Pacific. These movements were troublesome for European colonial administrations and gave the native islanders their first experience of open defiance of colonial rule.

Personal status movements provide immediate material and emotional benefits to members. Turner and Killian note that many religious sects attract adherents among the poor by providing food, shelter, medical care, and emotional security. The People's Temple provided such benefits in exchange for work, welfare, and social security checks. While the material benefits may seem meager by middle-class standards, they are often genuine improvements upon the lifestyles of the most disenfranchised poor. Other personal status movements provide emotional support and therapeutic relationships for members. Often these groups are formed to deal with problems that law enforcement, welfare, and medical

agencies ignore or can only partially alleviate. Groups are established to provide counseling and emotional support for victims of disease, rape, and drug addiction as well as to pregnant teenagers, child abusers, or single parents. Community agencies may sometimes refer people to these groups.

Participation-oriented movements can provide an organizational base upon which power orientations develop. The South Seas millennial movements evolved into nationalist movements. Synanon, a drug rehabilitation group with acknowledged success in the 1960s, acquired sizable California landholdings and became involved in armed confrontations with authorities in 1978.

For Turner and Killian, the history of a social movement reflects the interplay among power, value, and participation orientations. Social movements entail normative transformations for society and represent a molding of established and emergent practices, which may reveal new solutions to persistent problems. External opposition and support are major determinants in the direction of a social movement. Often social movements are undercut as established groups adopt and implement parts of the movement's program—the movement dies, but the program lives. Such was the case in the 1930s when the Roosevelt administrations implemented, in largely acceptable form, many programs first put forth by various socialist groups.

Summary

In summary, Turner and Killian's approach to collective behavior is a clear departure from the social contagion approach, utilizing conventional sociological views of normative and predispositional explanations of behavior. Turner and Killian develop an active view of social movements and identify external and internal factors that determine the character of movements. Turner and Killian do not claim to have developed a complete theory that specifies the essential conditions for the occurrence of collective behavior; instead, they claim to present a useful and extensive examination of processes that clearly shape the course of collective behavior.

The Value-Added Perspective

On Thursday, October 24, 1929, trading on the New York Stock Exchange began what promised to be another glorious day of profit making. During the previous five years, the trend in the market had been almost invariably upward. For those Americans with money to invest, "playing the market" had become an almost irresistible opportunity to amplify one's wealth. Stock dividends were of secondary concern—the rate of increase in the selling value of stock was the major attraction. What one bought today could be sold at a handsome profit three weeks from now. Blue chip stock, as well as newly formed and imaginatively financed issues in "investment trusts," were traded and retraded at ever increasing values. For the past few years, the market had perked along, trading 2–5 million shares a day, with only occasional and brief pauses in the upward trend in prices.

Thursday was to be different. Trading began heavily, and by 10:00 A.M. the ticker had dropped behind, unable to record the fast pace of trading. As the ticker fell behind, prices had begun to sag. More and more people began to sell, uncertain as to what was happening to prices other than that they were falling. There was also another concern—stop-loss orders. For their own protection, most brokers had standing orders calling for the sale of stock whenever a specified price was reached. As prices fell, they would cross increasing numbers of stop-loss orders, automatically dumping even more securities on the falling market. By 11:00 A.M. people were panic selling, and the floor of the Exchange resembled bedlam. The sound of this distress could be heard on the streets outside the Exchange; a crowd gathered, and police were sent out to keep order. The stock market crash of 1929 was underway. At the end of the day, stock averages had dropped by twelve points. Almost 13 million shares had been traded, exceeding the previous all-time high by more than 5 million.

Friday and Saturday the stock market was indecisive. Many stock analysts, politicians, and clergymen expressed the view in Sunday's papers and sermons that the worst was over. It had just begun. On Monday, more than 9 million shares were traded, and stock averages dropped forty-nine points. Tuesday, the ticker ran almost three hours behind as nearly 17 million shares were traded, and averages fell forty-three points. In less than a week, the stock market panic of 1929 had erased almost two years of gain. Investment trust stocks that survived had lost about two thirds their value of a week earlier. Even blue chips such as Westinghouse were selling at half their previous value.

In today's stock market, a three-day loss of 104 points would be considered a disaster. Adjusting for current prices, however, the 1929 crash would be the equivalent of today's market dropping 200–300 points. Stocks would continue to slide lower for another three years and not recover their early 1929 values for another decade. The most rapid and dramatic adjustments, however, had occurred.

Collective behavior episodes such as the financial panic that accompanied the stock market crash of 1929 are often described as "spontaneous," which usually indicates that the spontaneous collective behavior event was unexpected by authorities, spectators, and even the participants themselves. Often, such episodes seem to be triggered by an everyday, routine happening, such as a normal fluctuation in trading volume and stock prices. Many urban civil disorders of the 1960s are described as having been sparked by a routine arrest. Finally, the most exact meaning of the term *spontaneous* is "occurring without external cause." Applying this definition to collective behavior is somewhat problematic. It could be, and probably usually is, taken to mean that spontaneous collective behavior is caused solely by the *internal cognitive states* of participants: their individual attitudes, perceptions, and fears.

Closer examination of collective behavior events, however, invariably suggests causes apart from, or external to, the cognitive states of participants. Would, for example, the stock market panic have been as severe if the ticker had kept pace with transactions, or if there had been fewer stop-loss orders? Certainly, current federal regulations for investment groups and securities exchange would have slowed the selling. Likewise, many urban civil disorders started on weekends and during the late afternoon and evening, when people were relatively free from the competing demands of school and work. Arrests that precipitated initial phases of disorder were not as routine as often assumed. These arrests involved breakdowns in police communication procedure, lengthy delays in removing arrestees from the scene, and unusually large numbers of spectators.

All of the above suggest that collective behavior episodes, even seemingly spontaneous ones, can be viewed as the result of a *combination of causal factors*. No single factor by itself is sufficient to produce the event in question. However, several factors occurring together and in combination can produce a collective behavior episode. Neil J. Smelser's *Theory of Collective Behavior* (1962) presents a "several-factors-occurring-together" approach to collective behavior.

Collective Behavior and the Components of Social Action

In *Theory of Collective Behavior*, Smelser defines collective behavior as people's uninstitutionalized efforts to restructure the basic determinants of social behavior. These basic determinants—the components of social action—refer to the elemental forces, other than individual personalities, that order, regulate, and direct behavior within a society.

The most general component of social action within a society is the set of *social values*, or shared beliefs identifying the goals toward which the members of the society should strive. Sociologists often identify personal achievement, activity and hard work, affluence as a sign of virtue, efficiency and usefulness, progress, democracy, free enterprise, and belief in God as the dominant social values in the United States. Almost everything people do in the United States is judged in relation to these values. In many societies, those who wander the streets without jobs or money are ignored by authorities, but in the United States, it is generally viewed as fitting and proper that such people be arrested for vagrancy. The polluters of most industrial nations can quite convincingly justify their refusal to reduce pollution in terms of efficiency and cost effectiveness. In the United States, one of the most quick and certain ways to subject oneself to public denunciation, ridicule, and even death threats is to claim to be an atheist.

Societal norms are the second component of social action and are the explicit and implicit rules that govern the pursuit of values. Much of civil and criminal law in the United States directly and indirectly regulates the manner in which the value of personal achievement is pursued. Parents devote a great deal of time, effort, tears, and money to keep their children actively involved in school, sports, and the arts. Much conflict between generations is the result of young people subscribing to norms of personal achievement that differ widely from those of their parents.

The third component of social action is *organization of motivation*, which refers to the specific, implicit, and explicit requirements accompanying statuses, roles, groups, and organizations that constitute the social structure of a society. Much of what people do in society depends on the socially derived expectations for the ascribed statuses of men and women. In particular, societies set forth rather clear expectations of what work shall rightfully be carried out by men and what work shall rightfully be carried out by women. Social action within families is in large part directed by the expectations accompanying the roles of spouse, parent, and child. Finally, much social action is directed toward and judged in terms of fulfilling the demands accompanying group membership—being a good Shriner—and occupational role—being a good IBM executive.

The final and most immediate component of social action is the *situational facilities*— tools, skills, and knowledge of the environment—that people have at their disposal. Occupants of statuses and roles, and members of groups and organizations, have differing amounts of physical resources and knowledge that determine how easily and adequately they can meet the requirements of these positions. Some people have little difficulty in meeting parental role requirements because they have great situational facilities at their disposal: healthy children, adequate income, and relatively large amounts of unencumbered time to devote to children. Parents of physically or emotionally disabled children, parents with inadequate income, parents whose careers involve long absences from the home, parents with limited or inaccurate knowledge of child development, and many single parents have fewer situational facilities with which to meet parental role requirements. Consequently,

they have greater difficulty with, and derive less satisfaction from, their parental roles.

Restructuring the Components of Social Action. Institutionalized means are used in all societies to restructure the components of social action. In the Soviet Union, for example, the government has used the media as well as honorific and limited financial incentives to "create" societal values of higher worker productivity, having large numbers of children, and faith in the physical sciences. Institutionalized means are used to change organization of motivation, or social structure. Governments use taxes, tax credits, and transfer payments to promote or discourage the growth of groups and organizations. The Equal Rights Amendment (ERA) was an effort to restructure the legal and social expectations that accompany the status of women. Finally, situational facilities can be altered through institutionalized means. Some employers have made efforts to integrate the situational facilities of work with those of their employees' families. This includes such innovations as variable or "flex-time" work schedules, paternity leaves, child daycare programs, and family vacation programs. On a larger scale, the minimum wage, free public education, public libraries, and welfare programs are designed to expand the situational facilities available in the society.

The components of social action can also be restructured through uninstitutionalized means. That is, the restructuring occurs apart from, and at times counter to, traditional channels of authority and decision making, communication, and sources of political and economic power. For Smelser, this is collective behavior. The uninstitutionalized restructuring of values, norms, organization of motivation, and situational facilities occurs as *collective episodes*. Collective episodes are readily identified and relatively large-scale events that cluster in time and within certain parts of the social structure. Five general collective episodes constitute the field of collective behavior: (1) the panic, (2) the craze, (3) the hostile outburst, (4) the norm-oriented social movement, and (5) the value-oriented social movement.

Different collective episodes involve different components of social action. In panics and crazes, people's immediate concern is with situational facilities: getting to safety through a partially blocked exit, selling one's stock before prices hit rock bottom, or exploiting the rapidly rising price of silver bullion. Panics and the collapse of crazes are often preludes to hostile outbursts. Concern shifts to identifying and punishing the individuals, groups, and organizations responsible for the damage done earlier. Angry crowds may demand the removal of public officials. Minority groups become scapegoats and are attacked and expelled from the country. In the case of rebellions and revolutions, hostile outbursts may involve attempts to overthrow or totally restructure the government. In these cases, hostile outbursts may become part of larger-scale norm- and value-oriented social movements, as people begin to question the norms that govern relationships between groups in the society and the values that these norms reflect.

Summary. According to Smelser, social behavior within society is determined by the components of social action: social values, societal norms, organization of motivation, and situational facilities. In society, institutionalized means exist for altering the components for social action. Even so, there are times when people use uninstitutionalized means to alter the components of social action. This is collective behavior: collective episodes of uninstitutionalized efforts to alter the values, norms, organizations, groups, statuses, roles, and distribution of resources in the society. We now turn to Smelser's value-added explanation of why people depart from institutionalized means of change and take up uninstitutionalized means.

The Value-Added Determinants

As noted earlier, Smelser offers a "several-factors-occurring-together" explanation of collective behavior. Specifically, Smelser identifies five factors, or determinants, that together are sufficient to produce a collective episode. Smelser and others refer to this type of explanation as a "value-added" explanation of collective behavior.

The value-added explanation means, simply, that all five determinants must exist before a collective episode can occur. Further, the likelihood that a collective episode will occur increases as each determinant comes into being. In a sense, each determinant sets the stage for the remaining determinants. When four determinants are in place, for example, a collective episode is imminent. A hostile outburst, such as a race riot, can then be triggered by a seemingly insignificant event that fulfills the final determinant.

The value-added explanation also means that each determinant contributes to the character and general type of the resulting collective episode. Whether the collective episode takes the form of a panic, craze, hostile outburst, or social movement is a matter of how the determinants are organized. In the next sections we will consider the value-added determinants and the way each influences the character of collective episodes.

Structural Conduciveness. The most general value-added determinant of collective behavior is *structural conduciveness*. In the broadest sense, structural conduciveness refers to the basic parameters imposed on behavior by culture. Cultural values and norms entail world views within which collective behavior operates. For example, belief systems of the many cults and sects of recent years show great diversity, but this diversity is cast within the very general confines of monotheism, characteristic of Judeo-Christian and certain Eastern religions. These belief systems explicitly or implicitly take the view that man is created in God's image, thereby imbuing God with human characteristics. In developing their particular views, cults and sects have not freed themselves from the cultural constraints that prohibit development of pagan religions or the casting of animals and natural forces as deities. Cult and sect development among the South Sea Islanders, only marginally exposed to the religious views of European colonizers, often reflect the paganism of their earlier culture.

In the most restricted sense, structural conduciveness refers to immediate factors that facilitate communication and travel. The violent uprisings against European nobility during the Middle Ages had a decidedly local character, involving relatively few people and centering on specific grievances. As communication and transportation technology developed, and as increasing numbers of peasants were thrown off the land and congregated in cities, uprisings took on a more general character. Conditions of conduciveness that were the underpinnings of the French Revolution included greater levels of communication augmented by the printing press and improved overland transportation.

Smelser uses structural conduciveness in its most restricted sense in the analysis of panic. Panic flight is precluded in those situations where notice of impending danger is not given or when communication cannot occur among the threatened population. Panic occurs in situations where exits can only partially accommodate escape, but it will not occur if exits are readily available or are clearly and completely blocked.

Structural Strain.   The second value-added determinant of collective behavior is *structural strain.* For Smelser, all collective behavior re-

sults from some form of strain within the social system. Structural strain refers to inconsistencies between the values and norms of a society or to conditions of material deprivation established by the distribution of situational facilities of a society. Structural strain predisposes people to action but does not directly determine the content and direction of action. Pro- and anti-ERA movements and pro- and anti-abortion movements are opposing manifestations of structural strain at the level of societal values and norms. All are collective efforts to reconcile the inconsistency of societal values that emphasize the importance of the nuclear family with social norms of working women, small families, and high divorce rates.

Economic conditions such as inflation, unemployment, or rising prices of essential goods and services produce structural strain at the level of situational facilities. Nearly a decade of rising oil prices produced structural strain throughout the United States' economic system. This strain provided the basis for such diverse collective episodes as sporadic truckers' strikes, nationwide protest against American oil companies in October 1979, and anti-Iranian demonstrations a month later.

Generalized Belief.   The third value-added determinant is a *generalized belief* that prepares participants for action when structural conduciveness and strain are present. Generalized beliefs emerge through processes of rumor, milling, suggestion, and social contagion. A generalized belief eliminates uncertainty and provides focus for the collective episode and only coincidentally reflects a reasoned analysis or valid description of the situation confronting participants. For example, a generalized belief can explain economic deprivation as a result of imperialistic exploitation or as punishment for sins.

Value- and norm-oriented movements are based on generalized beliefs concerning the restoration, protection, or modification of social norms and the values they represent. Smelser states that classic religious doctrines such as Christianity and Islam often provide the belief component of social movements that reassert traditional norms and values. Recent events illustrate this point. The Iranian revolution of 1979 represented a retaking of power by Shi'ite Muslim leaders (*mullahs*) who had been displaced under the reign (1953–1979) of the Shah Mohammed Reza Pahlavi. The revolution reached a critical state in December 1978 when crowds celebrating Muharram (a Shi'ite month of mourning) were fired upon by the shah's police and the Iranian army. A general strike was called by the exiled Shi'ite mullah, the Ayatollah Khomeini. On January 16, 1979, the shah left Iran. Within weeks a revolutionary council of mullahs, under the leadership of the Ayatollah Khomeini, assumed power. During the following year, many traditional Muslim practices were reintroduced to Iran, such as the public flogging of criminals, traditional dress for women, and abolishing interest on loans or savings. The Ayatollah Khomeini's revolution was couched in Islamic rhetoric, and major events of the revolution coincided with Muslim holidays.

Hostile outbursts are based on generalized beliefs that place blame and express feelings of tremendous power to destroy, injure, or punish the offensive group or person. Immediately prior to the 1979 Muharram holiday, Iranian students seized the American Embassy in Tehran, taking the embassy staff hostage. The embassy was a focal point for daily anti-American demonstrations, and the chants and statements accompanying these demonstrations blamed the United States for the suffering inflicted on the Iranian people by the shah. Ayatollah Khomeini's revolution was seen as being imbued with the power of God, while the United States was described as a "defeated and wounded snake," powerless to end the seige. In the United States, sporadic anti-Iranian demonstrations occurred during the early days of the seige. Iranian flags (for burning) and Khomeini dart boards briefly enjoyed brisk sales. Iranian-owned businesses were boycotted, and the International Longshoremen's Association refused to handle Iranian cargoes. Participants in these activities usually described their actions as being intended to embarrass or punish Iran.

Crazes are based on generalized wish-fulfillment beliefs and fantasies of assured success. Smelser categorizes speculative booms, political bandwagons, fashion cycles, and religious revivals as crazes. Leaders in crazes may knowingly encourage such beliefs to further their ends. Generalized anxiety and fear provide the basis of hysterical beliefs that are in turn the basis of panic. The hysterical belief limits participants' awareness of alternatives, greatly reduces participants' capacity for rational thought in the face of threatening situations, and increases suggestibility to extreme levels.

Mobilization for Action. The fourth value-added determinant is the *mobilization for action*. Given conduciveness, strain, and a generalized belief, a susceptible population must yet be brought into action. Smelser's main focus in his conceptualization of mobilization is leadership. Leadership in the preliminary stages of mobilization for value- and norm-oriented social movements tends to be charismatic. At this stage the leadership's main concern is formulating ideology and programs for change. Once a movement shows evidence of success, it begins to gain members who join for reasons unrelated to the movement's original objectives. Success produces strange bedfellows. Intellectuals, Marxists, and military personnel moved to the side of Ayatollah Khomeini's Islamic revolution following the fall of the shah. As membership grows, the diversity of membership increases, and the movement becomes more central to national and international affairs, leadership must increasingly concern itself with administrative and tactical issues. As value- and norm-oriented movements grow, leadership must show increasing skills at resolving internal conflict. Leadership styles based on orthodoxy in the early stages of mobilization must change to those of accommodation in later stages. Finally, for movements to succeed, they must become largely institutionalized—the style of leadership used by the prophet and the revolutionary must be supplanted in degrees by those of the administrator. Very few leaders can fulfill these three roles with competence. More often, leadership personnel changes in response to these demands. Problems in leadership contribute to the failures and decline of social movements.

Leadership in the hostile outburst, craze, and panic is more elementary than in social movements. In these collective episodes, leadership of mobilization often derives from models rather than authority structures. The agitator or demagogue is the leader in the hostile outburst, and the mobilization accompanying a hostile outburst is described as following a "hostility curve." Initial hostilities, though small in scope, indicate an avenue for expressing grievance. Hostilities rapidly increase in scope and number. This later or derived state includes many hostile actions unrelated to the specific conditions that accompanied the initial outbursts. Such generalized hostilities provide an umbrella under which many groups can carry out their particular aims, such as looting, profiteering, or assault. In the final stage, hostilities rapidly decrease as social control is brought into play and the larger social order denounces this mode of expression.

The craze and panic follow similar mobilization curves. Leadership is primarily by example. Once initiated, speculation or panic flight rapidly increases at a furious tempo. Almost as rapidly, the craze and panic decline in scope and intensity, leaving the affected population in a state of emotional exhaustion.

Action of Social Control. The fifth value-added determinant in Smelser's model is *action of social control*. Institutions and leaders confronted by imminent or ongoing collective episodes can act to (1) prevent, (2) redirect, or (3) accommodate collective behavior.

1. *Prevention of collective episodes.* Institutions and authorities can act to alter conditions of conduciveness and strain. Regulation of financial institutions, such as installing quotas for trading volume, can act as a brake to prevent financial panic. Land reform programs are designed to alleviate the distressing poverty confronting landless peasants. Rumor control centers, presidential addresses, and propaganda can be used to dispel generalized beliefs. Action can be taken with respect to mobilization; leaders can be discredited, exiled, or even assassinated. Martial law or curfews can be imposed to quell hostile outbursts and panic.

2. *Redirection of collective episodes.* Collective episodes can be redirected. Leaders brought to national power through social movements frequently find it advantageous or necessary to redirect their constituencies' attention to external enemies while they establish workable domestic programs. One interpretation of the Iranian seizure of the American Embassy is that it was an attempt by Ayatollah Khomeini to divert attention from the failings of his revolution and to revitalize deteriorating Iranian unity.

3. *Accommodation of collective episodes.* Leaders may find it advantageous to accommodate certain forms of collective behavior. A politician's conditional recognition of a movement's goals can often guarantee financial and electoral support. Granting honorary and material concessions to movement leadership gives them a vested interest in the existing order. Given some authority, people often become staunch supporters of the social order from which that authority arises. Hostile out-

bursts may be tolerated by authorities as an alternative to terrorism or general revolution. The conditions of conduciveness, strain, and belief that underlie fashion crazes and financial panics are not seen by all authorities as undesirable. The sale of fallout shelter plans, hula hoops, T-shirts, pet rocks, and disco music, as well as gold and real estate, are a perpetual source of high profits for the skilled speculator.

The Logic of the Value-Added Approach

We began this presentation of the value-added approach to collective behavior with a brief description of the stock market crash of 1929, which Smelser has classified as a collective episode of panic. It seems appropriate to conclude this section by considering the stock market crash in terms of the value-added determinants. In so doing, we can illustrate the overall logic of the value-added explanation of collective behavior.

Structural Conduciveness. Our familiar ideas of profit motive, free markets, and free enterprise are not found in all societies. Many early societies, as well as a few small current societies, used barter systems instead of monetary systems. Throughout history societies have flourished without the benefit of money, trading chickens for pigs, bananas for potatoes, and horses for wives. Rates of exchange, such as ten chickens for one pig, were established not so much by immediate supply and demand but by centuries of tradition. The right to trade or otherwise dispose of property was also restricted by tradition. Trading could be carried out only during certain times of the year, only between certain people within the society, and only after the proper ceremonial rites had been observed. Within such societies, precipitous and large-scale transfer of property from one group to another was rare. Likewise, the total collapse of the worth of some barter

item was unlikely. In terms of the value-added approach, the conditions of structural conduciveness in small, traditional barter economies do not permit, or clearly work against, financial panic.

Such was not the case for the economy of the United States in 1929. Perhaps nowhere else on earth did conditions approach the ideal of immediate free trade of valued goods than on the floor of the New York Stock Exchange. The ownership of vast amounts of wealth could shift from one group or person to another with a gesture of the hand. Here the law of supply and demand worked rapidly, beautifully, and ruthlessly. The stock ticker conveyed the moment by moment results of these transactions to corporate board rooms and branch exchanges across the country.

Underlying all this were the investment trusts. The investment trust did not create new businesses or enlarge old ones; it simply allowed people to own stock in established companies by buying stock in the investment trust. In practice, the trust issued more of its own stock than it bought of established businesses. In effect, investment trusts allowed the volume of corporate securities to far exceed the volume of real corporate assets. The virtue of owning investment trust stock was in terms of its speculative value rather than in dividends. Investment trust stocks increased in value as long as confidence held in the stock market.

Finally, there were the stop-loss orders. Considered individually, a stop-loss order is a prudent measure to protect investments. A standing order to sell stock if prices dip to a certain level can automatically limit one's loss. If, however, stop-loss orders are for very large blocks of stock, or if there are many stop-loss orders in the market, the collective effect can be disastrous. Like a line of falling dominoes, stop-loss orders dump huge amounts of stock into an already falling market; the increased volume of unwanted stock further depresses prices and triggers more stop-loss orders.

In 1929 the conditions of structural conduciveness were such that vast amounts of wealth could be transferred within hours. Also inherent in these conditions was the possibility for vast losses in terms of the dollar value of stocks.

Structural Strain. Without structural strain, society is in a state of equilibrium. A variety of conditions within society can produce strain, which is the driving force behind all collective episodes. The uninstitutionalized activity of the collective episode is directed toward reducing structural strain. In the case of the stock market crash of 1929, a number of sources of structural strain increased the likelihood of a massive and potentially violent reorganization of the stock market.

Societal values are quite enduring, and we can assume that personal achievement and hard work were societal values, even in 1929. These values could have been a source of strain in the few years preceding the crash. The sense of a prudent and closely watched investment had given way to a feeling of easily acquired riches. The speculative profit of the last months in the stock market was not in keeping with the ideals of personal achievement and hard work. People with money to invest were, in a sense, taking advantage of a system that temporarily offered the chance for profit without the traditional responsibilities of ownership. This was clearly the case for those entering the market through the investment trusts, who indirectly owned stock in actual businesses. This era has often been described as a period of heedless speculation, although most investors must have occasionally reflected on the old axioms that "what goes up, must come down" and "all good things must end."

The ease with which they made money in the stock market may have caused occasional twinges of guilt and anxiety among people who normally placed a high value on personal achievement and hard work. But the most important source of structural strain lay in the economic conditions this speculation produced. Briefly stated, speculation pushed the market value of stock far above what was reasonable given the current corporate earnings and the general business climate.

In the final three months before the crash, there had been a broad downturn in most economic indicators. Steel production had declined by about 10 percent. Most factory output had declined, inventories were growing, and workers were being laid off across the country. Home building, which had been dropping all year, went into a dramatic June–September slump. Normally, the stock market makes fairly rapid downward adjustments to such developments, but this was not the case in the final months before the crash, as the stock market registered almost daily gains of at least five points. It was inevitable that business conditions would force an adjustment in stock prices.

Generalized Belief. In the fall of 1929, economic conditions clearly indicated that a large-scale adjustment in stock prices was in the offing. Nothing, however, indicated that the adjustment would take the form of a rapid and almost total collapse of the market. For such a violent reaction, a third value-added component was necessary—a generalized *hysterical* belief. Smelser identifies the generalized hysterical belief as a belief that assigns the power to destroy to ambiguous elements in the environment. This belief restricts people's attention to only one concern—escape. In this case, people's financial assets were endangered, not their physical safety.

In the sixteen months prior to the crash, many first-time investors entered the market. With investment simply a matter of putting money into the market and watching it grow, these investors had the confidence of professional stock analysts. When things started to get complicated on Thursday, October 24, and the real threat of total financial wipeout presented itself, these investors realized they were in over their heads. In a sense, the entire workings of the stock market suddenly represented an "ambiguous situation" to the novices. Escape, in the form of immediately dumping one's investments, seemed the only means of coping with the situation.

For the more seasoned investors, there were other fears and ambiguities. They knew that stock prices were out of line with current business conditions and that a downward adjustment was overdue, but the investment trusts were an unknown entity. Their stock had led the upward trend in the market in the past months. It was feared they might also lead the downward trend. Finally, they knew that the stop-loss orders could trigger a massive price slide.

After Thursday's drop in stock prices, many declared that the worst was over. Even the analysts of *The New York Times*, who had predicted disaster for more than a year, felt that the market had finally reached a realistic plateau. However, there were many rumors that major investors would soon be selling out. Perhaps such conflicting information only added to the novices' fear that they really knew little about the workings of the market. In any event, the many assurances of the weekend were insufficient to overcome the widespread concern of investors. Thursday had ruined some investors and reduced the wealth of many others by half. The fears of this latter group may have led the initial wave of heavy selling on Monday's market.

Mobilization for Action.   On Thursday, October 24, three of the five value-added determinants were in place; the next was mobilization for action. In the case of panic, this is the event (or events) that poses an immediate

threat and gives shape to generalized anxieties. The most immediate factor in the mobilization for action was the stock ticker failing to keep pace with transactions. This had happened several times before, but in those instances, the ticker had fallen behind in a rising market. Then, the only anxiety generated was that of waiting to find out how much richer one had become. Only once before, about eight months earlier, had the ticker fallen behind in a sagging market. It, too, had been a terrible day.

It is nerve-wracking to know that your stocks are falling but not by how much: you think that when the ticker catches up with transactions, your stock will be worthless. Smelser draws an analogy between this situation and trying to get to a partially blocked exit in a burning theater. If you move in an orderly fashion with the other patrons, the exit may be blocked before you reach it; if you dash ahead, you may escape. The rush to sell one's stock is the financial equivalent of dashing for the exit. In both situations, the mad rush adds to the confusion and may ultimately lead to large-scale tragedy.

During the three worst days of the stock market crash, the ticker fell behind within forty-five minutes after the opening of trading, and final prices were not available for at least two hours after the close of trading. During those awful hours, people were literally "selling blind."

The "models" available for action are another factor in mobilization for action during panic. Many accounts of those three days mention the behavior of influential and well-known bankers, brokers, and members of the stock exchange while they were on the trading floor. These prominent and influential people appeared nervous and worried. Their sell orders were given in a conspicuous manner. A flurry of rumors occurred each time these people left the trading floor to attend hastily called conferences. The apparent fear and indecision of major figures in the financial community prompted others to sell stock.

Action of Social Control.   The final value-added determinant is action of social control, which in this case refers to the actions of leaders and authorities to prevent or control panic. This can be done by *modifying other value-added determinants*. That is, leaders may provide information that can counter generalized beliefs and take actions that can alter structural conduciveness, reduce structural strain, or prevent mobilization. Throughout his discussion of action of social control, Smelser points out that a failure to act usually contributes to the scope and severity of the collective episode.

The inaction of leaders has been frequently noted as an aggravating factor in the stock market crash. On Friday, a group of bankers asked President Hoover to urge Americans to buy up the new "bargains" the market had just created. Hoover did not comply.

During the weekend, the newspapers were full of advertisements urging calm and declaring that the worst was over. On the floor of the Exchange, however, action had spoken louder than words. On Thursday at half past one, Richard Whitney, the acting president of the Exchange and floor trader for National City Bank, made large and conspicuous purchases of industrial stocks. The market immediately began a recovery that held Thursday's losses to only twelve points. Many accounts suggest that this purchase was calculated to give confidence to investors, but in any event, nothing of this sort was attempted on Monday and Tuesday. The market was left to fend for itself.

Finally, directors of the Exchange considered the idea of closing or shortening the hours of the Exchange to allow some sobriety to develop. It has also been suggested that events on Wall Street began to be affected by loss of sleep. Weary traders had begun to confuse, forget, and lose their clients' sell-orders. The first short day of trading did not come until Thursday. Wednesday's market had stabilized, however, and the "Crash of '29" was over.

Economic historians generally agree that by the fall of 1929, the stage was set for a large adjustment in stock prices. There is much less agreement regarding why the adjustment was so damaging. Smelser's value-added analysis of collective behavior offers an explanation of why the adjustment took the form of a sudden, widespread, and financially disastrous selling of stock.

The elements of Smelser's model—the components of social action, the value-added determinants, and the five types of collective episodes—are presented in Figure 2.2. The relationships among these elements are also illustrated. In later chapters, we will consider Smelser's value-added explanation of civil disorders and social movements.

The Social Behavioral/ Interactionist Perspective

Clark McPhail has devoted a great deal of time to teaching students how to identify, observe, and record collective behavior. He has directed field research teams in locations where crowds are generally found: at protests, political rallies, sports events, shopping malls, and airline terminals. These teams have made written and film records of crowd formation, marches, sit-ins, prayer services, spectator behavior, and crowd dispersal. They have made comparable records of routine movements of groups within shopping malls and on athletic fields, parking lots, and sidewalks. Throughout, they have paid considerable attention to recording the gestures and instructions people use to direct the activities and movements of others. In general, there has been a sustained interest in observing and recording crowd formation, or *assembling processes, behavior within gatherings*, and *crowd dispersal*. For

FIGURE 2.2 *Smelser's Value-Added Model of Collective Behavior*

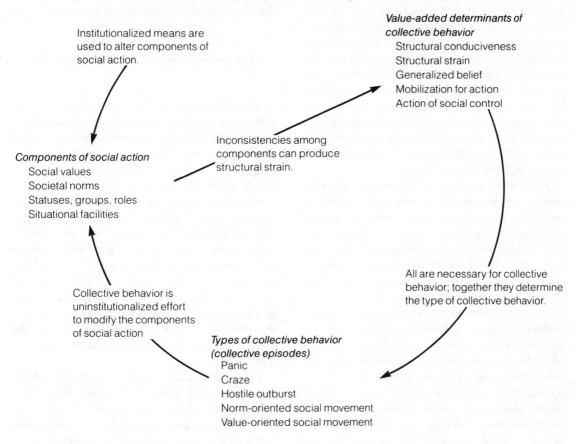

Institutionalized means are
used to alter components of
social action.

*Value-added determinants of
collective behavior*
Structural conduciveness
Structural strain
Generalized belief
Mobilization for action
Action of social control

Inconsistencies among
components can produce
structural strain.

Components of social action
Social values
Societal norms
Statuses, groups, roles
Situational facilities

All are necessary for collective
behavior; together they determine
the type of collective behavior.

Collective behavior is
uninstitutionalized effort
to modify the components
of social action

*Types of collective behavior
(collective episodes)*
Panic
Craze
Hostile outburst
Norm-oriented social movement
Value-oriented social movement

McPhail, these elementary patterns of behavior make up the events that have traditionally been viewed as belonging to the field of collective behavior.

The accumulating work of McPhail, his colleagues, and students is now generally regarded as a separate perspective within the field—the *social behavioral/interactionist perspective (SBI)*. The social behavioral/interactionist perspective is behavioral in the sense that collective behavior is conceptualized in terms of the *organization of convergent activity*, such as numbers of people marching, walking, or running in the same direction or to the same location. Chanting, singing, and gesturing by

many people with respect to a common object are convergent activities that occur within gatherings. These and other forms of convergent behavior necessarily precede or are a part of celebrations, protests, civil disorders, revolutions, disasters, and social movements.

McPhail's SBI approach is interactionist in the sense that convergent behavior is the result of meaningful interpretations, or instructions for response, supplied by participants and others. That is, instructions for response are cues to conduct that name, locate, and otherwise identify objects by denoting whether objects are good, bad, dangerous, and so on. Instructions may be verbal statements, such as "The

Russians are aggressors," or gestures, such as smiles, salutes, and "flipping the bird." Every society contains many *graphic identifiers*, including emblems, logos, and national flags. The golden arches of McDonald's and the letters *IBM* are identifiable the world over. People make a wide variety of responses to these cues to conduct. Through frequent interaction, people establish a more or less stable vocabulary of instructions, or shared interpretations, which constitute the meaningful objects within their social world.

While some instructions for response identify objects, others specify action with respect to these objects. Instructions for response specify movement toward or away from objects, and they include verbal statements, such as "Let's go to the Who concert next week," and the pointing and directing gestures used by police as they direct traffic at the scene of an accident. These instructions also tell people when activities are to begin, at what rate they are to be carried out, and when they are to end. Included in this category of cues to conduct are verbal statements, such as "When the militia opens fire, retreat to the jungle," written schedules that tell people when athletic events begin or trains depart, and hurry-up or slow-down gestures. People regulate their own and others' behavior with such instructions. With some imagination and persistence, investigators can observe many of these instructions. While people certainly provide some unobservable instructions to themselves (that is, thinking), they must provide audible or visible cues to others incident to convergent behavior.

From the standpoint of the SBI perspective, the organization of convergent activity, or collective behavior, results from immediate cues to conduct. The SBI perspective manifests a clear concern with what people are doing with and in relation to one another. How cues to conduct relate to convergent activity, and how both relate to the general concerns within the field of collective behavior, can best be made clear by considering the following examples.

Gatherings and the Assembling Process

The gathering together of people is a fundamental feature of social behavior. Many collective behavior events are preceded by and involve gatherings. For example, Wednesday, August 11, 1965, was a hot and humid day in Los Angeles. In the Watts section of the city, hundreds of people were sitting on their front porches, and children were playing on the sidewalks and in the street. A few people noticed a police car, with flashing lights, parked in the street. People began to walk toward the police cruiser and saw that two officers were in the process of arresting a young man for a traffic violation. The arrest entailed some shouting and shoving. Coincidentally, the young man's mother arrived on the scene and became quite upset.

As more and more people stood around the arrest scene, this gathering became increasingly conspicuous. Additional police cruisers and motorcycles began to arrive at the scene, with lights flashing and sirens on. This event could now be seen and heard for several blocks up and down the street, and people began to converge from even greater distances. Because of the large number of civilians and the snarl of police vehicles, police were no longer able to complete their arrest and leave the scene in an orderly manner. Before police made their way out of the congested area, citizens were injured and police vehicles damaged. Crowd activity continued throughout the Watts area until midnight. Late Friday afternoon, arsonists set several fires that again provided gathering points for crowds, and one of the largest racial disorders in our nation's history, the Watts riot of 1965, was underway.

Like collective behavior, routine social events are preceded by the gathering together of people. It is interesting to watch from one's office window as students trudge along sidewalks and between university buildings as morning classes begin. One can see faculty members hastily maneuvering their cars into parking spaces. Some faculty members arrive in the departmental office breathlessly clutching their lecture notes. They quickly check their mailboxes, exchange greetings, grab a quick cup of coffee, and then rush off to their classrooms. Students arrive in various stages of alertness, and typically, just after the lecture begins, a few stragglers wade over other students to unoccupied seats. Another day of classes has begun!

Assembling processes, through which gatherings occur, are a form of *convergent behavior*. McPhail and his students have made and analyzed film records of several short-range assembling processes, including student gatherings at street intersections during campus disorders, a gathering of people behind a student union prior to a campaign speech by Edmund Muskie in 1972, and the gathering of people in the parking lot of a football coliseum prior to the game and during halftime.

Using a questionnaire methodology, McPhail and Miller studied a medium-range assembling process that resulted in a late evening airport gathering of about four thousand students and townspeople prior to the arrival of a victorious basketball team. This assembling process began shortly after the radio broadcast of the game (about 8:30 P.M.) and culminated about midnight, when the team arrived. The distance from the center of campus to the airport was about ten miles. A few arrests were made, and newspapers carried descriptions of littering, theft, and minor vandalism at the airport. McPhail and Jane Bailey did a similar replication study of an assembling process that resulted in a gathering of about three hundred students and townspeople at the scene of an apartment house fire. Assembling began about 9:00 P.M. and occurred over a ten-block area.

Finally, this author has studied periodic assembling—the daily movements of students to an 8:00 A.M. first-period class taught by one of my colleagues. Using a questionnaire administered each day of class for three weeks, I obtained the names of people each student encountered prior to class and a description of the activities in which they engaged. Students who missed class filled out a similar questionnaire, detailing who they were with and what they were doing in lieu of class.

The SBI Explanation of Assembling. The studies outlined above suggest that the most essential event in the production and completion of assembling processes is that people receive *equivalent assembling instructions* establishing a location and time for an event and specifying movement to that location. The sights and sounds accompanying many events are sufficient to establish short-range assembling processes among people who are close enough to see, hear, and walk to the location of the event. Flashing lights, sirens, use of loudspeakers, and formations of uniformed police are among the many cues to conduct sufficient to establish that "something is happening," thereby creating a focal point for movement. The convergent gaze of onlookers provides cues as to the direction of the event. Convergent locomotion, such as walking, running, or marching, provides cues as to the direction and rate of movement toward the event. The size of the assembly itself has an effect on the assembling process; the larger the gathering, the more visible and noisy it is.

For medium-range assembling, word-of-mouth assembling instructions are important. These instructions can establish event locations outside people's immediate surroundings and at future times and dates; for example,

"Let's go to this afternoon's antidraft rally at the union." Medium-range assembling entails an amount of lead-time between the receipt of first assembling instructions and the pending gathering. It is therefore possible that people who have previously engaged in activities relevant to the gathering can be targeted for assembling instructions by others. For example, prior to the airport gathering, band members, student reporters and, perhaps, old alumni were sought out by others and given instructions to be at the airport when the team arrived.

While the receipt of assembling instructions seems to be necessary for the *initiation* of assembling movements, not everyone *completes* movement to gatherings. Completion of assembling movements depends on access to the event location. For medium-range assembling, walking or running to the location may be impossible or take too much time. Access to bicycles, motorcycles, or autos becomes essential and may also target vehicle owners for assembling instructions. Many students reported, for example, that they first learned of the airport event when others asked them to provide rides.

Competing instructions and demands are important factors in determining who completes assembling movements. Many people who started for the airport were deflected en route. For example, some students wanted or were asked by others to stop at bars, restaurants, or apartments along the way. While at these places, radio and TV announcements as well as people en route provided additional assembling instructions that occasioned further movement toward the airport. Some students, however, received no further assembling instructions and did not restart their trip to the airport. Competing demands such as work schedules, deadlines for class assignments, dormitory hours, and prior appointments encumbered the free time of some students and

resulted in their absence from the airport event.

In my study of periodic assembling, students who missed first-period class almost always reported being engaged in activities with other students who did not have a first-period class. Students with free periods frequently implicated fellow students in lines of activity, such as drinking coffee and conversing in the union, which resulted in absence from class.

In summary, for people to initiate and complete assembling movements, they must receive assembling instructions and have access to transportation and an amount of relatively free or negotiable time during which movement can occur. Given this, the completion of assembling movements also entails either an absence of competing instructions *or* recurring assembling instructions that keep people on the path, or trajectory, toward the assembly site (see Figure 2.3).

A more general theory of assembling must consider movements over greater distances to events of more than a few hours duration, or long-range assembling. In all likelihood, increased access to transportation facilitates such assembling movements and may expose participants to additional assembling cues, such as requests to provide rides for others or long-range verbal and written commitments to a chartered flight. As distance to the proposed assembly site increases, travel time and the proposed duration of the event extend the temporal commitment required of those initiating assembling movements. The initiation of assembling movements becomes increasingly dependent on rescheduling or "covering" competing commitments, such as getting another instructor to meet one's classes during the week of the annual American Sociological Association meetings.

Quite clearly, communication technology makes possible many of today's social events, and a general theory of assembling must ac-

FIGURE 2.3 *Assembling Process*

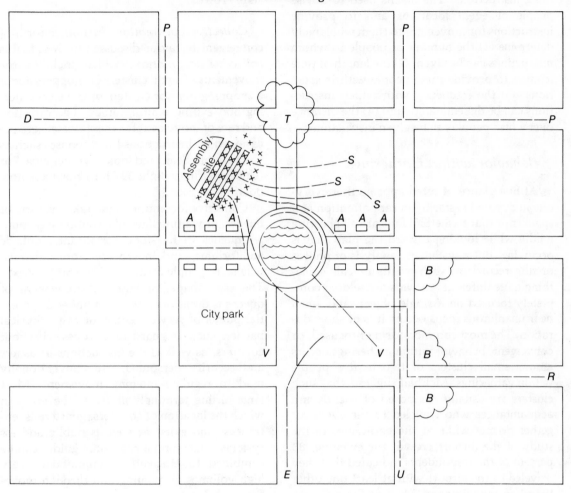

Assembling Movements

Long-range assembling

D   Antinuclear demonstrators

P   Police

U   Counterdemonstrators
    (unemployed construction
    workers from Sammy's Bar)

R   Television news crew

E   Street theater people

Short-range assembling

S   Picnickers who notice crowd
    move closer

A   Traditional bench sitters
    (elderly, winos, pigeon feeders)

B   Pedestrian shoppers who gather
    and watch crowd

T   Traffic jam—spectators and
    irate motorists

V   Hot dog vendors

count for the means of disseminating assembling instructions. The means used to advise people of event locations and to provide instructions for movement to them will largely determine (1) the number of people to whom instructions can be given, (2) the length of time it takes to provide these people with instructions, (3) the frequency with which instructions can be disseminated, and (4) the distance over which people can be given instructions.

Behavior within Gatherings

At first glance, it often appears that everyone in a crowd is staring in rapt attention at a speaker or that basketball fans are all cheering wildly while looking toward the play that is occurring. But a systematic analysis of photos or film records of such events reveals something quite different. Crowds are seldom completely focused on a single object, and when near unanimous focus occurs it is of short duration. The most common form of focused, or convergent, behavior within gatherings occurs among small clusters of two to five people within gatherings. McPhail suggests that such clusters are usually composed of friends and acquaintances who traveled to the event together or met while at the gathering. In the study of the airport crowd, for example, 83 percent of the respondents indicated that they traveled to the airport with at least one other friend or acquaintance. Most of these groups remained together at the rally and also returned together (75 percent and 87 percent, respectively).

This view of behavior within gatherings contrasts with the "unanimity of behavior" characterization offered by social contagion theory; it also contrasts with the assumption that crowds are composed primarily of elementary and transitory social relationships that contribute to crowd "instability." The influence of family members, friends, and organizational ties and demands must play a part in

the conceptualization, description, and analysis of crowds.

Collective Locomotion. Another form of convergent behavior discussed by McPhail is *collective locomotion*, which includes the movements of small clusters of shoppers about a shopping mall or clusters of travelers entering and exiting waiting areas. The direction and rate of movement for these clusters are occasioned by instructions for response, such as "Let's go into Sears and look at winter coats" or "United Airlines flight 327 for Phoenix is now boarding at gate 3."

Collective locomotion may take the form of queues, or waiting lines. We routinely encounter queues in fast-food restaurants, outside auditoriums, and in grocery stores, that is, whenever people await service, entry, or exit. The size, shape, and rate of movement of queues is occasioned by the number of potential points of service, entry, or exit. Physical barriers such as guard rails, ropes, checkout counters, as well as the instructions of ushers and security personnel, are conventionally used to regulate queuing movement. Most large airline terminals illustrate the ways in which the location of counters, guard rails, entrances, and exits, as well as public address systems, signs, and air terminal guides can be combined to efficiently accommodate very high volumes of queuing and through movement.

McPhail's SBI perspective explicitly introduces consideration of architectural design and crowd-management procedures to the field of collective behavior. Inconvenience and even tragedy can result when little attention is given to the regulation of high-volume queuing movement. On December 10, 1979, eleven people suffocated and others were injured in a crowd waiting outside Cincinnati's Riverfront Coliseum prior to a concert by the Who. Later accounts noted that many in the crowd had been intoxicated and rowdy. It is also clear, however, that the relatively unregulated "first-come, best-seated" festival seating arrangements, the unusually long wait, the use of only one entrance, and the lack of security personnel contributed to the size and density of the gathering. Neither promoters nor coliseum personnel attempted to establish orderly queuing when people began to arrive more than six hours prior to the concert. As the crowd increased in size, at the rate of about twenty-five people per minute, the opportunity to reposition people into queues soon faded. In the final minutes before the coliseum doors were opened, people were packed so tightly in the waiting area that police were unable to get to those who were being injured and suffocated. The concert went on as scheduled, and most of the audience was unaware that people had died. Within the week, ordinances had been formally proposed to ban festival seating and give Cincinnati police more crowd control authority.

Finally, a more concerted form of collective locomotion is marching, which includes the loosely parallel movement of demonstrators down a street as well as the highly choreographed routines of military precision marching teams. Ronald T. Wohlstein and McPhail have developed procedures for judging the degree of coordination (in terms of simultaneity, sequentiality, direction, and tempo) of collective locomotion. These procedures can be used to compare the degree of collective behavior displayed by various groups. They could be used, for example, to more exactly compare the marching characteristics of competing marching bands or to assess the effectiveness of various training and drill methods.

Taking a broader point of view, McPhail notes that the history of collective behavior and social movements is the history of people marching from place to place. Certainly, the organization and use of marches has been a major component of protest, rebellion, and revolution throughout history. From the He-

brews' march out of Pharaoh's Egypt to the latest march on the White House, people have used marches to present and press their claims on rights and resources. Revolutions often begin with the violent dispersal of marches. Joseph Stalin noted how the Cossack's whip and saber "rendered a great service" by infuriating marching street crowds and onlookers in pre-revolutionary Russia. McPhail identifies the march as a fundamental form of collective behavior. Consideration of how marches are organized and carried out, as well as the response of authorities to them, can give us a "nuts and bolts" understanding of protest, rebellion, and revolution.

Diaspora: The Process of Dispersal

McPhail uses the term *diaspora*, which derives from the Greek term meaning "scattering," to refer to the dispersal of gatherings. The dispersal of gatherings usually occurs routinely in response to instructions for dispersal or movement to different locations. Dispersal instructions and dispersal are occasioned by the termination time of events, most of which are known in advance. We know, for example, the time at which university classes are to end or the time at which a movie lets out. We can only approximate the termination time for athletic events such as football games, which terminate when two full halves have been played. The end of most events is an occasion for instructions specifying movement of small groups and individuals to other places, such as classrooms, dormitories, libraries, homes, bars, or restaurants. In these instances, dispersal is the result of people initiating movement to new locations and pending events.

The termination time for some gatherings, such as those at the scene of fires or beer parties, is quite indefinite, or open-ended. Often one can observe these gatherings decrease in size as the starting times for other activities approach. For example, I observed a gathering of

FIGURE 2.4   *Crowd Dispersal*

Cubs win! Cubs win! Thirty-four thousand people leave Chicago's Wrigley Field. The dispersals of crowds following sporting events are among the largest routine dispersal processes found in human social behavior. These and other large-scale dispersals usually occur without incident, but occasionally people are injured when dispersal processes break down. (Photo by Grant Bogue.)

approximately 150 people at the scene of a fire that started at 3:30 one warm and pleasant fall afternoon. About 4:45, the size of the crowd began to noticeably dwindle, even though firemen were still battling the blaze. The next day I discussed the fire with students who had been at the scene, and they said that they had

watched the fire until it was time to return to their dormitories and apartments for dinner.

The dispersal of gatherings usually occurs without incident. For example, I have delivered more than three thousand lectures to classes ranging in size from 10 to 280. In none of these instances did a class fail to disperse at the conclusion of the lecture, nor was anyone injured leaving the classroom. Sometimes, however, dispersal is problematic for both authorities and participants. McPhail considers the issues of the dispersal of crowds by police and emergency evacuations.

Crowd Dispersal by Police.   According to McPhail, the success with which police accomplish crowd dispersal by either providing dispersal instructions or using force is related to the fact that police are an organized group and many crowds are not. American police typically follow a pattern of requesting people in a gathering to relocate or refrain from specified activities: "Let's move along folks," "Please move back to your seats," or "You will have to stop making so much noise." Such instructions are usually complied with by all or a portion of the people in the gathering. Some within the gathering may offer instructions complementary to those provided by police, such as "C'mon, guys, let's go back to the dorm."

On the other hand, some people in a gathering may be either unable to hear the police or unable to move because of the density of the gathering. Finally, some within the gathering may provide alternate instructions, such as "We aren't hurting anybody; we aren't moving!" McPhail suggests that alternate instructions are provided by those who have traveled greater distances or have free time at their disposal. People organized under the auspices of interest groups, such as antinuclear groups, are more likely to provide alternate instructions than unorganized groups, such as the spectators at the scene of a traffic accident. When confronted with noncompliance and/or competing instructions, police can use force to disperse or arrest those in a gathering. Force, ranging from physically carrying people away from the gathering place to the use of lethal gunfire, can be used to control people in spite of their competing instructions and noncom-

pliance. Quite often in demonstrations, we observe police carrying away people who are loudly singing, "We shall not be moved." McPhail urges that theorists recognize the use of physical force in the control of human collective behavior.

Emergency Evacuations.   Though we seldom read about such events in the newspapers, even large numbers of people can usually evacuate theaters, restaurants, stores, auditoriums, and nightclubs under emergency conditions, without injuring themselves and others. McPhail suggests that when people are confronted with emergency evacuations, they provide "quite rational instructions for dispersal" in the direction of the exits known to them. This is in sharp contrast to the social contagion or panic image of emergency evacuations, which suggests that people are likely to become irrational and "stampede" at the first hint of danger (see box, p. 24).

Rather than accounting for the development of stampedes, the SBI perspective casts that problem as one of accounting for the deterioration and breakdown of initially sensible and rather orderly dispersal processes. Dispersal processes break down when toxic smoke and noise make it impossible for people to see and hear. When people cannot monitor one another's behavior or see exits and barriers to movement, controlled, coordinated dispersal becomes impossible. Narrow doors, hallways, and stairwells constrict movement and increase crowd density. It is in such *crowd extrusions* that people are crushed.

Under some circumstances, however, a successful evacuation is realistically impossible. When people are in overcrowded buildings with insufficient numbers of exits, and they are confronted with rapidly spreading fire giving off highly toxic and dense smoke, even controlled dispersal (which is impossible) will not allow all occupants to escape. The conditions

TABLE 2.1
Theories of Collective Behavior

Theory	Unit of analysis	Nature of collective behavior	Outcomes
Social contagion	Hysterical outburst	Episodic response to stress—homogeneous, intense, and rapidly transmitted behavior; individual suggestibility	Socially disruptive; once hysteria has run its course, population is temporarily immune to further outbreaks
Emergent norm	Emergent action in response to ambiguous situations	Collective definition of situations—emergent, temporary groups, and relationships	Collective behavior can lead to new forms of association within society
Value-added	Collective episodes: panic, craze, hostile outburst, norm-oriented social movement, value-oriented social movement	Collective behavior is a response to social strain directed toward a restructuring of the components of social action	Collective episodes can be disruptive for society; social control functions primarily to contain collective behavior
Social behavioral/ interactionist	Convergent behavior: assembling processes, behavior within gatherings, dispersal processes	Social behavior viewed as a result of cues to conduct; collective behavior is social behavior	Emphasis on the intermeshing of collective and routine social behavior; collective behavior can disrupt as well as augment routine social behavior

mentioned above are common to almost all stampedes cited in the panic literature. Under such circumstances, it is questionable whether the alleged panic had any substantial effect on the tragic outcome.

Sometimes it becomes necessary to evacuate entire communities. Recent rail accidents involving hazardous chemicals and accidents at nuclear power plants have underscored a general lack of preparedness for such evacuations. Police and civil defense personnel generally find it difficult to entirely evacuate communities. It is, for example, very difficult to locate all residents to provide them with dispersal instructions and other emergency information. Once notified, many residents provide alternate, conflicting instructions, such as "I'm going to stay and protect my property." In some instances, authorities resort to loading residents on trucks, buses, or helicopters in spite of their protests. For those leaving without such assistance, dispersal movement is often to the homes of friends and relatives in nearby communities. Many who evacuate soon confront authorities with demands to return to their homes, businesses, or jobs.

Migrations. Migrations are perhaps the largest scale upon which dispersal processes occur. Migrations are uniformly characterized by collective behavior theorists as highly individualistic, sometimes crazed mass phenomena. The SBI perspective, however, is similar to that of *human ecologists*, such as Amos Hawley, who characterize migrations as social phenomena produced by "forces of repulsion and attraction." Migrations are accompanied by statements of disdain for the place of departure and great praise for the proposed destination. Some migrations, such as occurred during Ireland's great potato famine of the 1840s, are largely the result of forced expulsion. Irish landowners provided passage to the United States for destitute tenants as a less expensive alternative to supporting these people in workhouses. Irish immigrants to the United States, likewise, paid passages for family and friends left behind in Ireland. Utilizing such arrangements, almost one third of Ireland's population departed for other countries in the 1840s.

Summary

In this chapter we have outlined and summarized four theories of collective behavior. In later chapters these theories will be our guides as we consider specific topics within the field. Table 2.1 summarizes much of what has been said in this chapter.

As we noted earlier, these are not the only theories of collective behavior. In later chapters we will introduce additional theories that provide still more insight into a wider range of issues than we have discussed to this point. Before we move on to specific topics within the field, however, we will attend to the problem of studying collective behavior.

◆ CHAPTER 3 ◆

Studying Collective Behavior

Collective behavior is one of the few remaining fields of sociology in which researchers can experience the satisfaction of developing entirely new methods and strategies of investigation. This is not to say that collective behavior research is easy or that there are no established research traditions within the field. Some collective behavior research involves unusually painstaking procedures of data collection and analysis. Firsthand observation of crowds even involves a degree of physical stamina and assertiveness not required in other areas of sociological investigation. Finally, some commonly used methods of investigation, such as survey research, are part of the methodological traditions of both general sociology and collective behavior.

The subject matter of collective behavior presents researchers with problems not encountered in most other areas of sociological investigation. These problems give the research a distinct character, which some critics describe as "makeshift." A more charitable and accurate characterization is that collective behavior research often shows many signs of being carried out under far less than ideal circumstances. In the first part of this chapter, we will examine three major problems encountered in doing collective behavior research. We will then consider recent attempts at resolving

these problems. Finally, we will examine a number of studies that illustrate how collective behavior research is conducted.

The Problems

Three major problems have hindered the development of systematic knowledge about collective behavior phenomena. First, there is the problem of unanticipated events, which make it difficult to develop carefully thought out and pretested research strategies. Second, there is the problem of studying the crowd. Studying the crowd is a more formidable task than conducting a door-to-door survey. Finally, there is the general problem of studying collective behavior under controlled conditions such as those found in psychology laboratories.

Unanticipated Events

One of the most compelling reasons for launching a research project is being suddenly confronted with the opportunity to study a dramatic and unexpected event. Foremost among the problems encountered when doing collective behavior research is that many collective behavior events are unanticipated. In practice, this means that collective behavior studies are often initiated with little if any preparation.

Consider the hypothetical example of sociologists at Average State University who, early one afternoon, hear news bulletins that a tornado has swept through a nearby community. Sociologists gather and confer with one another to determine whether a study can and should be attempted. Shortly, the go-ahead decision is made. Preparations may involve little more than grabbing notebooks and tape recorders, recruiting graduate students, and rushing to the disaster site.

Upon arrival, the research team's scholarly zeal quickly turns to indecisiveness. The visual impact of the tornado's destructive force is tremendous, and because they have no definite plan of action, the researchers may experience feelings of being hardly more than unwelcome sightseers. Valuable time is lost while the team familiarizes itself with the situation at hand and arrives at some consensus regarding specific research objectives.

Then the first interviews with survivors begin. Researchers have not had time to carefully construct or pretest a questionnaire, so unstructured interviews are used. The people interviewed are selected because they are nearby and willing to talk rather than by a purposive sampling plan. Some team members must stop interviewing people and run time-consuming errands or check out leads that yield little information. By late evening, the members of the research team are tired, cold, hungry, and in need of a hot shower. Hardly any interviews have been conducted during the past hour—the sociologists are "out of questions," it is too dark to write in the notebooks, and the tape recorder batteries are dead. The researchers now notice that some aspects of community life are returning to normal; the opportunity to study the early phases of disaster response has passed.

The weeks following the sociologists' initial fieldwork prove to be quite aggravating. Even though much valuable information was obtained initially, omissions become obvious as the analysis and writeup begin. The sociologists now realize what they "should have done." Important questions were not asked, key people were not interviewed, and information that seemed valuable at the time now turns out to be useless or redundant. Followup work is made difficult because the names and addresses of many interviewees were not obtained. Once these problems are recognized, however, plans are not made for resolving them in future research. Rather, the sociologists make the reasonable assumption that they will never have another opportunity to study a disaster close at hand.

The Crowd

A second major problem is created by the difficulties encountered in observing or otherwise studying crowds. Observing crowd formation poses many difficulties. Consider another hypothetical example: hundreds of people may converge on a courthouse to await the verdict in a murder trial. Such turnouts might well be viewed as a desirable show of civic involvement; occasionally, however, turnouts like these have preceded civil disorders (Cantril 1941).

In either case, studying crowd formation will help us understand how such events develop. Important questions include (1) how people were initially notified of the event, (2) which of these people initiated movement to the event, and (3) what activities occurred on the way to the event. In order to observe crowd formation, prior notice is necessary in order to deploy observers in the field. People typically converge on the assembly point in small groups. Therefore, the number of small groups that can be observed during any instance of crowd formation is limited to the number of available observers.

Once assembling processes have occurred, problems of observation are somewhat simplified, particularly for stationary crowds such as an audience at an athletic event. Observers may restrict their observation to a particular section of the crowd, such as the cheering section. On the other hand, crowds involved in celebrations, marches, demonstrations, or civil disorders often move from place to place. Systematic observation is more difficult in these instances, because observers must be able to move with the crowd.

Some explanations of crowd behavior cannot be tested through direct observation. Smelser's value-added model, for example, explains crowd behavior as a result of hostile, wish-fulfillment, or hysterical beliefs. Testing Smelser's theory, then, requires the use of interviews or questionnaires, which poses the problem of administering questionnaires or conducting interviews within the crowd. Initially, this idea calls up rather absurd images of the sociologist approaching a group of people looting a liquor store during a riot and asking them to fill out questionnaires.

Most researchers who have attempted to ascertain the beliefs, attitudes, and tensions of people engaged in crowd activity have conducted their research days, weeks, and even months after the fact. Using after-the-fact surveys requires making the assumption that beliefs, attitudes, and tensions that exist weeks after the event also existed during the event. Critics of this assumption argue, for example, that people who have been arrested or have battled the police are likely to express much more negative attitudes than they would have immediately prior to these confrontations. Logic dictates that beliefs, attitudes, and tensions be studied within the immediate context of the behavior they are assumed to direct. Common sense, however, seems to preclude

study of these variables within the acting crowd.

Controlled Study

The third general problem is the limited degree to which collective behavior can be studied under controlled conditions. Sometimes social behavior can be "created" in a convenient setting for the purposes of study. The early Hawthorne studies of worker productivity, for example, were carried out in a section of a Western Electric Company assembly plant set aside especially for the study. For almost nine years (1924–1933), studies were carried out that examined the effects of physical work environment, work rules, pay schedules, and the structure of work groups on productivity. The first analysis of this data took the form of cross tabulations and simple statistical tests. The results were surprising.

The initial analysis revealed that productivity tended to increase *regardless* of the work environment, work rules, pay schedules, or structure of the work group. Researchers interpreted these findings as indicating the strong influence of both the productivity norms established by the workers themselves and the fact that the workers appreciated being selected for special attention and study. Their consistently high productivity was interpreted as evidence that the workers were trying to be good experimental subjects. This finding came to be known as the *Hawthorne effect*, and it has long been a standard part of the literature in social psychology.

The Hawthorne studies yielded a vast amount of data, collected under nearly ideal conditions. These studies have been discussed, reexamined, and used for the development of sociological knowledge in many areas. In 1978, for example, Richard Franke and James D. Kaul submitted Hawthorne data to elaborate statistical analysis (regression analysis).

The conclusions drawn from this new and more comprehensive statistical analysis challenge many of the earlier conclusions drawn from the first analysis. Franke and Kaul argue that the Hawthorne effect has been greatly exaggerated and that the effects of work environment, work rules, pay schedules, and structure of the work groups were much stronger than the earlier analysis indicated.

Extensive bodies of data generated and collected under controlled conditions similar to those of the Hawthorne studies do not exist for those who study collective behavior. And it may seem unlikely that this kind of data will be generated in the future. One can, for example, set up different work group structures and determine their effects on productivity, but one cannot generate structural strain to see if it produces collective behavior as Smelser's model states. One can manipulate room illumination to determine its effect on productivity, but one cannot—or should not—scream "Fire!" in a crowded theater for the purpose of studying panic. In short, many forms of collective behavior cannot be created under controlled conditions for the purposes of research.

Solutions to the Problems

The three problems outlined above have long served as barriers to the systematic study of collective behavior. Much of the recent progress in the field of collective behavior, however, is a result of researchers providing solutions to these problems. In this section we summarize how these problems have been overcome.

Unanticipated Events

Researchers have made progress in developing procedures for studying unanticipated events, particularly in the area of disaster re-

search. Sociologists at Average State University were unable to foresee the disaster that struck a nearby community. Afterward, they saw little need for improving their research procedures because the likelihood of another disaster occurring in their vicinity was remote. But the latest *Statistical Abstract of the United States* reveals that each year brings forty to eighty tornadoes that kill people and cause at least $500,000 in property damage. Likewise, there will be between one and two hundred floods in which lives will be lost. There will also be twenty to thirty motor vehicle accidents, railroad accidents, fires, and explosions in which five or more fatalities per accident will occur. In this sense, unanticipated events do occur at rather predictable rates. The key to studying disasters is to be prepared to do a lot of traveling on short notice.

On the basis of such observations, the Disaster Research Center (DRC) at Ohio State University was established in September 1963. The DRC was a result of the work of Enrico L. Quarantelli, Russell R. Dynes, and J. Eugene Haas. On October 31, 1963, it responded to its first disaster, a multifatality explosion in the Indianapolis Coliseum. Since then, the DRC has conducted almost two hundred field studies of natural and technological disasters within the United States and in more than twenty other nations.

Field research for the DRC is conducted by teams of trained research associates selected from sociology graduate students at Ohio State University. These teams are prepared to leave for the site of any disaster on four hours' notice. Their field kits include DRC identification material, recording equipment, appropriate interview guides, and various information checklists. Enroute to the disaster scene, team members attempt to obtain new information from radio and newspapers in order to determine the conditions they will encounter. Once in the disaster area, team members establish a communication post to coordinate fieldwork and contact the DRC headquarters at Ohio State. Persons interviewed are selected on the basis of their proximity to and their involvement in the disaster. Particular attention is given to interviewing people in official and unofficial positions of authority. A careful record is kept of the names, addresses, and organizational affiliations of all persons interviewed, in case it becomes necessary to contact them again.

Debriefing sessions are conducted upon returning from disaster field trips. A team member is then selected to write a preliminary research memorandum describing the disaster, the team's field procedures, and the organizations studied. Other team members are assigned the tasks of preparing a detailed research report and filing all newspapers, brochures, and other materials collected. A list of all the people contacted or interviewed during the trip is compiled, and all tapes made in the field are catalogued. One team member is selected to write appropriate letters of appreciation and handle all follow-up correspondence.

The DRC is the only full-time disaster research group in the United States, and its contribution to the understanding of community responses to disaster is enormous. Its studies provide basic knowledge about group behavior and community life, as well as information that can be used to develop effective plans and programs for dealing with disaster. The DRC also serves as a repository for documents and materials collected by other agencies and researchers. This valuable library is open to all interested scholars and agencies involved in disaster planning. The DRC's training role should not be overlooked. Quarantelli notes that before the DRC was established, no more than twenty sociologists had direct field experience in the area of disaster study. Training students in disaster research remains a high priority. The DRC has provided intense training and field experience to more than one hundred graduate students, most of whom maintain professional commitments to disaster research or to organizations such as the National Transportation Safety Board and state civil defense agencies. DRC alumni also worked on the President's Commission on Three Mile Island.

The Crowd

Beginning in the late 1960s, Clark McPhail and teams of graduate students from the Universities of South Carolina and Illinois developed procedures for observing crowd activity. Initially, graduate students were sent out with tablets and pencils to record the activities of people in shopping malls and airline terminals. The first records were disappointing, consisting of cryptic comments and diagrams, erasures, and assumptions about what travelers and shoppers were thinking. No two records were alike, even though observers had attempted to describe the same people and activities. Most of these shortcomings were overcome through practice and giving priority to recording the rate and direction of people's movement, their direction of gaze, and their manual and vocal gestures. Codes were developed to facilitate the recording of the apparent age, sex, and ethnicity of people being observed. Field tactics were developed for positioning observers near or within stationary and moving crowds. Later, observation procedures were augmented by the use of 8-mm movie equipment. After this training period, observation teams were sent to dozens of rallies, celebrations, and strikes. Film and written records were made of short-range crowd formation, verbal and nonverbal gestures, the movement of crowds from place to place, and crowd dispersal.

No one has yet expanded these methods to obtain systematic data from various assembling processes for the purposes of comparison. To date, the only studies of these phenomena are the ones of medium-range assembling described in Chapter 2. These are the studies of the formation of a victory celebration crowd by McPhail and Miller (1973), the formation of a spectator crowd at the scene of a fire by Bailey and McPhail (1979), and the study of class attendance by Miller (1975). There have been no attempts to study the long-range assembling that precedes class reunions or annual conventions of groups such as the American Sociological Association.

At first thought, it seems unlikely that researchers could successfully administer questionnaires or conduct interviews within a crowd. Though newspaper and television reporters often enter the crowd to get a story, sociologists have been reluctant to enter the crowd to get their data. One exception is Quarantelli and Hundley's 1975 study of a campus disorder at the Universitiy of Ohio. The crowd phase of this disorder lasted almost six hours and included the blocking of vehicle traffic on streets near the campus, property damage, a protest march, and confrontations between students and police. A disorder of this magnitude and character clearly falls within the hostile outburst category of Smelser's model of collective behavior. Some data for this study were obtained with on-the-scene interviews conducted to determine the participation motives of those involved. Some interviewees attributed their presence in the crowd to feelings of hostility toward the police and university officials. The majority, however, expressed motives of curiosity, as well as desires to be with friends and share in the excitement. These findings contradict Smelser's explanation of hostile outbursts.

Adrian Aveni (1977) and a team of students also conducted field interviews within a celebrating street crowd following a University of Ohio football game. The purpose of this study was to determine social relationships within the crowd. People were randomly selected and interviewed to find out who they were with and who they had seen while on the streets. Altogether, 287 interviews were attempted, and 204 interviews were completed.

The studies of Quarantelli and Hundley and Aveni suggest that much more interviewing can be done in the crowd than has been assumed. This does not mean that we should interrupt looters to conduct interviews. Short of this, however, much can be done. Crowd activity is seldom as uniformly intense and focused as popular imagery suggests. Brief questionnaires can be administered, or short interviews conducted, during lulls in crowd activity. We need not interrupt a protest march to ask people questions about the assembling process or their motives for participation. Such information can likely be obtained beforehand, as people are waiting for the march to begin.

Controlled Study

Very little collective behavior has been produced and studied under controlled conditions. Further, the kind of collective behavior that has been produced may seem trivial in comparison to such events as civil disorders or the emergency evacuation of a crowded theater. Still, some progress has been made. Milgram, Bickman, and Berkowitz (1969) wanted to see to what degree groups composed of two to fifteen persons, all performing the same observable action, would draw passersby into their activities. Members of these stimulus crowds positioned themselves on a busy New York City sidewalk and, when signaled, all gazed upward at a window across the street. Motion pictures were made of the observation area for the sixty seconds during which stimulus crowds gazed at the window. Altogether, thirty one-minute trials were conducted. These researchers found that the number of passersby who stop alongside the stimulus crowd, or break stride and look up, increases as the size of the stimulus crowd increases.

A similar but unpublished study was conducted by McPhail and his students. In addition to the above, it suggested that the portion of university student passersby stopping alongside a stimulus crowd watching a karate demonstration depended on the time of day. The drawing power of stimulus crowds, at least for these students, decreased as class time approached.

Information regarding the drawing power of crowds can assist those whose job it is to produce crowds, such as the people who do advance work for political campaigns, celebrity tours, or advertising promotions. This information can also help police and traffic managers who control and sometimes disperse crowds. Finally, the procedures of manipulation and observation used in these studies can, with imagination, be used in the study of other facets of crowd activity.

In this section we have discussed problems encountered by those who study collective behavior. Because collective behavior events are unanticipated, it is difficult to prepare well thought out research plans for studying these events. The procedures of the Disaster Research Center illustrate the resources and tremendous commitment necessary for overcoming these difficulties. Beginning in the 1960s, sociologists made much progress in studying the crowd through direct and systematic observation, as well as through entering the crowd to conduct interviews. Finally, serious attempts have now been made to produce types of collective behavior under controlled conditions for the purposes of study.

Methods of Study

No single method of investigation can answer all the questions that have been asked about collective behavior. Information about collective behavior has been obtained through the analysis of historical material, survey research, simple and participant observation, and experiments. We will now review these research methods, which, taken together, are providing increased knowledge about collective behavior.

The Use of Historical Material

In his first "Outline of Collective Behavior" (1939), Blumer cited the "tulip mania in Holland in the eighteenth century" as an example of mass hysteria. Since then, the tulip mania example has been cited by Smelser (1962), Turner and Killian (1972), and Klapp (1972). While the tulip mania is thus recognized as a classic outbreak of mass hysteria or extreme form of "rapid, unwitting, and nonrational dissemination of a mood, impulse, or form of conduct," the evidence upon which this judgment is based is meager.

Only one historical account of the tulip mania has ever been cited in the preceding discussions of mass hysteria—the account by Charles Mackay (1932) in the third edition of *Extraordinary Popular Delusions and the Madness of Crowds.* This book was first published in 1841 and again in 1852. Mackay mades no claim that his work represents a complete or even careful history of the events he describes. In fact, in the preface to the 1852 edition, Mackay characterized his work as "sketches" and a "miscellany of delusions . . . a chapter . . . in the great and awful book of human folly." The tulip mania is described in the third and shortest chapter of *Extraordinary Popular Delusions.* Mackay states that the tulip mania occurred from 1634 to 1636. Interestingly, many of the discussions that cite Mackay's account place the tulip mania in the eighteenth century.

Upon examination, little in Mackay's account of the tulip mania illustrates events of a widespread and hysterical nature. Mackay presents entertaining anecdotes rather than detailed accounts of group processes involved in the event. Most of Mackay's chapter, for example, describes instances where people ate or otherwise ruined tulip bulbs—mistaking them for onions! It is difficult to reconcile the image of a nationwide, hysterical preoccupation for tulips with stories about people being unable to distinguish tulip bulbs from onions. Mackay also describes the elaborate system of measurement devised for marketing tulip bulbs, as well as their price fluctuations. While Mackay states that some bulbs did command extremely high prices, his accounts seem to imply that these were new or very rare varieties purchased by professional growers and serious speculators.

The use of Mackay's account of the tulip mania represents the rather casual use of historical material found within the social contagion literature. It is not difficult to find colorful descriptions of past moods, diversions, instabilities, and fanaticism compatible with the social contagion point of view. It is from such sensationalized accounts that much of the supporting evidence for the social contagion perspective is drawn. More detailed and careful historical accounts usually reflect underlying economic, political, and social forces that shape events more than they illustrate the "hysterical" nature of events. The question of relevance at this point is: "What constitutes an acceptable level of historical scholarship?"

The Work of George Rudé. Shortcomings in the use of historical material within the social contagion perspective become more obvious when contrasted with the work done elsewhere in the field. A very good example of extensive and careful use of historical material is George Rudé's *The Crowd in the French Revolution* (1959). Rudé masterfully uses historical analysis in describing the socioeconomic composition and motives of crowds during the French Revolution. Many accounts claim that

the scum of French society—the ruffians, criminals, prostitutes, vagabonds, and insane—were the most active in the Revolution. These derelicts were motivated by bribery and the quest for loot. Other accounts portray participants in heroic terms—the "noble poor," motivated by the lofty ideals of liberty, freedom, and equality. Rudé notes that these opposing characterizations have never been carefully evaluated from the standpoint of surviving records, most of which are preserved in the French National Archives.

Rudé examined police records for the years 1787–1795 and those of the revolutionary government's Committee of General Security of 1793–1795. These were the years of the revolutionary crowd: the preliminary skirmishes between crowds and police, the taking of the Bastille, the march on Versailles, the fall of the monarchy and the Reign of Terror, and the unsuccessful counterrevolution of 1795. These records contain lists of those killed, wounded, arrested, or who had complaints placed against them. Rudé notes that these records concern a minority of all participants but that the size of these records concern a large enough group, or sample, that general conclusions can be drawn from them. Rudé also examined lists of claimants for pensions and compensation for time lost under arms during the years 1792 and 1793. During these years, the revolutionary government also conducted surveys of its police agents. In these surveys agents reported the reactions of small property holders and wage earners to the events of these years. Rudé also utilized statistical lists compiled during the revolutionary period reporting the movement of wages and the prices of bread, meat, butter, eggs, sugar, wine, coffee, candles, and soap. It is from such historical material that Rudé constructs an image of those most active in the French Revolution and draws conclusions about their motives.

Rudé concludes that the revolutionary crowds were primarily composed of wage

earners, shopkeepers, small traders, housewives, craftsmen, and workshop masters.
Very few of those killed, wounded, or arrested
had previous police records, and of those who
did, few were for major offenses. In contrast,
the leaders of the Revolution were drawn
largely from the owners of large businesses, the
professions, and the liberal aristocracy. While
the ideals of liberty, freedom, and equality
were often prominent among the expressed
motives of the revolutionary crowds, the most
constant motive throughout the popular uprisings of this period was the desire to obtain a
stable and increased supply of inexpensive
bread and other essentials. Rudé notes that police records contain very few references to
bribery, or "paid participation," and he indicates that very little looting—other than the securing of weapons—occurred during these disorders.

Rudé's image of the participants in the
French Revolution lies somewhere between the
extremes of derelicts and noble poor. Those
participating were neither riffraff nor heroes.
They were mostly members of the emerging,
urban, industrial social order—a new social
order against whose interests the monarchy
largely stood. The revolutionaries were motivated by a concern for liberty, freedom, and
equality, but these motives were tempered
with the practical concern for a reasonable and
stable standard of living.

The work of Rudé has been widely acknowledged as providing genuine insight into
the makeup and actions of crowds during the
French Revolution. The question remains, however, whether the findings from this specific
historical analysis apply generally to other political and industrial conflicts. One might easily suspect that the large-scale upheavals studied by Rudé are, in many ways, quite different
from the various smaller and more frequent
protests, strikes, military coups d'etat, and localized rebellions that make up much of modern social conflict.

The Work of William A. Gamson.   In order to obtain a more general understanding of
the prior conditions, the dynamics, and the
outcomes of political and industrial conflict,
comparisons must be made among a *representative sample* of groups involved in conflict.
This task involves three major problems. Foremost among them is specifying what constitutes a *group*. Once a working definition of a
group is established, we must ascertain the universe of all groups that fit this definition,
which involves a systematic and exhaustive
search of the historical record for references to
these groups. Finally, we must obtain similar
amounts of necessary information about each
group and the conflict in which it took part.

William A Gamson (1975) developed a
methodology to overcome these problems in
his analysis of social protest. First, he developed a working definition of a protest, or *challenging*, group. For Gamson, a challenging
group is involved in mobilizing a constituency
among people who were unorganized with respect to a particular issue or problem. A challenging group also has a clear, external target
of influence, such as employers, legislators, or
police. The challenging group must have demonstrated the capacity to take such actions as
petitioning, demonstrating, striking, attacking
authorities, raising money, or holding meetings. Finally, challenging groups have names
and a clear conception of membership in the
group.

Gamson restricted his attention to challenging groups that existed in the United States between 1800 and 1945. He then addressed the
task of searching history books for references
to any and all groups that could possibly be
considered as a challenging group. This search
had to be systematic and exhaustive. A team of
researchers examined the indexes of a series of
general and specific histories that included the
years between 1800 and 1945. The indexes were
searched for the names of organizations, be
they General Motors or the Iowa Socialist

League, and a master card file of more than 4,500 organizations was compiled. These organizations were placed into at least one of seventeen categories, including agricultural, labor, ethnic, women, religious, professional, business, socialist/communist, peace, veterans, cranks/crackpots, and sports/recreation. These categories served as a basis for selecting general and specific history books from which descriptive information would be drawn. Seventy-five books were selected, including the *Dictionary of American History, The Oxford Companion to American History,* and specific histories such as *History of Woman Suffrage,* Elizabeth Stanton, et al., and Louis Filler's *A Dictionary of Social Reform.* Each volume was searched for references to any of the organizations in the card file. The final dozen history books yielded minimal amounts of new information, and so the list of "all organizations in the United States from 1800 to 1945" was considered complete. From this file, a random sample of 467 organizations was selected, of which 64 met the criteria of being a protest or challenging group. These organizations and the conflicts they were party to constituted the *database* for the rest of Gamson's analysis.

At this point, we should consider the degree to which procedures such as those outlined above can produce a "true" sample of those organizations that expressed grievances, advanced causes, and challenged authorities between 1800 and 1945. Clearly, we cannot judge the representativeness of this type of sampling in the same way that we judge the samples used by Gallup Poll.

We can gauge, somewhat, the representativeness of Gamson's sample by considering the kinds of organizations likely to have been overlooked by historians. Many "crackpot" groups, secret societies, and small, short-lived groups are likely to go unnoticed or be considered unworthy of serious attention. Each of these types, however, is represented in Gamson's sample. Compared to the stated objectives of other groups, those of the League of American Wheelmen (1880–1905) may have received more than a few laughs. This group attempted to organize bicyclists to demand the removal of restrictions on the use of bicycles, including the prohibition of riding in the street. Similarly, the Society for the Promotion of Manual Labor in Literary Institutions (1831–1833) had as its goal the improvement of physical fitness among college students. Gamson's search unearthed one acknowledged secret society—the Order of Secularists—an organization of atheists of the 1860s. Finally, nine of the groups in the final sample had "lifespans" of three years or less. It is impossible to assess how many kinds of groups were not immortalized by historians. Still, Gamson's sample contains groups manifesting a wide range of interests.

There is also the question of whether Gamson located all, or a suitably large portion, of the groups actually mentioned by historians. Certainly, he consulted only a small portion of United States history books. Still, those examined covered a very *wide range* of historical interests, geographic areas, and groups. There is no noticeable bias toward overselecting books dealing with the history of a given region, such as the Eastern United States, or with particular topics, such as labor and business groups. Finally, Gamson concluded his search only after reaching a high level of diminished returns, that is, when the search stopped yielding realistic amounts of new information.

The completeness of Gamson's search can be gauged through *replication.* For example, using Gamson's method of gathering historical data, would other researchers come up with appreciably more groups than Gamson? There is no compelling reason to think that they would. However, replication would provide a greater level of confidence in this method of gathering data.

Gamson next turned to the task of ascertaining the nature and outcomes of the conflicts in which these challenging groups were involved. As it would be impossible to interview the people involved in most of these conflicts, Gamson, in effect, "interviewed" the history books.

A questionnaire containing 113 questions was composed, including the following:

What was the size of the challenging group?

What were the group's formal goals?

Who were the primary antagonists of the challenging group?

What types of police activity, such as legal arrest or illegal harassment, were directed against the group?

What types of public relations attempts were made by the group?

To what extent did other groups extend support to the challenging group?

What skills did the leadership of the challenging group possess?

There were a number of questions about the outcome of the challenging group's efforts—whether they received formal recognition by employers, as in the case of trade unions, or obtained formal concessions or agreements such as the passing of requested legislation or changes in formal policy.

Researchers examined the history books for specific answers to these questions and included photocopies of relevant passages on each questionnaire. In some instances, other sources, such as contracts or the minutes of challenging group meetings were consulted to obtain answers. These procedures involved about eighty hours of work for each questionnaire. Complete interview schedules were obtained for fifty-three of the sixty-four organizations in the sample. This is comparable to a response rate of 83 percent for a conventional survey. This response rate is generally viewed as quite satisfactory in most survey research.

The completed questionnaires were then coded in the same way that conventional interviews are coded, and the coded information was tabulated and analyzed. The information allowed Gamson to answer questions about the nature and outcomes of nearly a century and a half of protest in the United States. We will consider the findings of this study in Chapter 12.

This method of historical analysis is described in much greater detail in Gamson's *The Strategy of Social Protest* (1975). These research procedures allowed Gamson to systematically and comprehensively gather information from the historical record. Much can be learned from *qualitative*, case-by-case historical analysis such as Rudé's. Work such as Gamson's, however, represents a *quantitative* approach to the historical record. Making the historical record speak in quantitative terms yields information that can be analyzed and interpreted with the statistical tools of modern sociology. In turn, quantitative information allows us to more meaningfully compare the many collective behavior events of the past with those of the present. This methodology sets a new standard of scientific rigor by which research utilizing the historical record must be judged.

Surveys and Official Statistics

A very large portion of the data used in sociology is obtained through surveys and official statistics. These are the primary sources of data in the large body of riot participation research conducted in the late 1960s and early 1970s. Altogether, the many studies of riot participation use information about or from thousands of people and dozens of disorders.

One of the first tasks in studying riots is to determine who is and who isn't a riot participant. The most obvious and frequent solution to this problem is to assume that those who have been arrested at the scene of the disorder are rioters. Most riot participation studies compare samples of respondents arrested on riot charges with a control sample of nonarrestees drawn from the community in which the riot occurred. A few studies, such as that of Strasel and Larkin (1968), simply provide a descriptive snapshot of the accused rioters by analyzing information provided by people at the time of their arrest.

In most of these studies, it is acknowledged that being arrested as a rioter does not always mean that the person has engaged in violent, destructive, or "riotous" activity. That is, there are degrees of riot involvement, ranging from being on the streets after an imposed curfew to stoning police or being caught in the act of firebombing a building. Some studies take the arrest charge into account. For example, Strasel and Larkin excluded curfew violators in their sample of Washington rioters; they restricted their sample to those charged with burglary II (the category for looting) and other crimes, such as assault, committed during the riot period.

A smaller number of studies utilize surveys conducted in riot communities a few weeks or months after the disorder. In these postriot surveys, respondents indicate what they did and saw during the disorder. From this self-report information, researchers have constructed several categories of involvement, including *actives*, or persons who reported being involved in or close at hand to shootings, stonings, and looting; *counterrioters*, who reported that they went out and tried to talk others into "cooling it"; and *inactives*, who reported staying at home or only observing the riot from their porches or yards.

The primary purpose and focus of riot participation studies has been to determine the personal characteristics and attitudes that dispose people to participate in riots. Studies of arrestees use information from official records made in the process of booking and pretrial investigation. For example, the *D.C. Bail Agency* was the source of data in Strasel and Lar-

kin's study. The scope of the information was limited by the purpose of the bail agency, which is to determine the character, reliability, and community ties of individuals for whom a bail determination is being made. The bail questionnaires were administered by volunteer law students and attorneys of the federal bar.

The information obtained for the purpose of bail determination was quite extensive and included age, race, sex, place of birth, marital status, physical and mental health, criminal records, length of residence, educational level, employment status, occupation, and take-home pay. Fifty-five relevant prisoner attributes were either listed or deducible from the original questionnaire items. In like manner, other researchers have constructed detailed socioeconomic profiles of those arrested during riots. Such information, however, has little direct bearing on the attitudes and opinions of those arrested. Arrestees' attitudes and opinions have been obtained largely through the postriot surveys discussed above.

The postriot surveys solicited respondents' statements about police malpractice or brutality, overt discrimination by employers, merchants, and "whites in general," as well as respondents' political participation and expectations for the future. From these responses, researchers constructed hundreds of attitude/opinion indexes and compared them with people's involvement in rioting. We will discuss specific findings of these studies in Chapter 11. Here it is sufficient to note that the results of riot participation research have been disappointing—at least as far as discovering a riot-prone personality is concerned. About all this research has shown is that, overwhelmingly, riot participants tend to be young, black, and male, as opposed, for example, to being old, white, and female. Of the hundreds of additional socioeconomic characteristics, attitudes, and opinions that have been examined, few are clearly or highly associated with riot

FIGURE 3.1 *Photographing the Crowd: The Problem of Foreshortened Perspective*

A. How many people are in this picture? Are the people in the rear of the crowd standing closer together than those in the front? Foreshortened perspective makes it difficult to answer these questions. (Photo by Grant Bogue.)

participation. Unfortunately, the surveys and official statistics now available provide little additional information that would allow the testing of alternate explanations of riot participation.

Simple Observation: The Use of Film Records

It is relatively easy to make film records of compact crowds in shopping malls, waiting areas of airline terminals, and on sidewalks. It is usually most convenient to shoot film from balconies or windows overlooking these areas. Analyzing these films, however, in order to es-

tablish the precise number of people in the crowd, their spatial arrangements and movements presents some difficulty. This is the problem of *foreshortened perspective*—a distortion in the film record that results from the height of the camera position above the surface upon which the crowd is located and the size of the area filmed (see Figure 3.1). The lower the elevation of the camera and the greater the area filmed, the greater the distortion in the film record. Theoretically, we can eliminate this problem only by shooting from directly overhead. Foreshortened perspective makes people closer to the camera appear to be mov-

B. It is somewhat easier to count heads and judge distances between people in this picture because the camera is at a higher elevation above the crowd. This reduces foreshortened perspective distortion. (Photo by Grant Bogue.)

ing more rapidly than those farther away, even though they are moving at the same speed. Foreshortened perspective also makes it appear that shorter people closer to the camera are standing very near taller people farther from the camera, when, in fact, these people may be located some distance apart.

Ronald T. Wohlstein (1977) has devised a method of compensating for foreshortened perspective. His solution to this problem is of particular interest in that it involves relatively simple procedures and requires no special equipment beyond the cameras, lenses, and projectors used in making the original film rec-

ord. Basically, Wohlstein's correction method involves filming a grid laid out on any large floor from the same angle and at the same magnification (or lens setting) as the initial film record. This creates a foreshortened matrix (see Figure 3.2) that can be marked on the projection screen, thereby providing reference points for calculating all distances in the picture. The procedure is a bit more complicated than this brief description indicates, but it has been verified to allow less than three degrees of error in estimating angles and less than a foot of error in estimating the positions of people and objects in the picture.

FIGURE 3.2   *Analyzing Photos of the Crowd: The Foreshortened Matrix*

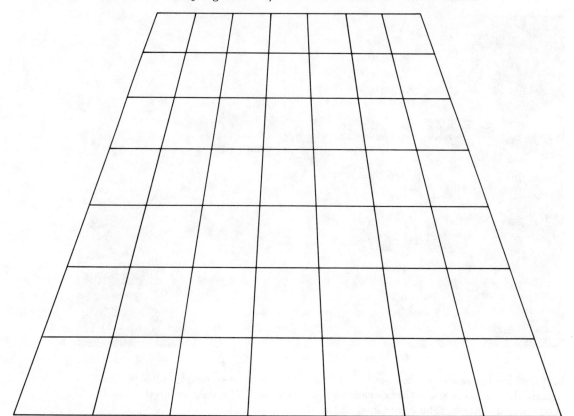

If one knows the lens setting and the elevation of the camera, a foreshortened matrix can be constructed (Wohlstein 1977). When a slide of film is projected on this matrix, accurate measures of distance between objects in the picture can be obtained.

Participant Observation: Studying Groups from the Inside

Participant observation involves a researcher becoming a participant in or member of a group in order to study the group. This method of investigation usually involves considerable time, effort, and emotional and personal commitment to the research act, and in some instances it even poses physical danger to the researcher. Why, then, would a researcher use this method of investigation? Researchers use participant observation to study groups from the inside in order to learn (1) what meanings people attach to their actions, (2) how groups are organized, (3) what is the interplay between group members, and (4) how a group takes action with respect to others.

Little of the above is visible to an outsider, and these things may be deliberately and systematically concealed from such investigators as sociologists, newspeople, and police. Some aspects of group decision making and tactics may even be concealed from portions of the membership. Even though groups may often grant interviews or allow the administration of questionnaires, it is generally assumed that only superficial information can be gained by outsiders. In short, participant observation can provide information unattainable through other methods of sociological investigation.

The most important participant observation study in the field of collective behavior is John Lofland's *Doomsday Cult* (1966, 1977), a study of the early and largely unsuccessful days of an evangelical group that came to international prominence in the 1970s. In the beginning of his study, Lofland told members of the "Divine Precepts" group that he was a sociologist and that he would maintain the anonymity of the group in any of his later writings. Given the obscurity of the group at that time, this promise seemed quite easy to keep. Later events made the Divine Precepts and other pseudonyms used by Lofland quite transparent. Though Lofland has remained true to his initial promise and continues to use the initial pseudonyms, it is quite clear that Lofland studied the American branch of the Reverend Sun Myung Moon's Unification Church, whose followers are popularly known as the Moonies. Noting this, and without further comment, the Divine Precepts pseudonym used by Lofland will be maintained throughout this text.

Lofland's study began in 1962 when he was approached by a Divine Precepts recruiter to come and hear the "good news" the group had to pass along. Lofland attended a few meetings and then indicated that he did not wish to become a Divine Precepts adherent but did want to study the group. The group consented to this arrangement and during the next thirteen months, Lofland attended meetings, provided transportation, helped set up group residences and offices, and edited some group literature. He obtained extensive biographical information and history of Divine Precepts involvement from the twenty-three people who com-

posed the initial active core of the group. He observed the group's planning of recruitment drives and the conversion of a few new members. In March 1963, the group leader requested that Lofland either join or leave the group, so Lofland terminated the participant observation phase of his study. In all, he generated more than nine hundred pages of single-spaced typed notes and several hours of tape-recorded notes during this time. His findings regarding recruitment, conversion, and maintenance of faith were first presented in *Doomsday Cult*, dealing with the Divine Precepts' more recent history and successes. We will review Lofland's particular findings in Chapter 14.

Participant observation has provided the field of collective behavior with information that would have been difficult if not impossible to obtain through other means. The observations of participants in many types of collective behavior are another valuable source of information. The accounts of major and minor revolutionary figures, for example, provide insights into the covert processes of revolutionary groups. Some accounts were intended by their writers to be widely read, such as Chairman Mao's various books of quotations and Hitler's *Mein Kampf*. Such works provide insights into the world view of revolutionary groups. At the other end of the continuum are works that served as underground organization and training manuals for revolutionary groups prior to their wider publication. Examples include Joseph Stalin's *The Russian Social Democratic Party and Its Immediate Tasks*, Kwame Nkrumah's *Handbook of Revolutionary Warfare*, Carlos Marighella's *Minimanual of the Urban Guerrilla*, and Abraham Guillen's *Philosophy of the Urban Guerrilla*. The ideological bases of these writings are implicit and nondoctrinaire; these works, in many respects, are the "how-to" books of street fighting and insurrection, providing insights into the organization and tactics of guerrilla groups.

Experiments in Collective Behavior

We noted earlier in this chapter that very little collective behavior has been produced and studied under controlled conditions. The ability to control and manipulate what is being studied is the essence of the experimental method. The lack of experimental examination of collective behavior results in part from the prevailing definitions of collective behavior. If we assume, as does the social contagion perspective, that collective behavior involves extreme emotion, then it is difficult to justify terrorizing or otherwise exciting people for the purposes of study. If we assume, as does the value-added perspective, that collective behavior always involves structural strain and large-scale events, then experimental examination is precluded. That is, we cannot produce and manipulate structural strain and other elements of the value-added process to see if they indeed cause various types of large-scale collective behavior. At best, we can make *comparative studies* among nations experiencing different levels of political violence and civil strife. We will consider such studies by Gurr (1969) and Davies (1969) in later chapters. On the other hand, the SBI perspective seems, at least superficially, more compatible with the logic of experimental examination. Milgram, Bickman, and Berkowitz (1969), for example, controlled the size and activities of stimulus crowds to assess their impact on passersby.

Alexander Mintz: A Study of Panic.   An early and widely cited experiment in the field of collective behavior is Alexander Mintz's (1951) study of nonadaptive group behavior. In this experiment, Mintz designed a procedure to simulate an emergency escape situation to determine the conditions under which group cooperation breaks down and individualistic, nonadaptive responses occur. Mintz placed fifteen to twenty-one aluminum cones in a large

glass jug, the neck of which was large enough to accommodate only a single cone. Each cone had a string attached to it. The bottom of the jug was fitted with a valve that allowed water to enter it (see Figure 3.3).

Subjects were handed a string and told that as soon as water started to enter the jug, they could withdraw their cone. Subjects were shown that only one cone at a time could escape from the jug and that nonadaptive "jam-ups" would occur if this procedure were violated. Subjects could successfully complete the experiment if their cones escaped dry.

In the initial trials, no jamup responses occurred and everyone escaped with dry cones. Mintz concluded that one reason for these successes was that groups usually established a "one-cone-at-a-time" plan of action in informal conversations prior to beginning each trial. In later trials, Mintz secretly recruited accomplices in the groups of subjects and instructed them to incite emotions. The accomplices were asked to swear, yell, and scream once the trial was underway. The accomplices succeeded in arousing the emotions of the subjects, but despite this disturbance, no jamups occurred.

Mintz was able to induce jamups only after he forbade pretrial conversations and set up a reward-and-fine condition. Subjects received a quarter if their cones escaped dry and were fined a dime if their cones got wet. Finally, to eliminate the effects of excitement, Mintz placed a partitioned screen around the jug so that subjects could not see one another. Under these arrangements, nonadaptive jamups occurred frequently.

Mintz's study could be characterized as a study of "panic," but this is inaccurate because Mintz dismissed emotional arousal as a key factor in the occurrence of nonadaptive group behavior. Instead, Mintz argued that the reward structure was the key ingredient in nonadaptive group behavior. From Mintz's study, it is also clear that factors of communication (pretrial conversations) and lack of mutual sensory access (the partitioned screen) greatly contributed to the incidence of nonadaptive jamups. (For further discussion of communication and sensory access, as these factors relate to evacuation disasters, see Chapter 9.)

A True-to-Life Study of Rebellion. An experimental study utilizing a more "true-to-life" situation was conducted by William A. Gamson, Bruce Fireman, and Stephen Rytina (1982). In this study, representatives of a "research organization" requested groups of subjects to engage in blatantly unethical and potentially illegal acts. Groups often encounter *unjust authority* in the real world and are faced with the decision of complying or rebelling. Gamson, Fireman, and Rytina designed their experimental study to ascertain the conditions under which groups choose and carry out rebellion.

The experimental scenario began with newspaper ads that solicited subjects for research being conducted by Manufacturer's Human Relations Consultants (MHRC). Participants would be paid ten dollars, and the research session would last about two hours. People who phoned for further information were told that the research would involve one of four topics. These topics were brand-name recognition, product safety, community standards, and research in which subjects would initially be misled about the purpose of the study. Callers were then asked to schedule an appointment for the research session.

Research sessions were held in a motel suite equipped with desks and portable videotaping equipment. When subjects arrived, they were asked to sign an agreement specifying that their participation was voluntary, they were aware the sessions would be videotaped, and that the tapes would not be used for commercial purposes. Each participant was then paid, given a name tag, and a cover letter that explained, in

FIGURE 3.3 *Experimental Study of Panic*

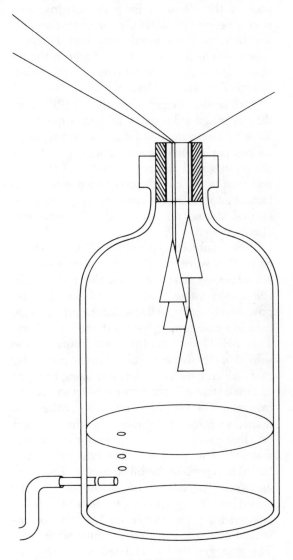

A sketch of the apparatus used to study nonadaptive group behavior, or panic, in the laboratory. Mintz (1951) found that by creating a reward structure and greatly limiting mutual sensory access among the subjects, he could produce frequent nonadaptive jam-ups of cones in the neck of the bottle.

general terms, the aims of MHRC and the purpose of the research. Each session involved twelve people: the MHRC coordinator and his assistant, nine naive subjects, and a person who posed as a naive subject. Later in the research session, this person would act to mobilize rebellion against the MHRC.

Each session began when the MHRC coordinator asked subjects to fill out a questionnaire to assess their opinions regarding large oil companies, business practices, people engaging in sexual affairs, the rights of citizens, and trust in the courts and government. Such factual information as subjects' age, sex, race, marital status, religion, and education was also requested.

When subjects completed the questionnaire, they were told that the research session would consist of a panel discussion to ascertain community values and standards for the purpose of obtaining reliable information to be used in a case coming before the federal court. The MHRC coordinator then informed the subjects of the issues involved in the particular case, which involved a lawsuit being brought against a large oil company by a service station manager. The oil company had revoked the manager's franchise, stating that the manager was living with a woman to whom he was not married. The manager's lifestyle made him "unfit" to represent the oil company. The manager's suit charged that the oil company had invaded his privacy and that his lifestyle neither affected his performance on the job nor offended contemporary community standards. The manager further claimed that the company had taken action against him because he criticized the company's pricing policies in a televised interview.

The MHRC coordinator then asked the subjects to discuss whether they would be concerned if the manager of a local gas station pursued this type of lifestyle. Almost without exception, subjects expressed little concern with the station manager's living arrange-

ments. The MHRC coordinator entered the room, shut off the videotape recorder, and asked the subjects to discuss whether they would do business with a person like the station manager. He then instructed three or four subjects to argue as if they were offended by the station manager's behavior. He then turned on the recorder and left the room.

After a somewhat confused and strained discussion, the MHRC coordinator entered the room and asked the subjects to discuss whether someone like the station manager is bad for the community. He then asked three more people to argue as if they were offended by unmarried cohabitation. As in the first instance, the request to act offended was not recorded.

The next time the MHRC coordinator entered the room, he asked subjects to summarize their feelings regarding the station manager's conduct. While the videotape was again stopped, he asked all subjects to act as if they were offended by the lifestyle in question.

Finally, the coordinator entered the room and asked subjects to sign affidavits stating that they were aware that the videotapes would be used in court. At the conclusion of this encounter, which was often quite abrasive, subjects were immediately informed that they had been participating in an experimental hoax. Subjects were then requested to fill out another questionnaire, which asked a wide range of information dealing with what they had planned to do had not this research situation been a hoax.

Thirty-three groups participated in this study. Participants tended to be younger, better educated, and more middle class than a cross section of the adult population from the community in which the study was conducted. Still, these groups were not grossly unrepresentative of their community, which would have been the case had the groups been composed entirely of men or college students.

In almost all of the groups, some form of individual or collective resistance to the MHRC was encountered. While the person posing as a naive subject was to attempt to initiate resistance in subtle ways, subjects usually offered resistance without prompting. Resistance took various forms. Individually, subjects remained silent, disclaimed their negative statements, or acted in a sarcastic manner during the taping. Some offered open resistance by refusing to sign the final affidavits, and a few took direct action, such as seizing the participation agreements signed at the beginning of the experiment or openly threatening to seize the videotapes. Finally, some members made plans to meet later and expose the tactics of the MHRC to the courts.

In summary, four groups never developed a rebellious majority, four groups "fizzled" when the rebellious majority eventually signed the final affidavits, in nine groups the majority refused to sign the final affidavits, and sixteen groups maintained unanimous resistance. In none of the thirty-three sessions, however, did the MHRC coordinator openly threaten or intimidate subjects.

In their subsequent analysis of the videotapes, the researchers utilized Erving Goffman's (1974) symbolic interactionist terminology to analyze how rebellion developed. In Chapter 13 we will have need to consider in greater detail the development of rebellion, and this experiment sheds light on the process. Here it is sufficient to note that necessary ingredients of rebellion include *organizing acts*, which increase the capacity of rebels to act as a unit. Groups confronting the MHRC were composed of mutual strangers. During the course of the experiment, those groups in which people engaged in friendly conversation and developed a minimal sense of solidarity and loyalty were much more capable of rebellion than those groups in which members remained strangers to one another. *Divesting acts*, which include statements that negate fears of "making a scene" and question obligations to authority, facilitate rebellion. Finally,

reframing acts are necessary; these are acts that loudly and clearly call attention to the wrongdoings of authority.

Gamson, Fireman, and Rytina's research clearly indicates that rebellion is not easy, particularly among groups who do not share a long history of interaction. Still, their research shows that ordinary people, with no prior experience of working together, were able to openly and actively resist unjust authority. The courage to rebel seems to be in greater supply than the knowledge of how to rebel.

Summary

Our purpose in this chapter has been to describe and illustrate the methods that have been used to study collective behavior. We began by noting that those who choose to study collective behavior take on some rather interesting but formidable challenges not found elsewhere in the field of sociology. First, there is the challenge of studying unanticipated events. Second, there is the problem of studying mobile and acting crowds. Finally, there is the issue of studying collective behavior under controlled conditions. The Disaster Research Center (DRC) has developed tactics to get trained investigators, using proven research strategies, to disaster sites on short notice. Since the 1960s, other researchers have developed methods of observing and entering crowds for the purpose of systematic and controlled investigation.

In the second part of this chapter, we reviewed the methods used to study collective behavior. The examination of historical material tells us much about collective behavior. Some historical accounts, such as Mackay's brief description of the tulip mania, have been used to support the social contagion image of collective behavior. A careful examination of this material, however, calls into question the assumptions of the social contagion perspective. Rudé, on the other hand, provides a model of rigorous historical analysis in his qualitative investigation of the composition, actions, and motives of the revolutionary crowd. Gamson developed a methodology for the systematic and comprehensive search of the historical record. These procedures yield quantitative information that can be analyzed and interpreted using the statistical tools of modern sociology.

Survey research is the most prominent method of sociological investigation. Survey research, however, cannot be used with the same precision and assurance in the field of collective behavior that it can in most other areas of sociology. The results of survey methods in the study of riot participation were meager. Some researchers, however, have used modified survey methods within the crowd and have obtained useful information.

Perhaps the most promising methodological development in the field of collective behavior has been the efforts to directly and systematically observe collective behavior events. Direct observation coupled with procedures for conducting interviews within the crowd represent the first real penetration of the crowd for the purposes of obtaining systematic sociological data.

Lofland's participant observation of the Doomsday Cult has provided valuable insights into recruitment, conversion, and maintenance of faith. There is also a wealth of observation by participants that can provide valuable insights into groups that often conceal their internal processes from outsiders.

Finally, we have briefly considered experimental methods. Experiments involve the control and measurement of key variables. Theories of collective behavior must use many variables that cannot be controlled or directly measured; hence, few collective behavior experiments have been conducted. We first considered Mintz's experiment in nonadaptive group behavior, or panic. This experiment has generally been interpreted as illustrating the impact of "reward structure" within the panic-producing situation. Mintz's study also shows how diminished sensory conditions contribute to nonadaptive responses. Gamson, Fireman, and Rytina conducted an experimental study of rebellion in response to "unjust" authority. These researchers utilized a more true-to-life experimental situation than did Mintz. Their experiment illustrates the possibility of simulating more elaborate and carefully monitored situations in the study of collective behavior phenomena.

The use of experimental methods holds promise of greatly expanding our knowledge about some areas of collective behavior. A precondition for the use of experimental methods is the development of procedures for indentifying, observing, and recording collective behavior phenomena. As was noted above, perhaps the most important advance in the field of collective behavior has been the recent attempts to observe and record collective behavior firsthand.

COLLECTIVE BEHAVIOR IN EVERYDAY LIFE

CHAPTER 4

Rumor and Communication

Rumors are usually thought of as unreliable stories from unknown or questionable sources that are passed indiscriminately from one person to another. We often use the term *rumor* to mean the same thing as lies, falsehoods, slander, and libel. Those who pass along rumors are referred to as rumormongers, gossips, or busybodies. This popular conception is quite similar to some of the sociological views we will discuss in this chapter. Occasionally, however, we hear a story that strikes us as just a rumor at the time, but we later learn that the story is true. Some sociological approaches to rumor acknowledge that rumors may sometimes convey accurate information.

We will first consider some "false" and some "true" rumors. There is little difficulty in presenting examples of false rumors; presenting examples of true rumors, however, is more problematic. This is not because there are very few instances of true rumors. Rather, when we read stories in gossip columns, hear stories from our friends, or hear stories from "unidentified" sources through the media, we simply cease to think of these stories as rumor once they have been borne out by subsequent events.

Some False Rumors

Often, rumors are passed around for a considerable length of time before they die out.

Then, years later, they reappear in a slightly modified form. Sometimes rumors acquire variations as they are passed from one region of the country to another. A few rumors are truly international travelers, hopping from nation to nation. Some rumors endure for so long or reappear so often that it is difficult to draw a sharp distinction between them and legends or folklore. For the most part, these rumors sound plausible, but even rigorous attempts to verify them have failed.

Product Rumors

Nearly everything we consume in our daily lives is made by someone else, somewhere else, so it is not unreasonable that we often talk about the cleanliness and safety of the products we use. One type of rumor is the *product rumor*. Stories about the questionable properties of a product carry clear potential for cutting sales and damaging the reputation of manufacturers. Such stories also carry the potential of damaging the sales and reputations of competitors. Consequently, the Federal Trade Commission has heard numerous cases of people and organizations spreading false information about products.

Chesterfield's Leper. In the fall of 1934, and for at least ten years afterward, rumors circulated that a leper had been discovered working in the Chesterfield cigarette factory in Richmond, Virginia. A companion rumor held that the leper story was untrue and had been started by Chesterfield's competitors or by religious groups opposed to smoking. In fact, no leper had ever been discovered working in any cigarette factory. Even though Liggett and Meyers Tobacco Company eventually offered a $25,000 reward, the source of the rumor was never found (Jacobson 1948).

Coca-Cola's Unfortunate Worker.   During the 1950s, a rumor circulated that a worker in a Coca-Cola bottling plant had fallen into a vat of cola and drowned. Because of the cola's acid content, the body had been almost completely dissolved when the accident was discovered a few days later. Various versions of this rumor circulated and, depending on the region of the country, the worker was identified as a Negro, a Japanese, a Mexican, or a derelict.

Wormburgers.   Beginning in 1979, rumors circulated that McDonald's hamburgers were made out of processed earthworms. This rumor was made more plausible by bonafide news stories a few years earlier that scientists were experimenting with earthworms as a usable source of protein. Variants of the rumor included stories that scientists had perfected the worm protein and that McDonald's had secretly purchased the formula. Investigators concluded that the stories first started in Chattanooga, Tennessee. In recent years, other fast-food chains have been vulnerable to this type of rumor.

K-Mart Snakes.   In 1981, rumors circulated that a woman customer had been bitten by a very poisonous snake while shopping at a K-Mart store in Detroit. At the time, she was trying on a coat made in Taiwan, and the snake was in the sleeve. Somehow, a poisonous snake had laid eggs in bundles of clothing headed for the United States, and the snakes had hatched enroute to Detroit. The woman

barely survived the bite, and she lost an arm because of the venom. K-Mart officials, reporters, and even herpetologists were unable to verify the story. No one-armed woman has brought suit against K-Mart, nor have any hospitals reported amputating a woman's arm because of snakebite.

Disaster Rumors

During disasters, people must often make quick decisions based on information that comes to them in unusual ways. Sometimes this information is wrong. Occasionally, people are warned of danger when no danger is present, but they take protective action on the basis of such information. These events have been referred to as *pseudo disasters* and have been considered instances of true panic.

The Burst Dam.   On Wednesday, August 17, 1955, Hurricane Diane hit the tri-state area of Pennsylvania, New Jersey, and New York. One town, Port Jervis, New York, was particularly hard hit by flooding. On Friday evening, the mayor declared the city in a state of emergency and turned the town over to civil defense. Friday evening and early Saturday morning, numerous reports that a large dam had broken circulated through Port Jervis and other nearby towns. At one point, fire sirens were sounded to warn of the coming flood. In fact, the dam in question was holding firm. Still, nearly 75 percent of the area's residents heard these rumors, and about one third of those who heard them made some attempt to leave the threatened area (Danzig, Thayer, and Galanter 1958).

Nuclear Accident.   On November 13, 1973, people near the Barsebäck Nuclear Power Station in Sweden heard a radio broadcast warning people that there had been a very large and dangerous radiation leak. In fact, the power station was still under construction and no radiation leak had occurred. The fictitious news bulletin, eleven minutes in length, had been part of a public interest talk show dealing with the risks of atomic energy. The bulletin had been preceded and followed by announcements that it was fictional. Within an hour of the broadcast, however, and for the next few days, radio and newspaper stories reported widespread panic reactions in southern Sweden. An investigation of the event was carried out at the request of the Swedish Board of Psychological Defense. The findings of this study indicate that the extent of the panic caused by the broadcast was much less than the media had reported. So the Barsebäck panic turned out to be a double error: the news bulletin that started it all was fictitious, and the later stories of widespread panic were exaggerations (Rosengren, Arvidson, and Sturesson 1975).

Atrocity Rumors

In times of conflict, rumors of atrocities committed by one's enemies circulate widely. These stories portray the other side in the most villainous of terms. In wartime, such rumors can boost military recruitment and home-front morale. Atrocity rumors carry particular impact when opposing groups are in daily and close contact with one another. Such is the case with rumors that are part of race riots.

Alfie's Stamp Collection.   In England during World War II, the story was often told of the family who had received a letter from their eldest son, who was in a German prisoner of war camp. The letter said that the Germans treated prisoners well, that the camp was comfortable, and that the food was "almost as good as home." The stamp on the envelope, the letter said, should be of some interest to the youngest son, Alfie, who collected stamps. Because the family had no son named Alfie, they became suspicious. When the stamp was steamed off the envelope, the family was horri-

fied to read the message "they have torn out my tongue."

The likelihood that such a letter could have been received was remote; letters from POWs were not stamped, and letters containing stamps would have been closely examined. Attempts to locate the family to whom the letter was sent failed. After the war, it was discovered that much the same story circulated in Germany. This time the son was writing from a Russian prison camp, and the hidden message read "they have cut off my feet" (Jacobson 1948).

Raped Women and Dead Babies.   On Sunday night, June 20, 1943, fighting broke out between groups of white sailors and black civilians on Belle Isle, one of Detroit's public beaches. Within an hour, fighting had spread throughout the downtown area of Detroit. Stories of how the fighting started were passed along as gangs of whites and blacks attacked one another, overturned cars, and stopped buses and streetcars. For the whites, fighting started because "Negroes had raped and killed a white woman on Belle Isle"; for the blacks, fighting started because "whites had thrown a Negro woman and her baby off the Belle Isle Bridge." As the riot continued into Monday, the story was broadcast over the radio that carloads of armed blacks were headed from Chicago to Detroit. None of these stories were correct. Adding to the atmosphere of hate, the Ku Klux Klan distributed antiblack, anti-Jewish, and anti-Catholic literature during the riot. The riot lasted little more than twenty-four hours, yet thirty-four people were killed and more than $2 million worth of property was destroyed.

Some True Rumors

It is easiest to discuss "true" rumors in situations where initial stories are dismissed as rumors by government officials, politicians, reporters, and editors. It is more difficult to recognize true rumors in those situations where no previous denials have been given. In these instances, we seldom realize that the information has been passed along through the same interpersonal channels that transmit less accurate information.

Meteorites

For ages, human beings have seen meteors streak across the sky. Some of the oldest written histories describe meteors or "shooting stars." But it wasn't until about two hundred years ago that people made the connection between the blazing trails in the sky and meteorites—the actual mineral residue that survives atmospheric entry and hits the earth. Until then, authorities were puzzled and sometimes amused or annoyed by stories peasants told of rocks falling from the sky.

The thought of rocks falling from the sky was totally contrary to the views of the universe and creation held at the time. Even the peasants were confused by what they had seen. They called meteorites "lightning stones" or "thunder stones," and they thought that the stones had magical properties. Norwegian peasants, for example, thought that thunder stones were useful to women in labor and that they would aid in the delivery of the child.

In the 1780s, scientists began to offer explanations of the rocks that fell from the sky. These explanations included "fossils," "tools of ancient men," and "tips of lightning bolts." Some suggested that the stones might have fallen from the sky but were ordinary stones that had been picked up by strange winds or hurled great distances by volcanic explosions. By the 1790s, however, scientists noted similar chemical and physical characteristics of thunder stones from around the world. Finally, between the years 1790 and 1795, spectacular meteor showers occurred in England, France,

Germany, and Italy. Hundreds of witnesses told of seeing thunder stones falling from these exploding fireballs. In 1795 German physicist E. F. Chladni wrote a small book advancing the argument that thunder stones were the residue of meteors that traveled through space. In a very obliging fashion, the Italian meteor shower provided direct confirmation of his theory a few months later. The peasants were right—stones did fall from the sky (Westrum 1978)!

The Atomic Bomb

For a week after the atomic bomb was dropped on Hiroshima, survivors tried to explain the horrible destruction that had occurred. Many survivors had seen or heard reports of the incendiary raids on other Japanese cities. The total devastation of Hiroshima, however, was beyond comparison. Minutes after the bomb detonated, the smell of oil hung in the air. This led many to speculate that the lone American bomber that flew over the city before the blast had sprayed finely vaporized gasoline into the air. The gasoline had then been detonated with an aerial flare. This view was given credibility when abnormally large, oily raindrops began to fall. Some thought the Americans were dropping more gasoline to kill the survivors.

Another explanation was offered. A prominent physician suggested that fine magnesium powder rather than gasoline had been dropped and that it had been ignited by electrical sparks from trolley cars.

Another common theory held that a very large incendiary bomb had been dropped. It was described as a "Molotov flower basket," which consisted of a number of smaller incendiaries that had scattered across Hiroshima and been ignited simultaneously.

Finally, another explanation was discussed. Some suggested that Hiroshima had been destroyed by the energy released when the smallest known particles were somehow split. Survivors referred to the weapon as the "original child bomb," but no one fully understood this idea. It was another interesting rumor (Shibutani 1966).

U.S. Atrocities

As opposition to the Vietnam War grew in the United States, stories of the savage nature of the conflict began to circulate. There were abundant stories about Viet Cong atrocities. Occasionally, stories circulated that Americans had also committed atrocities. Stories appeared in many local "underground" and decidedly anti–Vietnam War newspapers. These stories included the court-martial of Captain Howard B. Levey, an army physician who refused to train Green Berets. Dr. Levey claimed that to do so violated medical ethics, because the Green Berets used their medical knowledge for political ends, including torture of the enemy and exchanging care for information and cooperation.

As the war continued, stories were told and also printed in the underground press of how American troops tortured and killed prisoners and also shot or napalmed civilians. Almost always, military and government officials flatly denied these rumors, which was easy to do, considering the sources. In a few instances, it was acknowledged that civilian casualties had occurred but that these had been accidents or the result of misidentification. The wanton killing of civilians was not the way Americans fought wars.

Finally, in the spring of 1970, major newspapers and magazines carried stories of the Mylai 4 (Songmy) massacre. Mylai was a small hamlet in South Vietnam. On March 16, 1968 (it took nearly twenty months for the story to reach the public), five hundred women, children, and old men were shot down and bayoneted by American troops. Perhaps even more disturbing, the Mylai disclosure brought forth a number of reports about other, similar incidents involving American troops in Vietnam. Mylai served to further divide an already divided nation.

The Assassination of Sadat

On Tuesday, October 6, 1981, afternoon television shows were interrupted by a special bulletin. An assassination attempt had been made on President Anwar L. Sadat of Egypt. Live television and video replays showed the attack. Army troops fired into the reviewing stand where Sadat and other Egyptian officials were seated. It was a brutal attack. The cameras showed many people, their bodies horribly ripped by bullets.

Within moments of the shooting, CBS carried a report that Sadat had been killed. This report came from a camera crew at the scene. Within moments, however, the State Department issued a statement that Sadat was alive. This statement was followed shortly by Egyptian reports that Sadat had not only survived the attack but was uninjured. The most credible report was issued about forty-five minutes after the shooting. State Department officials claimed to have spoken with Sadat by telephone. News bulletins were interspersed with video replays of the attack, interviews with government officials, ambassadors, and journalists. Nearly ninety minutes of uninterrupted coverage was devoted to the event. Finally, Egyptian officials issued a statement: Sadat was dead; he had died almost instantly on the reviewing stand.

The Mass Hysteria Perspective

Discussions of mass hysteria emphasize that under conditions of intense collective excitement, people lose their ability to distinguish fact from fancy, and they become excitable, suggestible, uncritical, and irrational. Many events that have been identified as mass hysterias could aptly be described as "hysterias of rumor"; that is, fantastic stories come to dominate the conversations of people. Orrin E. Klapp (1972:116) describes rumor as the medium of anxious hysteria. In anxious or rumor hysteria, there is no real threat to people. Imaginary threats, however, are embodied in the content of rumors that rapidly circulate through the distressed population.

The nature of rumor and the rumor process is derived from people's psychological transformations during mass hysteria. Because people are excited, they spread rumors rapidly and indiscriminately, and because they are suggestible, they pass along the most outlandish stories as fact. Because people are uncritical and irrational, they spread rumors that usually run counter to established views and the statements of authorities. Rumors are seldom accurate, but they are internally consistent—a consistency that is based not on critical consideration but on "paranoid logic" (Klapp 1972:251).

Communication during rumor is free flowing; people willingly depart from the channels on which they rely for everyday communication. They give word-of-mouth communication the same or greater credibility than they give the established media. People may spread rumors through the use of hastily written leaflets, exchange rumors with total strangers, or pass on overheard conversations. In the deliberate transmission of product rumors, advertising agencies used teams of field workers to work stores, subways, train stops, and other places of routine public gatherings. Feigning real conversation, these workers would loudly praise or condemn a given product or manufacturer, and eavesdroppers would then pass the story on to others (Jacobson 1948:159–186).

Stories and images fashioned by rumor usually serve the psychological needs of those who invent or pass along the rumor. According to Klapp (1972:116), likely rumor participants include the uneducated. Increasing levels of education tend to insulate people from the gullible acceptance of rumor. Other likely participants include those with pent-up hatreds, aggressions, or other tensions. Spreading rumors allows for the expression of feelings that would be otherwise held in check by psychological and social constraints.

Though people may have conscious or unconscious motives for involvement in the rumor process, participants are not totally free from group constraints. That is, motives alone do not shape the content of rumor. People tend to fabricate or distort information to fit the central theme of the rumor (Klapp 1972:251). For example, perpetrators of violent crimes are identified as members of minority groups in the rumor process long before police investigation is complete. Evidence counter to this view is ignored. Motives for the crime, weapons used, and injuries inflicted are all molded to fit prevailing minority group stereotypes. The facts that emerge during investigation, however, may be quite contrary to the image of the crime conveyed by rumor. Sometimes the facts will be accepted because the rumor process has run its course and excitement has diminished. As the facts come to be accepted, few people recall the fantastic stories that circulated days earlier.

In general, people who hold this perspective view rumor as both a mechanism and a manifestation of mass hysteria. Rumor is the mechanism through which mass hysterias occur, because rumor can excite the people who participate in the exchange. Rumor also creates the bizarre images on which hysterical action is based. Rumor is a manifestation of hysteria because it clearly shows the operation of suggestibility and diminished critical ability.

The Emergent Norm Perspective

For Turner and Killian (1972:32), rumor is the process through which people develop shared definitions of unstructured and ambiguous situations and is therefore, "the characteristic mode of communication in collective behavior." In the early phases of disaster recovery, for example, there is often very little clear and certain information indicating the extent of damage, death, and injury, or the likelihood of further danger. People must evaluate and pass along information that is often incomplete or contradictory, and the group must choose between competing views of the situation. In such unstructured and ambiguous situations, rumor provides both needed information and a sense of certainty about the situation. The sense of certainty develops in part because the group attends to some features of the situation and ignores others during the rumor process. Rumor provides the basis for emergent norms that give direction to the activities of the collectivity.

Sensitization

In general, communication during rumor is more open and free flowing than usual. Turner and Killian (1972:37–40) account for this in terms of increased interpersonal sensitivity within the crowd. This sensitization occurs during the milling process, which includes both "wild" and "mild" activity. An example of intense milling would be people's rapid movement and shouting as they converge on the scene of an accident, while low-key milling would be restless movements and polite but pointless conversations that occur when people wait for an overdue train. Even silence and subtle gestures can sensitize people to one another and communicate moods. Milling, in whatever form it takes, sensitizes people to those around them through the mechanism of mutual role taking.

As people become sensitized to one another, spontaneous communication usually develops between those who do not ordinarily interact. Such communication is open and unguarded, and polite conversations between strangers may be surprisingly intimate and candid. Even the norms of communication that exist between friends and neighbors may become more relaxed. For example, someone may telephone friends at mealtime or at hours later than usual to pass along information. In general, interpersonal sensitization accounts for the rapid spread of rumors.

Suggestibility

Turner and Killian (1972:32–38) point out that group consensus emerges much more quickly than usual during the rumor process, which gives the appearance of increased suggestibility. It is not, however, the kind of suggestibility that occurs because of emotional arousal or diminished critical ability. Suggestibility during rumor arises because of the uncertainty of the situation. With increasing uncertainty, the greater are the fluctuations in people's judgment when they attempt to describe the situation confronting them. For example, through rumor, people may initially provide extreme estimates of the numbers of people injured in a disaster. Some may suggest that few people are injured, while others suggest that many are injured. Given such extreme initial judgments, consensus is reached in a surprisingly short time. For Turner and Killian, it is the uncertainty of the situation and not emotional arousal that increases individual susceptibility to the suggestions of others.

Selective Definition

In the rumor process, the group chooses between alternate and competing definitions of the situation, closely attending some views while ignoring others. Turner and Killian (1972:47–50) point out that during the rumoring and milling that preceded some lynchings, information pertaining to the guilt and villainy of the victim was attended to very closely. On the other hand, information that suggested innocence and appeals to "let the law handle it" were ignored. The selective definition of a situation provides the basis for shared action. It provides the standards by which group behavior is judged.

Keynoting. Selective definition occurs in three steps, the first of which is *keynoting*. Keynoting establishes the general boundaries within which later decisions will fall and the assumptions upon which proposed action is based. In the case of some lynchings, keynoting establishes that the victim is guilty and deserving of severe punishment. Keynoting also establishes that "taking the law into their own hands" is a reasonable community response. In a sense, the fundamental assumptions are set at this stage: the victim is guilty, and a lynching is appropriate. As more people vocally agree with these propositions, other crowd members find it increasingly difficult to express views that run counter to the emerging theme. The absence of open expression of counterviews adds to the impression that keynotes are the feelings of the majority.

Symbolization. The next step in the process of selective definition is *symbolization*. Turner and Killian argue that communication normally occurs largely through cognitive symbols. The object of cognitive symbols is separated from the feelings that the object arouses in the user. Terms such as *my worthy opponent*, *the accused*, or proper names are cognitive symbols. Usually such terms do not call out uniform emotional responses. Selective definition involves the use of mystical symbols that do arouse uniform emotional responses among the audience. Mystical symbols include name-calling and inflammatory terms such as *commie, atheist, bastard, honkey, gook, kike,* or *nigger.* This type of symbolization simplifies the situation and neutralizes norms that might inhibit the crowd from unrestrained action toward the object of the symbol. The open and frequent use of such derogatory terms often signifies a "point of no return" in the development of collective hostile actions.

Coordination. Finally, selective definition involves *coordination.* Statements that call attention to the separate interests of the collectivity do not permit unified action. Particularistic statements can be used to hinder the development of hostile actions. Police, for example, may call crowd members by name and ask them to leave, saying "People like you should know better than to act this way." Ministers may remind people in the crowd that their actions are not in keeping with "what you learn in church." City officials may remind people that their actions "degrade their fine town." The effective coordinating symbol must emphasize features of the situation and identities that a wide range of people may respond to in a uniform manner.

Rumor and Crowd Action

Activities and symbols that simplify the situation, eliminate ambiguity and conflicting views, and provide the basis for uniform response are the fundamentals of crowd action. Emergent norms and a sense of certainty grow together and reinforce one another. It is through the rumor process that such symbols and norms develop (Turner and Killian 1972: 55). Rumor is the characteristic mode of communication in collective behavior.

The Value-Added Perspective

For Smelser, rumor fills an important role in the development of collective episodes. Specifically, rumor is necessary for the development of generalized belief. Rumor is also an important part of mobilization for action. In many respects, Smelser's discussion of rumor runs parallel to that of the mass hysteria perspective.

Generalized Belief

According to Smelser, beliefs that prepare people for action are present in all collective behavior, but generalized belief differs from those that are part of everyday action. Generalized belief reduces ambiguity created by conditions of structural strain. In order to reduce ambiguity, generalized belief is simplistic; it necessarily does not reflect the complexity of situations revealed by careful scrutiny. Generalized belief also prepares people for collective action by creating shared or common objects, giving focus to anxiety or discontent, and fostering consensus.

Given the nature of generalized beliefs, it is obvious how rumor is instrumental in their development. As a form of communication, rumor creates simplistic views of complex or ambiguous situations. It also creates common objects, gives focus to conscious and unconscious motives, and fosters a sense of certainty and consensus. The characterization of generalized beliefs and rumor are so similar that Smelser sometimes uses the two terms interchangeably (Smelser 1962:82–84).

Panics are based on generalized hysterical beliefs that transform an ambiguous (and sometimes harmless) situation into a definite and potent threat. Fear-laden rumors of impending disaster, descriptions of crimes, and stories of monsters and UFOs provide the basis for generalized beliefs. Such rumors eliminate ambiguity by creating an object that is sure to harm or destroy anyone in its path. Even though these rumors foster fear, they also provide predictability and structure.

Crazes are based on hysterical wish-fulfillment beliefs. Rumors of fortunes made in land or commodity speculation reduce ambiguity in financial dealings. Hysterical wish-fulfillment beliefs portray the possibility of wealth in unrealistic terms—as a "sure thing." Rumors also play a role in the transformation of crazes into financial panics. Bankruptcy rumors, rumors that the big investors are selling, or rumors of embezzlement are enough to turn bold speculators into panicked sellers.

Hostile outbursts are based on generalized hostile beliefs. These beliefs portray the object of attack in bold, simple, negative terms. Rumor entails the use of mystical or emotion-provoking symbols. Generalized hostile beliefs also include a feeling of omnipotence—a belief that the crowd has the power to remove, punish, or destroy the object of attack. In the case of attacks against authority, these beliefs may well be unfounded. They are fostered by rumors describing the ineffectiveness of authorities or their lack of resolve to fight against the crowd. Rumors may also exaggerate the strength of the crowd or the likelihood that others will rise up with the crowd when attacks commence.

Norm- and value-oriented social movements are based on beliefs that envision the reconstruction of a deteriorating normative and value structure. These beliefs are created by rumors describing the decadence of the existing society. Bizarre stories about satanic rock groups, promiscuous sex, horrendous crimes, political corruption, dangerous environmental pollution, and wanton use of drugs portray today's society in dire need of drastic reform. The belief that the social movement's program is certain to bring about desired changes is also necessary for continued reform efforts.

Mobilization for Action

Once generalized beliefs are in place, it is necessary to bring people into action. According to Smelser, this occurs through the action of leadership. For panics and crazes, leadership may simply take the form of models of appropriate action. Sometimes these models are concocted in the rumor process. Rumors of bankruptcy or that big investors are selling out may have no basis in fact. In hostile outbursts, leadership is often emergent and may come from people who spread reports of police brutality or pass out hate literature. The leadership of social movements can assume many of the characteristics of leadership within formal organizations. Leaders of social movements are often in a position to manipulate information through the use of planted rumors. Leaders may also have access to telephone numbers, computerized mailing lists, and the established media. Smelser acknowledges that leaders may manipulate information sent through these channels. Regardless of the way in which information is conveyed, calls to action must be expressed in unambiguous and emotional terms.

Collective Behavior and Rumor

The mass hysteria, value-added, and emergent norm perspectives differ in many fundamental ways. In their view of rumor, however, they are much alike. The mass hysteria perspective and, to a great extent, the emergent norm perspective characterize rumor as conveying simplistic, often inaccurate, and emotion-provoking images of ambiguous situations. Smelser adopts this view of rumor, which fits quite conveniently with his view of collective behavior. Collective behavior is based on generalized beliefs—simplistic and emotion-provoking explanations of ambiguous situations created by structural strain.

Classical Approaches to Rumor: Gordon W. Allport and Leo Postman

Shortly after the United States entered World War II, rumor became a serious national concern. People told and retold stories of how our losses at Pearl Harbor were far greater than our government officials would admit. Some stories told that our entire Pacific Fleet and nearly all of our military aircraft had been destroyed and that our entire West Coast was defenseless. In fact, our losses at Pearl Harbor were greater than officials could admit publicly, so these stories were of considerable annoyance to those who had to mobilize a nation for war. Pearl Harbor stories became so troublesome that about ten weeks after the attack (February 23, 1942), President Roosevelt spoke out. His "fireside chat" radio broadcast accurately described the extent of the damage and did a great deal to restore confidence in our military situation. Still, the stories continued for months afterward. Throughout the war, government agencies such as the Office of War Information maintained active rumor control programs. These programs included public speakers, special newspaper features such as the "The Rumor Clinic" of the *Boston Herald-Traveler*, and, of course, the "Loose Lips Sink Ships" posters.

During this time, Gordon W. Allport and Leo Postman carried out a series of studies on the rumor process. Allport and Postman (1965:ix) defined *rumor* as "a specific (or topical) proposition for belief, passed along from person to person, usually by word of mouth, without secure standards of evidence being presented." Even though people may begin their remarks with the phrase "It's only a rumor, but . . . ," the implication is that fact is being presented.

Allport and Postman (1965:33–34) were the first to state the "basic law of rumor": *The in-*

*tensity of rumor is the product of the impor-
tance of the subject to the individual and the
ambiguity of the evidence pertaining to the
topic at issue.* According to Allport and Postman's law, rumor is most likely to occur when
people are intensely interested in a topic and
little definite news or official information is
available. Rumor is unlikely when people have
little interest in a topic and/or official information is plentiful.

An Experiment in Serial Transmission

Using their definition and basic law of rumor, Allport and Postman devised an experiment to show how rumors are transmitted. Interestingly, their experiment was conducted
before audiences. Allport and Postman argued
that this would not contaminate the results because in real life rumors are often passed along
within groups. Further, they conducted the experiment a few times without an audience and
obtained essentially the same results. They
tried their experiment before a wide range of
audiences; including college undergraduates,
army trainees, community groups, patients in
an Army hospital, participants in a teachers
conference, police officials, and children in a
private school.

The specific procedures used by Allport and
Postman have been described as creating a *serial transmission* pattern of communication.
They selected six or seven volunteer subjects
from the audience and sent them from the
room, then selected another person to act as an
"eyewitness." Next, Allport and Postman
called one subject back into the room and seated the subject so that he or she could not see a
picture that was being projected onto a movie
screen. The pictures were usually line draw-
ings of various scenes, including a combat
scene, an accident scene, a street scene, and the
interior of a crowded streetcar. The pictures included males and females, whites and blacks,

signs on buildings and vehicles, clocks, and
ambulances. The eyewitness then described
about twenty details of the picture to the first
subject.

After the eyewitness described the picture, a
second subject was brought into the room and
seated next to the first. The first subject then
retold the eyewitness account to the second
subject. Then the third subject was brought in
and seated next to the second subject, who told
the third subject about the picture. The researchers continued the process until the final
subject described the picture. During the experiment, subjects were not allowed to interrupt or question one another or ask for repeti-
tions. Allport and Postman justified this
feature of the experiment by claiming that rumor spreaders seldom ask for clarification in
real life.

In nearly every instance, the description
given by the last subject bore little resemblance
to the eyewitness description or the picture.
Many details were lost in retelling, some details were exaggerated, and sometimes details
were added that did not occur in either the picture or the eyewitness account. Still, Allport
and Postman concluded that their procedure
probably did not distort information as much
as real-life rumoring.

Leveling.   Allport and Postman note that
the distortions that occurred in the retelling of
descriptions was not haphazard. Rather, three
major patterns of distortion were evident from
their data. The first pattern was *leveling.* As a
rumor is transmitted, it tends to grow shorter.
Nearly 70 percent of the details provided by
the eyewitness are lost in the course of five or
six word-of-mouth transmissions (Allport and
Postman 1965:75). In particular, times of day
(shown by clocks in the picture), numbers of
people, names appearing on signs, and kinds
of vehicles are lost. Often the final description
contains no more than four or five of the original details.

Sharpening. The second pattern of distortion is *sharpening*, which refers primarily to the details that survive through a number of transmissions. Why are certain details retained? Allport and Postman attribute this selective perception and retention to the subjects' individual prejudices and interests. Very seldom are the racial identities described by the eyewitness lost during transmission. Other features of the eyewitness account are maintained when presented in a novel or odd fashion. One eyewitness described an adult as "remonstrating" a boy because the boy had "stolen vegetables from a market." The term *remonstrating* was maintained through subsequent retellings. Descriptions of movement, such as running, jumping, falling, striking, or throwing are maintained fairly well. Finally, familiar symbols, such as crosses on the church and the names of popular entertainers are maintained.

Assimilation. The final pattern of distortion is *assimilation*. Details are leveled or sharpened depending on the general theme of the story. In pictures of combat, military objects and actions are maintained more than nonmilitary parts of the picture, such as birds, clouds, or buildings. Some assimilation is consistent with racial stereotypes. In one picture, for example, a black man was shown talking to a white man who was holding what appeared to be a straight razor. In the retelling, the straight razor often ended up being held by the black man! Assimilation often reflects people's special interests. Women, according to Allport and Postman, often remember clothing and signs in store windows, while army trainees and police more often remember times of day, vehicles, and weapons. Finally, some assimilation involves adding details that are not in the picture or part of the eyewitness description. This often takes the form of assuming the motives and identities of people in the pictures. Blacks were often described as "zoot-suiters"

and troublemakers, while whites were often described as "defense plant workers," as "going to or coming from work," and as victims of harassment.

Summary

According to Allport and Postman, rumors are by definition inaccurate. People have little interest in ascertaining the source or accuracy of information contained in rumors, because rumoring primarily serves motives other than information seeking. Rumors help to "relieve, justify, and explain underlying tension" (Allport and Postman 1965:36–38). Rumors, for example, that portray the Soviet Union in a very negative fashion are heartening to those who advocate a strong military stance against Russia. Rumors are a means of projecting one's own feelings, and discrimination, prejudice, and even race hatred become "reasonable" responses in the face of rumors detailing the vicious nature of other ethnic groups. The bad conduct of others becomes a reasonable explanation of one's own negative feelings (Allport and Postman, 1965:40–41). Active involvement in rumoring is also a way to relieve guilt. Stories about bizarre sexual misconduct by public officials and entertainers make our "everyday" sexual transgressions seem tame by comparison. Finally, rumoring may simply be a way of "seeking attention," "feeling important," and "filling awkward gaps in conversations" (Allport and Postman 1965:46–47).

Discussion

Allport and Postman characterize rumoring more as serving personal motives than as a process of information seeking or communication. In many ways, this characterization runs counter to their "basic law of rumor" which states that the intensity of rumoring is due to the importance of the subject to people and the availability of information. After laying out the basic law of rumor, Allport and Postman say little about how to determine the "importance of events" and the "supply of information." Much of what Allport and Postman say about rumor would lead us to examine the psychological characteristics of people involved in rumoring (which is virtually everyone!) rather than the situational context in which rumors occur.

The serial transmission experiment used to study the rumor process strips away much of the context within which rumor processes occur. In everyday life, people exchange information with people they know. People can judge, at least superficially, the "reliability" of the person offering information. Further, they usually receive information from more than one person, as well as from the media, allowing for "working triangulation," or checks for consistency. These communication network features are totally lacking in Allport and Postman's experimental design. Finally, contrary to Allport and Postman's claim, as information is transmitted by word of mouth, people do question one another about sources and inconsistencies and do ask for elaboration. In brief, Allport and Postman's experimental design does not include conditions of *redundancy* (more than one source of information) and *reciprocity* (being able to question the teller of information) that are found in most real-life situations. The conditions under which Allport and Postman studied rumor are more likely to be found in a highly structured, impersonal setting than in, say, a university dormitory or party of friends. Perhaps the serial transmission arrangement produces the enormous amounts of distortion observed by Allport and Postman. Put another way, under conditions of minimal redundancy and reciprocity, almost any kind of information will be severely distorted.

It is difficult to reconcile Allport and Postman's conclusions that word-of-mouth transmission greatly distorts information with the fact that preliterate societies could store and transmit vast amounts of information, seemingly without distortion, for hundreds of generations. More to the point, in everyday life—to the discomfort of many public and corporate officials—rumors often turn out to be true.

Allport and Postman's work occurred at a time when any kind of systematic information about how the rumor process operates was sorely needed. Their work gave incentive to those whose job it was to protect vital military information, such as troop movements and cargo destinations. There was a clear need to counter fears about our military weaknesses, untrue stories that generated racial tensions, and untrue stories that undermined cooperation with such programs as food rationing. Perhaps the most important outcome of Allport and Postman's work was that it provided a stimulus for further studies of communication and rumor.

Rumor as News: Tamotsu Shibutani

Tamotsu Shibutani's (1966) interest in rumor also began with World War II experiences. Shortly after the attack on Pearl Harbor, thousands of Japanese Americans were evacuated from the West Coast and confined in relocation centers in the Midwest. Later in the war, many young men from these camps volunteered for military service, some of which was in occupied Japan. Shibutani made fieldnotes while observing rumor processes firsthand as those around him speculated about what would happen to them next. Unlike Allport and Postman, Shibutani studied rumors in their natural setting rather than under controlled conditions. Later, he also compiled records of rumors that had occurred among other groups from the mid-1800s to the 1960s.

The classical approach of Allport and Postman's characterizes rumor as inaccurate, exaggerated, or outlandish information that primarily serves the psychological needs of the people passing on the rumor; only coincidentally does rumor provide useful or accurate information. Shibutani turns the classical view around. For Shibutani (1966:17), rumor is a recurrent form of communication through which people attempt to construct a meaningful or "working" interpretation of a threatening or ambiguous situation by pooling their intellectual resources. The collective result is not necessarily inaccurate, exaggerated, or implausible. Shibutani acknowledges that rumor can relieve anxiety and be shaped by the psychological needs of people. For the most part, however, rumor is primarily a substitute for news, which is usually supplied through institutional channels (see below); rumor is news that develops outside of institutional channels. In short, rumor is "improvised news."

Established Channels of Communication

In everyday social life, most communication occurs through established channels. Much information is transmitted through formal or *institutional channels*. Institutional channels refer to most of the news media as well as to the formal channels of communication that exist in bureaucracies. Institutional channels are well organized and are characterized by a stable set of rules, officers performing clearly defined roles, and well-established procedures that can be followed by interchangeable personnel. Within most institutional channels, there are fixed standards of what is acceptable news, procedures for obtaining news, prescribed routes of transmission, verification procedures, and codes of reliable conduct. Participants in institutional channels are held personally accountable for their perfor-

mance, and there are agreed-upon sanctions for misconduct (Shibutani 1966:21).

Even within the media and bureaucracies, not all routine communication is handled through established channels. Enduring *auxiliary channels* of communication are interwoven with institutional channels. Auxiliary channels refer to the established or recurring patterns of interpersonal communication within our daily lives. Auxiliary channels are composed of family members, friends, neighbors, and work associates with whom we normally exchange and discuss information. Auxiliary channels supplement institutional channels. Within bureaucracies, for example, auxiliary channels are utilized to obtain clarification of "official" communication, correct bureaucratic errors, and resolve problems not mentioned in the "rulebook." In some instances, auxiliary channels may entirely supplant institutional arrangements, as in disasters or for carrying out illegal activities such as embezzlement or employee theft. Major areas of everyday living, such as family life and most shared activities between friends and neighbors, are also constructed through auxiliary channels of communication.

Conditions Giving Rise to Rumor

Allport and Postman's basic law of rumor states that the intensity of rumor is the product of the importance of the subject to the individual and the ambiguity of the evidence pertaining to the topic at issue. Shibutani (1966:57) restates this law in somewhat different terms: "if the demand for news . . . exceeds the supply made available through institutional channels, rumor construction is likely to occur." In other words, when institutional channels fail them, people move outside institutional channels for information.

Perhaps the most obvious situation in which people rely on rumor for communication is when institutional channels have broken down. This condition exists during disasters when local newspapers or radio and television stations are unable to operate or are unable to provide up-to-the-minute information. A similar situation exists when totalitarian governments shut down the media in times of political crisis.

Another situation in which people rely on rumor for communication is when the credibility of the media is suspect. This condition exists when the only media allowed to operate is government sponsored or strict censorship is enforced. Censorship increases rumoring, even when the censorship is voluntary and most citizens agree with it on principle. This type of situation existed in the United States during World War II. The media generally followed a policy of voluntary restraint in reporting stories having to do with the war. In principle, most Americans agreed that this policy was necessary for national security. Still, rumors circulated about disastrous military casualties, profiteering, waste, and corruption.

Finally, people rely on rumoring for news about topics that are ignored by the media because they are in poor taste, potentially libelous, or nonsensical. Through rumor, people often attempt to ascertain the exact details of mutilations in murders and accidents, the sexual and personal quirks of public figures, and UFO or Bigfoot sightings.

Types of Rumoring

If unsatisfied demand for news is moderate and collective excitement is mild, then rumor construction takes place through *critical deliberation*. For the most part, people use the auxiliary channels of communication that have been established through everyday interaction. Social control, though informal, is present. Most participants retain their critical ability; reports are checked and cross-checked for plausibility and reliability of sources. The definitions that emerge tend to be consistent with cultural axioms (Shibutani 1966:94).

Deliberative rumoring is not that different from the way we draw conclusions, arrive at decisions, and form opinions in everyday life. Shibutani (1966:94) points out that most ambiguous situations are resolved through joint deliberation and that most decisions one makes in the course of a day are predicated on unverified reports. People rely to a large extent on what they hear from others, and they usually find such information sufficiently reliable for meeting the challenges of daily life. Such information is not *rumor*, the term being reserved for those accounts of which one is suspicious; most information on which people base their lives, however, cannot meet high standards of verification.

If unsatisfied demand for news is very great and collective excitement is intense, then rumor construction occurs through spontaneous interchanges. Shibutani refers to this type of rumoring as *extemporaneous rumoring*. That is, people depart not only from institutional channels but from auxiliary channels as well. Reports are accepted from almost any source—acquaintances, strangers, and even overheard conversations. Under conditions of increased anonymity, personal responsibility for information is minimized. Extemporaneous rumoring departs significantly from the communication that occurs in everyday life. Under conditions of extemporaneous rumoring, the greatest amount of confusion and distortion of information occurs.

Shibutani (1966:128) argues that extemporaneous rumoring occurs only under extreme and infrequent circumstances. Even then, rumoring is not haphazard or unrestrained by previous experiences and statements of possible outcomes. Rumor content is still largely limited by considerations of plausibility. Social reconstructions, or rumors, are circumscribed by the basic culture of the group, and most rumors are consistent with cultural axioms. Implausible proposals are selectively eliminated on the basis of what seems sensible in terms of what is already taken for granted. Situations marked by intense tension and extemporaneous construction may provide the conditions necessary for the development of drastically different beliefs. This type of collective consensus is a major step in processes of social change.

Interaction during Rumor

Shibutani notes that the classical view treats *rumor* as a noun rather than as a verb. In the classic sense, a rumor is an object, like a brick, that can be handed from one person to another. In Allport and Postman's study, the rumor is a "fixed combination of words" that "stimulates one person, undergoes certain modification while passing through him, and then departs to stimulate someone else" (Shibutani 1966:8). The classical view recognizes that rumor is a *social* phenomenon only in the sense that more than one person is involved in its transmission; that people acting together in any enterprise are intertwined in a complex web of social relationships is ignored (Shibutani 1966:8).

Emergent Roles in Rumoring

Shibutani (1966:13) views rumor as "a collective transaction, involving a division of labor among participants, each of whom makes a different contribution." Because people involved in the development of a rumor do not have identical vocabularies, interests, and perceptions, the transaction as a whole can not be explained in terms of individual motivations. The career of a rumor is not a process of unilinear development, as in serial transmission experiments. Instead, Shibutani suggests the collective rumor transaction involves a "division

of labor" in which people occupy identifiable roles. The most obvious role in rumor development is that of the *messenger*, the person who brings pertinent information into the group. Another role is that of the *interpreter*, who tries to put the news into context and evaluates it in terms of past events and likely outcomes. Within almost any group is the *skeptic*. Occupants of this role express doubt about the authenticity of information, demand proof, and urge caution. The role of *protagonist* emerges when someone advocates one interpretation or plan of action over others. There is also the role of *auditor*, the spectator who says relatively little. This role is important because debate is frequently carried out with an eye toward winning over the uncommitted participants. Finally, there is the role of the *decision maker*, who takes the lead in deciding what should be done. Shibutani suggests that there is no necessary or close correspondence between personality types and the roles people come to occupy in the rumor process. In fact, a person may change roles during an encounter, perhaps initially occupying the role of auditor, then the role of messenger, and finally that of protagonist.

Stereotypes

Shibutani takes issue with some of the stereotypes concerning the psychological processes involved in rumoring. One stereotype is, that when confronted by rumors, people lose their critical abilities and do not verify the information on which they are acting. Shibutani notes that in normal, everyday situations, people seldom verify information before they act on it. Instead, they must rely on the "taken for granted" nature of social life. People ask total strangers for directions to important destinations; people give money to strangers, assuming they will receive the product that is promised; they accept at face value uniforms, badges, and professional diplomas. People probably could not get out of the house in the morning if they attempted to verify even a small portion of the information they act on daily!

In everyday life, people usually verify information only after they have acted on it. This occurs when events do not turn out as planned. People make inquiries when the goods they order fail to arrive, and they check credentials when hired workers fail to perform as expected. About the only time information is consistently verified beforehand is when it is someone's job to do so. There is a growing demand for the services of businesses that verify information on résumés and employment application forms.

Shibutani suggests that in problematic situations such as disasters, people can no longer rely on the taken for granted nature of social life. Immediate and effective action is clearly necessary, and people may actually attempt to verify more information than usual. When people act on unverified information contained in rumors, it is often because opportunities for firsthand verification are unavailable.

Another closely related stereotype is that of suggestibility: people are willing to consider and sometimes act on the most outlandish of rumors. According to Shibutani (1966:108), people are suggestible only to the extent that they uncritically accept ideas inconsistent with their own standards. In disaster situations, where survival often depends on accurate information, people usually retain their critical abilities. People may give consideration to seemingly outlandish information because to do otherwise would be dangerous. In conflict situations such as war, rumors concerning the strength of opposing forces and battle tactics must be carefully evaluated. This "defensive pessimism" is a kind of realism that makes people consider, at least momentarily, even the most bizarre information. It also makes survival on a battlefield possible. Finally, people's critical outlook is heightened when they are aware of the possibility of being cheated or tricked. Sometimes this type of caution can result in paralyzing indecision, making concerted group action difficult (Shibutani 1966:125–127).

Discussion

Shibutani approaches the study of rumor from the standpoint of naturalistic observation rather than experiment. He conceptualizes rumor in a way quite different from the classical view of Allport and Postman. For Shibutani, rumor is in many ways like the kind of communication we use in solving everyday dilemmas. Rumor is a collective process in which people combine their intellectual resources when institutional channels of communication have failed. Then, people must rely almost entirely on the auxiliary channels of communication used in everyday interaction with family, friends, and neighbors. Under extreme conditions, people may depart from even these auxiliary channels and utilize information from any available source. Still, the outcome of rumor processes is constrained by plausibility, consideration of likely outcomes, and the people's culture. Perhaps the most significant idea in Shibutani's approach to rumor is that rumor is basically similar to the types of communication that occur in everyday life. In this sense, Shibutani's approach to rumor can accommodate both the idea that rumor is sometimes quite divergent from what most consider "accurate" accounts of events and the fact that rumors sometimes turn out to be true.

Communication in Collective Behavior

The kind of communication on which collective behavior is based does not appear to be substantially different from the kind of com-

FIGURE 4.1   *Patterns of Communication: Serial and Social Transmission of Rumors*

SERIAL TRANSMISSION
(Allport and Postman)

Eyewitness

Serial transmission tends to distort information. In part, this is because those involved in the transmission of information are mutual strangers. Further, there is little if any redundancy in the communication network, that is, there is only one eyewitness source of information. Finally, there is little reciprocity, only one-way communication links exist between participants.

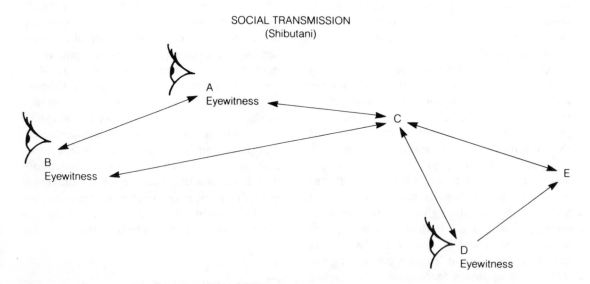

SOCIAL TRANSMISSION
(Shibutani)

Social transmission is much less likely to distort information than serial transmission. This is because many of those in the communication pattern know one another and interact frequently. Further, in social transmission there may be several eyewitness sources of information providing greater redundancy of information. Also, there is greater reciprocity among participants; most communication links are two-way and each individual can communicate with a number of other participants in this pattern. Redundancy and reciprocity provide "working triangulation," which produces accurate information.

munication that occurs in other areas of everyday life. Some writers (Shibutani 1966; Turner and Killian 1972), while emphasizing these similarities, still claim that people engaged in collective behavior readily utilize anonymous sources for news. In part, this is because identifiable sources are absent. Even this moderate view, however, must be qualified.

First, some research indicates that information provided by anonymous sources is less likely to be transmitted from person to person than information from known sources. Rosnow and Fine (1976:63–80) discuss two experiments in which a rumor was started by a "known" and authoritative source—a teacher and a guidance counselor. A third experiment was conducted among a group of undergraduates during campus orientation. The source of the rumor was a student assistant to the experimenter, and who constituted an "anonymous" source within the group. The researchers found that rumors provided by the teacher and guidance counselor were much more likely to be repeated and passed through two or more exchanges than rumors provided by the anonymous student. These findings clearly run counter to the notion that "rumor flourishes from anonymity."

Second, other research (Aveni 1977; Miller 1979) indicates that the number of identifiable sources of information available within crowds may be much larger than we might expect. This is particularly the case for crowds that form within or near residences and workplaces. For example, neighbors may rush from their homes and gather at an auto accident in a nearby intersection. Friends and even family groups may gather at the picket lines during strikes, and friends may attend protest rallies together. Aveni (1977) surveyed a milling street crowd following a university football game and found that a majority of those interviewed (74 percent) were accompanied by one or more friends. Most (64 percent) also said that they had seen relatives and friends from class, work, residences, and hometowns on the streets after the game. Miller (1979) also found that a majority of student respondents (77 percent) were with friends while they prepared to attend a large, impromptu pep rally following an upset victory by their university's basketball team. Further, most respondents (76 percent) said they accompanied these people to the rally, stayed near them while at the rally, and returned to campus with them. In a sense, many normal, everyday social relationships are extended into the crowd and other collective behavior situations as well. These social relationships, in the form of identifiable others, give collective behavior continuity with everyday life.

Designative and Prescriptive Aspects of Communication

The SBI approach to collective behavior emphasizes the importance of *instructions for response* for the occurrence of convergent behavior. Some conceptions of rumor, particularly in the classical view of Allport and Postman, identify rumoring as primarily an "extension of people's innermost fears, wishes, or guilt." At best, this view places rumor at the periphery of communication processes. In contrast, Shibutani attributes a much more prominent communicative role to rumor. Rumor provides definitions of reality and represents collective answers to problems facing groups. This and similar characterizations place rumor within one category of instructions for response. Stewart (1969) refers to this category of instructions as *designations*: activities that name, locate, and otherwise identify objects by denoting whether objects are good, bad, dangerous, and so on. Rumors, regardless of their source, accuracy, and plausibility are designations. Rumors create images of groups; rumors tell us what kind of people our leaders, celebrities, enemies, work associates, and neighbors "really" are; rumors tell us who is responsible for many of life's tragedies. Rumors establish what has happened, what is happening, and what is likely to happen.

Studies of rumor do not tell us precisely how these designations are used in the development of new lines of conduct. For example, we know that false stories of rapes and murders circulated during the Detroit race riot of 1943 (see Chapter 11). We also know that many rioters who spoke to police and reporters during the riot used these stories to justify their actions. We do not know, however, how many people heard these stories and then went out and attacked someone. It may well be (and some riot research lends indirect support to this assertion) that only a small portion of those hearing the atrocity stories became involved in the rioting. Further, some people quite likely became involved in the rioting before they heard the atrocity stories. In short, rumor studies tell us about leveling, sharpening, assimilation, roles in the rumoring process, and rumor in ambiguous situations. Rumor studies tell us very little about how rumors become the basis for convergent behavior.

Rumors and Convergent Activity. Before designations, or designative rumors, can serve as the basis for convergent behavior, action specifications must occur with respect to the objects established by the rumor. Action specifications are referred to as *prescriptions* (Stewart 1969). Designations *and* prescriptions are necessary for the organization of convergent behavior. For example, designations establish the setting: "An accident has occurred on the corner and several people are injured!" Prescriptions specify activity: "Get the first-aid kit and let's go help!" In the absence of action specifications or prescriptions, designative rumors do not provide the basis of convergent behavior. In order to understand the effects of rumor, we must identify conditions under which they are likely to be accompanied by prescriptions.

Objects Established by Designative Rumors. Rumors are likely to be accompanied by prescriptions for action when they identify or create an object toward which some immediate action can be taken. As such, a large portion of what is called rumor hardly ever serves as a basis for concerted behavior beyond idle conversations. This is particularly true for rumors that pertain to the personal lives and dealings of public figures. Rosnow and Fine (1976:81–93) refer to derogatory "personal life" rumors as *gossip*. Their main criterion for classifying this type of information as gossip is its triviality. For most people in the United States, rumors about the royal family of England fall within this category. Rumors about the personal lives of entertainers also fall within this category. For most people, personal life rumors are almost totally devoid of any potential for action beyond prescriptions to buy (or avoid buying) the tabloids in which these stories are published. About the only people to take action with respect to these types of rumors are the injured parties, as when Carol Burnett sued the *National Enquirer* for libel.

Occasionally, people are in a position to actually make a decision or take some action with respect to the object of the personal life rumor. Stories about the misconduct of public officials are more likely to be accompanied by specific prescriptions for action near election time. Prescriptions such as "Let's vote against the jerk!" among the constituency can serve as the basis of action with respect to the rumor. Likewise, derogatory stories about entertainers may reduce movie attendance or record sales. Product rumors, such as McDonald's wormburgers or K-Mart's poisonous snakes, may clearly generate prescriptions to avoid the product, although the harmful effects of these particular rumors have not been documented.

Established Conflict.   Rumors are likely to be accompanied by action specifications when they occur in the context of an already established conflict. Rumors (both accurate and inaccurate) of police brutality were followed by assembling instructions in the urban riots of the 1960s. Blacks assembled at the scenes of arrests, raids, and shootings. Brutality rumors were consistent with the deterioration of white police–black civilian relationships in many cities. During wartime, atrocity rumors serve to boost recruitment, public support for the war, and austerity measures. Conversely, rumors of atrocities committed by one's own troops, such as the Mylai massacre of the Vietnam War, seem to create considerable dissension and debate.

Proximity.   Rumors about groups or individuals are more likely to be accompanied by prescriptions for action when these groups live in close proximity to one another and/or interact frequently. In the Detroit race riot of 1943, for example, rumors that whites had thrown a black woman and her baby off a bridge and that blacks had raped and killed a white woman occurred on an evening when the streets and public beaches were congested with crowds of whites and blacks. Congestion further increased when the factory shifts changed and workers crowded onto buses and streetcars. Fighting broke out near crowded housing projects and at major intersections. Similar conditions existed in the urban riots of the 1960s.

Availability.   Designative rumors are more likely to be accompanied by prescriptions for action when there is increased availability to carry out additional activities. Though people nearly always gather at the scene of accidents, fires, and disasters, assembling is more extensive when these events occur during time periods within minimum competing demands on those who assemble. Fires and accidents draw bigger crowds during noon hours, after the dinner hour, and on weekends. For most of us, holidays and vacation periods represent blocks of unstructured time during which we can schedule extemporaneous activities, such as visiting a disaster site.

Spatial availability, or proximity, can also increase the likelihood of action specifications (McPhail 1983). Reports of arrests in progress, accidents, fires, and disasters, as well as the sights and sounds that accompany these events, are more likely to generate assembling instructions among those who are close by. Bailey and McPhail (1979) interviewed a sample of participants in a gathering at an apartment house fire and a comparative sample of people who knew of the event but did not attend. More than half (55 percent) of those interviewed indicated that they learned of the event by word of mouth. Subsequently, most of these people received suggestions to assemble from others.

Previous and Ongoing Activity.   Designative accounts are likely to be accompanied by prescriptions for action among people who have previously participated in activities related to the prospective object or event. Accounts of the Detroit race riot of 1943 often note that members of the Ku Klux Klan and white and black "hoodlums" were the most likely to initiate violent attacks. Civic and religious groups were the most active counterrioters in Detroit, as well as in the riots of the 1960s. During the campus disorders of the 1960s, some people repeatedly participated in rallies and demonstrations. Finally, fundamental religious groups have been active in efforts to combat the influence of "satanic" rock and roll groups. This is not to say that rioters are all criminals, that campus disorders were started by "professional agitators," or that religious fundamentalism attracts only "fanatics" or paranoid individuals. Rather, these groups constitute "publics" with respect to particular issues.

Prior participation in events related to a given issue can result in others' identification of individuals (and groups) as likely recruits for participation in pending events of a similar nature (McPhail 1983). Likely recruits are then targeted for instructions to participate in pending events. Interest groups often compile membership lists with names, addresses, and telephone numbers to facilitate block recruiting. In like fashion but in a less formal manner, rumors and prescriptions for action can be transmitted through the auxiliary communication channels of family, friends, work, and neighborhood groups. Occasionally, prescriptions for action are addressed to nonmembers in the form of leaflets, posters, and speeches. Thus, fundamentalist Christian groups send speakers before PTA meetings to warn against and organize resistance to "satanic music."

Discussion

Research by McPhail and Miller (1973) on the assembling process and research by McPhail (1983) and others on behavior within gatherings have utilized designative and prescriptive activities as explanatory variables. This treatment of communication clearly falls outside the traditional boundaries of rumor studies. The above discussion of communication within collective behavior summarizes the views developed so far. These ideas will have to be developed to a much greater degree than they are at present. In all likelihood, the results will be in the direction of a general theory of communication rather than a theory of rumor.

Summary

The popular images of rumor are not that different from those set forth in the mass hysteria, emergent norm, and value-added theories of collective behavior. The rumor process is characterized as transmitting inaccurate, exaggerated, and dangerously simplified definitions of situations confronting people. From this standpoint, rumor is an "inferior" form of communication. This view is consistent with the idea that collective behavior is "inferior" to normal social behavior.

The serial transmission studies of Allport and Postman support and amplify the above characterization of rumor. Information transmitted serially and by word of mouth is greatly distorted in the process. According to Allport and Postman, information is distorted because of the individual biases, fears, and misperceptions of rumor participants. A critical examination of the serial transmission model, however, suggests that distortion occurs because of the lack of redundancy and reciprocity designed into the experiment.

Shibutani's study of rumor transmission in natural settings provides additional support to the criticism of serial transmission. When people receive information from several sources and are free to question those who provide information, the amount of distortion is greatly reduced. Shibutani also suggests that people usually retain a critical stance toward information transmitted outside customary channels.

The SBI perspective does not approach communication during collective behavior from the standpoint of rumor. Instead, collective behavior, or convergent activity, results from designative and prescriptive activities. Rumors are designative in character, and they establish objects toward which subsequent action can be taken. Prescriptions specify the activity that is to occur. Without additional prescriptive activity, rumors do not produce convergent activity beyond conversation.

In order to understand the impact of rumors during collective behavior, we must also understand the circumstances under which prescriptions occur. Many rumors do not establish objects toward which immediate convergent activity can be directed. Rumors are likely to be accompanied by prescriptions when the objects established are near at hand, and prescriptions are likely to occur when people have time available for extemporaneous activity. Finally, prescriptions for action often occur when rumors accompany an ongoing conflict, and they are likely to accompany designative rumors when people have previously participated in related activities.

Rumor is one of the earliest topics studied in the field of collective behavior. The early studies have led to the nearly axiomatic assumption that rumor is an "inferior" form of communication. Since then, there has been relatively little interest in the study of rumor. Recent theoretical and empirical developments in the field, however, dictate that we must once again look at rumor. Perhaps greater gains can be made if we attempt to develop a general theory of communication rather than a theory of rumor.

CHAPTER 5

Mass Hysteria

Mass hysterias are capricious, unpredictable, and contagious. In the theoretical frameworks of Blumer, Klapp, and Smelser, mass hysteria is the most elementary, transitory, and least differentiated form of collective behavior. Blumer (1969) describes mass hysteria as an instance of widespread and "relatively rapid, unwitting, and nonrational dissemination of a mood, impulse, or form of conduct" that disrupts social routines and authority patterns. For Smelser, panics and crazes are shaped by *hysterical beliefs,* which greatly restrict people's normal concerns to those of individual flight and escape (panic) or unrealistic wish fulfillment (craze). Mass hysteria can take almost any form, including widespread *physical symptoms* of nausea, dizziness, trembling, and fainting. Mass hysteria can also be manifested in widespread excitement such as fantastic rumors, rejoicing, celebration, morbid preoccupation, mourning, or fear.

Mass hysterias are transmitted through a process of mutual excitation—which Blumer calls circular reaction—during which people's behavior comes to be guided by aroused emotion rather than social norms. The actions of people involved in mass hysteria show an alarming degree of intensity, restricted focus, and unanimity. People lose their critical abilities and begin to believe almost anything consis-

tent with their hysterical frame of reference. These beliefs often make those involved in mass hysteria seem stupid, gullible, and dangerous.

In Chapter 3 we noted that the early tulip trade in Holland traditionally has been cited as an example of mass hysteria. More recent events, such as "mob action" (Myers 1948) and a religious gathering awaiting the miraculous appearance of a saint (Tumin and Feldman 1955), have also been described as mass hysteria. Most of what are referred to as "studies" of mass hysteria, however, are little more than journalistic accounts of events witnessed by the authors. In some cases, the authors happened on the event quite by accident and were not prepared to make systematic fieldnotes. Authors who did have prior notice of an event made no real attempt to assess the relative levels of involvement among active participants, spectators, and passersby. In other words, the authors of these accounts failed to consider unanimity and intensity of involvement as evidence of mass hysteria. Instead, they concluded that they were observing mass hysteria largely because the events they witnessed struck them as being distasteful or frightening or reflecting superstition.

Beyond the dozens of journalistic case studies, however, the mass hysteria perspective has fostered very few empirical, or quantitative, studies. There are probably no more than seven mass hysteria studies in which investigators actually interviewed people to objectively compare those closely involved in the event with those having lesser involvement. These few studies and their findings speak to the issues we will raise in this chapter.

We will begin by considering four unusual events that later became the subjects of quantitative mass hysteria studies. Subsequently, we will see that the mass hysteria studies have generated a number of questionable findings and have left several unresolved questions regarding unusual events. Given these shortcomings, we devote the final section of this chapter to a consideration of another unusual event, which we'll examine from the standpoint of the SBI perspective.

Unusual Events and Mass Hysteria

The four unusual events described below involved the spread of a strange fear, affliction, or definition through a group of people. Participants in these unanticipated outbreaks seemed to have greatly impaired critical abilities because they rejected or ignored the "commonsense" and "official" explanations of the problem and acted on the basis of their own interpretations. Such characteristics prompted researchers to study them from the standpoint of mass hysteria. Some of the descriptive material used in the presentations below was obtained from these studies. The reaction to the "War of the Worlds" broadcast was studied by Hadley Cantril (1966), and the phantom anesthetist episode was studied by Donald M. Johnson (1945). The June bug epidemic was studied by Alan C. Kerckhoff and Kurt W. Back (1968), while James R. Stewart (1977,

1980) maintains a continuing interest in cattle mutilations.

The War of the Worlds

Probably the most widely known event to be generally considered a mass hysteria occurred on Sunday evening, October 30, 1938. Orson Welles and his CBS Mercury Theater group presented an adaptation of one of H. G. Wells's then lesser-known short stories, "The War of the Worlds," which described a nineteenth-century Martian invasion of England. The Mercury Theater adaptation was set in the present (1938) and took place in the United States. Perhaps Welles's most consequential decision was to use an "open format" during the first half of the show. Instead of using the conventional dramatic format of background music, narration, and dialogue, the first announcements of the Martian invasion took the form of simulated news bulletins, interrupting a program of dance music. Welles's second most consequential decision was to use the names of actual New Jersey and New York towns, highways, streets, and buildings when describing the movements and attacks of the Martians.

These two decisions, plus the fact that most listeners tuned in eight to twelve minutes late and therefore missed the Mercury Theater theme and introduction, set the stage for what was to follow. Thousands of people across the United States assumed they were listening to real news bulletins and public announcements. A substantial portion of these listeners became very frightened and attempted to call police, the National Guards, hospitals, newspapers, and radio stations for information. In addition, people tried to contact family members, friends, and neighbors. By the time Mercury Theater's first station break came, informing people they were listening to a CBS radio drama, most of the broadcast's damage had been done.

The next day, newspapers across the country carried stories of terrorized people hiding in basements, panic flight from New Jersey and New York, stampedes in theaters, heart attacks, miscarriages, and even suicides. During the months that followed, these stories were shown to have little if any substance, yet today the myth of "War of the Worlds" stampedes and suicides persists as part of American folklore. One clear and certain result of the broadcast, however, was a number of Federal Communication Commission regulations, issued within weeks of the broadcast, prohibiting the use of the open format in radio drama.

The Phantom Anesthetist of Mattoon

About midnight, Friday evening, September 1, 1944, police in Mattoon, Illinois, investigated a most unusual case. A woman and her teenage daughter claimed that a mysterious prowler had stood in the shadows outside an open window and sprayed an irritating gas into their house. The gas made the women nauseated and very dizzy. Mattoon police found no evidence of a prowler but were again called to the residence later in the evening when the woman's husband saw a man run from their yard.

The *Mattoon Daily Journal-Gazette* carried a front-page story of this incident the next day. The story prompted two other families to report to police that they had been gassed in their homes a few days earlier. In both instances, however, the victims had initially attributed their symptoms to other causes and had seen no prowler. On Tuesday evening two more attacks were reported, and on Wednesday three attacks were reported. There were no attacks on Thursday, but during the weekend twenty attacks were reported to police. Symptoms

usually included temporary paralysis, eye and mouth irritation, dizziness, and nausea. Other Mattoon residents and a few victims claimed to have seen the prowler and described him as tall and thin, dressed in black, and wearing a black skullcap.

The thought of someone lurking about the yards of Mattoon and spraying homes with a potentially lethal gas produced considerable wariness. Mattoon police records indicate a substantial increase in the number of calls reporting prowlers during the two weeks of gas attacks. Some newspaper stories stated that townspeople were buying special locks for their windows, keeping loaded guns beside their beds, and had organized neighborhood patrols to apprehend or at least frighten off the gasser.

Newspaper coverage of these happenings was quite extensive, particularly in Illinois and the rest of the Midwest. Newspapers as far away as England made occasional reference to the phantom anesthetist. Early stories indicated that out-of-town newsmen were suffering headaches from the aftereffects of the gas. A chemist from the Illinois Criminal Investigation Laboratory tentatively identified the gas as chloropictin. By September 12, many news reports began to contain elements of skepticism and sarcasm. A week later, most newspapers referred to the anesthetist story as a case of mass hysteria. The residents of Mattoon were frequently depicted as simple-minded, frightened about nothing, or seeking publicity. Altogether, twenty-nine gassing reports and about seventy prowler calls had been received by Mattoon Police. Some accounts indicate that no gassings occurred after September 12, while others indicate that occasional gassings were reported for years afterward.

The June Bug Epidemic

In June 1962, a female worker in a southern textile mill broke out in a severe rash and complained of nausea and dizziness. The next day, several women and at least two men reported to the mill infirmary with the same symptoms. Workers insisted this ailment was caused by bites from insects that had infested the last shipment of fabric from England. During the next four days, a total of sixty-two of more than nine hundred mill workers complained of this bug bite syndrome and either received medical attention or were absent from work. Sixty-two ill workers was not an unusual number for a mill this large, but the type of illness was quite unusual.

At the peak of the outbreak, plant managers decided to briefly close the mill in order to locate the source of the ailments. Health officials from the mill and the Communicable Disease Center of Atlanta found only two biting insects in the entire plant. They were also unable to detect pollutants that could cause such symptoms. The mill was then sprayed for insects, primarily to soothe the fears of the workers. Management and health authorities then concurred with the earlier judgment of local physicians that the symptoms were psychogenic in nature or a manifestation of mass hysteria. Workers were understandably skeptical of this explanation, but in any event, no more bug bite ailments were reported.

Cattle Mutilations

The first major episode of cattle mutilations occurred in Nebraska and South Dakota from late August to early November 1974. Cattlemen reported the discovery of cattle that appeared to have been killed and partially dismembered. In many instances, the sex organs, tongues, and ears were reported to have been removed, and some cattle appeared to have been drained of blood. During this period, between seventy-five and one hundred reports of cattle mutilations were received by state police, veterinary health authorities, and newspapers.

Speculation varied as to what or who could have caused such bizarre occurrences. In 1967 much publicity had been given to the discovery of Snippy, a dead and mutilated pony, shortly after a Colorado UFO sighting. One of the first explanations offered for the cattle mutilations was that they were the work of the occupants of spacecrafts from other planets. Another explanation grew out of the reported sighting of a hairy, manlike beast in the general area of several mutilations. Zoology students from the University of Nebraska tried to track down "the thing" with absolutely no success.

Perhaps the most widely accepted explanation of cattle mutilations was that blood cult members were sneaking about and killing cattle to obtain organs and blood for their dark ceremonies. This explanation seemed quite plausible, given the lurid descriptions during 1970 and 1971 of the Charles Manson "Helter Skelter" family. If some cultists were able to kill and mutilate people, they could certainly do the same to cattle.

Initially, most law enforcement and veterinary authorities in Nebraska and South Dakota seemed to agree with the "mysterious mutilation" description of cattle deaths. At the peak of the outbreak, however, some authorities began to cast doubt on this explanation. Veterinarians at the Universities of Nebraska and South Dakota said that autopsies performed on a few of the mutilated cattle indicated that the animals had died of natural causes. They suggested the mutilations and absence of blood were the combined result of small scavengers, such as coyotes, feeding on the dead animals and normal post-mortem decomposition. Some authorities began to describe the cattle mutilations as a "collective delusion," posing no real danger to cattle or people.

Since this first cattle mutilation episode, others have occurred in Colorado, Illinois, Iowa, Kansas, New Mexico, Oklahoma, and Texas. As recently as August 1981, the Iowa Cattlemen's Association offered a $1,000 reward for information leading to the conviction of people who "steal, mutilate, or kill cattle belonging to an association member."

Three Other Unusual Events

Three other unusual events have been examined using the mass hysteria framework. In 1967 a graduation ceremony at an English girls' school was halted by an epidemic of fainting. In a brief "head count" analysis of the event, Moss and McEvedy (1967) determined the approximate numbers of fainters and nonfainters in the graduating class. The testing of nuclear weapons and the threat of nuclear war have been viewed as the anxieties underlying two other outbreaks of hysteria. Following atmospheric testing of hydrogen bombs in 1954, people in and around Seattle, Washington, began to report mysterious "pitting" damage to auto windshields. Medalia and Larsen (1958) studied the incidence of windshield-pitting reports and the spread of windshield-pitting rumors and beliefs. This incident was shortly followed by a nationwide rush to buy fallout shelter plans. Though the federal government offered free shelter plans, magazines carried hundreds of advertisements for "better" plans. Some shelter plans were indeed better than the government's, while others probably constituted mail fraud. Levine and Modell (1965) conducted a national survey to determine the characteristics of households buying fallout shelter plans and constructing shelters.

Empirical Focus of Mass Hysteria Studies

Events that prompt mass hysteria studies comprise three general and distinct elements. First, the *unusual and unverified experiences* of people give the hysterical incident much of its noteworthy character. Such experiences include interpreting a radio drama as a real news event, being attacked by a phantom anesthetist, being bitten by a strange bug, or finding one's cattle dead and partially dismembered. These occurrences are unusual from the standpoint of everyday experience, and they are unverified in the sense that authorities debunk or refuse to substantiate the victims' claims. Authorities are usually the first to suggest that the unusual and unverified experiences are a manifestation of hysteria.

Second, there is *mobilization* with respect to the unusual and unverified experiences. Mobilization includes people fleeing to escape Martian attacks or workers collectively demanding that management "do something" about bug bites. Mobilization also includes the formation of neighborhood patrols to apprehend or scare off prowlers or cattle mutilators. Most often, mobilization rather than the unusual and unverified experiences is the most disruptive of normal social relationships.

Finally, there is the *general preoccupation* with the unusual and univerified experiences and accompanying mobilization. General preoccupations involve large portions of the population hearing about the unusual and unverified experiences and mobilization. This news serves as a topic for conversations and perhaps arguments but little else. General preoccupation is the most extensive but least disruptive element of these unusual episodes. We will now consider the manner in which these three elements of unusual events have been approached in mass hysteria studies.

Unusual and Unverified Experiences

From a quantitative standpoint, the mass hysteria studies fail to show that unusual and unverified experiences are as widespread as mass hysteria theory suggests. In some studies, more than one table must be examined and footnotes cross-checked to determine the number of people and approximate portion of an available population who had unusual and un-verified experiences. None of the quantitative studies show that even a slim majority of the available population reported such experi-ences. Moss and McEvedy (1967) state that about 30 percent of the students in an English girls' school succumbed to "hysterical dizzi-ness, fainting, headaches, and vomiting." Can-tril's (1966) study of "The War of the Worlds" broadcast concludes that about 20 percent of those listening to all or part of the broadcast exhibited hysterical panic reactions. During the A-bomb fallout shelter panic of 1962–1963, only about 12 percent of U. S. households bought plans for shelters of stockpiled sup-plies, and less than 1 percent of households ac-tually built a shelter (Levine and Modell 1965). Kerckhoff and Back (1968:13) concluded that about 10 percent of the first-shift textile mill workers, or 6 percent of all workers, experi-enced bug bite symptoms. Only 6 percent of the respondents in the Seattle windshield-pit-ting epidemic of 1954 reported they had any direct experience with windshield damage (Medalia and Larsen 1958). Johnson's 1945 study of the phantom anesthetist shows that less than 1 percent of the population of Mat-toon claimed to have been gassed or made prowler calls to the police. Finally, the number of cattle mutilations reported by Stewart (1977, 1980) means that less than 1 percent of area farmers made such reports. Quantitative studies show that the occurrence of unusual and unverified experiences within available populations is limited and, in some instances, quite rare. Nonetheless, these studies discuss the experiences as if they were being reported by a substantial majority of the available pop-ulation.

Without question, listeners were frightened by the "War of the Worlds" broadcast; Mat-toon residents were convinced their dizziness and nausea were caused by the phantom's gas; workers were hospitalized for days with rashes, rapid heart beat, and nausea during the

June bug epidemic; and farmers were con-vinced their cattle had died in a mysterious manner. Those who studied these events from the standpoint of mass hysteria described these reactions as "almost exclusively psychogenic in nature" (Kerckhoff and Back, 1968:12). In oth-er words, from the standpoint of mass hyste-ria, fear reactions to the "War of the Worlds" broadcast were abnormally severe, given the nature of the show. Likewise, it was concluded that the physical symptoms reported in the phantom anesthetist and June bug episodes had no organic cause, and that the mysterious cattle mutilations were either totally imagi-nary or the work of scavengers combined with normal decomposition. Not surprisingly, few of the frightened listeners or those reporting being gassed or bitten or finding their cattle mutilated accepted the psychogenic explana-tion of their experiences.

All the mass hysteria studies conclude that the unusual and unverified experiences had psychogenic causes. There are some major questions as to how researchers reached this conclusion. For example, in those instances where all or a majority of the victims were women, this fact alone is considered part of the proof that hysteria caused the afflictions. Johnson (1945:245) notes that "those who suc-cumbed to the 'mental epidemic' were mostly women. . . . This supports the above analysis and puts the 'phantom anesthetist' of Mattoon, in some respects at least, into a familiar psy-chological pattern."

In general, the mass hysteria studies give considerable weight to the hysteria explana-tions suggested by authorities *before* the stud-ies were initiated. It should be noted, however, that in most of these episodes, authorities *ini-tially* gave considerable credence to the inter-pretations of the victims and only began to back away from this stance later in these epi-sodes. Authorities are usually acting with re-spect to immediate, practical problems, such as getting employees back to work or restoring order in the community, rather than evaluating competing theories of collective behavior. Intense public concern and publicity accompanying these unusual and troublesome events is usually short lived, and attributing the cause of such events to "mass hysteria" is one way of laying them to rest. When they use the judgment of authorities as the primary means of ascertaining the "hysterical" nature of these events, mass hysteria studies lose a great deal of their scientific merit.

The weakness of the psychogenic explanation is perhaps most obvious when we consider the reactions to the "War of the Worlds" broadcast. Again, we should emphasize that the "War of the Worlds" was not an ordinary radio drama. As mentioned above, the first half of the show used an open format in which the entire story line was developed through the use of simulated news bulletins and on the scene reports. The second half of the show used a conventional dramatic format. Many discussions of the "War of the Worlds" read as if listeners panicked at the very beginning of the broadcast and remained terrorized throughout the show and much of the evening. In fact, a ten-minute segment in the first half of the broadcast caused most of the trouble.

Following the show, newspaper columnists and public officials expressed dismay at the "incredible stupidity," "gullibility," and "hysteria" of listeners. Many popular accounts claim that the broadcast was interrupted several times for special announcements that a play was in progress. Listeners, however, had apparently been too panicked to notice them. These extreme psychogenic assumptions are, for the most part, unwarranted and inaccurate. For example, other than Mercury Theater's one-minute introduction (which most listeners missed), the station break at the middle of the broadcast, and the signoff, there were no announcements, special or otherwise, to indicate that a play was on the air. Further, Mer-

cury Theater was being presented by CBS as a public service broadcast, and there were no commercials from which listeners might conclude that they were listening to a drama (Houseman 1948).

Cantril (1966) and Houseman (1948) indicate that most listeners, and virtually all of those who became frightened, tuned in Mercury Theater about twelve minutes after it began. These listeners joined the broadcast during an on-the-scene news report from a farm near Grovers Mill, New Jersey—an actual town located between Princeton and Trenton—where a large meteor had landed. Welles's careful direction meticulously created all the character of a remote broadcast, including static and microphone feedback and background sounds of autos, sirens, and the voices of spectators and police.

Twelve minutes from the beginning of Mercury Theater newscaster Carl Phillips (played by radio actor Frank Readick) was concluding a rather awkward interview with a Mr. Wilmuth, the owner of the farm where the meteor had landed. Phillips broke off his interview with the annoyingly inarticulate Mr. Wilmuth by providing listeners with a detailed description of the meteor. During this description, Phillips called the listeners' attention to mysterious sounds coming from the meteor, and then the meteor suddenly opened. Phillips fought to maintain his composure as he described the incredible and horrible creatures emerging from the pit where the meteor had landed. Background sounds of angry police and confused, frightened, and milling spectators provided a brilliant counterpoint to Phillips's stammering narration. At this point, Phillips signed off temporarily to "take up a safer position" from which to continue the broadcast.

For what seemed a very long time, a studio piano played "Clair de Lune," filling in the empty airspace. Finally, an anonymous studio announcer broke in with, "We are bringing you an eyewitness account of what's happening on the Wilmuth farm, Grovers Mill, New Jersey." After more empty airspace, Carl Phillips returned. Apparently unsure of whether he was on the air, Phillips continued to describe the monsters. The tempo of his reporting increased until Phillips was almost incoherent. In the background, the sound of terrified voices, screams, and the monsters' strange fire weapon merged into a chaotic and hair-raising din. Then, abruptly, there was dead silence. After an unbearably long period of empty airspace, the studio announcer broke in with, "Ladies and gentlemen, due to circumstances beyond our control, we are unable to continue the broadcast from Grovers Mill. Evidently there is some difficulty in our field transmission" (Cantril 1966:17–18). This segment of the boadcast lasted less than five minutes, but, according to later interviews, it caused most of the fright.

The technical brilliance of the broadcast aside, how could an event as seemingly unlikely as a Martian invasion be readily interpreted as real? Part of the answer to this question lies in the fact that the monsters were never clearly identified as Martians until several minutes after Carl Phillips's segment of the broadcast. It is likely that some people who became frightened later concluded that they were listening to a play when the monsters were finally identified as Martians (Cantril 1966:171). Another reason so many listeners became confused and frightened was Frank Readick's interpretation of an on-the-scene news reporter. Readick was inspired by the eyewitness description of the explosion of the zeppelin Hindenburg, which had occurred on May 6, 1937, at Lakehurst, New Jersey. In this world-famous broadcast, the reporter was describing the uneventful landing of the Hindenburg when it suddenly exploded with spectacular and deadly force. The reporter struggled to remain co-

herent, and his tearful, second-by-second description was heard by millions. The day of the "War of the Worlds" broadcast, Readick spent hours listening to the Hindenburg recording (Houseman 1948). His interpretation of the Martian attack created a sense of *déjà vu*. The emotion, the stammering, and even the tempo of Carl Phillips's narration reminds one of the Hindenburg disaster. Frank Readick's blending of the real and imaginary must have been very disconcerting for those who had heard the Hindenburg broadcast eighteen months earlier.

After Carl Phillips's "death" and until the first station break, the broadcast consisted of a collage of news bulletins, public announcements, and on-the-scene reports. Taken *sequentially*, these bulletins and reports seemed to describe the Martians' utter destruction of the New Jersey National Guard, a devastating Martian advance across New Jersey, and, by the end of the first half of the show, massive nerve gas attacks on New York City. Events of such magnitude could hardly occur in a period of less than fifteen minutes. About 25 percent of the listeners who had become frightened quickly concluded that they were listening to a radio drama because of this time distortion and other internal inconsistencies of the broadcast (Cantril 1966:106–107).

Most of the frightened listeners did not perceive the impossibility of a fifteen-minute sweep of the East Coast by Martians. Cantril describes these people as experiencing the most severe symptoms of panic: their critical abilities had been so swept away that they continued to believe the impossible. Cantril's data, however, suggest an alternate interpretation of this group's behavior. Quite simply, many of Cantril's interviews suggest that listeners perceived the reported events as occurring *simultaneously* rather than sequentially. Nothing in the first part of the broadcast definitely stated that the Martians who had landed at Grovers Mill were the same Martians who, moments later, were reported to be marching across New Jersey or attacking New York City. Listeners who failed to perceive a time distortion in the broadcast had not necessarily lost their critical abilities. Rather, they were perceiving the news bulletins and on-the-scene reports as an understandably confusing and disordered collage of information pouring in simultaneously from all across the nation.

The psychogenic, or hysteria, explanation of people's reactions to the "War of the Worlds" broadcast severely underplays the unique and unsettling character of the show. Cantril poses the question: "Why did this broadcast frighten some people when other fantastic broadcasts do not?" He provides a partial answer when he considers the realistic way in which the program was put together (Cantril 1966:67–76). Houseman (1948) provides even more insight when he discusses the "technical brilliance" of the show that emerged under Orson Welles's direction. If we take into account the unique character of the "War of the Worlds" broadcast, we needn't speculate that psychogenic mechanisms caused people to lose their critical ability and then to panic. Rather, Orson Welles and his Mercury Theater staff of excellent writers and actors innocently conspired to "scare the hell out of people" for Halloween. They succeeded in scaring the hell out of 20 percent of their listening audience.

In summary, the quantitative mass hysteria studies fail to show that the unusual and unverified experiences are widespread. In some instances, these experiences are reported by a very small portion of an available population, and in no instance are they reported by a majority. The quantitative studies also fail to clearly substantiate the hysterical nature of unusual and unverified experiences. Some studies have relied almost totally on the judgment of law enforcement or medical authorities that the reported experiences are of a hysterical nature. Cantril, on the other hand, fails to take the unique features of the "War of the Worlds"

broadcast into account when he concludes that the fear reactions were hysterical in nature.

Mobilization

Mass hysteria studies generally fail to distinguish mobilization as a distinct element of the episodes that prompted the investigations. Cantril, for example, alleges that panic flight occurred during the "War of the Worlds" broadcast but does not systematically examine his data to determine the extent or characteristics of this flight. Cantril also notes that telephone switchboards at CBS, local radio stations, police, and hospitals were flooded with calls from hysterical people. Again he made no systematic attempts to ascertain the nature of these calls. Likewise, Johnson (1945) noted that Mattoon residents formed neighborhood patrols during the anesthetist incident, but he did not attempt to find out when these patrols occurred or determine their size, composition, and activities. Such types of mobilization are probably more burdensome to authorities and disruptive of social routines than are the unusual and unverified experiences.

Even though the mass hysteria studies fail to systematically examine mobilization, they do present information that, when carefully considered, provides some insight into this process. Though Cantril's data does not document the claim that the "War of the Worlds" broadcast produced substantial amounts of panic flight, a few of his interviews suggest that some people started to pack belongings in preparation for movement before they found out the news bulletins were a play. In only one instance, however, does Cantril (1966:54) discuss a person attempting to get away from the Martian attack, without regard for future consequences. Cantril received a letter from a man who spent $3.25 of his meager savings to buy a ticket to "go away." After the man found out it was a play, the letter continued, he realized he no longer had enough money to buy a pair of workshoes. The last part of the letter contained a request for size 9B workshoes. Houseman (1948:82) reports that Mercury Theater received a similar request for size 9B workshoes which they sent in spite of their lawyers' misgivings. The story of the man who decided to forgo workshoes in order to escape the Martians has a decided ring of the apocryphal.

Cantril (1966:207–208) also notes that interviews were conducted with nine people who heard the broadcast over their car radios, only three of whom reported becoming "extremely frightened." Being in an auto presents people with an immediate means of flight. In all three instances, the drivers reported handling their cars in a reckless manner; however, none appear to have been fleeing the Martians. One driver tried to get home quickly to be with his family, another drove to "rescue" his girlfriend, and the third drove to find his parish priest. The kinds of reactions Cantril describes as "panic flight" actually appear to be similar to the efforts people usually make to contact family and friends during disasters. Additional support for this *disaster reaction* image comes from accounts describing unusually heavy traffic through Grovers Mill following the broadcast. Similar convergence on accident and disaster sites is quite typical and may even hinder rescue and recovery efforts. (We discuss disaster reactions in Chapter 9.) There seem to have been many similarities between people's reactions to the "War of the Worlds" broadcast and people's initial adaptive reactions to real disasters. In the case of the broadcast, however, people learned very quickly that they were listening to a play.

Cantril (1966:60) notes that accounts of telephone calls flooding switchboards of radio stations, newspapers, and police stations are confirmed by statistics provided by the American Telephone Company. These statistics indicate a 25–40 percent increase in telephone call volume throughout northern New Jersey during, and for an hour following, the broadcast.

Cantril and others cite instances where radio stations, newspapers, and police received "hysterical" calls from sobbing and incoherent people. However, Cantril's data seems to suggest that other types of calls were more frequent. Some callers requested information, such as which units of national guard were being called up or whether casualty lists were available. Some people called to find out where they could go to donate blood. Some callers were simply angry that such a realistic show was allowed on the air, while others called CBS to congratulate Mercury Theater for the exciting Halloween program. Unfortunately, it is now impossible to determine the relative frequency of each type of call. Finally, we cannot know how many of these telephone calls were between households. It seems reasonable, however, that many callers just wanted to chat with their families and friends about the exciting show they had just listened to on the radio.

Johnson (1945:233–234) states that neighborhood patrols were established in Mattoon during the phantom anesthetist episode. In the final days of the disturbance, the commissioner of police put a note in the *Mattoon Daily Journal-Gazette* requesting that men and boys discontinue the patrols "because some innocent person might get killed." How large and how extensive these patrols were cannot be ascertained from Johnson's study. It is apparent, however, that Johnson obtained most of his information about these patrols from newspaper accounts. Later in this chapter we will show how newspaper accounts often exaggerate the number and extent of such patrols. In any event, Johnson does note that photographs of these patrols, which appeared in a number of newspapers, were posed by news photographers.

Mass hysteria studies tell us relatively little about mobilization with respect to unusual and unverified experiences. Cantril's study does suggest similarities between mobilization with respect to the "War of the Worlds" broadcast and reactions to disasters. Also, a portion of the phone calls made during and immediately following the show were for the purpose of obtaining information, volunteering services, or simply commenting on the broadcast. Johnson's study of the phantom anesthetist suggests that neighborhood patrols were not as extensive as newspaper accounts claim.

General Preoccupation

Mass hysteria studies give attention primarily to the general preoccupation element of the episodes in question. Kerckhoff and Back (1968) devote a great deal of their analysis, for example, to various aspects of the belief in bug bites among mill workers. Medalia and Larsen (1958) restrict their study to determining which groups were the most likely to believe in windshield pitting. Stewart's (1977, 1980) analysis focuses primarily on the relationship between sources of information and types of belief about cattle mutilations.

Mass hysteria studies usually begin by discussing the unusual and unverified experiences and mobilization, which affect only a minority of the population. Then the analysis subtly shifts to the beliefs accompanying the episode, which often includes virtually the entire population. This shift from unverified and unusual experiences and mobilization to general preoccupations gives the impression that a population is almost unanimously involved in the episode. The elements of unverified and unusual experiences, mobilization, and general preoccupation, however, represent substantially different levels of involvement. People reporting unusual and unverified experiences may suffer physical symptoms as well as becoming targets of scrutiny by authorities. Their normal family lives and work routines may be disrupted by ridicule or momentary celebrity status. Those involved only to the extent of mobilization also confront disruptions in normal routines, if

only to the extent of irregular mealtimes and lack of sleep. However, those involved only to the extent of general preoccupation may discuss, debate, and certainly form opinions about the strange events occurring in their vicinity, but do little else. In his most recent consideration of the nature of mass hysteria, Stewart (1984) suggests we use the term *collective delusion* rather than mass hysteria to refer to episodes that primarily involve the spread of beliefs rather than physical symptoms.

When sociologists start to study the episode, perhaps weeks after it occurred, they tend to focus on the general preoccupation element. That is, studying unverified and unusual experiences and mobilization will almost certainly include finding some of the individuals involved. This in itself may be difficult, and perhaps expensive. Once located, these people may be reluctant to talk to sociologists who have already concluded how "hysterical" they had been. The unavailability and reluctance of gas attack victims, for example, contributed to the limited scope of Johnson's phantom anesthetist study.

Faced with such difficulties, sociologists may simply administer a large number of questionnaires or conduct telephone interviews to obtain socioeconomic information and people's beliefs about what happened. Thus Kerckhoff and Back (1968:53) administered a questionnaire to mill workers, the results of which indicated that about 90 percent of the workers thought the bug bite illness had a real rather than a psychogenic cause. Medalia and Larsen's (1958) telephone survey indicated that about 95 percent of Seattle residents had formed an opinion about the cause of windshield pitting. Finally, Stewart's (1977, 1980) survey indicates a similar pattern of widespread dissemination of information and formation of opinions about cattle mutilations.

Explicitly or implicitly, mass hysteria studies equate general preoccupation with the more direct kinds of involvement that are part of unverified and unusual experiences and mobilization. This aspect of mass hysteria studies gives the superficial appearance of demonstrating that the hysteria is affecting nearly the entire available population. While nearly all the population may be involved at the level of general preoccupation, this involvement has been shown to have little consequence. Kerckhoff and Back (1968) conducted their survey more than two months after the June bug epidemic. Almost all the workers believed that the cause of the disruption had been bug bites. The repeated denials of this view by plant managers and health authorities had done little to convince workers otherwise. More important, in spite of a persistent and almost unanimous belief in bug bites, work routines at the mill had returned to normal within a week of the first bug bite reports. Likewise, Johnson indicates that Mattoon residents continued to believe strongly in the phantom anesthetist months after the first attack. This belief, however, appears to have been insufficient to produce another wave of "hysteria."

In summary, mass hysteria studies have failed to substantiate either the widespread prevalence or the hysterical nature of unverified and unusual experiences and mobilization that make up the incidents under investigation. Mass hysteria studies have shown that during these episodes, there is nearly complete dissemination of information regarding unverified and unusual experiences and mobilization. This general preoccupation, or dissemination of quite interesting information throughout a population, does not necessarily reflect the workings of hysteria, nor does it seem to make a later recurrence of such incidents more likely.

Explanations of Mass Hysteria

Though mass hysteria theory states that *circular reaction* is both the cause and the mechanism through which mass hysteria is transmitted (see Chapter 2), this assertion has never been examined. In part, this is because mass hysteria studies are conducted weeks and months after the episode at issue. Researchers, therefore, have no opportunity to observe the "crowd interaction" and "intense interstimulation" that are part of circular reaction. Kerckhoff and Back (1968) came closest to examining such interaction when they attempted to determine the sequence in which bug bite victims succumbed. They found that the first few victims tended to be social isolates. Then, as the affliction spread, it tended to occur more frequently within identifiable friendship groups. In the final stage, the affliction tended to occur randomly, afflicting isolates and friendship groups alike. Kerckhoff and Back (1968:115) compared this last stage to a "crowd response."

Mass hysteria studies have offered two general explanations for hysteria. The first explanation states that mass hysteria results from *social strain*. According to this view, mass hysteria is a "safety valve" that allows people to discharge, in a relatively harmless way, anxieties caused by social strains such as economic downturns or threats of war. A second explanation, not entirely unrelated to the first, is that people having certain inferior socioeconomic attributes are more prone to involvement in mass hysteria than others. In discussions of mass hysteria, researchers consistently claim that young people, women, and those having little formal education are more likely than others to become involved in mass hysteria. As the social strain explanation suggests, persons with inferior socioeconomic attributes, such as having a low income or an insecure job or owning little property, have a much greater tendency to become part of mass hysteria episodes than people not subjected to these strains. Researchers have tested various aspects of the social strain and inferior socioeconomic attribute explanations in mass hysteria studies.

Social Strain

In their theoretical statements, Blumer, Smelser, and Klapp all claim that social strain is one of the necessary causes of mass hysteria. Social strain refers to the "feelings of frustration and protest over an existing mode of life" (Blumer 1969:25), an "anxiety provoking effect of an ambiguous environment" (Smelser 1962:141), or "tensions within individuals caused by strains in the larger social system" (Klapp 1972:160). In all the mass hysteria studies, either directly or indirectly, researchers address the issue of social strain. Their approach, however, is to determine the nature of the strain that "caused" the hysteria rather than to learn whether strain and hysteria are actually related phenomena. That is, these researchers have failed to construct quantitative measures of social strain that can determine comparative levels of strain prior to and following the episode in question. Instead, they simply speculate about what may have concerned people prior to the event. Thus, Cantril (1966) questioned listeners about their fears of war in Europe, and Kerckhoff and Back (1968) examined workers' economic hardships and job satisfaction. In this manner, almost any conceivable personal complaint or fear can be seen as evidence of social strain. Stewart (1977, 1980), for example, argued that because the price of beef was at an all-time high during some cattle mutilation episodes, this created anxiety among farmers that the price would soon drop.

Inferior Socioeconomic Attributes

In all the mass hysteria studies, researchers have examined socioeconomic attributes on the assumption that certain "types of people" are more susceptible to hysteria than others. This assumption has had a considerable impact on the way in which mass hysteria studies are conducted. As we noted above, researchers have given little attention to the task of determining the nature of unverified and unusual experiences and mobilization, while they have given considerable attention to the task of determining the age, sex, economic, occupational, and educational characteristics of the available population. Consequently, the results of mass hysteria studies generally claim to show that young people, women, and people having low incomes, low occupational prestige, and low educational attainment are more likely than others to succumb to mass hysteria.

While these studies present support for the above relationships, the mass hysteria data consistently suggest that these relationships are quite weak. Thus Medalia and Larsen's (1958) data show that women were more likely than men to believe in windshield pitting. The actual difference between the beliefs of men and women was so small, however, that it was essentially meaningless.

In other studies, researchers seem to have forced the methods and findings a bit to fit the assumption that women are more susceptible than men to hysteria. In Kerckhoff and Back's 1968 study, for example, three of the sixty-two bug bite victims were men, one of them among the earliest and most severely stricken. But Kerckhoff and Back excluded these male victims in order to simplify the analysis. Further, they made no empirical comparisons between female victims and males who were not affected. In the case of the phantom anesthetist of Mattoon, Johnson (1945) concluded that only 3 percent of the twenty-nine gas attack victims were males. This was inconsistent with his initial description of the episode, where he mentioned four instances in which women were with their husbands at the time of the attacks. These couples were described as being upset and showing symptoms of gassing. Had these four husbands been included among the twenty-nine gassing victims, then men would have accounted for nearly 15 percent of the reported casualties. At the beginning of his article,

TABLE 5.1
Quantitative Mass Hysteria Studies

Study	Independent variables	Dependent variables	Percent of available population affected
Moss and McEvedy (English girls' school)	Inferred stress, sex, age	Fainting, vomiting	33
Kerckhoff and Back (June bug epidemic)	Inferred stress, sex	Fainting, vomiting, rash	20
Cantril ("War of the Worlds")	Inferred stress, education, sex, region of U.S.	Fear reaction, flight	20
Levine and Modell (Fallout shelters)	Socioeconomic status, home ownership	1. Purchasing fallout shelter plans 2. Building shelters	12 1 of group 1
Medalia and Larsen (Windshield pitting)	Inferred stress, education, sex	Reporting windshield damage	6
Johnson (Phantom anesthetist)	Inferred stress, sex, income	Vomiting, rash, sighting of prowler, calls to police	less than 1
Stewart (Cattle mutilations)	Income, education, occupation	Reporting cattle mutilations	less than 1

Johnson also noted that groups of men and boys patroled the streets of Mattoon, but he did not include this type of male mobilization in his final analysis. In short, Johnson clearly underplayed the extent of male involvement in the phantom anesthetist episode. He concluded, "As might be predicted from the psychological and psychiatric literature, those who succumbed to the 'mental epidemic' were mostly women."

Discussion

In his 1895 work *The Crowd*, LeBon argued that crowds have the emotional qualities of inferior forms of evolution, such as women, savages, and children. This statement gave rise to or at least reflected a bias that continues to the present day. Women, nonwhites, young people, and those having little education, income, or social prestige are the most likely candidates for active involvement in mass hysteria. Largely, the inferior socioeconomic attribute assumption has been accepted on the basis of faith and a bit of casual observation. Very few quantitative studies of mass hysteria have been conducted. Table 5.1 summarizes the variables and findings of seven quantitative mass hysteria studies. In these studies, researchers do not examine circular reaction; instead, they develop and test inferior socioeconomic attribute explanations of mass hysteria. Generally, however, the data from these studies show only minimal support for the mass hysteria image and explanation of collective behavior.

An Alternate Approach to Unusual Events

The preceding discussion places great emphasis on the shortcomings of the quantitative mass hysteria studies. But any negative assessment of these studies must be tempered with the realization that they were also the *first* and for decades the *only* quantitative studies within the field of collective behavior. It wasn't until the late 1960s, when interest (and funding) in civil disorder, protest, social movement, and political violence research peaked, that quantitative studies became the norm within the field of collective behavior.

Since the late 1960s, quantitative research efforts have all but ignored the study of unusual events (Stewart's study of cattle mutilations is an exception). Certainly research in the areas of civil disorder, protest, social movements, and political violence is important; however, events similar to the reaction to the "War of the Worlds" broadcast, the phantom anesthetist episode, or the June bug epidemic are also worth studying. As one commentator put it, "The study of such seemingly strange events . . . is important, I think, precisely because such phenomena must cause us to examine more closely our assumptions about ordinary, everyday life."

Such unusual events are not a thing of the past. People still grossly misinterpret information from the media. People still see and become excited about flying saucers, or UFOs. (We will consider this particular type of unusual event in Chapter 6.) People still report seeing and being frightened by "monsters" in their communities. In the next section of this chapter, we will consider a monster sighting episode from a standpoint other than the mass hysteria perspective.

Many of the preceding criticisms of the mass hysteria perspective are derived from the social behavioral-interactionist (SBI) perspec-

tive. It is from the standpoint of the SBI perspective, for example, that researchers break down unusual events into the components of unusual and unverified experiences, mobilization, and general preoccupation. These elements call our attention to the potentially observable aspects of odd episodes that have been confused or ignored in mass hysteria studies. The analysis of the "War of the Worlds" broadcast is an attempt to account for people's reactions in terms of "cues to conduct" rather than relying exclusively on inferences drawn from their socioeconomic attributes. Most of the criticisms of the mass hysteria perspective in this chapter grew out of the study of an event that had all the superficial characteristics of a classic case of mass hysteria. We will now discuss this event from the standpoint of the SBI perspective.

The Enfield Monster: The Episode

On Thursday, April 26, 1973, the *Carmi Times* (Carmi, Illinois) carried a story that described a face-to-face encounter with a "weird creature" in the nearby town of Enfield (population 760). The informant, Mr. M., claimed that he had been alarmed by scratching at his front door at about nine o'clock the previous evening. When he opened the door, he was confronted by a three-legged creature, about five feet tall. The visitor was gray, had a flat body, wide head, and two large pink eyes. Greatly alarmed, Mr. M. fired a pistol at the creature, which "hissed like a wildcat," sprang from the porch, and ran northward into the underbrush beside a nearby railroad track. Mrs. M. quickly phoned the state police, who later claimed to have discovered unusual animal tracks near the house. During the disturbance, about sixty residents of Enfield converged on Mr. M.'s property and discussed the event.

By Thursday afternoon, the news director of radio station WWKI in Kokomo, Indiana, had been dispatched to Enfield. The station broadcast reports that at least three other residents of Enfield had seen "something strange." Most prominent among the reports was that of a ten-year-old boy who lived near Mr. M.'s house. The boy claimed that about an hour before Mr. M.'s sighting, the creature "jumped out of some bushes, stomped on his feet, and tore his tennis shoes to shreds." According to subsequent newspaper accounts, he ran home "in hysteria."

The next day, the AP and UPI news services were carrying the Enfield story. The *Champaign-Urbana News Gazette* ran an article claiming the investigating officers had described Mr. M. as a "rational and sober" person and that the creature's tracks were "shaped like a dog's" but had "six toe pads." The article also noted that schoolchildren told Mr. M. that they had seen a similar creature near the ballpark. The article concluded with Mr. M.'s statement that there were probably more than one creature and that "they were not from this planet."

On Monday, April 30, the *Carmi Times* reported that Mr. M. had received more than 250 telephone calls over the weekend. One call had come from a government representative who claimed that many similar incidents had occurred since 1967 and that they were usually associated with UFO sightings. During the weekend, an anthropologist had interviewed Mr. M., examined the tracks of the creature, and decided that the tracks were definitely not those of a kangaroo. The article also noted that plaster casts of the tracks were en route to an undisclosed laboratory for "closer examination." Two local men had spent the weekend searching for the creature, without success. The article concluded by suggesting that a bear was wandering about the Enfield area.

There was little newspaper or radio coverage of events in Enfield for the next few days. Renewed interest was shown, however, when on Sunday, May 6, Mr. M. reported to radio station WWKI that he had sighted the creature about 3:00 A.M. on the railroad tracks near his home. Later that Sunday, WWKI's news director and three companions revisited Enfield. This search party later reported that they observed an "apelike" creature standing in an abandoned barn near Mr. M's house. They claimed to have recorded some of the creature's cries and fired a shot at it before it ran off.

By Monday, May 7, events in Enfield were again on the wire service network, and stories appeared in the *Chicago Daily News*, the *Moline Dispatch*, the *Champaign-Urbana Courier*, and the *Alton Telegraph*. Mr. M. was also interviewed by Wally Phillips of radio station WGN, Chicago, and this telephone interview was broadcast live throughout the Midwest.

On Tuesday, May 8, the White County sheriff arrested five young men from outlying communities after Enfield residents complained of gunfire. The men stated that they had heard radio reports about the monster and had come to Enfield to photograph the creature. They brought shotguns and rifles "for protection" and claimed to have sighted a creature and fired at it. The hunters were charged with hunting violations and posted bond.

On Wednesday, May 9, accounts of the arrests appeared in several Illinois newspapers. The *Carmi Times* accompanied descriptions of the arrest with statements from Enfield residents expressing fears that monster hunters might accidentally shoot people or livestock. It was also suggested that some of the "experts" visiting Enfield had no academic credentials or affiliations with universities and were little more than thrill seekers. The article concluded by noting that local newspeople and law enforcement agencies continued to receive telephone calls from various magazines and television and radio stations.

On Thursday, May 10, our five-person research team arrived and began to conduct interviews throughout Enfield. We left Enfield about noon on Saturday, May 12. On Sunday, an anthropology graduate student from the University of Illinois arrived in Enfield. Later that day, UPI releases quoted the student as suggesting that the Enfield monster was probably a wild ape, such animals having been reported sporadically throughout the Mississippi watershed since 1941.

On Monday morning, May 14, Wally Phillips of WGN, having somehow heard of our investigation, contacted us by phone. The interview was broadcast live, and we attempted to avoid speculating about the identity of the monster. We did, however, note the potential danger that "monster hunters" posed for local residents.

By Tuesday, May 15, almost three weeks after the first monster sighting and a week after the arrest of the five monster hunters, the *Carmi Times* included only two items concerning the Enfield monster. One item discussed the building of a calf pen by an Enfield resident who, when asked by a neighbor, claimed he was constructing a "monster pen." The other item reported that an Ohio woman was sure that the Enfield monster was her pet kangaroo, missing for more than a year. She offered a $500 reward for its return. The Enfield incident ended on these whimsical notes (Miller, Mietus, and Mathers 1978).

The Enfield Monster: Methods of Investigation

One of the most important aspects of our study was that our five-man research team arrived in Enfield *during* the episode. Within the first hour, we were struck by the discrepancy between what radio and press reports led us to believe was occurring in Enfield and what we actually saw the morning our research team entered the town. Instead of seeing anxious and agitated people milling through the streets, nervously speculating about when the monster would be sighted again, we encoun-

tered a tranquil scene of small-town community life. People greeted one another outside the post office, children were chattering as they leisurely walked to school, and the small cafe and filling station were opening for business. Friendly greetings were extended to us, and when we explained that we were in Enfield to conduct a study, the residents cooperated fully.

During the first morning, we conducted several interviews in which we attempted to assess "monster beliefs" and to administer an anxiety scale we had designed to quantitatively assess the level of social strain accompanying this event. The people we interviewed put forth considerable effort to carefully answer the questions we asked. After about two hours, however, we decided that we needed a research strategy meeting. We assembled the research team and drove to a secluded rest area a few miles outside Enfield. At this strategy session, we decided that we were clearly failing to obtain the essential who, what, when, and where information about the events occurring in Enfield. Therefore, we decided to abandon our efforts to measure monster beliefs and social strain and instead focus on finding out as much as possible from residents about the events occurring in their community.

Enfield's street pattern enabled us to easily divide the community into four sampling areas. We used a community influential–reputational approach (Hunter 1963) to select fourteen people to be interviewed, including Enfield's postmaster, the managers of the local recreation center, the diner and service station, and general store, and the high school principal and teachers. Such people represent traditional clearinghouses of information in small rural communities. Also, these people occupy public positions that enable them to observe and report on the pervasiveness, intensity, and content of discussions about topics of local concern. We conducted another seventy-three interviews with people available in the four sampling quadrants. We purposely selected more people from the quadrant where the sightings took place. We also spoke with but did not formally interview a few farmers from the surrounding area and people from Carmi, Illinois. Finally, we interviewed the White County sheriff and the editor of the *Carmi Times*. From these people we obtained a sufficient amount of descriptive material to construct the following analysis.

The Enfield Monster Episode: An Analysis

Events such as those that occurred in Enfield have traditionally been studied from the standpoint of mass hysteria. Had others studied the Enfield monster episode, it too might have been declared to be mass hysteria. But our theoretical approach, the questions we asked, and the people we talked to led us in a different direction.

Unusual and Unverified Experiences. As we interviewed Enfield residents, we saw no compelling reason to attribute the monster sightings to psychogenic causes. In part, this was because the actual number of monster sightings was much smaller than we had been led to believe from earlier newspaper and radio reports. Mr. M.'s frequent statements to the news media that "others in his community had seen monsters" created the impression that a large number of sightings had occurred. During our time in Enfield, however, we were not able to locate any of the "other people" who had seen the monster.

We did interview the boy who had his tennis shoes "ravaged" by the monster. This incident turned out to be a practical joke. The boy and his parents told us that they invented the shoe-tearing story to tease Mr. M. and have some fun with an out-of-town newsman.

The White County sheriff told us that news stories describing the men he arrested on May 8 as a "monster hunting expedition" were an ex-

aggeration. He described the hunters as just "out drinking and raising hell." According to the sheriff, they only mentioned the monster briefly during their questioning.

Our investigation revealed that there were perhaps no more than three firsthand monster reports. These were the April 28 and May 6 sightings reported by Mr. M. and the May 6 sighting by the WWKI news team. These three reports hardly constituted an "epidemic" of monster sightings. Such findings are consistent with those of the mass hysteria studies discussed earlier in this chapter. That is, in episodes of this kind, the number of unusual and unverified experiences is smaller than initially thought and represents only a small portion of the available population.

We also saw no need to attribute monster sightings to psychogenic causes, given the rugged woodlands surrounding Enfield. In this area of southern Illinois, it is not unreasonable to assume that Mr. M. or the radio news team had actually seen an animal. As to the kind of animal it might have been, the suggestions of those we interviewed included large dogs, calves, bears, deer, and wildcats. Some suggested that exotic pets, such as apes or kangaroos, were responsible for the monster reports. Finally, some people tactfully suggested that Mr. M. had a notoriously active imagination and had probably been shooting at shadows. In any event, we interviewed only one person who felt that Mr. M. had indeed seen a monster from outer space.

Mobilization. The convergence of people toward or dispersal from scenes of unusual and unverified events, the formation of neighborhood patrols, and the subsequent movements of hostile or celebrating throngs have been cited as evidence of mass hysteria. Mass hysteria issues aside, these instances of mobilization are differentiated phenomena, frequently consisting of or at least preceded by *assembling processes*. A necessary condition for an assembling process is that people be notified of an event occurring at some distant location. A facilitating condition for the initiation of assembling processes is a large number of people in general proximity to one another, with a period of free or uncommitted time at their disposal. These time frames generally include early evening or "afterwork" hours, weekends, and holidays. For example, the first monster sighting occurred about 9:30 P.M. and was accompanied by pistol shots and the arrival of state police vehicles. Subsequently, about fifty to seventy-five neighbors gathered at the site of the disturbance. In contrast, no assembling processes accompanied Mr. M.'s second monster report.

Smelser's discussion of hysteria suggests that in the later stages of such outbreaks, people reach a stage of emotional "burnout" or saturation, and they become almost immune to further excitation. Events that earlier caused great excitement now pass, seemingly, without notice. Mr. M.'s two monster sightings and the reaction to them invite this type of interpretation. Our analysis, however, suggests that the quite different responses to these two sightings was due almost entirely to the kinds of cues to conduct accompanying each incident. In contrast to the first sighting, Mr. M.'s second sighting occurred at a less favorable time (3:00 A.M.), no pistol shots were fired, and no state police vehicles were dispatched. In all likelihood, many Enfield residents remained unaware of the second sighting until they read the *Carmi Times*.

Increasing distance from the location of an event decreases sensory access to cues that something is occurring. Persons who can neither see nor hear the event depend on face-to-face communications, phone calls, or mass media announcements for instructions that establish the existence of the event and specify movement toward (or away from) the location of the event. Newspaper stories and radio dis-

patches notified people throughout Illinois and parts of Indiana, Ohio, Missouri, and Kentucky of the happenings at Enfield.

An issue that must be addressed is how such extensive notification is produced. In this instance, notification of the event was facilitated by Mr. M.'s active pursuit of newspeople. For example, following the second sighting, Mr. M. called an Indiana radio station rather than the state police. Further, Enfield events may have been given play in the media because the monster stories provided some relief from other, more ominous issues. Flooding was seriously delaying spring planting in southern Illinois, the Vietnam War was still to be resolved, and Watergate disclosures were beginning to surface. Editors and station managers may have welcomed these monster stories for their contrast to an unusually long and depressing series of events.

Once people throughout Illinois and adjoining states had been informed of the Enfield events, mobilization occurred across this larger area. There were patterns to this mobilization. For the most part, news teams, anthropologists, hunters, and sightseers traveled to Enfield on weekends, when people traditionally schedule their outings. Some mobilizers, however, were clearly unencumbered by the familiar commitments of work. Four of the five hunters arrested on May 8 were unemployed, and the other hunter was on military leave.

Though mobilization processes have been acknowledged only to the extent that they represent mass hysteria, our analysis suggests an alternate interpretation. Mobilizations result from *processes of notification* through which people learn of the location of an event. Mobilizations also result from *differential availability*, or people's differential access to periods of negotiable or uncommitted time within which participation in mobilization processes can be scheduled.

General Preoccupation. The mass hysteria approach focuses primarily on the extent to which reports of unusual and unverified experiences are spread and believed. The rapid and widespread dissemination of all types of information, however, is a common and necessary feature of contemporary social life. A statement such as "A state police car just parked in front of Harry's house" may sensitize people to such events. Such necessary information is not itself sufficient for the organization of innovative or disruptive activities. At minimum, statements such as "Let's go see what is happening" must occur before further activities are organized with respect to these events (McPhail and Miller 1973:724).

The mass hysteria approach has attended to the spread of information but has failed to acknowledge whether, or examine how, this information is used to construct activity divergent from the usual. Enfield residents seemed to be well informed of recent happenings in their town. Their frequent discussions of these events were restricted to casual conversations, jokes, and inconsequential bull sessions in homes, cafes, and other meeting places. Schoolchildren had composed a few monster poems which they recited for us.

The only discussions that we know disrupted usual kinds of activities were the interviews we conducted. Business proprietors, teachers, mail carriers, and housewives stopped what they were doing to answer our questions. The only other consequence of "monster conversations" were mentioned by a few residents who complained that their children were now "afraid to go out at night," "became frightened by small noises," and "had bad dreams." One resident reported that she cautioned her children to stay away from Mr. M.'s house because they might get shot by "some fool." Finally, someone placed a barricade sign near the train tracks where the monster was first reported. The sign read "Danger! Monster Crossing!"

Of all our respondents, the White County sheriff was perhaps the most vehement in his denial that a monster had been sighted. Yet because of his organizational position, his routine activities had been disrupted more than those of any other person we interviewed. He stated that the arrests and legal dealings with the hunters, telephone calls from newspapers across the nation, and complaints from county residents had greatly hindered him and his staff in carrying out their other duties. The preestablished or institutionalized relationships within a community, rather than who believes information and who doesn't, are a key consideration in accounting for how routine activities are disrupted.

Discussion and Summary

Perhaps the best way to conclude this chapter is to compare our study of the Enfield monster with what probably would have been done if this episode were studied from the standpoint of mass hysteria. Table 5.2 is designed to facilitate this comparison.

Our analysis of a monster sighting in Enfield, Illinois, illustrates the utility of the social behavioral/interactionist approach for understanding unusual events that in the past have been considered to be mass hysteria. With this approach we begin by ascertaining, from firsthand investigation, the general character of *differential participation* in the episode. In Enfield, only three unusual and unverified events, or monster sightings, had occurred, though newspaper and radio accounts led us to believe that monster sightings were much more frequent. With respect to mobilization, respondents reported that fifty to seventy-five people gathered at Mr. M.'s house after state troopers arrived. Fewer than ten people mobilized for the purpose of hunting the monster.

TABLE 5.2
The Enfield Monster: A Comparison of Two Approaches

Element	Mass hysteria	Social behavioral/interactionist
Unusual and unverified experiences	Reliance on newspaper reports; monster sightings are psychogenic and the result of stress; stress inferred from current national and international events and the socioeconomic characteristics of Enfield residents	Reliance on firsthand investigation; determination of number and circumstances of monster sightings; acknowledment that some monster sightings could have been animals
Mobilization	Reliance on newspaper reports; mobilization viewed as further evidence of mass hysteria, but not examined as a separate element of episode	Reliance on firsthand investigation; determination of extent of mobilization; examination of communication processes preceding mobilization; examination of availability
General preoccupation	Primary focus of study; attention given to the variety of monster beliefs, comparison of beliefs, and socioeconomic attributes; most likely, weak relationships are obtained	Determination of extent to which monster information and discussion disrupted routine activity; determination of the nature of these disruptions

Regarding general preoccupation, virtually everyone in the community discussed the event with friends and neighbors. Our data show that the type and extent of participation varied considerably. In mass hysteria studies, researchers usually fail to make such distinctions and consider these diverse types of participation as equivalent to one another. They would view all types as symptoms of mass hysteria.

We did not interpret these events as evidence that everyone "took leave of their senses" or abandoned the forms of conduct they normally use when dealing with more familiar problems. The processes of notification that accompanied monster reports were similar to those sights, sounds, and media announcements that inform people of street accidents, civil disorders, sports rallies, and public meetings. Mobilization processes tended to occur in

the evenings or on weekends, and they involved those who were relatively unemcumbered by competing institutional demands. The pervasive, community-wide discussion of monster events during this time frame did not disrupt preestablished community routines. The spread of monster information and the question of whether or not it was believed would have been a primary focus of a mass hysteria study.

The occupants of institutionalized positions are usually relied on by locals and outsiders to determine what is happening in a community. Monster sighting events created major problems of accommodation for local law enforcement agencies. Similar overload problems are frequently encountered by police following disasters and spectacular crimes or during presidential visits and holiday celebrations. In mass hysteria studies, researchers usually consider communication overload as evidence of aroused emotion.

Mass hysteria was the first theoretical perspective within the field of collective behavior. It fostered an early interest in unanticipated, unusual, and, to some observers, senseless and possibly dangerous episodes of collective emotional displays. A few mass hysteria studies represent the first attempts to quantitatively examine collective behavior.

Today, most research in the field of collective behavior proceeds from other theoretical perspectives. Unfortunately, this shift has also resulted in an almost total loss of interest in the kinds of unusual events that are part of the mass hysteria tradition. These events tell us much about the assumptions we make about reality and about what we take for granted in ongoing social life. We can suggest and hope that more recent theoretical perspectives will be brought to focus on such events.

CHAPTER 6

UFOs

There are many references to puzzling or frightening aerial phenomena throughout the written history of human society. Some contend that biblical passages such as Ezekiel's "heavenly wheels" represent ancient wonderment at something that today would be considered a UFO. Throughout the Dark and Middle ages, European chronicles are sprinkled with stories of great fireballs, flying ships, and even flying people. In none of these episodes does it appear that these aerial phenomena had any tremendously disruptive impact on the societies that witnessed them. Perhaps this is because such occurrences could be easily accommodated within the prevailing religious and mystical belief systems, or basic culture. Thus, such occurrences were viewed as merely another kind of omen, angel, or demon.

At the beginning of the twentieth century, such widely acceptable explanations were not available; new explanations and accommodations became necessary. In this chapter we will examine how UFOs became a part of our basic culture and social structure. We will first consider the types of UFO reports that lie at the heart of the matter. Our work here is made somewhat easier by using the sixfold typology or classification system developed by astronomer and longtime UFO investigator James Allen Hynek (Hynek 1972:25–35). The categories describe a continuum of strangeness of UFO reports. The most frequently reported and least "strange" events are *nocturnal lights*. Next, there are *daylight disks* and *radar/visual* reports. Finally, there are the *close encounters*. Close encounters of the first kind are reports in which people claim to have had a close-at-hand experience with a UFO. Close encounters of the second kind are similar to the first kind except that tangible physical effects on the observer, on the land, or on animate or inanimate objects are reported. Finally there is the close encounter of the third kind, in which the sighting of UFO occupants is reported. Hynek uses this typology throughout his discussion and analysis of UFO reports. In addition to Hynek's typology, we will often draw on material presented in David M. Jacobs's (1975) *The UFO Controversy in America* and Margaret Sachs's (1980) *The UFO Encyclopedia.*

UFO Sightings and Incidents

Dr. David R. Saunders of the Center for UFO Studies began a computerized cataloguing system (UFOCAT) for UFO reports in 1967. UFOCAT draws reports from the files of UFO investigation groups, journals, and books. Though most reports concern events occurring in the United States, the catalogue includes reports from all over the world. The intitial UFOCAT (1945–1973) contained nearly eighty thousand entries, and it has been updated to include more than one hundred thousand entries. UFOCAT gives us a clear indication of the very large number of UFO reports available for analysis. The following events illustrate the kinds of UFO reports that have been made through the years.

Nocturnal Lights

One of the most famous instances of nocturnal lights occurred in and around Lubbock, Texas, from August to October 1951. The first sighting occurred about 9:30 P.M. on Saturday, August 25, when four faculty members of Texas Technical College observed a formation of twenty to thirty pale lights moving across the sky. Two more formations were observed before midnight. These sightings were reported to local newspapers, but, surprisingly, no one else reported seeing these lights.

The next sightings occurred on Friday, August 31, and this time many people across Lubbock witnessed the lights. Radar at the nearby Air Defense Command briefly tracked a single object at thirteen thousand feet, traveling at nine hundred miles per hour. Further confusion arose when an amateur photographer offered to sell three photographs of the lights to the newspapers. While an analysis of the photos and negatives showed no signs of tampering, the photos themselves were dissimilar to the descriptions given by witnesses.

Weeks after these sightings, air force and private UFO investigators inquired into the Lubbock lights. Several people from rural areas surrounding Lubbock said that they knew the answer to the mystery—flocks of night migrating birds. The streetlights of Lubbock illuminated the light undersides of migrating plover, giving the appearance of high-altitude, rapidly moving, luminous objects. This explanation was later verified to the satisfaction of most of the witnesses and other resi-

dents of Lubbock. The Lubbock lights are now generally considered to be one of the classic cases of UFO misidentification.

Daylight Disks

On June 5, 1947, Kenneth Arnold was conducting an air search near Mount Rainier, Washington. Arnold, a co-founder of the Idaho Search and Rescue Pilots Association and an experienced mountain pilot, had taken off from Chehalis, Washington, at about 2:00 P.M. and had been flying for about forty-five minutes. Arnold was startled by a very bright flash of light as he turned his airplane toward Mount Rainier. A few seconds later, he observed another bright flash of light, which came from the vicinity of nine crescent-shaped craft flying in an echelon formation at about his altitude. Arnold watched the craft maneuver for several minutes and, using his pilot's knowledge of trigonometry, calculated their speed at more than a thousand miles per hour.

When Arnold landed at the small airport at Yakima, Washington, he discussed the sighting with airport personnel and other pilots. They speculated that Arnold might have observed guided missiles from a nearby guided missile base. Arnold then flew on to Pendleton, Oregon, where he tried unsuccessfully to contact the FBI. Finally, he talked to the editor of the *Eastern Oregonian* and his story was released to the wire services.

In the days that followed, Arnold was the center of considerable attention, which he neither sought out nor retreated from. Arnold described the movements of the craft as similar to a saucer skipping over water, and William Bequette of United Press International then coined the term *flying saucers*. Within weeks, this term had become part of our language, and it is still the most popular term used to describe UFOs.

Not surprisingly, Arnold's interest in UFOs has continued since his famous sighting. In

1948 Arnold's story appeared in the first issue of *Fate* magazine. In 1952 Arnold and Ray Palmer of *Fate* magazine published *The Coming of the Flying Saucers*. Arnold also investigated several UFO sightings in the 1950s and sighted and photographed other UFOs in 1952. Arnold has both suffered ridicule and enjoyed admiration since his sighting of the flying saucers; and more than thirty years after his Mount Rainier sighting, he is still asked to "tell his story" to interested groups.

Radar/Visual UFO Reports

One of the most recent radar/visual UFO sightings occurred on May 14, 1978, near Pinecastle Electronics Warfare Range, Ocala, Florida (Sachs 1980:228). Pinecastle is a training facility for navy pilots. Between 10:00 and 10:15 P.M., the duty officer received two telephone calls from civilians who reported seeing bright flying objects in the area. Fearing that an air crash had occurred, the duty officer quickly ascertained that no known military or civilian aircraft were in the area.

As the tracking radar warmed up, the radar operator observed a cluster of lights moving in a northerly direction. When the radar became operational, an object was located sixty miles north of Pinecastle. Another object was located three miles north of Pinecastle, and then another three miles south. These latter two objects were observed visually, appearing as bright white and orange lights. Radar/visual contact was maintained with these two objects for about ten minutes, with the radar indicating speeds from five miles per hour to more than sixteen hundred miles per hour. Finally, the objects disappeared after circling the base. Eight naval personnel had observed the objects either visually or on radar. Civilians from nearby areas continued to make inquiries about their own sightings.

Some investigators claim that this sighting was the result of bright stars, aircraft sightings,

confusion, and faulty radar equipment. Others, however, feel that this explanation contains too many improbable occurrences. In either event, the Pinecastle incident is quite typical of the dozens of radar/visual reports made since the first one at Goose Bay, Labrador, in 1951.

Close Encounters of the First Kind

Some UFO reports involve much more than the sighting of distant objects performing puzzling maneuvers. A small proportion of UFO reports are of *close encounters*, in which people claim to have seen a UFO at an uncomfortably close range. It is difficult to attribute these reports to the misidentification of birds or stars.

A close encounter of the first kind was reported on October 18, 1973, near Mansfield, Ohio. Captain Lawrence Coyne and his three-man crew were returning from their annual flight physicals, flying an Army Reserve helicopter. It was about 11:00 P.M. and the weather was calm and clear. Coyne was alerted by Sergeant Robert Yanacsek that they were being paced by another aircraft on the eastern horizon. After observing what they assumed to be the aircraft's lights for a few moments, they saw the lights begin to close on the helicopter. As the lights rapidly approached, Coyne put the helicopter into a steep dive to avoid collision. The lights continued to close on the rapidly descending helicopter until all four men could clearly see that the lights were on a wingless, cigar-shaped craft. The craft took a position above the helicopter, focusing a green spotlight on them. Meanwhile, copilot Lieutenant Arrigo Jezzi had been attempting to contact Nashville Air Control, initially to find out what other aircraft were in the area, then to warn of their likely crash. The radio, however, had stopped transmitting or receiving.

The strange craft stayed with the helicopter for a few moments and then quickly departed.

When Coyne regained stable flight, the helicopter was at an altitude fifteen hundred feet higher than when they had attempted to dive. The UFO appeared to have been able to pull the helicopter to a higher altitude. Shortly after the UFO departed, the radio began to work properly. Some investigators attribute this UFO incident to a near collision with a meteor and resulting cockpit confusion. The event was witnessed from the ground, however, and the witnesses support the contentions of the aircrew (Sachs 1980:187–188).

Close Encounters of the Second Kind

On the evening of August 19, 1952, Mr. D. S. Desvergers was returning four boys to their homes in West Palm Beach, Florida, following a Boy Scout meeting. It was a clear evening, and as they drove down a country road, their talk turned to recent sightings of UFOs. It was during this conversation that Desvergers slowed and then stopped the car. About a hundred yards from the road, amid a palmetto and scrub pine woods, was an erratically flashing, electric blue light. After watching the light for a few minutes, Desvergers announced that he was going closer to investigate. He told the boys to wait in the car and go for help if he was not back in fifteen minutes.

As he entered the woods, Desvergers began to smell an ammonialike odor. When he moved close to the place where he had last seen the light, he felt a distinct sensation of heat. To keep his bearings, Desvergers occasionally pointed his flashlight up into the foliage above him and looked at the stars. He had wandered in the woods for about five minutes and, because the light had not reappeared, was about ready to return to the boys. He looked up at the stars but could not see them. He raised his flashlight and his heart dropped—instead of seeing foliage and stars, he was looking at bright polished metal. He realized instantly

that he had wandered under an enormous craft of some sort. He started to back away and, still staring upward, noticed a small port in the seamless metal skin. Before he could turn and run, a ball of flame dropped from the port and engulfed him. At that point, Desvergers fainted.

When he regained consciousness, the boys and a deputy sheriff were near him. According to their account, Desvergers was trembling and hardly able to talk. His arms and hands had been slightly burned, and his cap was singed. It wasn't until several hours later that Desvergers was able to relate the earlier part of his encounter.

Air force and civilian investigators interviewed Desvergers and sent his cap to an FBI lab to ascertain the nature of the scorch marks. This analysis quickly revealed that the burns on the cap were made with a cigarette. Later, it became clear that this entire close encounter of the second kind was a hoax.

Close Encounters of the Third Kind

The most bizarre UFO reports are those in which people report seeing the occupants of UFOs. A close encounter of the third kind was reported by Charles Hickson and Calvin Parker. The encounter occurred about 9:00 P.M., October 11, 1973, in Pascagoula, Mississippi. Hickson and Parker were fishing near the shipyards where they worked when they heard a humming noise. Moments later, a translucent craft appeared on the riverbank and two humanoid occupants "floated" toward them. Parker fainted, and Hickson, though terrified, was unable to move. The occupants of the craft floated Hickson and Parker into the craft and gave them brief physical examinations. The two men were then floated back outside the craft, which disappeared a moment later after emitting a humming noise. During this time, the occupants did not talk to Hickson or Parker, nor did they communicate to them through telepathy.

About a half hour later, Hickson and Parker arrived at the sheriff's office in a state of terror and confusion. After interrogating them, the sheriff was firmly convinced that their terror was genuine. Hickson and Parker were repeatedly interrogated by air force and civilian investigators. Lie detector tests were administered, and hypnotic regression was attempted with Hickson. Under hypnosis, Hickson became frightened and incoherent. Within weeks, Parker was hospitalized for a nervous breakdown and since his release has avoided publicity. Hickson, on the other hand, enjoyed a brief period of near celebrity status and appeared on several talk shows. He also marketed his taped narration of the incident. These attempts to profit from the event led some investigators to suggest that the entire incident was contrived by Hickson to make money. However, investigators who have actually interviewed Hickson, often on several occasions, dismiss the con man hypothesis (Sachs 1980: 241–242).

What Are UFOs?

As the above examples show, the total UFO phenomenon has many aspects, including incidents that range from people sighting lights in the night sky to others who earnestly claim to have been taken aboard alien spacecraft against their will. To these incidents we must add the obvious and admitted hoaxes. After some investigation, most UFO incidents can be given an earthly explanation. Beyond this, however, there is little consensus. We will consider three explanations that have been given for the UFO phenomenon and then look at this phenomenon from the standpoint of collective behavior.

The Extraterrestrial Hypothesis

The most intriguing hypothesis suggests that UFOs are spacecraft from other planets,

and some UFO experts argue that there is enough evidence to accept or at least seriously entertain the *extraterrestrial hypothesis*. Thousands of people have reported seeing saucerlike, cylindrical, or other wingless craft doing aerial maneuvers that clearly surpass the performance of any known aircraft or missile. In some instances these craft have left physical traces: imprints on the ground, burned and broken shrubbery and trees, and chemical residues. In a few cases, metallic pieces of these craft have been obtained. Physical analysis has determined unusual alloy combinations, levels of purity, and density. Finally, there are the abduction incidents, in which people claim to have been taken aboard alien spacecraft. Often, victims can recall details of these abductions only through hypnotic regression. Many of these accounts have stood up well under repeated interrogation and lie detector tests.

Other experts argue that the evidence for the extraterrestrial hypothesis is neither clear nor convincing. We will discuss this issue in the next section. At this point, however, it is worth noting that those who oppose acceptance of the extraterrestrial hypothesis often describe those who do as "self-styled" experts (Jacobs 1980:123–138). Whatever else this label implies, it is a form of debunking that does not focus on the merits of the evidence.

By definition, anyone who studies UFO phenomena is a "self-styled" UFO researcher—regardless of their conclusions. Universities do not offer degrees in UFO research, nor does the U.S. Bureau of the Census include UFO Investigator as an occupational category. UFO research is a marginal and eclectic field in which experts credentialed in many fields of the natural and social sciences have participated. Further, some UFO investigations have been carried out by people who are not expert in any scientific field. Finally, UFO research has been undertaken by the federal government and private organizations. It is not surprising, then, that great diversity exists in the investigation procedures, the handling and interpretation of information gathered, and the conclusions reached in UFO research. Neither those who accept nor those who reject the extraterrestrial hypothesis can lay claim to doing orthodox and flawless research.

The Terrestrial Hypothesis

If there is any consensus among UFO investigators, it is that most UFO sightings turn out to be the misidentification of stars, meteors, aircraft, and weather balloons. Atmospheric conditions such as temperature inversions may make misidentifications more likely. Temperature inversions, in which the air at ground level is several degrees cooler than air at higher altitudes, can occasionally distort the appearance of stars and other lights and can also create weather target radar images. These often quite technical explanations are referred to here as the *terrestrial hypothesis*.

The terrestrial hypothesis is part of the "official explanation" of UFO phenomena. On January 22, 1948, after almost seven months of widely publicized UFO sightings, the United States Air Force instituted Project Sign to investigate and identify UFOs. Shortly after it began, Project Sign encountered adverse publicity and was reorganized and named Project Grudge. In March of 1952, Project Grudge was expanded and renamed Project Blue Book. Project Blue Book was continued until 1969, when it was terminated on the recommendation of a review panel headed by Dr. Edward U. Condon of the University of Colorado. The Condon Committee Report concluded that the study of UFO phenomena had little scientific merit. With the exception of the inconclusive Project Sign, all officially commissioned research adopted the terrestrial hypothesis and concluded that UFOs were not spacecraft.

Even before the Condon Committee issued its final report, some experts were challenging its conclusions. Among the concerns expressed was that as many as 25 percent of the cases reported to Project Blue Book had, after investigation, been classified as "unidentified." Defenders of the Condon Report and other official findings correctly pointed out that when investigators are unable to identify a UFO, it does not mean that people have seen an alien spacecraft.

Official reports use a similar though faulty logic. The error in this logic is most obvious in the large number of cases in which UFOs are identified as meteors. Several known meteor streams regularly pass near the earth, producing annual meteor showers in late July and early August. Even though this is a time of peak meteor activity, it is obvious that not all bright moving lights in the sky during July and August are meteors. The official reports, however, identify nearly all nocturnal lights and fireball UFOs occurring in July and August as meteors, concluding that no further investigation is necessary.

Similarly, official reports use the temperature inversion and weather balloon explanations in a blanketlike fashion to account for UFO phenomena. Clearly, temperature inversions can distort the appearance of bright lights and stars and also produce false radar images. But official reports attribute all UFO sightings and radar trackings occurring during temperature inversions to these weather conditions. The weather balloon explanation is frequently abused in the same manner. If a weather balloon has been recently launched within five hundred miles of a UFO sighting, then it is assumed that people saw a weather balloon.

The Hoax-Hysteria Hypothesis

Experts on both sides of the UFO controversy agree that many UFO reports are deliberate hoaxes. The UFO experience claimed by the Florida scoutmaster, for example, was quickly determined to be a hoax. Most UFO photographs have turned out to be hoaxes, and some

FIGURE 6.1   *UFOs*

Thousands of UFO photographs have been analyzed by those who study UFOs. Only a very small number of these are regarded as photos of genuine UFOs. Most UFOs on film turn out to be lens reflections, dirty or damaged negatives, and other photographic artifacts. A few photos, like the one above, are simply fakes. (Photo by Grant Bogue.)

physical traces of UFOs, such as landing marks and burned foliage, have been faked to add credibility to UFO reports. Many UFOs have turned out to be pranks, such as railroad flares carried into the sky by kites or balloons (Sachs 1980:145–147). It is not surprising, then, that some investigators are unwilling to seriously consider reports made by teenagers, close en-

counter reports, or UFO artifacts and quickly classify them as hoaxes.

When careful investigations of close encounter sightings occur, attempts are made to ascertain the reputations of the people involved. Almost any eccentricity or disorderliness can be used as grounds for classifying the report a hoax. If witnesses have an interest in science fiction literature or ties to a UFO organization, then their accounts are routinely challenged on these grounds. This "reputational analysis" is essentially intuitive and, at times, has verged on character assassination.

People who make UFO reports are frequently overwhelmed by news reporters and UFO investigators. Their integrity is directly challenged and they are often severely ridiculed. In some cases, the notoriety has been so severe that witnesses have quit or lost their jobs and moved to another community. The negative responses invariably encountered by witnesses have given investigators reason to doubt some of the hoax "confessions." Admitting to a hoax is one way to end an unpleasant situation.

Some close encounter sightings have been classified as likely hoaxes primarily because witnesses have tried to capitalize their stories. UFO witnesses, for example, have appeared on television and radio talk shows and have sold their stories to publishers. In one instance, townspeople tried to turn an alleged UFO landing site into a tourist attraction. Although the profit motive can serve as a reason for a hoax, many UFO witnesses who attempt to profit from their stories, appear to do so hesitantly and often only at the urging of others.

The *National Enquirer* and many magazines and organizations offer prizes for the best UFO story of the year, the best UFO photograph, or physical evidence of UFOs. This "bounty hunter" approach to the UFO question encourages hoaxes. Knowledge about UFOs would be greatly furthered if these resources were used to train investigators and to support ongoing research programs.

Some UFO witnesses have steadfastly adhered to their stories through repeated interrogation by police, UFO investigators, and psychiatrists. Hypnotic regression has also been used to allow witnesses to recall the details of their experiences. Hypnotic regression is used in many areas of conventional psychiatry to get people to recall repressed or forgotten incidents from their childhood, battlefield experiences, or other traumatic occurrences, and information so obtained is generally assumed to reflect the reality of earlier experiences. On this basis, then, investigators have concluded that "something very real and very frightening" has happened to some UFO witnesses. Although this conclusion may be valid in some instances, it must be noted that people other than UFO witnesses can be made to "recall" UFO abductions under hypnotic regression (Lawson 1980). Naive subjects give vivid, detailed descriptions of the interior of spacecraft and also express confusion and fear. There are many similarities between these descriptions and those provided by UFO witnesses. That people can vividly "recall" imaginary events through hypnotic regression has rather far-reaching implications not only for the study of UFO phenomena but for the field of psychiatry as well.

Finally, there is the hysterical contagion explanation of UFO phenomena. In many ways, UFO phenomena seem to fit the "rapid, unwitting, and nonrational" characteristics of hysterical contagion. UFO investigators have noted, for example, that on nights shortly following major UFO sightings, groups of people gather to excitedly watch the lights of radio transmission towers. Even in cases of known hoaxes, others in the vicinity have sometimes claimed to have seen the UFO. In the next section of this chapter, we will begin to consider UFO reports from the standpoint of social contagion and other collective behavior theories. The question "What are UFOs?" will be left unanswered. More than thirty years of official and unofficial investigation has failed to provide an answer to this question—at least an answer that satisfies most of those interested in UFOs. We can state without equivocation only that UFOs exist as an enduring feature of our basic cultural and social life.

UFOs and Collective Behavior

Casual observers and UFO experts alike attribute many UFO sightings to social contagion, or mass hysteria. This is a temptingly obvious characterization considering the bizarre stories provided by excited or frightened people. We will first examine the social contagion explanation of UFO phenomena.

We will then consider the social history of UFOs. The emergent norm perspective of collective behavior provides much insight into this history. The modern idea that UFOs are the vehicles of space travelers began to emerge just before the beginning of this century. By the 1960s, this idea was fully developed and amply reflected in our popular culture. By then, hundreds of organizations were engaged in studying UFOs and UFO witnesses and were pressuring Congress for funds to "answer the UFO question," or were passing along messages from the space visitors. In many ways these groups are similar to groups formed to deal with more prosaic social problems.

The Mass Hysteria Perspective

Neil J. Smelser and Orrin E. Klapp cite UFO phenomena as one of several manifestations of social contagion. In a strict sense, Smelser does not regard UFO phenomena as value-added panic, or a collective flight based on a hysterical belief. He does, however, describe outbreaks of UFO sightings as involving widespread terror, bodily symptoms of fright, anxiety, and fantastic beliefs (1969:142).

In contrast, Klapp identifies outbreaks of UFO sightings as enthusiastic contagions that give evidence of magical wish fulfillment. It is assumed that space visitors are benevolent and intend to use their knowledge to benefit humankind.

Smelser and Klapp argue that UFO sightings are decidedly episodic in their occurrence,

strongly suggesting the work of contagion. Klapp (1972:133) uses data reported by Dr. J. Allen Hynek to support this view. This same data is summarized in Table 6.1, which also includes the source of the information and the yearly differences in UFO sightings.

Table 6.1 shows three major UFO waves, peaking in the years 1952, 1957, and 1966. The year-to-year fluctuations in the number of UFO reports are not as extreme as the hysteria explanations imply. The peaks of 1957 and 1966, for example, represent less than a doubling in the number of UFO reports from the previous year. In fact, in only one instance does the number of UFO reports show marked fluctuation. From 1951, the number of UFO reports increased more than tenfold in 1952 and then dropped to less than a third that number in 1953.

The year 1952 is often referred to as the year of "flying saucer hysteria." It should be noted, however, that in March 1952, Project Grudge was expanded and upgraded to Project Blue Book. Project Blue Book was given more publicity, the number of field investigators was substantially increased, and investigation procedures were made more rigorous. Some of the increase in UFO reports, particularly during the summer of 1952, is due to the improved reporting and recording procedures of Project Blue Book. It should also be noted that during Project Blue Book's sixteen years of full operation, the annual number of reports obtained always exceeded 186, the largest yearly total obtained through Project Grudge. Rather than showing peaks of hysteria, Table 6.1 shows the effects of improved reporting and recording procedures, and it demonstrates that the occurrence of UFO reports is not as erratic as those who offer the hysteria hypothesis have suggested.

Since the end of Project Blue Book, UFO reports have been tabulated and investigated by a number of private UFO organizations. These groups lack the resources, full-time staffing, and visibility that were part of Project Blue Book. Consequently, fewer UFO reports have been recorded since 1969. Nonetheless, the tallies compiled by these organizations indicate that ten to twenty UFO sightings are reported monthly across the United States. There was a marked increase in UFO reports in 1973 and another in 1978. UFOs are not, as some suggest, merely a quaint part of the popular culture of the 1950s and 1960s.

What about the hundreds of sightings that are classified as close encounters? In close encounters, witnesses report being within fifty feet of the landed UFO, and in a few instances they report entering the UFO. In short, can people grossly misperceive aircraft, streetlights or other common objects so close at hand? Some UFO investigators have attributed close encounter experiences to group-induced hysteria (Menzel and Boyd 1963:138). Under conditions of emotional stress, great excitement, and group pressure, susceptible people are often alleged to become so detached from their critical abilities that they see things that aren't there.

Group influence and suggestibility have long been topics of experimental investigation. The nature of suggestibility as demonstrated in the laboratory is quite different from that assumed in the hysteria explanation of close encounters. It should also be noted that in about half of the close encounters, witnesses report that they were alone at the time of their experience.

The classic studies of group influence and suggestibility conducted by S. E. Asch (1958), for example, indicate that naive subjects can be made to misperceive something as simple and unambiguous as the length of lines. In Asch's study, naive subjects were placed in groups of eight people who had been previously coached to give false judgments as to the length of lines. Each member, in turn, was to announce aloud which two of five lines were the same length. Faced with unanimous announcements of in-

TABLE 6.1

Pattern of UFO Sighting Reports in the United States, 1947–1968

Air Force project source	Year	Annual total reported sightings	Percent increase or decrease from the preceding year
—	1947	79	—
Sign	1948	143	+81
Grudge	1949	186	+30
Grudge	1950	169	−9
Grudge	1951	121	−28
Blue Book	1952	1,501	+1,140
Blue Book	1953	452	−70
Blue Book	1954	429	−5
Blue Book	1955	404	−5
Blue Book	1956	778	+93
Blue Book	1957	1,178	+51
Blue Book	1958	590	−50
Blue Book	1959	364	−38
Blue Book	1960	514	+41
Blue Book	1961	488	−5
Blue Book	1962	474	−3
Blue Book	1963	399	−16
Blue Book	1964	526	+32
Blue Book	1965	887	+69
Blue Book	1966	1,060	+20
Blue Book	1967	937	−12
Blue Book	1968	392	−58

SOURCE: Original data reported in *Christian Science Monitor*, April 2, 1970, by Dr. J. Allen Hynek, then director of Lindheimer Astronomical Research Laboratory, Northwestern University.

correct judgments, 25 percent of the subjects remained independent in their judgments and gave entirely correct answers. However, another 25 percent of the subjects capitulated to the group by making incorrect judgments in one half or more of the trials.

Are some of the very dramatic and strange close encounter reports the result of similar processes of suggestibility that distort the witnesses' judgment? This seems unlikely if we consider the Asch studies further. Nearly all of the subjects who yielded to the unanimous majority later reported that they did so because they thought they had "misunderstood the instructions" or "didn't want to ruin the experiment," even though they had clearly perceived the majority response as incorrect (Asch 1958: 176–179). Those who report close encounters do not indicate that they are trying to appease other witnesses who are wrong in their judgments.

Finally, Asch conducted a series of trials where the majority was not unanimous. The presence of even a single dissenter almost totally eliminated the compliance effect (1958:179–180). Reports from witnesses to the same close encounter usually contain conflicting elements and alternate interpretations. As Asch's studies show, these inconsistencies eliminate extreme compliance with the group.

Laboratory findings regarding social influence illustrate what Turner and Killian refer to as the *normative constraint* that operates in groups and crowds (1972:21–25). People's actions do influence one another. In natural settings, however, these actions are not uniform enough to produce the extreme influences claimed by the mass hysteria explanations of UFOs and other collective behavior phenomena.

The UFO as an Emergent Social Phenomenon

Turner and Killian's emergent norm perspective offers more insight than the mass hysteria perspective into the history of UFO phenomena. The first modern UFO flap occurred during the winter of 1896, when thousands of people reported seeing mysterious airships hovering, cruising, or racing in the skies across the United States. Many explanations were offered

at the time, including secret inventions, hysteria, and hoaxes. Though a few people attributed the airships to visitors from other planets, this explanation did not become popular for another forty years. For Turner and Killian, much of collective behavior involves people developing new, collective definitions of problematic events. We will briefly consider the emergence of the extraterrestrial explanation of UFOs in the following section.

Mystery Airships

The first repeated sightings of UFOs in the United States took place in November and December of 1896 and March through May of 1897. Sightings were reported in nineteen states from California to West Virginia. The most common term used to describe the reported objects was *airships*. Many of the descriptions would seem to describe dirigibles, zeppelins, or blimps. However, the first known dirigible flight in the United States did not occur until three years later, and the first practical dirigible, the *California Arrow*, was not flown until 1904. In the 1890s there was a general expectation that someone would soon invent a successful powered flying machine. Many patents had been issued, and dozens of inventors, including the Wright brothers, were busily experimenting with powered flight. It is unlikely that such experiments were the cause of numerous and widespread airship reports, although "experiments" was one of the most popular explanations offered at the time. In much the same way that UFOs are currently explained, several astronomers stated that bright stars had been mistaken for mystery airships. Some people argued that the airships were hoaxes, and indeed some of the later incidents proved to be hoaxes. A few suggested that the airships were advertising gimmicks for cigarettes or circuses. Finally, some skeptics wrote off the airships to gullibility, stupidity, or too much whiskey.

An extraterrestrial explanation was occasionally suggested: the airships were exploration vehicles from Mars. The "canals" of Mars had been discovered about twenty years earlier, which led to the belief that Mars had an earth-like climate and intelligent life. This explanation, however, was not as popular as the "secret inventor" explanation (Jacobs 1975:28–29).

Dozens of encounters with the airship crews were also reported. A few witnesses described the crews as monsters who spoke a strange and frightening language. Most witnesses, however, described the crews as gentlemen who introduced themselves as inventors. Often, the airship crews mentioned the confidential nature of their flying machine and asked witnesses not to tell others about what they had seen. Another common theme to the encounters was that the aircrews requested food and water or borrowed tools.

While most accounts described what could possibly have been dirigibles, zeppelins, or blimps, several accounts were similar to more recent descriptions of UFOs. A few airships were described as egg shaped, metallic, and able to accelerate "like a shot out of a gun." Reports of night sightings often mentioned bright, pulsating, white, orange, red, and blue lights. There were some reports of airships flying in formations.

The airship sightings did not precipitate government-sponsored investigations or the founding of any private investigation groups. In fact, it appears that the airship mystery was soon forgotten, perhaps because the mystery airships never returned. Also, the airship reports were soon to be outdone by news stories and pictures of the successful flights of the Wright brothers and other early air pioneers. The airships of 1896 and 1897 probably received more consideration after 1947 than when they occurred.

Foo-Fighters

The twentieth-century history of the UFO began during World War II when Allied, German, and Japanese aircrews reported being intercepted, followed, and occasionally harassed by fireballs and disk-shaped objects. Aircrews referred to the phenomenon as "foo-fighters" and considered them to be enemy secret weapons of some sort. The United States Fifth Army's explanation was that foo-fighters were mass hallucinations induced by the stresses of air combat (Jacobs 1975:35–37).

Ghost Rockets

In 1946 "ghost rockets" were reported in Sweden and continued to be reported throughout Europe until 1948 (Sachs 1980:123). These cigar-shaped UFOs and fireballs were given some attention by the United States and Swedish military, primarily to find out if the Soviet Union was conducting rocket experiments. It was generally concluded that most of the ghost rockets were misidentified aircraft.

Flying Saucers

In early 1947, many people across the United States began to report UFOs to their local authorities and newspapers. These reports were given scant attention until Kenneth Arnold's sighting of nine "flying saucers." At first the press reported sightings in a straightforward manner. This stance soon became more cautious, and in spite of the great amount of UFO or flying saucer activity reported, no concrete evidence for the existence of these strange craft was obtained. Caution changed to open skepticism and ridicule as some blatantly absurd reports were given and numerous hoaxes were revealed. Finally, the UFO phenomenon fell into further disregard as followers of the occult and other marginal groups began to adopt and adapt UFOs to their particular interests (Jacobs 1975:xi). To the present day, the established media has maintained a skeptical stance toward UFO reports. What attention is given is usually in terms of human interest, hysteria, or "silly season" stories (Jacobs 1975:278).

The Stage of Formal Organization

The mystery airships of 1896 and 1897 were forgotten as soon as the glamour of early aviation captured the public imagination. After World War II, however, flying saucers became a matter of much greater concern to the United States government and to numerous civilian groups that sought to answer the flying saucer question.

The Air Force Projects

Despite early and growing skepticism, the United States Air Force instituted Project Sign in January 1948 in order to ascertain the nature of flying saucers and determine whether they presented a threat to national security. In 1950 Project Twinkle was undertaken to obtain photographs of the green fireballs being reported frequently in northern New Mexico (Sachs 1980:261). The Washington Air National Guard equipped aircraft with cameras to obtain pictures of UFOs. These projects came under immediate criticism as either "extremely inadequate, given the scope of the problem," or a "waste of taxpayers' money." None of these UFO projects, however, were ever top-priority air force projects, and they were poorly funded. Project Twinkle was terminated after only six months of operation, and no photographs of fireballs were obtained. At one point, Project Blue Book had only two field investigators and was briefly directed by an enlisted man.

UFOs as a Public Relations Problem

By 1953 the air force was satisfied that most UFOs were misidentifications, hysteria, or hoaxes and did not pose a threat to national security. Consequently, the UFO phenomenon became as much a problem of public relations as it was a problem to be investigated (Jacobs 1975:89–107). There seemed to be no real need to continue Project Blue Book other than to avoid the outcry from UFO buffs and organizations if the project were canceled. Project Blue Book was continued until 1969. After 1953, sighting investigations were carried out as training exercises for Air Intelligence Service Squadron personnel. Thereafter, Project Blue Book involved little more than the compiling of air intelligence reports and investigating a few of the "unidentifieds."

In 1957 the number and kinds of UFO reports again brought the UFO phenomenon to public attention. While the air force argued that these were nothing more than the usual misidentifications, hysteria, and hoaxes, private UFO organizations pushed to have congressional hearings. The purpose of hearings was to upgrade the scientific study of UFOs and to get the air force to disclose what it really knew about UFOs. By late 1957, however, the number of UFO reports was beginning to decline, and so did congressional enthusiasm.

In 1966 the number of UFO sightings returned to the 1957 level. On April 5, 1966, the House Armed Services Committee held the first and to date the only open hearing on UFOs. It was decided at this brief meeting that a scientific committee should be appointed by the air force to investigate selected UFO sightings and evaluate Project Blue Book.

By the end of 1968, the number of UFO sightings had declined to their lowest level since 1959 (see Table 6.1). It was in the context of lower than usual UFO sighting reports that the Condon Committee issued its congressionally mandated report. The report concluded that the air force had done an excellent job of studying UFOs and that UFOs had a number of terrestrial explanations. The Condon Committee Report concluded that there was no longer any reason to continue Project Blue Book.

After the Condon Committee Report, many UFO organizations underwent a rapid and marked decline in membership. Several UFO magazines went out of business (Jacobs 1975: 256). The number of UFO reports submitted to private UFO investigation groups indicated that there had been a clear decline in UFO sightings from the levels of the 1950s and 1960s. Many felt the UFO had departed the American scene.

The decline in UFO sightings, however, was only temporary. By 1973 the number of UFO reports approached those of 1952, 1957, and 1966. This time the air force remained outside the controversy, which was easy because the disputes accompanying UFO sightings had calmed considerably. In 1973 the media seldom ridiculed UFO reports, and charges of hoax were less frequent and less bitter. There were many reasons for this change in public reaction. UFO sighting reports had become "tame stuff" compared to what had, since 1966, become commonplace to the American public. The report that someone had observed an automobile-sized, egg-shaped object take off at high speed seemed much less dramatic to the millions of people who had watched live television coverage of several *Saturn V* launches. The report that someone had observed humanoid pilots scampering around their UFO hardly compared to the drama of watching Neil Armstrong take the first step on the surface of the moon. The occasional blurred photos alleged to be UFOs hardly compared to the brilliant photo essays of the Gemini and Apollo space missions published in *Life* magazine. Any possible threat the UFOs posed now seemed to be matched equally, or even to be exceeded, by those of our own making. We were discovering the worldwide threat of pollution and were being continually reminded that we had finally created nuclear arsenals clearly capable of destroying our planet.

The scientific study of UFOs also seemed to have attained a degree of respectability not enjoyed earlier. Perhaps this was because scientists had succeeded in demystifying themselves in the eyes of the public. During the late 1960s and early 1970s, there was an increase in the number of celebrity scientists. People such as Jane Goodall, Marlin Perkins, Jacques Cousteau, and Carl Sagan allowed the American public to see scientists as quite likable, articulate, and dedicated people, in marked contrast to the "egghead" image given to scientists during the 1950s. Their popular books and television shows greatly increased public awareness of the nature of scientific investigation and the scope of scientific interests. If scientists studied the social life of chimps, catalogued the density of ocean plankton, and speculated about the nature of antimatter and black holes in space, then why not study UFOs?

The books of James Allen Hynek seriously addressed the methodological and analytical problems involved in studying UFOs. Previous serious discussions of UFOs were primarily devoted to, for example, how temperature inversions could produce false radar images (cf. Menzel and Boyd 1963). Hynek's *The UFO Experience: A Scientific Enquiry* (1972) clearly stands apart from earlier books written about UFOs. It presents, foremost, a scientific methodology for classifying and studying UFO reports.

The character of the UFO phenomenon has changed through the years. When people first began to report strange airships in the sky, it was largely attributed to mysterious inventions, hysteria, or hoaxes and promptly forgotten. The next time large numbers of people reported strange craft in the sky, it was treated as a possible threat to national security and worthy—though just barely—of official investigation. Much controversy and bitter debate surrounded the UFO phenomenon until the mid-1960s, when the government concluded its UFO studies and the number of UFO reports decreased substantially. When large numbers of people began to see UFOs in the 1970s, much had changed. Scientists who expressed interest in studying UFOs and the people who reported them were subject to less ridicule than before. Most UFO reports seemed less fantastic now that people's frame of reference had been expanded to include the drama and spectacle of real space travel. The possible threats that UFOs could pose seemed small in comparison to the much more imminent threats of pollution and nuclear war. Finally, the scientific establishment had shed some of the aloofness and mystery attributed to it by the media of the 1950s. The scientific study of UFOs was resumed by individual scientists and private organizations.

Public Awareness of UFOs: The Gallup Polls

The Gallup poll included its first UFO items on August 15, 1947, less than eight weeks after Kenneth Arnold's widely publicized sighting. The poll indicated that fully 90 percent of the adult population had read or heard about UFOs. By comparison, fewer people were able to recognize pictures of Dwight D. Eisenhower (83 percent) and Douglas MacArthur (76 percent). This poll offered little to support the notion, however, that the United States was in the grip of a flying saucer hysteria or scare. The most frequent answer given to the follow-up question "What are flying saucers?" was "optical illusions, imagination, and hoaxes" (39 percent). Less than 5 percent of those polled indicated that UFOs were Russian secret weapons or alien spacecraft. Later in the poll, people were asked what was the most important problem facing the United States, and 45 percent of the respondents indicated either in-

flation or foreign policy. Less than 1 percent mentioned flying saucers. On May 20, 1950, the Gallup poll again asked about flying saucers. This time 94 percent had heard or read about UFOs. Five percent of these people said UFOs were "something from another planet" or "Russian weapons." While almost everyone knew about flying saucers, few perceived them as a threat.

The Gallup poll did not ask UFO questions again until May 8, 1966. This time "UFO" was substituted for "flying saucer" and additional questions were asked. Ninety-six percent of the national sample had heard or read about UFOs, and 5 percent of these people claimed to have seen a UFO. Pollsters asked whether UFOs were real or imaginary. Forty-six percent said UFOs were real, 29 percent said they were imaginary and the rest had no opinion. This question was ambiguous compared to the earlier polls in which people were asked "What are flying saucers?" People who claimed that UFOs were real may have had in mind "real" optical illusions as well as "real" spacecraft.

The UFO polls since 1966 also show that an increasing number of people think that there is intelligent life on other planets in the universe. Only one third felt this way in 1966. By 1978, however, the majority of those polled (51 percent) and almost 70 percent of those under thirty thought that there was intelligent life elsewhere. These findings are summarized in Table 6.2.

Since 1966, Gallup polls have consistently shown that better-educated people are more likely to believe that UFOs are real and that there is life similar to ours on other planets. These findings run counter to the mass hysteria view that less-educated people are likely to believe in UFOs and are therefore more susceptible to hysterical influences. These findings are summarized in Table 6.3.

The results of these surveys indicate continuing interest in and knowledge of UFOs in the United States. Questions posed since 1969

TABLE 6.2
Public Awareness and Definition of UFOs

Gallup poll question	Response	Percent by year				
		1947	1950	1966	1973	1978
Have you ever heard or read about flying saucers [UFOs]?	Yes	90	94	96	95	93
Are flying saucers from other planets?	Yes	1	5	—	—	—
In your opinion are they something real or just people's imagination?	Real	—	—	46	53	57
Do you think there are people somewhat like ourselves living on other planets in the universe?	Yes	—	—	34	46	51

SOURCES: *The Gallup Poll: Public Opinion 1935–1971*, Vols. 1 and 3 (New York: Random House, 1973), pp. 666, 911, 2004. *The Gallup Poll: Public Opinion 1972–1977*, Vol. 1 (Wilmington, Delaware: Scholarly Resources, 1978), pp. 213–215. *The Gallup Poll: Public Opinion 1978* (Wilmington, Delaware: Scholarly Resources, 1979), pp. 161–163.

TABLE 6.3
UFO Beliefs and Education

Gallup poll question	Response	Level of education	Percent by year		
			1966	1973	1978
In your opinion are [UFOs] something real or just people's imagination?	Real	College	51	62	66
		High school	51	55	57
		Grade school	33	41	36
Do you think there are people somewhat like ourselves living on other planets in the universe?	Yes	College	37	58	62
		High school	38	47	53
		Grade school	25	39	24

SOURCES: *The Gallup Poll: Public Opinion 1935–1971*, Vol. 3 (New York: Random House, 1973), p. 2004. *The Gallup Poll: Public Opinion 1972–1977*, Vol. 1 (Wilmington, Delaware: Scholarly Resources, 1978), pp. 213–215. *The Gallup Poll: Public Opinion 1978* (Wilmington, Delaware: Scholarly Resources, 1979), pp. 161–163.

show that about 10 percent of the population claims to have seen a UFO at some time during their life. Interestingly, these surveys suggest that UFOs have never been generally perceived as a threat by the American public. Finally, the results of these polls run counter to the notion that the UFO phenomenon appeals primarily to the less educated.

UFO Organizations

In the last section of this chapter, we will consider various UFO organizations that have maintained membership and programs over an appreciable length of time. There are three major types of organizations. *UFO investigation groups* are often headed or advised by credentialed scientists interested in studying UFO phenomena. The general membership of such groups includes field investigators and those who simply receive periodic mailings. The second type of UFO organization is the *contactee group*, whose leaders and members claim to have been contacted by people from other planets. The stated purpose of these groups is to spread the messages given them by the extraterrestrials. The third type of UFO group could best be termed *UFO cults* (cf. Buckner 1965). These groups claim that UFOs are sent by God for the salvation of humankind. Beyond their general interest in UFO phenomena, these groups have little in common and are frequently at odds.

UFO Investigation Groups

The first civilian UFO investigation group to be established was the Aerial Phenomena Research Organization (APRO). APRO was established in 1952 by Coral and James Lorenzen, and it has a staff of seven, with a five-person board of directors. This group also utilizes about fifty professionals in the physical and social sciences as advisers. APRO was established, in part, out of dissatisfaction with the procedures used by the air force in investigating and reporting UFO phenomena. APRO is international in scope, with about three thousand members and five hundred field investigators in the United States and fifty other countries. Independent of APRO, Coral and James Lorenzen have authored and coauthored several popular books about UFOs.

In 1956 the National Investigations Committee on Aerial Phenomena (NICAP) was established by T. Townsend Brown. Marine Corps Major Donald E. Keyhoe became director of NICAP in 1957 and served until 1969. Keyhoe often brought NICAP into controversy with frequent charges that the air force was engaging in a coverup of the UFO phenomenon.

In part, this was because Keyhoe saw NICAP as having a dual role: investigating UFO sightings and lobbying for congressional and scientific investigations of the UFO phenomenon (Jacobs 1975:145–157).

The board of governors of NICAP includes U.S. senators, businessmen, and military officers. Prior to the Condon Committee Report, NICAP claimed more than 12,000 members worldwide; currently, NICAP membership stands at about four thousand. NICAP maintains about seventy-five field investigators across the United States. Among NICAP publications is the monthly newsletter, *UFO Investigator* (Sachs 1980:213).

The Mutual UFO Network (MUFON) was established in 1969 by Walter H. Andrews, Jr., John Schuessler, and Allen R. Utke. MUFON has an advisory board of seventy professionals in the physical and social sciences, more than a thousand member/investigators, and chapters in almost every state and several nations. MUFON sponsors an annual UFO symposium for scientists, engineers, and authors and publishes the *MUFON UFO Journal*.

In 1973 Dr. James Allen Hynek founded the Center for UFO Studies. The center has no official position regarding the nature of UFOs; its goal is to provide both a public source of reliable UFO information and an international clearinghouse to which people can report their UFO experiences without fear of ridicule (Sachs 1980:52). A computerized catalogue of UFO reports, "UFOCAT," is maintained and available to those studying UFOs. MUFON assists the center in its field investigations. The center is not a "membership" organization; it is composed of invited scientists and other academics willing to actively investigate and study the UFO phenomenon. The monthly *International UFO Reporter* is available by subscription.

Dr. James Allen Hynek, director of the Center for UFO Studies, has long been involved in the study of UFOs. He was an astronomical consultant to Projects Grudge and Blue Book from 1948 to 1968. He was also chairman of the Department of Astronomy and director of Dearborn Observatory at Northwestern University from 1960 to 1975. For nearly thirty-five years, Hynek has been an advocate for the scientific study of UFOs. Since the termination of Project Blue Book, groups such as the center for UFO Studies have become the only sources of reliable information on UFOs.

The UFO investigation groups described above are all nonprofit organizations. During the course of the many disputes surrounding the UFO issue, critics charged these groups with having vested financial interest in keeping the UFO controversy alive, but this charge appears to be largely unfounded. NICAP, for example, has been for most of its existence a "bare bones" organization. Organizers of these groups have occasionally written popular and profitable books that helped these organizations continue operations, but for the most part, these organizations are far from lucrative undertakings. They continue to function because of the dedication of their organizers and members.

Contactee Groups

Contactee cases differ from close encounters of the third kind, in which witnesses such as Charles Hickson simply report observing humanoids. Contactee cases involve persons who claim to have socialized with the occupants of UFOs, often on a continuing basis. Contactees frequently claim to have been given messages from, or given missions to perform by, the occupants of UFOs. Most UFO investigation groups have refused to investigate contactee claims because of their apparent likelihood of being hoaxes.

The Amalgamated Flying Saucer Clubs of America (AFSCA) was founded in 1959 by contactee Gabriel Green. AFSCA has fifty-six hundred members worldwide and more than a hundred unit directors. AFSCA has no formal investigative program; instead, it holds that flying saucers obviously originate from our solar system and other galaxies: space people have fed false information to our probes of the solar system to make us think the planets are uninhabitable. The mission of AFSCA is to assist the space people in their efforts to contact the leaders of the world. The space people offer solutions to most of our planet's problems, but our leaders refuse to take their advice because to do so would decrease their own power and influence.

AFSCA sells tape-recorded messages from the space people, books, photographs, and even bumper stickers. One of the popular bumper stickers reads "Flying saucers are real, the Air Force doesn't exist" (Sachs 1980:13). At the urgings of visitors from Alpha Centauri, founder Gabriel Green has been a candidate for the presidency of the United States and the California legislature.

The National Investigations Committee on UFOs (NICUFO) was established in 1967 by contactee Frank E. Stranges. As the name implies, NICUFO is patterned much along the lines of NICAP. The purpose of this organization is to investigate UFOs, giving particular attention to contactee cases, which have generally been ignored by most UFO investigation groups. While NICAP continues to hold reservations regarding the extraterrestrial origins of UFOs, NICUFO claims to have proven that UFOs come from Earth and other planets. Further, UFOs have been on Earth for at least four thousand years. Like NICAP, NICUFO has a board of directors, but it consists largely of contactees, including Donald Fry, Gabriel Green's running mate for the presidency in 1972.

NICUFO has about one thousand members. Membership rights and benefits include a 10 percent discount on all NICUFO literature, a 20 percent discount on NICUFO-sponsored conventions, workshops, and lectures, and a subscription to NICUFO's *Confidential Newsletter*.

UFO Cults

In 1947 the Universal Industrial Church of the New World Comforter was established by contactee Allen-Michael. The church has about seventy-five members, and the group claims to maintain telepathic contact with space people. According to the group, the purpose of UFOs is to bring peace, freedom, and security to Earth through *Uni-Communism*. The system of Uni-Communism would grant to each person ample food, clothing, shelter, and care. The church takes into its fold people who have had UFO experiences and can no longer cope with society. According to the church's precepts, Christ was a Venusian contactee, and the people from Venus provided Christ with much assistance (Sachs 1980:349).

Mark-Age was established in 1960 by Charles B. Gentzel and Nada-Yolanda. These contactees claim that Nada-Yolanda, also known as Pauline Sharp, is the present earthly speaker for the spiritual government of the solar system. Christ, or Sanada, is part of the program of earthly enlightenment being conducted by the spiritual government, and he is scheduled to return to Earth by the year 2000. UFOs have guided earthlings throughout our evolution and in the year 2000 will help us attain a new cycle of fourth-dimensional existence. Mark-Age provides its members and other interested people with meditation tapes, home study courses, and counseling and training in the ways of the New Age (Sachs 1980: 189).

The Universaurian foundation was established in 1962 by contactee Zelrun W. Karsleigh, LeRoy Roberts, and A. H. Albrecht. Karsleigh claims to be in telepathic contact

with space people and therefore serves as the main guide for the foundation. The Universaurian belief systems includes the dissemination of information provided by the highly evolved space people. The space people desire to eliminate the fear and misery that exist on Earth. If this fails, the space people will transport selected and perfected people to other planets before Earth is destroyed.

The Universaurian Foundation claims 420 members in Portland, Oregon, Syracuse, New York, and Phoenix, Arizona. A library of UFO, scientific, and religious books is available to members. The group meets three times weekly throughout the year, except in August, and sponsors speakers in the area of UFOs, extrasensory perception, and other interesting topics. *The Voice of Unarius*, the group's monthly magazine, presents and discusses the latest messages from the space people (Sachs 1980:349–350).

Summary

There are references to puzzling and often frightening aerial phenomena throughout recorded history. In recent years people have attributed such UFO occurrences to extraterrestrial visitors. The modern era started with the mysterious airships of the 1890s and reached its full development with the flying saucer terminology of the late 1940s and early 1950s.

We began this chapter with a description of some typical UFO incidents: nocturnal lights, daylight disks, radar/visual sightings, and close encounters. This now familiar classification scheme for UFO incidents was first set forth by Hynek.

There have been more than one hundred thousand reported sightings of UFOs since 1947. Some UFO investigators claim that all UFO sightings result from the misidentification of such familiar objects as aircraft and stars, the effects of certain atmospheric conditions, hysteria, and hoaxes. Other UFO researchers conclude that a sizable number of UFO reports are genuine and that the extraterrestrial hypothesis cannot be dismissed. The investigation of UFO reports is difficult, and neither camp can lay claim to having the superior research methodology.

The mass hysteria perspective of collective behavior identifies outbreaks of UFO sightings as a type of mass hysteria. For Smelser, UFO flaps represent widespread terror and for Klapp they represent hysterical wish fulfillment. An examination of UFO reports indicates that fluctuations in the annual volume of reports is not as extreme as suggested by the definition of social contagion. Some of this fluctuation is certainly due to the procedures used in obtaining reports.

Asch's (1958) classic line-judging study illustrates that group influence is capable of distorting people's judgment. The conditions that led to distorted judgment in Asch's study, however, are seldom found during UFO sightings.

The emergent norm perspective offers some insights into the social nature of UFO phenomena. Present explanations of UFO phenomena have emerged through a process of collective definition. The explanations offered for the mystery airships included stars, hysteria, hoaxes, and visitors from Mars. These explanations have been elaborated on during the course of subsequent outbreaks of UFO sightings.

Following World War II, when flying saucers were seen as posing a possible military threat, numerous governmental and private organizations have sought to scientifically study them. Though official government interest has ceased, private groups continue to study UFO-related phenomena.

The Gallup polls indicate that UFOs have become a permanent feature of popular culture. About half the adult population believes that there is intelligent life similar to ours on other planets and that UFOs are real. There are few major differences in these beliefs that can be accounted for in terms of people's level of education.

Finally, UFOs have also spawned a number of groups that take a nonscientific interest in UFOs. These include numerous contactee groups who claim to have received messages from the space people and seek to pass these messages on to the rest of us.

CHAPTER 7

Fads and Fashion

Fads and fashion were among the earliest concerns of sociologists. This may seem surprising, because most of us view fads and fashion as part of the "lighter side" of social life. George Simmel (1904), however, argued that fads and fashion play an important role in modern society. Through fads, people can experience a "sense of identity and unity" with groups to which they aspire or belong. Fashions are expressive symbols that communicate people's status and prestige within society. Thorstein Veblen (1912) noted that through conspicuous adherence to fashion, people find a socially acceptable way to advertise their wealth to others.

With respect to fads and fashion, most theories of collective behavior take the classic statements of Simmel and Veblen as their starting point. They depart from these statements, however, in their emphasis on the apparent spontaneity, novelty, and intensity of fads and fashion. While the classic theories emphasize the integrative aspects of fads and fashion, theories of collective behavior usually emphasize the disruptive aspects.

Fads and fashion occur within nearly every sphere of social life in modern society, most obviously in the areas of clothing, personal adornment, and grooming. Commentators often note that the dress and decoration of women are more prone to fads and the whims of fashion than those of men, although such differences are probably overstated. Men had their white buckskin shoes, bolo ties, DA haircuts, and lamé shirts in the 1950s. If they dig far enough into their closets, many men can find the narrow ties and belts, madras shirts, and perhaps even a Nehru jacket they wore in the 1960s.

If one ever remodels an old house, many remnants of past fads and fashions of interior decoration come to the surface. Alternating layers of wallpaper and wall paint tell us what designs and colors were "in." During the late 1950s, vivid pink and black bathroom tile were popular. In the 1960s, solid colors were the thing, and beautiful woodwork and cabinets were painted to match the walls. Flawless hardwood floors were covered with wall-to-wall carpets. Stained and etched glass, once casually discarded from American homes, has now returned as a popular decorative item.

Some fads center on novelty items. If we search through our closets, garages, and basements, we are likely to find hula hoops, lava lamps, wood-burning sets, beaded curtains, beanbag chairs, pet rocks, Rubik's cubes, and deely boppers. Though we would not now have the nerve to sell many of these things at a yard sale, they were once prized possessions.

There are also activity fads. These include the dance marathons of the 1930s, the jitterbug contests of the 1940s, and the eating contests, panty raids, and phone booth stuffing of the 1950s. In the early 1960s, a Kennedy family tradition, the twenty-mile hike, was copied around the country. The 1970s brought us toga parties and streaking. Break dancing is part of the 1980s scene.

Three Kinds of Fads

In this chapter we begin with a description of three separate kinds of fads. The first is the fantastic burst of sales of citizens' band (CB) radios in 1976 and 1977. This is a *useful product fad*, or the widespread purchase and use of an item that has obvious and tangible benefit to the user. The next fad episode is the sale of Cabbage Patch Kids dolls during the Christmas season of 1983. This is a *novelty product fad*, or the purchase and use of an item that has little practical value for the user. Finally, there is the streaking fad during the spring of 1974. This is an example of an *activity fad* in which variations of an activity are publicly displayed, usually within a crowd setting.

Citizens' Band (CB) Radios

Citizens' band (CB) radios came into use on October 4, 1958, when federal regulations were changed to permit their operation. Licensing was much less stringent than for ham radios, in part because they were designed to have a range of less than ten miles. Taxicab companies and local delivery services were the first businesses to use the CB radio extensively; noncommercial and recreational uses were rare. The growth in CB licenses and sales was steady, holding at about one hundred thousand licenses and radios a year.

Annual sales suddenly increased about twentyfold during the gasoline crisis of 1973. During that year, 2 million CB licenses were issued, most of them to long-distance truck driv-

ers, who found that CBs helped them locate filling stations that sold diesel fuel. The CB also proved valuable in keeping truckers informed about road conditions and accidents and for relaying emergency messages. Also, the CB was a welcome diversion for truckers who just wanted to talk to one another during the long hours on the road. Soon, truckers had evolved their own jargon, nicknames or "handles," and rules of CB etiquette.

Motorists who spent a great deal of time on the highways, such as sales representatives and commuters, began to use CBs. Farmers put radios on their tractors and trucks. They were very useful for relaying messages between house and field, coordinating fieldwork, and herding livestock. Farmers and ranchers also used CBs to organize night patrols when theft and cattle rustling became more common.

The greatest increase in CB sales came in 1976, when more than 11 million CB units were sold. Most commentators attributed this increase to the fifty-five-mile-per-hour national speed limit that was enacted that year. The CB radio was used to thwart police enforcement efforts. Truckers and motorists began to "convoy," or drive in large groups at high speeds. Drivers of oncoming vehicles were able to notify speeders of the location of police in time for the convoys to slow to "double nickels."

That year, CB radios began to appear on everything from family autos to bicycles and golf carts. There were also numerous spinoff items, including jewelry boxes, banks, cologne bottles, and salt and pepper shakers designed to look like CB radios. Toy CB radios were sold for use on tricycles and kiddy cars. Model truck kits appeared on the shelves of hobby shops. Numerous books on CB jargon were published. Elaborate locking and alarm systems were marketed to prevent the theft of CBs.

CB jargon invaded popular speech. Tractor-trailer rigs became "eighteen wheelers," state police became "smokeys," and exceeding the speed limit became putting "the pedal to the metal." The term *10-4* was often substituted for saying yes, of course, or all right. People adopted handles like the truck drivers, calling themselves such names as Nitro, Big Red, Hotshot, the Professor, Rubber Duck, Ditch Witch, and Squirrely Shirley.

Songs about truckdrivers and truck driving, such as C. W. McCall's "Convoy," broke out of the country and western field and into the Top Ten. Television shows such as "B.J. and the Bear" capitalized on the CB radio–truck driver–state police theme. The second most popular film of 1977 was Burt Reynolds' *Smokey and the Bandit*, in which truckers used CB radios to evade the police.

CB clubs were established across the nation. Some of them were primarily social in nature, allowing people who had talked over CBs to meet face to face. These clubs also allowed people to exchange the latest technical information, make trades, and purchase equipment in large volume. Other clubs, such as Radio Emergency Action Citizen Teams (REACT), were established to relay emergency information and monitor weather. These groups often sought to work closely with police in the area of surveillance and disaster assistance.

In addition to evading enforcement of the fifty-five-mile-per-hour speed limit, CB radios were put to other "outlaw" uses. Burglars used CB and scanner radios to monitor police transmissions, and CB prostitutes used the radios to proposition truckers and motorists in or near interstate rest areas (Klein and Luxenburg-Ingle 1980a, 1980b). Finally, during this period CB radios became a very popular theft item (Gutschenritter 1977). They were stolen and hocked from coast to coast and some thieves were arrested with hundreds of stolen CBs in their possession!

CB radios presented other problems as well. Some operators illegally modified antennas so that they could skip their signals over hun-

dreds of miles. Some cheaply built, poorly maintained, or damaged CB sets interfered with radio, television, and stereo reception. The use of CB radios near construction sites posed the threat of detonating explosives. Numbers of people were electrocuted and injured or killed in falls while erecting antennas. CB radio clubs worked to promote CB etiquette and a positive image within the community. They also urged the safe use of radios and reported "skippers" to the authorities. Still, in many communities, CB radios came to be regarded as a nuisance.

General interest in CB radios began to decline during 1978, and by 1980 some commentators were claiming that the CB phenomenon was dead (Keerdoja and Sethi 1980). This is an exaggeration, of course. Many of the CB clubs formed during the 1970s remain active. Truckers, taxi drivers, delivery services, farmers, ranchers, and motorists still use CB radios. Still, the use of CB radios is far below what it was during the peak activity of 1976 and 1977.

Cabbage Patch Kids

In 1974 a very flexible synthetic fabric (Polly Doll) was introduced to the home needlecraft market. The material was used for making dolls. With proper stitching, one could make chubby but hauntingly lifelike faces, hands, and feet. Soon craft shows and bazaars across the country featured dolls that were crafted to look like grandmas and grandpas as well as infants.

Georgia artist Xavier Roberts established Original Appalachian Artworks in 1977 and began to sell "little people." He moved his sales/showroom into a former medical clinic in Cleveland, Georgia. Because the dolls were handcrafted, no two were identical. Further, depending on the quality of the sewing, the size of the doll, and the clothing, prices ranged from about $50 to $1,000. At Roberts's "hospital," dolls were "delivered" from under cabbage leaves by employees dressed in nurses' uniforms. New "parents" of the little people had to vow undying love for their new doll and were given adoption papers. Many of the most expensive dolls were bought by adults for themselves. By 1983 Roberts had sold more than two hundred thousand dolls.

Coleco Corporation and Original Appalachian Art Works negotiated a licensing agreement that allowed Coleco to market their version of the doll under the label of Cabbage Patch Kids. By using the latest robot technology, Asian manufacturers were able to retain the handcrafted appearance of the original dolls while manufacturing them in mass quantities. Cabbage Patch Kids were introduced in February 1983 and sold for about $30. Coleco also included adoption papers. If purchasers returned the papers, they received a note of thanks and, a year later, a birthday card for the doll.

Initially, retailers placed modest orders for the 1983 Christmas season. It did not appear that Cabbage Patch Kids would sell any better than other dolls, and it was also feared that the season would be characterized by generally weak sales. Coleco, however, set out on a nationwide advertising blitz, and by mid-November retailers were placing new orders. As Christmas approached, Coleco was scrambling to meet demand. In regions where dolls were in very short supply, ads were stopped altogether out of fear that false advertising charges would be brought by consumer groups. At this point, Coleco was chartering planes to bring in two hundred thousand dolls a week from their Hong Kong factories.

These cherubic little dolls seemed to inspire a very un-Christmaslike rowdiness in people. In Charleston, West Virginia, a near riot was reported when about five thousand people crowded into a department store that had advertised a new shipment of dolls. In Wilkes-Barre, Pennsylvania, a woman broke her leg in a disorderly crowd waiting for a department store to open. Some stores set up special Cabbage Patch waiting lines in an effort to end shoving matches and angry squabbles between customers.

It is not surprising that a black market in Cabbage Patch dolls began to emerge. Newspapers carried classified ads offering dolls for resale at grossly inflated prices. Those who knew how to make the dolls capitalized on their skills in the weeks before Christmas. Advertisements offered "counterfeit Kid dolls" at prices up to $200. In New Jersey, the FBI arrested counterfeiters with more than one thousand dolls in their possession.

There were other ways to cash in on the Cabbage Patch Kids. Stores that were able to acquire only a few dolls used them as promotional items. One store, for example, kept their dolls in the vault of a local bank and used them as prizes in a daily drawing. Churches and civic groups raffled off the dolls. Charity auctions were held, with reports that some dolls brought as much as $1,500.

Predictably, sales declined after Christmas, but by then Coleco had sold nearly 2.5 million Cabbage Patch Kids. No other doll has sold so well in its first year. Whether the Cabbage Patch Kids have the staying power of Mattel's Barbie and Ken dolls remains to be seen. Coleco is optimistic, because they are also marketing auto safety seats, tricycles, strollers, and clothing for the sweet little things. They will also have to send out more than 2 million birthday cards in 1984.

Streaking

What would you do if you were eating lunch and someone ran naked through the restaurant? What would you do if you saw a small crowd of naked people running down the street? In early March of 1974, you probably would not have been perplexed. Rather, you would know immediately that you had just witnessed a streaking. Total or partial nudity had been known for many years on and about college campuses, taking the form of "mooning," pranks, and initiation rituals. Still, none of this equaled the rash of streakings that occurred from February 11 (the acknowledged date of the first true streak) until March 15, when no one seemed to care anymore.

Evans and Miller (1975) concluded that one or more streaking incidents occurred on at least 123 colleges and universities during the outbreak. In addition, dozens of restaurants, shopping centers, high schools and junior colleges, a few state legislatures, and at least one baseball training camp were streaked. For a time, nothing was sacred, as Wall Street, St. Peter's Square, and the Eiffel tower were also streaked.

Evans and Miller discerned a pattern in the campus streaking incidents. On any given campus, a daring individual or small group would streak, often at night. Rumor and local media usually made the incident widely known by the next day. After that, other streaks occurred, climaxing in a preannounced streak-in. These streaks usually drew large crowds and the media to await the first sign of bare bottoms, tops, and everything else. During these streaks, innovations such as streaking on bicycles, motorcycles, roller skates, and wheelchairs occurred. Nude dancing, stripteases, and mass moonings were interspersed in the festivities. Streak-ins usually lasted about two or three hours. Afterward, smaller, unannounced streaks would occur. After a few days, the cycle occurred again. After about the third streak-in, interest faded rapidly, and students used their spare time to pursue other things.

Streaking was generally restricted to the college-age population, although streakers as young as eleven and as old as sixty-five occasionally appeared. Streaking was most likely to occur on or near large public universities. There was no discernible pattern of diffusion among universities. Small universities and pri-

vate institutions, as is usually the case, had a much lower incidence of streaking. Streakers were predominantly male, although women were well represented. For the most part, it was a lighthearted episode. Police made few attempts to capture or arrest streakers, and campus authorities made little effort to put a halt to it (Evans and Miller 1975).

Numerous explanations were offered, though none seemed particularly convincing. Evans and Miller suggest that streaking may have reflected a general attitude of disdain for existing social conditions. Beyond this, they suggest, simply, that it was a lot of naughty fun.

The Nature of Fads and Fashion

Numerous attempts have been made to define both fads and fashion, and there are several common elements to these definitions. For example, both fads and fashion are part of "conspicuous consumption" and occur with respect to superficialities (for example, Simmel 1904; LaPierre and Farnsworth 1949; Lofland 1981; Schaefer 1983). The superficial nature of fads and fashion does not refer to the degree of excitement or to the financial and emotional investments found in them. Rather, it refers to the fads' short life expectancy and the likelihood that fad and fashion items will be outmoded and replaced before their serviceability ends. Because of this aspect of fads and fashion, we see perfectly usable clothing and furniture being discarded or sold at yard sales because they are "out of fashion."

Additionally, fads and fashion follow much the same pattern of development and decline (e.g., Penrose 1952; Meyersohn and Katz, 1957; Lofland 1981). This pattern is characterized by an initial *latent period*, in which the object of the fad or fashion is known only within a limited and often small group. Then there is the *breakout period*, during which the first group introduces or other groups "discover" the fad item. Next there is the *peaking period*, in which use of the new item is defined as a fad or fashion and people enthusiastically adopt it as such. During the peaking period, competing items, such as other forms of recreation or fashion, are ignored. Innovations on the theme of the fad, such as contests for the first, best, or most, occur frequently. Finally, there is the *decline period*, in which the fad or fashion rapidly fades. In the case of fashion, it is always replaced by something else. Use of the fad or fashion item may totally disappear or again be restricted to a small group.

Finally, fads and fashion serve much the same ends in society. Simmel argued that human beings possess two competing impulses—unity and differentiation. First and foremost, people desire a secure feeling of acceptance or belonging to groups of which they are a part (unity). Second, people desire a sense of self-identity and autonomy (differentiation). Fads and fashion can accommodate these competing impulses more or less simultaneously. Personal involvement in a fad or adherence to a particular fashion communicates a sense of unity, comradeship, and belonging to a group. Involvement also sets individuals apart from the "rest of society" and establishes them as "trend setters" or at least "in tune with the latest happenings" in society. Fads and, in particular, fashion communicate a sense of one's own personal identity and social status. Fad and fashion, then, give people a clear sense of both unity and differentiation.

How do fads and fashion differ from one another? To begin with, the concept of fashion is most often applied to dress, grooming, and personal adornment. Discussions of fads typically include these areas but are seldom limited to them (Sann 1967). Several discussions emphasize that fads are less predictable, and their life cycles shorter and more intense, than fashion (for example, LaPierre and Farnsworth

1949; Penrose 1952; Lofland 1981; Schaefer 1983). Fads are also seen as more trivial than fashion. Fashion may manifest trends that allow a person to wear a style of clothing for a few seasons and still remain in step. Clothing fads, on the other hand, seldom last more than a few months. Fashion usually communicates economic status much more clearly than fads. Finally, some have argued that fashion is more enduring than fads. Fashion often comes to characterize historical periods, whereas most fads are soon forgotten, leaving little trace of their passing.

The Social Origins of Fashion

Simmel was among the first to argue that fashion, as a dynamic means of social differentiation, does not exist in primitive social systems. For Simmel, primitive social systems include tribal systems or caste systems such as those of India and Sri Lanka. A caste system is characterized by a nearly total absence of social mobility from one group to another. People's social status is strictly ascribed at birth, and everyone is expected to remain within their caste throughout their life. Primitive social systems also include what Simmel referred to as "classless" societies, such as the hunting and gathering societies of many American Indians or the early horticultural societies of New Guinea. The social structure of these societies is assumed to be relatively simple and undifferentiated. Not only are these groups very small, they generate little economic surplus. Consequently, there are few differences in wealth among members.

Primitive societies are therefore characterized by little social differentiation. In caste systems, social differentiation is not only limited, it is also inflexible. Simmel offers a twofold explanation for the kind of social differentiation found in primitive societies. First, Simmel assumes that the imitation impulse is much more developed among primitive people than is the differentiation impulse. According to Simmel, the primitive mentality mistrusts and even fears that which is new or different. For Simmel, the development of the impulse toward differentiation is a mark of civilized people. Second, the imitation impulse is reinforced by a heightened need for unity within primitive societies, which arises because primitive groups are more directly subject to the adversities of nature, such as disaster, disease, and famine, than are more civilized peoples. Only a united and highly cohesive group can stand against such constant testing.

Saying that fashion does not exist in primitive social systems does not mean that clothing, grooming, and personal adornment are unimportant. In these societies, both obvious and subtle differences in dress and decoration convey such important dimensions of social status as one's age, kinship, marital status, occupation, past exploits, and religion. These styles, however, are dictated by tradition and are relatively unchanging. They do not exist as a dynamic or variable means of conveying status. Primitive societies utilize more or less permanent differences in style, rather than fashion, as a basis of limited social differentiation.

As societies grow in size and their technology becomes more complex, there is an accompanying pressure toward social differentiation. Some people acquire new skills, others remain masters of old skills, and still others possess few skills. Greater differences in wealth develop among members and become ingrained in the social structure. New opportunities for power present themselves. According to Simmel, all these conditions heighten the need for increased social differentiation. Further, it is a need for social differentiation of a new sort—a type that is flexible enough to reflect constantly changing social relationships.

Fashion meets this need. Various elites attempt to differentiate themselves from others by way of new or exotic items of dress, grooming, or personal adornment. Because the elite is in an enviable position with respect to other groups in the society, many try to copy the styles of the elite. Simmel notes that in modern societies, it may take very little time before large numbers of people are also using the same colors, fabrics, hem lengths, and trouser styles as the elite. In order to successfully differentiate themselves from others, people must change styles. Simmel refers to this constant cycle of change in styles as fashion. In modern and wealthy societies, the fashion cycle is institutionalized, wherein fashion houses compete with one another each season for the nod from the elite. Shortly thereafter, manufacturers race to bring the "latest" fashion to the racks of the clothing and department stores of the world.

Women and Fashion.   Simmel claimed that women are far more conscious of fashion than men, in part because there is less psychological diversity among women, as a group, than among men. The limited psychological diversity of women contributes to their adherence to fashion or the "social average." On the other hand, Simmel argues that fashion gives women compensation for their lack of clear status position in a society where so much of individual identity rests on occupational skills and profession. For his time, Simmel set forth a rather contemporary sounding hypothesis, namely, that as women acquire more equal footing with men in terms of occupational and professional opportunities, fashion would become correspondingly less important to women.

The Natural History of Fads

Just as there are many predictable elements to the fashion cycle, so are there regularities in the origins, growth, and decline of most fads. Penrose (1952), Meyersohn and Katz (1957), and many others have have attempted to trace out the "natural history of fads." What follows is a composite of these discussions.

Latent Period. Meyersohn and Katz (1957) conclude that fads are not born but rediscovered. That is, fads often involve items that were once commonplace among limited constituencies such as ethnic, regional, or occupational groups, or collectors and hobbyists. For example, one of the most successful novelty items of all time, the hula hoop, started as a bamboo hoop used in gym classes in Australia. A plastic version was introduced into the United States in 1958 by the Wham-O Manufacturing Company, and before the fad subsided a year later, 30 million hula hoops had been sold (Sann 1967). Many of the moves (for example, backspins, swipes, knee spins, and splits) in break dancing, the urban phenomenon of the 1980s, come from a very athletic style of dancing found among southern rural blacks, which dates back to the 1930s. If one looks carefully, nearly every fad can be found to have its mundane predecessor.

Breakout Period. The latent period ends when the fad item is adopted by groups outside the original constituency. This early diffusion occurs primarily through interpersonal contact, with media playing a secondary role. Diffusion is enhanced when members of the original constituency actively promote the new item. CB radios were originally sold almost exclusively through truck dealerships, at truckstops and service garages, and through specialty catalogues. Once groups other than truckers started to purchase the radios, manufacturers recognized their wider sales potential. By the time the national speed limit was enacted, CB radios were just beginning to be found in department stores.

Early adopters often take their cues from the original users. Motorists who bought CB radios mimicked the truckers' style of using it,

often with hilarious results. Coleco took great care to retain the Cabbage Patch Kid ritual established by Xavier Roberts.

In the breakout phase, originators and early adopters are usually ignorant of the extent to which the use of the object has spread. Adoption reaches a point, however, when people cannot help but notice that something is happening. At this point, a statistical fad becomes a real fad (Meyersohn and Katz 1957).

Peaking Period. The peaking phase begins when the media acknowledge and name the fad. Diffusion then occurs through both interpersonal and media channels. Usually, a groundswell of adoption occurs immediately after the fad is given a name and attention by the media.

Later adopters are more likely to be innovative in their use of the fad item than early adopters. Later adopters still tried to mimic truckers when using CB radios, but they were less concerned with CB etiquette. Before the CB radio, truckers customarily used Channel 19, and Channel 9 was reserved for emergency use. As more and more motorists acquired radios, Channel 19 became virtually useless for truckers, and Channel 9 was often used for idle chatter. New CB users frequently interrupted or "walked over" the transmissions of serious users. Other kinds of innovations occurred as well. CBs were mounted on all sorts of vehicles, including bicycles and skateboards! Others began to interfere with nuisance innovations such as "skipping" and using illegally powerful radios. Young children transmitted without supervision.

At their peak, fads may produce a large "coattail" effect. This includes writing popular songs about the fad and quick merchandising to capitalize on the fad. Some merchandising, such as counterfeit Cabbage Patch dolls, may be illegal, while other merchandising, though legal, may be blatantly opportunistic. Manufacturers rushed poorly designed and cheaply built CB radios and accessories into production. During the Davey Crockett fad of 1955, the logo was used to sell everything from toy guns to refrigerators.

It is not surprising that as the fad peaks, original users often come to view the fad with contempt. Truckers were infuriated by novice and thoughtless users. The Cabbage Patch fad created a shortage of Polly Doll fabric, which raised the ire of needlecrafters across the land.

Decline Period. Some fads fade slowly, while others disappear overnight. Widespread adoption creates the conditions for a fad's decline. A theoretical "saturation point" is reached, beyond which the fad ceases to be a novelty; then, adherence to the fad becomes the mark of the boor. Knowledge that all fads ultimately die can be a self-fulfilling prophecy, as merchants delay or reduce orders for fad items in anticipation of the fad's passing.

The natural history of fads is such that fads rarely leave substantial traces of their passing. Items that once were eagerly sought are discarded or put away in closets, basements, and garages. If any traces remain, it is because use of the fad item has returned to the original constituencies of the latent phase.

Discussion. The natural history of fads describes social phenomena with which we are all familiar. Still, efforts to describe a typical pattern of fad growth and decline have focused on *product fads*. It is somewhat difficult to apply this natural history to *activity fads*, such as goldfish swallowing or streaking, which often have little if any commercial aspects.

The natural history of fads fails to explain why fads sometimes remain highly localized events. Many fads occur only within the boundaries of a high school, college campus, or region of the country and fail to catch on elsewhere.

Finally, the natural history of fads suggests that fads are so trivial that they seldom leave traces of their passing. It must be remembered, however, that numerous items that have fundamentally transformed our lives were initially regarded as fads. A small sampling from this list includes automobiles, airplanes, movies, radio, television, and business and home computers. Other fad items remained to enrich our leisure time, including ten-speed bicycles, games such as Monopoly and Scrabble, barbecue grills, Polaroid cameras, and frisbees.

The natural history of fads emphasizes their trivial nature, and indeed many fads are trivial. On the other hand, what we call fads are also an important component of cultural diffusion. We will now examine fads and fashion from the standpoint of theories of collective behavior.

Fads and Fashion as Collective Behavior

Simmel only hinted at the unpredictable, irrational, and wasteful aspects of fads and fashion, focusing instead on their consequences for social integration and differentiation. Others, such as Tarde (1903) and Park and Burgess (1924), reversed this focus and instead described fads and fashion primarily as a form of social pathology. Sapir (1937), for example, identifies fads as something "unexpected, irresponsible, or bizarre" and socially disapproved. Viewed in this manner, fads and fashion clearly fall within the domain of collective behavior.

The Mass Hysteria Perspective

According to Herbert Blumer (1969), fads are a form of social contagion, characterized by collective excitement that attracts and infects spectators and bystanders. As they catch the spirit of the fad, participants lose their self-consciousness and become attentive only to the immediate situation. For Orrin E. Klapp (1972), fads and fashion represent a temporary subordination of individual identity to mass identity. Fads and fashion are not a source of group solidarity as Simmel suggests, but a pathological loss of self-identity to the group.

For Blumer, such social contagions as fads are caused by underlying conditions of social unrest, such as economic uncertainty and fear of war. For Klapp, an important underlying cause of fads is boredom with the social relationships found in modern society.

Klapp states that recent fads and fashions are fundamentally different from those of thirty or forty years ago. Fads such as goldfish swallowing barely exceeded the limits of acceptable conduct. Fashions such as designer jeans still functioned much as Simmel suggested—as a means of communicating status. Recent fads and fashion, however, have left the range of tolerated freedom and threaten the basic norms of society. Fads and fashion no longer communicate status; they threaten to destroy status. Thus, goldfish swallowing gave way to panty raids, which in turn gave way to public nudity in the form of streaking. The CB fad had an outlaw character not found in earlier fads. Punk fashions reflect a level of hostility and decadence not witnessed before in America.

According to Klapp, fads and to an extent, fashions, serve a safety valve function for society. They allow people to act on tensions and impulses in a way that leaves the basic social institutions intact. If, however, tensions (including boredom) become extreme, then even safety valve outbursts can threaten the social structure.

The mass hysteria perspective emphasizes the lack of predictability, seeming irrationality, intensity, and infectious nature of fads and fashion: they constitute a form of social pathology. Still, even social pathology can serve a hidden positive function for society. Fads and fashion can help release collectively felt tensions while leaving the social structure intact. However, as Klapp suggests, under conditions of extreme stress, even fads and fashion can threaten the social structure.

The Value-Added Perspective

According to Neil Smelser, collective episodes of fads and fashion are common instances of the craze, or mobilization for action based on a positive wish-fulfillment belief. Such beliefs embody a greatly inflated view of the craze item's worth and blind people to possible alternative and substitute items in their environment. Crazes can occur in the economic sphere of social life and include speculative booms in securities, land, and commodities as well as "get rich quick" schemes such as chain letters (Sann 1967). In the political sphere, crazes take the form of bandwagons for political candidates and utopian schemes such as the Townsend retirement plan of the 1930s (Sann 1967).

For Smelser, fads and fashion largely operate in the expressive sphere. They are, as Simmel suggests, a means of expressing differential prestige and status. Fads and fashion, and their status-expressive components, enter into all aspects of social life, including clothes, architecture, vehicles, conversation, and the arts. They can even extend into medical treatment (Penrose 1952) and psychotherapy (Rosen 1979).

Fads and fashion are collective episodes caused by the combined effect of a number of societal conditions that Smelser identifies as the value-added components. How these components combine to produce fads and fashion will be the focus of the following discussion.

Structural Conduciveness. The most general necessity for fads and fashion is a differentiated social structure in which people are formally free to openly express their economic and social status. This view runs parallel to Simmel's view of fashion in modern social systems. Even in highly differentiated societies, however, people may not be free to use dress to communicate status. Clothing styles may be set by laws (sumptuary legislation) that prohibit the wearing of certain items or the use of certain products by the "masses." In regimented societies such as the People's Republic of China, dress may be largely restricted to workers' uniforms. Military dress is severely restricted, and to a certain degree, school dress codes may limit the spread of fads and fashion.

Fads and fashion are encouraged in societies with marketing systems that can rapidly disseminate products. Research and development is given high priority in economies in which inventions can be rapidly translated into new consumer items. These social systems can also produce less expensive versions of nearly any product. Fashion behavior may be more structured than fad behavior: in the fashion industry, leadership is fairly well defined, and a responsive marketing system is geared to a seasonal fashion cycle.

Structural Strain.   Structural strain may be a more or less permanent feature in an open and differentiated society, taking the form of an ingrained status consciousness that carries over to such things as clothing, autos, and home furnishings. The rapid availability of cheaper copies, as well as institutionalized fashion cycles in these areas, virtually guarantee that such items will lose their uniqueness and exclusiveness.

Strain is heightened by the uncertainty of when to abandon a particular fashion item. The upper classes desert a fashion as soon as it no longer differentiates them from others who have adopted it. For the less affluent, the fashion item represents a relatively larger investment, and they will endure greater stress before abandoning it. Strain also results from the

uncertainty of which new item will be adopted in the next fashion cycle.

Generalized Belief.   Smelser describes the generalized belief that is part of fads and fashion as a "wish-fulfillment fantasy." Elements of this belief are an implicit part of open and differentiated societies. For example, the get rich quick mentality is an established cultural belief that does not have to be created for every speculative outburst. Likewise, the desire to be "in fashion" is a stable attitude shared by most people. These beliefs need only be excited and sharpened by the presence of other conditions. This underlying state of "psychological readiness" explains why fads and fashion are perhaps the most volatile and frequently observed episodes of collective behavior.

Mobilization for Action.   For Smelser, mobilization for fads and fashion often occurs through preexisting channels. This is most obvious in the case of fashions. Leadership is already established in the form of fashion houses and reputable designers who service a fairly definite and exclusive clientele. In turn, these designers rely on a responsive and widely based system of distribution.

In the case of fads, the media are quick to cover such matters as a source of light filler for the news. Likewise, manufacturers, merchandisers, and retailers are constantly alert for unexpected opportunities to capitalize on collective whims. Beyond this, leadership in fads is largely by example. Public figures can give tremendous impetus to fads.

As a type of hysteria, fad and, to a lesser degree, fashion interaction is characterized by imitation and suggestion. Once leaders have started a fad or fashion, much interaction is among anonymous individuals. Fad and fashion are also characterized by a type of intensity not found in other forms of social behavior. A seemingly irrational and mindless attitude emerges that takes the outward form of abandonment or inattention to other suitable and less expensive alternatives to the current fad or fashion.

Smelser also notes that fads and fashion consist of real and derived phases. For fashion, the real phase consists of the adoption of styles among the upper classes. The derived phase is characterized by a substantial trickle down of the fashion into the lower classes and its abandonment among the upper classes. For fads, the real phase consists of the early adoption of an item, its subsequent labeling as a fad, and the groundswell of adoption that follows immediately thereafter. The derived phase is characterized by innovations on the fad theme and coattail effect such as the indiscriminate use of the Davey Crockett logo.

Actions for Social Control.   Authorities rarely intervene in fads or fashion. Exceptions occur when laws are violated in the course of the collective episode. For example, the Interstate Commerce Commission (ICC) tried to force trucking companies to remove CB radios when drivers used them to evade enforcement of the speed limit (Klein and Luxenburg-Ingle 1980a). The FBI arrested counterfeiters of designer jeans and Cabbage Patch dolls. Local police sometimes made attempts to arrest streakers (Evans and Miller 1975).

Other forms of social control are inherent in fads and fashion. Speculative booms are kept from getting totally out of hand by the inevitable apprehension over grossly inflated prices. Fads decline because of loss of novelty caused by widespread adoption and the exhaustion of opportunities for innovation. Both fads and fashion are held in check by the desertion of leaders. Finally, fashion cycles are regulated by the approach of the new season.

Discussion.   The value-added approach to collective behavior characterizes fads and

fashion as a type of hysterical craze. Smelser restricts fads and fashion to the expressive sphere of social life. Following Simmel, Smelser characterizes them as a means of expressing status and prestige in an open and differentiated society.

Unlike Simmel, Smelser argues that fads and fashion contain elements of hysteria. Fads and, to some degree, fashion are unpredictable in their incidence and content. Both are based on widely held fantasies. Fads and fashion lead people to ignore other immediate opportunities for gratification and gain. Leadership is largely through the mechanism of imitation and interaction among anonymous individuals.

In other respects, the value-added model complements the natural history of fads described earlier. The real phases of mobilization roughly correspond to the latent and break out stages of fad development. The derived phases of mobilization correspond to the peaking stage. Finally, Smelser's comments about the social control of fads and fashion run parallel with descriptions of the decline of fads.

The Emergent Norm Perspective

Turner and Killian (1972) argue that fashion tends to reinforce established status distinctions. Items such as oceangoing yachts, Paris originals, private jets, and Rolls Royces do not trickle down to the less affluent. Less expensive substitutes for these items serve more to mark one as a member of an anxiously aspiring group than to convey higher status. Fads, on the other hand, may establish status and prestige at variance with the conventional scale, because pacesetters of a fad can come from any social stratum. Today's klutz can become tomorrow's champion at skateboarding, dancing, or video games.

Turner and Killian state that most descriptions of fads tend toward overdramatization.

Further, fads are equated more closely with the compact crowd than is justified. In the compact crowd, mood and attention are sustained in part because participants have no chance to relax and survey their own behavior. The fad, however, is sustained with constant interruptions, as people attend to their families, jobs, and community.

Fad involvement can be intermeshed with other activities partly because it does not consist of simple, mindless imitation. Recruitment is not through the interaction of anonymous individuals but through interaction nets that already exist in neighborhoods, schools, and workplaces. These nets account for the selective clustering of fad adoption. Social support found in these nets is essential for maintaining the fad and justifying the behavior of the faddist. Likewise, indifference or opposition to a fad is not treated with much toleration. Fads are accompanied by strong informal pressures to participate and penalties for those who resist. The "selective inattention" that is part of fads is not due to contagion that blinds people to other opportunities for amusement or gain. Instead, it results from the normative constraint that operates in all areas of social life.

Fads are characterized by differential involvement. Some participants are firmly committed and actively involved, while others' involvement is short lived and sporadic. Still others restrict their involvement to spectatorship and kibitzing. Finally, some take a exploitive attitude and attempt to capitalize on fads.

There is a tendency to emphasize the spread of fads among people who are somewhat detached from the stable aspects of society, such as adolescents or those with little education and low incomes. Turner and Killian argue that no abnormal degree of isolation or insecurity is necessary for faddish behavior. People do, however, trivialize the behavior of adolescents and others of low social standing. Thus we often describe clothing styles among teenagers as "fads," while adults adhere to "fashion."

Finally, Turner and Killian suggest that the dynamics of fads also apply to the transmission of important cultural items. They present Penrose's (1952) analysis of the growth and decline of therapies within the practice of medicine. Likewise, the growth of "deviant epidemics" such as anti-Semitism, vandalism, or recreational cocaine use follow many of the same lines as fads. Fads and fashion are one of the ways that social change is brought about.

The SBI Perspective

McPhail has yet to specifically address fads and fashion. Still, many elements of his social behavioral/interactionist (SBI) approach are immediately applicable to issues raised in the previous discussions. Like the emergent norm approach, the SBI approach sets forth a differentiated view of fad behavior. Fads generally involve crowds, from those gathered at a panty raid to shoppers waiting to buy Cabbage Patch Kids, which are preceded by assembling processes. A wide variety of activity occurs in fad crowds, ranging from people stuffing themselves and others into phone booths to idle conversations.

Assembling and Behavior within a Panty Raid Crowd.   Not all fad activity transpires in crowds, but when it does, it is preceded by assembling processes. One of the last and largest panty raids at the University of Iowa occurred in late April of 1967. Earlier in the week a 2:00 A.M. fire alarm had roused about seven hundred male students from their dormitory and sent them into the streets. It was a cold and misty evening, and as the students huddled gloomily, a basketball player shouted "Panty raid! Panty raid!" About fifteen students left the crowd and headed toward the women's dorms. Campus police stopped the small group, however, and ordered them back to the dorm in a threatening and abusive manner. That morning at breakfast, the dining hall was the scene of heated conversations. Students took the earlier actions of the police as a challenge. If they were going to threaten fifteen pajama-clad guys who were clowning around, the students would show them what a *real* panty raid was like on Friday night.

During the next two days, word-of-mouth assembling instructions were augmented by notes and signs on classroom walls and in dormitory hallways. These signs announced the location of a gathering place from which the raid would be launched. They also announced the time at which the gathering would commence, which, incidentally, was about fifteen minutes after the closing of campus-area taverns and the library.

A crowd of five to six hundred formed at the gathering place and then moved toward the women's dormitories. They were stopped by state police at an intersection about three blocks from the dormitories and near the fraternity row. The crowd at the intersection, as well as chants, cheers, shouts, and the flashing lights on police cars created a focal point for further assembling. In about twenty minutes, the crowd had grown to nearly five thousand by drawing members from passersby and residents of fraternities and other off-campus residences. Additionally, "messengers" had left the crowd and returned with people from more distant locations. Finally, the police dropped their barricade, and thousands of people dashed toward the dormitories.

The crowd that milled about the dormitories was not composed exclusively of young college males. Many female students were in the crowd, as were teachers, townspeople, reporters, and police. The crowd seemed composed primarily of small groups of people who arrived together and apparently knew one another, rather than isolated individuals. Chants

of "Pants! Pants! Pants!" applause, and numerous loud cheers were raised as undergarments, sheets, pillowcases, sanitary napkins, and trash were thrown from dormitory windows. Most of the items were caught before they hit the ground.

Police kept people away from dormitory doors and off fire escapes. As groups moved from one dormitory to another, many clusters of people engaged in happy conversations. A large portion of people in the crowd simply stood around and watched the spectacle. After about an hour, the crowd began to thin as contingents returned to the men's dormitories or moved off quietly in other directions. The great panty raid of 1967 was over.

Timing of Fads. The timing of fads is not as random or haphazard as some claim. The SBI perspective suggests that fad activities are interspersed with other activities, including those of family living and work. While fad activities do sometimes disrupt or supplant ordinary routines and schedules, on the whole, they usually mesh rather well with these demands. This is because people typically carry out fad activities with family members, roommates, friends, neighbors, and others they know well and with whom they associate on a day-to-day basis. Further, involvement in fad activities peaks during lunch hours, evenings, weekends, and at other times when people are likely to have free time. Perhaps this is why many conclude that fads leave no trace of their passing.

Many fads occur on college campuses. Paul Sann (1967) describes an admittedly nonrandom sample of these fads. Of the ones that include dates, descriptions indicate that the fads struck in late May and early June. Nearly all of the streaking incidents occurred during the week of Saturday, March 2, to Saturday, March 9, 1974. The panty raid described above occurred on a Friday night in late April.

As one reflective student put it, "These things occur after midterms, when it's too soon to start booking for finals."

Fad Origins.　What about the origins and promotion of fads? The SBI perspective cannot tell us why one item becomes a fad while similar items fail to do so. Of course, other collective behavior perspectives do not tell us this either. The SBI perspective does suggest, however, that fad items are not adopted in a "mindless" way, as is often suggested. In the case of CB radios, hula hoops, pocket calculators, or frisbees, there may be no nonfad item of immediately comparable use that is ignored. Even novelty items are purchased with hard-earned money and then used intensively with family, roommates, friends, and neighbors. Compared to other recreational costs, fad items may be a "good deal" or at least a comparable value. Finally, fad items frequently provide people with happy and long-remembered experiences.

Is it possible to promote any single product and turn it into a fad? The answer appears to be no. Most product fads are aggressively promoted by an organization keyed to quick and flexible market responses. This explains little, however, because many nonfad items are promoted in the same way. Once an organization has inadvertently produced a fad item, it often tries to come up with another and has little success in doing so. Wham-O seems to have the best track record in this regard, having introduced the hula hoop, frisbee, and superball. The ability of Wham-O executives seems to be intuitive: they play-tested the hula hoop on children in their own neighborhood and at cocktail parties—a far cry from anything scientific.

While there seems to be no sure-fire formula for producing fad items, sometimes fads reveal or perhaps create new markets for further exploitation. The CB radio certainly helped to increase the electronic sophistication of the American public. People who couldn't initially fathom the workings of even the most elementary electronic devices were soon able to talk confidently about coaxial cables, band widths, amplitude, the finer points of antenna design, and rules of the Federal Communications Commission (FCC).

Many people went into business for themselves by retailing CB radios. Merchants who had sold nothing more sophisticated than toasters broke into the CB market. Electronic specialty shops such as Radio Shack, Allied Electronics, and Pioneer Electronics enjoyed tremendous growth and became household words during the boom. As CB sales faded, these merchants began to move into other electronic items, such as video recorders and business and home computers.

The Decline of Fads.　It is often argued that fads decline because of "psychological satiation." Fads reach a point of diminishing returns that minimizes the novelty of adoption: people become bored or exhausted, and they regain their senses. Little else seems to explain the decline of activity fads such as panty raids and streaking.

For product fads, however, other explanations are possible. The decline in CB sales, for example, can be explained in terms of an obvious decline in utility. That is, at the peak of the fad, novice users, skippers, and walkovers greatly reduced the usefulness of radios for on-the-road communication. Further, by 1978, sunspot activity had reduced the range and clarity of CB transmissions. Many CB units simply wore out after more than a year of intense use. They were not replaced, in part because people were traveling much less than they were in 1976. Inflation and unemployment also cut deeply into the disposable income of the main cohort of recent CB adopters, middle- and low-income blue-collar workers. Clearly, this explanation does not apply to decline in sales and use of novelty items such as hula hoops or deely boppers.

Summary

Fads and fashion were among the earliest concerns of sociologists. Simmel and Veblen, for example, saw fads and fashion as a way of communicating status within open and differentiated societies. Others, such as Tarde and Park and Burgess, emphasized the seeming contagious and irrational nature of fads and fashion. These later views brought fads and fashion into the field of collective behavior.

The mass hysteria perspective emphasizes the irrational and disruptive aspects of fads and fashion. Klapp, for example, argues that modern fads and fashion work more to destroy status distinctions than to reflect them.

The value-added perspective views fads and fashion as one type of hysterical craze. Fashion represents the most nearly institutionalized form of craze behavior. Fads and fashion arise from stresses in the social system, namely, concerns over the expression of status. Both are based on common cultural fantasies: the hope to get rich quick and the desire to be in fashion. Mobilization during outbreaks of fads and the fashion cycle is largely though imitation and interaction among anonymous individuals. Internal mechanisms of social control keep fads and the fashion cycle in check.

The emergent norm perspective presents a differentiated view of fads and fashion. Fashion functions more to reinforce status distinctions than to allow people to express higher status. Fads allow people to attain a type of status and prestige that is at variance with the conventional scale. The intensity and uniformity of fad behavior are often exaggerated. Differential participation in fads and fashion can range from committed involvement to spectatorship to exploitation. People conform to fads and fashion because of normative constraint rather than contagion and mindless imitation. Fads and fashion can occur in important as well as trivial areas of human endeavor, and they can be an important source of social change.

The SBI perspective also presents a differentiated view of fads and fashion. Fad activity often occurs in crowds, which form through the same assembling processes as do other crowds. Many, if not most, participants in fad crowds are accompanied to the scene by family members, roommates, friends, and neighbors. For those in the crowd, fad-related activity is neither unanimous nor continuous. Participation in fad activity is intermeshed with the demands of routine and previously scheduled activities. Consequently, fad activities peak during lunch hours, in the evening, and on weekends, when people have free time at their disposal. Fads can create and enlarge distribution systems and point out potential new markets. Finally, the decline of fads is due in part to competing demands.

COLLECTIVE BEHAVIOR AND
THREATS TO THE SOCIAL ORDER

CHAPTER 8

Migrations

Human migrations are usually sad. People who leave their native lands have often been uprooted by disaster, famine, poverty, racial or ethnic hatred, and war. People who migrate seldom travel first class. Migrations of thousands of miles have been accomplished on foot. Migrations by sea are usually carried out under miserably crowded, unsanitary, and dangerous conditions. Hunger, disease, and death are usually the migrants' constant companions. In the process of migration, families are separated and broken. The migrants' sense of ethnic identity is challenged. Migrants are often viciously exploited—they are sold shoddy goods and impure foods and are sometimes simply robbed of their meager resources. Those who migrate are seldom welcomed by the receiving country.

In this chapter we begin with a description of two migrations. First, we will consider the migration of the Irish to the United States in the 1840s and 1850s. This was one of Western society's greatest migrations, precipitated by famine and political upheaval. We will then consider the recent migration of Cubans to the United States—the Freedom Flotilla of 1980—which illustrates how migrations acquire political overtones. Next we will briefly consider migrations as mass behavior, and finally we will examine migrations as differentiated phenomena.

The Irish Migration

The migration of the Irish is one of the largest migrations in human history. During its peak years, 1846–1855, more than 2 million people migrated from Ireland and England to the United States and Canada. The deep rooted reasons for this migration are many. People stood in three distinct relationships to the land in Ireland. First, there were the *landlords*, many of them residing in England, who owned 80 percent of Ireland's farmland. Below the landlords were *leaseholders* and *middlemen*, who seldom actually farmed the land but used it as a source of rental income. The *tenants* and *farm laborers*, who paid rents to the leaseholders and middlemen, actually farmed the land.

This system was quite inefficient as far as food production was concerned, but it did serve other purposes. The landlords were free to pursue other interests, such as politics and hunting, while the leaseholders and middlemen were able to obtain a substantial return on their capital by squeezing the tenants and laborers. Finally, the tenants and laborers were able to earn a meager subsistence from the land. Access to a little plot of land and the garden crops it could produce was all that distinguished this group from the paupers who wandered the countryside or sought charity in the cities.

As the middle of the nineteenth century approached, things began to change. For the leaseholders and middlemen, the dawning industrial revolution and expanding trade were beginning to suggest better uses for land and capital. The status of the tenants and laborers became increasingly precarious.

Disaster struck in the spring of 1846, when the potato and most other food crops were destroyed by blight. Starving and unable to pay their rents, thousands of laborers were dispossessed. When the blight reappeared in 1847, the leaseholders and middlemen began to rapidly divest themselves of their properties and seek other investments. Meanwhile, thousands of Irish died of starvation and disease. The British Parliament did little to ease their plight, largely because of the almost universal assumption among Western governments that if you feed starving people, you destroy their character and encourage idleness.

A few positive efforts were made, however. Grain imports were increased, causing a rapid drop in the price of corn. But regardless of how much the price of corn fell, it was still too expensive for the Irish. A program of soup kitchens was started, but this program was weakened by corruption from the beginning and did not provide even minimal nutrition to those who depended on it. Finally, in 1847, in an effort to increase relief funds, Parliament extended England's Poor Laws to include Ireland. Under the Poor Laws, landlords were charged a rate, or tax, based on the number of paupers residing in their county (Smith 1962:36–37). Ironically, this law did much to hasten and enlarge the emigration.

Suddenly faced with the possibility of being taxed according to the number of paupers residing in their county, landlords felt that it would be cheaper to pay passages to the United States and Canada than to pay the rates. To "encourage" tenants and laborers to accept passage, a policy of "shoveling out" and "tumbling

of houses" was undertaken. Landlords hired gangs of toughs to evict tenants and laborers. Families, infants, widows with children, the elderly, and the sick or dying, were thrown from their cottages. Their personal belongings were often destroyed or stolen in the process. Then, amid tears and protests, the cottages were "tumbled," or smashed to the ground. Some gangs boasted of being able to tumble sixteen cottages in a day. Some tenants built *scalpeens*, or temporary shelters, from the wreckage of their cottages. A few landlords did not use such brutal tactics, instead offering their tenants passage and traveling expenses if they would agree to leave. Whether tenants agreed to leave or were shoveled out, passage to the United States and Canada seemed a better alternative than the disease-ridden workhouses.

Most emigrants probably never realized that the landlords had no legal basis for compelling them to leave Ireland. This private program of deportation was a major factor in the early stages of the Irish migration. Some landlords deported as many as two thousand people. When large numbers of tenants were leaving, landlords chartered ships rather than buying passages. After leaving their former tenants in Quebec, Halifax, New York, or Boston, landlords loaded their ships with cargo for the return voyage to England, allowing them to offset some of the charter costs. Parliament took little notice of this private deportation program. In one instance, a landlord eloquently defended his actions to Parliament by noting that his former tenants would prosper in the United States and Canada and would therefore buy more British goods than if they had remained in Ireland. Perhaps he was correct.

After 1850, private deportations declined in importance as word came back from the United States and Canada from those who had emigrated earlier. Brothers, sisters, sons, daughters, cousins, and husbands wrote frequent letters to their families describing life in the new lands (Schrier 1958:18–42). More important, they sent money and tickets to their families. More than $3 million was sent back to Ireland between 1847 and 1856 (Coleman 1972:204).

The Irish migration was not typical of most migrations because about equal numbers of men and women emigrated. Initially, larger numbers of men were emigrating, but the number of women and children among the emigrants began to increase rapidly after 1850. Then, single women began to emigrate in appreciable numbers, as demand for Irish maids began to grow among affluent families in the United States.

The emigrants left from the ports of Belfast and Liverpool. Here, they were preyed upon by "runners" who stole the baggage of those waiting to board ships. An emigrant's baggage sometimes contained all his or her worldly possessions, and its loss could mean tragedy. Runners also separated emigrants from their money by selling them conterfeit ship tickets and worthless medicines to prevent everything from seasickness to cholera. They referred emigrants to dishonest merchants and boardinghouse operators. The crimes of the runners became so outrageous that Parliament instituted several investigations and, at one time, even considered establishing a government-run emigration facililty.

More than 90 percent of the emigrants traveled steerage class. We discuss these accommodations later in this chapter; here it is sufficient to note that steerage conditions were dangerous. There were Passenger Laws designed to protect emigrants somewhat from the avarice and blatant disregard for life and limb shown by booking agents, captains, and crews. However, it was virtually impossible to enforce most of these laws, even if funds had been made available to do so. One law, for example, forbade swearing by the passengers in order

that a wholesome atmosphere be maintained aboard ship.

Emigrants Become Immigrants

Irish immigrants arrived primarily at the Ports of Quebec, Halifax, Boston, and New York. Immigrants had to wait aboard ship, sometimes for almost a week, until Immigration Authority doctors examined them. If typhus or cholera were found, the ship would be immediately quarantined for one month. The ill among the immigrants were sent to military hospitals such as Wards Island in New York Harbor. In these facilities whole families perished. The quarantine procedures were only partially effective. Runners, even more predatory than those of Belfast and Liverpool, boarded and departed from waiting ships at will. The bedding and clothing that had been soiled during passage, and other possibly infected refuse, were thrown overboard before doctors arrived, washing ashore within hours. Sometimes, to speed Immigration Authority clearance, the ill would be smuggled off before the doctors arrived. Captains and crew were unlikely to report suspected typhus or cholera deaths in order to avoid being held in quarantine. Consequently, Quebec, Halifax, Boston, and New York were swept by outbreaks of typhus and cholera in 1847, 1849, and 1852.

The Irish appeared an unsavory lot when they climbed upon the docks of New York and Boston. Malnutrition, near starvation, and the six to fourteen weeks spent in the crowded filth of steerage had all taken their toll. Additionally, about one third of the immigrants were illiterate (Schrier 1958:20). The most common fear expressed in Boston and New York was that these immigrants would soon become paupers. While a surprisingly small proportion of these immigrants became indigent, still, within a short time the majority of those receiving public assistance in New York and Massachusetts were Irish immigrants.

Boston, being smaller than New York, was particularly hard pressed by the arrival of the Irish, some of whom were coming by foot and rail from Canada and Nova Scotia. Bitter concern was expressed that Britain was turning the United States into another Botany Bay by sending convicts among the emigrants. In an effort to deter immigration and to fund relief efforts, Boston and New York imposed $2.00 and $1.50 head taxes, respectively. In addition to the head tax paid by each immigrant, bonds were demanded for aged, injured, ill, or any other immigrant that authorities thought might become a pauper. Obviously, this left a great deal to the discretion of the authorities.

The Supreme Court decided against head taxes in 1849 and pauper bonds in 1875. Both the tax and bond were viewed as unconstitutional restraints on commerce (Coleman 1972:231–235). In 1847 citizens petitioned the Massachusetts Legislature to spend less money on immigrants. By 1854 the Know-Nothing party had made Irish immigration a national political issue. Local Know-Nothing leaders provoked attacks on Irish laborers and Catholic churches. But the party, which disseminated anti-Irish and anti-Catholic literature from 1850 to 1856, collapsed in 1856 after it was soundly defeated by the new Republican Party.

Anti-Irish and anti-Catholic sentiment ran deep but was diffused in part by the growing national division over slavery. The sons of these immigrants would fight and die in the American Civil War. After the war, those arriving from Ireland would be joined by emancipated blacks, Scandinavians, and Chinese. Together, these immigrants would build a railroad across a continent.

The Freedom Flotilla

During 1979, about one hundred thousand Cuban Americans visited their homeland. For most, it was a chance to renew family ties. For some, it was also a chance to show off the prosperity they had attained in the United States. The designer jeans, pretty dresses, digital wristwatches, and cameras drove home to many Cubans that their economy was still unable to provide, even in short supply, goods that were readily available in most American shopping centers. This glimpse of prosperity came at a time of high unemployment for the Cuban people. Blight had ruined the sugar and tobacco crops, and most sugar mills and cigar factories were closed until the next harvest.

In the early months of 1980, small groups of Cubans began "fence hopping"—entering the Peruvian and Venezuelan embassies to seek political asylum. Most of these people stated they wished to leave Cuba to join families in the United States. Stories of these incidents appeared occasionally in the U.S. press as interesting little vignettes that illustrated the discontent of Cubans with their political system. Finally, on Easter weekend of 1980, a group of Cubans entered the Peruvian Embassy to request political asylum. Cuban officials attempted to remove these people and, failing to do so, issued a public statement that any other Cubans who were unwilling to work and live within the socialist system could join those at the embassy and leave Cuba. Within forty-eight hours, about fifteen hundred people had converged on the Peruvian Embassy. By midweek, this number had grown to more than five thousand persons. This number of people so overloaded the Peruvian Embassy that it soon represented a health and safety hazard. By the end of the week, arrangements had been made for the transfer of these people to Havana Airport for flight to Costa Rica, France, Venezuela, West Germany, and Peru. The United States reluctantly agreed to accept thirty-five hundred of the Cubans.

By now, the Peruvian Embassy had become a focal point for large, daily, antidefector demonstrations. Those leaving were being characterized as selfish people who were selling themselves for a pair of designer jeans. President Castro publicly described the emigrants as "delinquents, antisocial elements, bums, parasites, homosexuals, gamblers, and drug addicts." He cautioned the governments admitting these Cubans that they were opening their doors to a flood of people that would be hell for them. Despite such denunciations, Cuban officials attempted to provide the emigrants with safe passage to the airport. Still, those leaving were harassed and attacked along the way. At least a thousand emigrants remained in the Peruvian Embassy during the last week of April.

The focus and character of this unfolding event changed considerably when Cuban officials ran newspaper notices stating that anyone who had relatives willing to pick them up could leave Cuba. The place of departure was Mariel Harbor Naval Base, thirty miles west of Havana. Telephone lines were flooded as Cubans tried to reach relatives in the United States. As soon as the news of Mariel Harbor spread through Miami, anti-Castro groups began to organize the Freedom Flotilla. Dozens of Cuban-American work boats and yachts departed on the two-hundred-mile voyage to pick up relatives. Within days, these boats were joined by hundreds of others, including those who were charging up to $1,500 per relative brought from Cuba.

Mariel Harbor became heavily congested, and the Cuban Navy had to oversee harbor traffic and the loading of emigrants. This was interpreted as harassment by those returning from Cuba. Initially, boats were picking up the relatives of Cuban Americans who chartered them. As the numbers of Cubans converging on the harbor increased, officials began to demand that returning boats be fully loaded with emigrants. Consequently, many people were disappointed that after chartering a boat to Cuba, they had to return with a boatload of strangers, sometimes without the family members they had set out to find.

The first Cubans to arrive were given sixty-days parole visas and, if needed, room and board. This procedure soon became impractical as thousands more Cubans arrived. A receiving area was established at Miami's Tamiami Park, where Cubans were screened by FBI and immigration officials. It was soon apparent that about half of those arriving had no relatives in the United States. Private relief agencies began to mobilize sponsorship drives for these people. Still, the processing of refugees was so slow that the population of the receiving camp climbed steadily. By May 20, more than thirty thousand Cubans had arrived by boat, and additional refugee camps were set up at Key West, Florida, and Fort Chaffee, Arkansas.

The United States had initially agreed to accept thirty-five hundred refugees, but by the end of May, more than sixty thousand Cubans had entered the country. Newspapers predicted that another two hundred thousand refugees would be arriving. Increasingly frequent complaints were being expressed that a large portion of the refugees were "common criminals." Cubans released from the reception centers were given food stamps, housing, and, often, jobs in restaurants and hotels. Black leaders in Miami began to complain that it was easier for a Cuban refugee to get food stamps and a job than it was for most American citizens. Even the Ku Klux Klan started to hold anti-Cuban rallies.

In mid-May, U.S. officials began seizing boats in Miami Harbor in an effort to reduce the number of arrivals. This was met with bitter protest from boat owners and parts of the Cuban-American community. Countercomplaints were voiced that the refugee situation was having a negative impact on the South Florida tourist trade: people did not wish to vacation amid such turmoil. The number of sponsorships by relief organizations were beginning to decline. For many Americans, the height of ingratitude seemed to have been reached when about one thousand of the seventeen thousand Cuban refugees at Fort Chaffee rioted. The Cubans complained about being detained with violent criminals, poor treatment by authorities, and the living conditions at the camp. By early June, the U.S. Coast Guard imposed a full blockade against the Freedom Flotilla, greatly slowing the arrival of refugees. Since Easter, at least one hundred thousand refugees had arrived.

The aftermath of the Freedom Flotilla has been bittersweet. Obviously, thousands of people benefited materially by coming to the United States. However, in early June of 1980, Miami was shocked by three days of rioting, chiefly by blacks. More than thirty people died, and about $90 million of property damage was sustained. Afterward, black leaders complained of the seemingly preferential treatment given the Cubans by state and voluntary welfare organizations. It was also noted that during the height of the Freedom Flotilla, boatloads of Haitians were being detained and even turned away from our shores. The economic and political conditions in Haiti are even more severe than in Cuba; however, all the Haitian refugees were black.

It now seems likely that Cuban officials allowed and probably encouraged an appreciable number of habitual criminals and derelicts to depart from Mariel Harbor. Sporadic outbursts occurred at Fort Chaffee, where more than a thousand "unplaceables" were detained until 1982. Finally, hundreds of refugees requested to be returned to Cuba, and at least one airliner was hijacked to Havana by refugees.

Similarities in the Irish and Cuban Migrations

The Irish migration during the Great Famine and the Cuban migration during the Freedom Flotilla occurred more than a century apart. Yet there are similarities in the two migrations. Both were carried out by people facing stark economic conditions who had been given a glimpse of substantially better conditions elsewhere. Further, neither group was fully welcome in their homeland. Both migrations illustrate the importance of family ties. Both groups were exploited during their departure and journey to the new land. The Irish were exploited for what little wealth they carried with them; the Cubans, for propaganda purposes in the game of international politics.

Neither group was fully welcome in the land of their choosing, and they were viewed as potential burdens on the welfare services of the United States. The arrival of both groups precipitated civil disorders. Both groups were feared to contain common criminals, and both groups did. In each instance, however, the general public overlooked the fact that the offspring of common criminals become some of our more substantial citizens and, sometimes, noteworthy politicians. Finally, in both instances, a small number of those who emigrated soon decided to return to their homelands. The two or three thousand Irish per year who chose to return were relatively free to do so. The Cubans who wish to return, however, are hindered in their efforts by the modern intricacies of foreign relations and extensive bureaucracies.

Migrations as Mass Behavior

Blumer identifies migrations as one of several kinds of *mass behavior*, which he characterizes as the behavior of groups composed of anonymous individuals responding in parallel fashion to a common event or idea (1939:78). Within the mass there is little if any communication, coordination, or control. There may be a sense of pursuing a common goal, but instead of generating a sense of cooperation in the mass, a sense of competition arises. The mass behaves in terms of anonymous individuals working to answer their own needs. The form of mass behavior is determined by individual lines of activity rather than by concerted action.

Turner and Killian's brief discussion of migrations proceeds much along the lines set forth by Blumer. Turner and Killian discuss migrations as part of the *diffuse crowd*, which also includes such phenomena as fads, crazes, and deviant epidemics (1972:111–141). They characterize migrations as involving "a certain amount of social contagion and we feeling, even though in the final analysis, the activity remains primarily individualistic" (1972:136).

Most collective behavior discussions, then, characterize migrations as homogeneous and individualistic in nature. From this standpoint, migrations are motivated by people's overblown, hysterical images of a "promised land" where they will find unlimited opportunity or at least shelter from their current misfortunes. There is minimal cooperation, and much competition, among migrating people, caused either by the excitement of reaching the promised land or by the desire to get there before others.

Perhaps it might be fruitful to analyze some migrations from the standpoint of mass behavior. The 1849 gold rush to California may have involved unrealistic views of attaining wealth and may have been characterized by individualistic competition. We could consider the drift of U.S. population to the Sun Belt states in terms of individual or family decisions made with respect to such things as rising energy costs in the northern states and increased job opportunities in the South. These migrations, however, are not typical of most human migrations.

Migrations as Differentiated Phenomena

Migrations are complex and differentiated phenomena. This characterization is funda-

mentally the opposite of the mass behavior characterization. Migrations arise from multiple rather than single causes, and they involve concerted behavior rather than homogeneous, individualistic action. Migrations involve various expressed motives from numbers of sources rather than a single, compelling vision of the promised land. Migrations involve *dispersal processes* and *collective locomotion*, which we discussed in Chapter 2.

Migrations can be seen as taking place along a continuum. At one end of the continuum are groups who set out proudly and with great fanfare to go to a new land of opportunity. Examples of this extreme form of migration are hard to find, although this may not be too inaccurate a characterization of some wagon train departures from St. Joseph, Missouri, heading West in the 1840s and 1850s. At the other end of this continuum are migrations that are aptly described as a *forced dispersal* of people with little regard for their welfare or ultimate destination. An example of this extreme form of migration, perhaps, was Pol Pot's Khmer Rouge forced dispersal of the urban populations in Kampuchea (Cambodia), in 1975. Most human migrations fall between these two extremes.

Dispersal Processes: Mobilization and Departure

In Chapter 9 we noted that flight from a disaster area is an infrequent occurrence. Authorities who attempt to evacuate people from threatened or dangerous areas often encounter resistance. Following even partial evacuations, people usually attempt to return to their communities before it is entirely safe to do so. In short, it is usually difficult to get people to leave their homes and community for even short periods of time.

Given the normal tendency for people to remain in their home community, even under extremely adverse conditions, what gives rise to migrations? If we can make any generalization, it is that many migrations have been preceded by the sudden appearance of circumstances that, for all practical purposes, make it impossible for people to continue their traditional or accustomed way of life. It is obvious that human beings are extremely adaptable to changing circumstances. But if the change is sudden, stark, and far reaching, the capacity to adapt can be exceeded.

Many human migrations have followed disasters of such magnitude that large areas were rendered virtually uninhabitable by the survivors. The only natural forces seemingly able to produce disasters of such scope are disease and climatic shifts; the only manmade force is war. The migration of the Irish to the United States was precipitated by a disastrous potato blight that for three consecutive years, 1846–1849, totally devastated Ireland's food production. For the past twenty years, areas of eastern Africa have been swept by a deepening drought. The desert is rapidly destroying areas that for thousands of years produced crops, provided grazing land for cattle, goats, and sheep, and supported large populations. The migration of starving people to the refugee camps of Somalia are the result (Kohl 1981:756–775).

The impact of such disasters is increased by the failure of governments to make concerted efforts to alleviate the plight of those affected. In Ireland, for example, the colonial government and Parliament made no provision, aside from the workhouses, for the tenant farmers and farm laborers who were the first affected by the famine. In eastern Africa, the countries of Ethiopia, Kenya, and Somalia continue to devote substantial portions of their national resources to fighting border wars, while drought refugees swell the refugee centers in Somalia to a combined population of more than 2 million. The occupants of these camps are mainly women, children, and old men. Young men have joined or have been forced to join the armies of Kenya, Ethiopia, and Soma-

lia, or they have migrated farther north, seeking work in the Arabian Peninsula oil fields. Kenya and Ethiopia view international relief efforts as "indirect military aid," relieving Somalian men of their familial obligations so that they can go fight (Kohl 1981:761). Migrants often face desperate situations in terms of securing their livelihood, when governments are unwilling or unable to help them.

Authorities Initiate Migrations.   In some instances, authorities may be hostile rather than simply indifferent to the migrants. Landlords tumbled cottages to "encourage" dispossessed tenants to accept passage out of Ireland. The armies of Somalia, Kenya, and Ethiopia steal the sheep, goats, and cattle of Somalian migrants. Finally, some migrations result from open attacks on minorities by majority religious, political, or ethnic groups.

The practice of driving out the unwanted provides some of the grimmest historical examples of "righteous" brutality. If the victims survive the initial attacks, numbers of them migrate to different areas. Thus millions of people who were identified with the United States during the Vietnam War have been driven out of Laos and Kampuchea and into refugee camps in Thailand. Likewise, almost a half a million people left the southern part of Vietnam after the war, migrating by boat to Hong Kong and Malaysia. Some of these "boat people" eventually found their way to Europe and the United States.

The migrations considered in the above examples are the result of authorities encouraging the migration of undesirables or using violence in an attempt to expel them. Sometimes authorities are attempting not to expel a group but to enslave or exterminate them. In these instances, groups migrate in spite of the efforts of authorities. Perhaps the clearest example of this type of migration was people's escape from Nazi-controlled areas of Europe between the years 1936 and 1945. Hundreds of thousands of Jews, Catholics, and other Eastern European groups escaped through the underground. Those migrating needed fake passports, travel permits, and places to hide, eat, and rest, as well as transportation. Groups such as the Society of Friends, also known as the Quakers, have a long history of providing such things out of humanitarian concern. Other groups have provided these services at high cost.

Migrations Initiated in Other Ways. Certain migrations are initiated out of despair and hunger. Daily, hundreds of emaciated and starving people come out of the desert areas of Kenya, Ethiopia, and Somalia, or the jungles of Laos and Kampuchea, and arrive at refugee camps. People are starving in areas that once exported food or at least provided an adequate livelihood. Today, because of war and fractured social structures, food production is one tenth of what it was formerly. Large populations have simply been cast adrift to fend for themselves.

Clearly, not all migrations involve the breakdown of social structures or harassment by authorities. Some groups initiate migration on the basis of requests and other information from those outside their country. Countries with a high demand for labor may advertise abroad for workers to fill these jobs. Even after the worst of the Irish famine years, wealthy American families continued to advertise and pay passage for Irish women to serve as maids. West Germany utilizes temporary workers imported from other countries to regulate the nation's labor supply, and Arabian oil fields employ workers from all over the world. Initially, many of these work agreements are viewed as temporary, both by the host country and by the migrant groups. The host country plans to send the migrants back once they are no longer needed; the migrants plan to return to their homes and families once they have earned a considerable amount of money. Often, this is just what happens; occasionally, however, migrants establish social ties and remain in the host country.

Collective Locomotion: The Journey

The mass behavior conception of migration emphasizes the contagion and excitement among migrating people as they individualistically strive to reach their destination. Turner and Killian point out that aroused emotion is not sufficient to sustain a social movement (1972:247–250). Rather, organizational structure and a program of action are necessary to sustain a social movement. In like manner, it seems clear that excitement is not sufficient to sustain a migration. Once a migration is underway, excitement quickly gives way to weariness and thoughts of decent meals and soft beds (cf. Walker 1966). Any additional excitement that occurs en route is usually caused by fear for one's survival. As with social movements, a degree of social structure and cooperation is needed to sustain a migration.

The Flight of the Nez Percé. On June 17, 1877, Companies F and H of the United States First Calvary attempted to force a group of 650–750 Nez Percé Indians onto Idaho's Fort Lawpi Indian Reservation. The battle of White Bird Canyon that followed was a culmination of this and earlier disputes. Thirty-four soldiers were killed and seven wounded. Only two warriors were wounded, and no Nez Percé were taken to the reservation.

Following the battle, the group decided to make a break for the Canadian border in the hope of obtaining sanctuary. The band was led by several chiefs, including Joseph, Looking Glass, and Yellow Wolf. For the next eleven weeks, this band of warriors, women, children, and elderly were pursued by at least ten separate U.S. Army units of infantry, cavalry, and artillery.

Their flight took them across some of the most rugged terrain in North America. The Nez Percé fled southward, down the Bitterroot Mountain Range between Idaho and Montana, then bore eastward into Wyoming and through what is now Yellowstone National Park. Then they headed northward through the mountains of central Montana. When they were within sixty miles of the Canadian border, they were overtaken in the Bear Paw Mountains. Here, the Nez Percé held off a cavalry and artillery siege for three days in freezing rain and snow.

Finally, the main body of Nez Percé, led by Chief Joseph, surrendered. Chief Looking Glass had died in the siege, and Chief Yellow Wolf and a few dozen Nez Percé who had been separated from the main group escaped into Canada. Altogether, 418 Nez Percé surrendered, including 147 children, 65 elderly, and more than 40 wounded. In the eleven weeks since they left White Bird Canyon, this group had traveled a bit more than seventeen hundred miles (Beal 1963).

Throughout this ordeal, the Nez Percé social structure and discipline endured. This was a major reason that they were able to successfully evade the U.S. Cavalry for so long. Chiefs Joseph, Looking Glass, and Yellow Wolf maintained their authority and acted as chief strategists, frequently seeking advice from other chiefs and subchiefs in the group.

The Nez Percé engaged the U.S. Cavalry eleven times in addition to the battles at White Bird Canyon and the Bear Paws. The warriors' success in these battles was due to their coordinated offensive and defensive maneuvering. Effective in their own right, the warriors' tactics were additionally confusing to the soldiers because the Nez Percé were not "fighting like Indians." Finally, a factor in their evading the U.S. Cavalry was the Indians' ability to set up and strike camp quickly and to gather food on the move. This was quite an accomplishment for a group that was not traditionally nomadic.

Most of the responsibilities in this area were assumed by the women, children, and elderly (Beal 1963).

Steerage. The transportation of migrants is usually quite lucrative, as exemplified by the steerage accommodations aboard ships. During the age of the great ocean liners (1850–1950), first- and second-class passengers were referred to as ladies and gentlemen, while third-class, or steerage, passengers were referred to as males and females. Until the 1920s, virtually all steerage passengers from Europe to the United States were emigrants, in part because steerage passage cost a small fraction of what other accommodations cost. Nonetheless, steerage fares represented one third of the shipping company revenues and more than half their profits during the age of the great liners (Maddocks 1978:58).

Between 1850 and 1920, more than 30 million people had crossed in steerage, mostly under wretched conditions. There were usually only two toilets for the entire steerage sections, and the canvas bunks were only eighteen inches wide and frequently four tiered. Agents often overbooked steerage, adding to the crowding. Such close confinement contributed to the filth and stench as well as to the spread of disease. Death rates ran as high as 10 percent on some voyages.

Steerage passengers were kept strictly apart from the other passengers: they were boarded and departed from separate gangways. If any above-deck areas were made available, these were the small freight-handling decks. First- and second-class passengers enjoying their fine meals, entertainment, and recreation facilities were often quite unaware of the disease, filth, and misery on the decks below them. At the end of the voyage, steerage passengers were required to scrub and dry the steerage areas before leaving ship.

These distinctions were maintained under all conditions, including disasters at sea. During the sinking of the *Titanic*, on April 15, 1912, armed crewmen guarded the passages leading up from steerage decks and only opened them after most of the lifeboats were away. The old nautical rule of "women and children first" was replaced with "steerage last." In all, 1,503 men, women, and children died in the sinking of the *Titanic*. Twelve percent of the women and only 1 child in first and second class died, 40 percent of the women and 53 of the 76 children in steerage died. The survival rate of men in first class was greater than that of children in steerage (Broom & Selznik 1968:175). The heavy death toll among steerage passengers in the *Titanic* disaster was not atypical. Emigrant ship passengers make up the bulk of those lost at sea throughout maritime history.

Exploitation of Migrants. Those who exploit migrants are not just the petty criminals, typified by the runners who preyed on Irish immigrants. Such exploitation can become virtually institutionalized as established groups profit from the migrants' plight, and if laws are broken in the process, the legal restitution to migrants is slow in coming. In 1834 Alabama speculators were paying Creek landowners about ten cents on the dollar for their estates. As the Creek people were to be removed by the U.S. Army to the Oklahoma Indian Territory, it was a buyers' market. Speculators urged the Creeks to sell quickly before the artificially depressed prices went even lower. The federal government largely ignored this early white-collar thievery (Jahoda 1975:143–159).

In 1837 the Chickasaw people were being removed from Mississippi to the Oklahoma Indian Territory. For this unwanted action, the Chickasaws were obliged to reimburse the United States government for the expenses of transporting them westward. Rations were to be provided by private contractors. Altogether, the Chickasaws paid about $200,000 for spoiled pork, flour, and corn, and were billed

another $700,000 for rations they did not receive. It took the Chickasaw people fifty years to obtain settlement from the government for the food not delivered, spoiled food, and baggage lost during their removal (Jahoda 1975:172).

Migrations: Arrival

For many migrants today, the end of a difficult journey is often an indefinite stay in a refugee camp. Cubans from the Freedom Flotilla were detained at Fort Chaffee, Arkansas, for nearly three years. Some refugees were intimidated and attacked by the violent among them. Although all but a handful of the refugees eventually found sponsors, it was a long and emotionally draining wait. Even today, a few of these Cubans live in a bureaucratic limbo, their legal status uncertain.

While the accommodations at Fort Chaffee are austere, some refugee camps are little more than "dying grounds." Medical authorities question whether refugees in the camps of Thailand and Somalia receive enough food to sustain life over an extended period of time. Few of those who arrive ill or in the advanced stages of starvation can be saved. Population densities have exceeded fifteen hundred people per acre in these camps, overburdening the water and sewage facilities. Tuberculosis, measles, dysentery, malaria, and even leprosy are in evidence in these camps. Humans are living on the edge of survival. If the food and water trucks are delayed even hours, the death rates rise dreadfully. Little is known about the social organization of these refugee camps. They are administered and tended jointly by the United Nations Commission for Refugees, various private relief organizations, and the governments of the countries within which they are located. Among the refugees themselves, fundamental social units such as the family and even the village seem to endure.

At the other end of the continuum are immigrant communities within host countries. In American cities there are neighborhoods named Germantown, Poletown, Little Italy, El Barrio, or Chinatown. Within these communities native languages are spoken, native newspapers published, traditional foods served, and other native customs and social relationships are maintained. These communities provide recent and many not so recent immigrants with employment, information, companionship, and a place to either find relief from the pressures of assimilation or avoid assimilation altogether. Within these communities, immigrant organizations such as the Puerto Rican Young Lords party or the Chinese *tongs* provide everything from political voice to illegal goods and services. In many respects, immigrant communities are more cohesive and complex in their social organization than the larger communities surrounding them (Schaefer 1979:289–328). Immigrant communities are clearly not distinguished by a sense of individualistic competition, which is part of the mass behavior characterization of migrations.

Summary

This chapter began with descriptions of two migrations: the Irish migration to the United States in the 1840s and the Freedom Flotilla migration of Cubans to the United States in the spring of 1980. Although these two events are separated by over a century, they are similar in several ways: both groups left countries with economies and governments that were under severe strain from agricultural failures. Those who left were not fully welcome in their own country. Both endured great hardship during their travel and encountered resistance upon their arrival in the United States.

There are perhaps fifty million people living in refugee camps throughout the world today. They are migrants who have fled from drought, war, and religious and racial hatred. It is this kind of migration that is of interest to those who study collective behavior.

Historically, though, the collective behavior literature has had a great deal to say about riots, rebellions, and revolutions but relatively little to say about the migrations that often accompany them. Blumer and Turner and Killian discuss migrations from the standpoint of mass behavior and the diffuse crowd. From this point of view, migrations are similar to fads and crazes; that is, they involve aroused emotions, social contagion, and are homogeneous and individualistic phenomena.

In this chapter we develop an alternate point of view. Migrations are complex and differentiated phenomena, involving processes of dispersal and collective locomotion. We have briefly considered the social conditions and the actions of authorities and the migrants themselves that are necessary for initiating dispersal. Collective locomotion, or the actual journey, involves varying degrees of social organization. Part of the character of migrants' journey results from the vulnerability of migrants to exploitation by established groups. Migrants today live under a wide range of conditions, from the disease-ridden refugee camps in Thailand and Somalia to largely self-contained immigrant communities within many cities in the United States.

CHAPTER 9

Individuals in Disaster

The agents of disaster include fires and explosions, floods, tornadoes, hurricanes, and earthquakes, as well as airplane crashes, train wrecks, and the sinking of ships. Disasters often strike without warning, and when they do, people face unexpected and unfamiliar problems that demand direct and prompt action. There is the obvious problem of sheer survival at the moment when disaster strikes. During impact, individuals must confront and cope with their fear while at the same time looking to their own and others' safety. After disaster impact, people encounter numerous problems demanding life-and-death decisions as they carry out rescues and aid the injured. During disasters people must make do with what is at hand: people with needed information are missing; utilities have been knocked out; shelter is in short supply; and transportation systems are in shambles. *Improvising* is the key activity in disaster response. In this chapter we will examine how individuals improvise to cope with the many problems that are created by disasters.

Of course, a range of other problems accompanies disasters. These are the problems confronted by organizations, communities, and societies. Police and fire departments, for example, are usually the first organizations to respond to disaster, undergoing important transformations as they do. Communities are also transformed by disaster. In particular, communities are greatly altered as outside agencies and organizations arrive to provide assistance. Finally, some societies are better able than others to channel resources to disaster-struck regions. We will consider these problems in Chapter 10.

Two Disasters

In this chapter we focus on individuals in disaster, beginning with the description of two disasters that affected people who were brought together by circumstances. The first is the multifatality evacuation of Gulliver's Discothèque in Port Chester, New York. This event is typical of *stampede panics*—part of the popular imagery often used to describe fatal theater, nightclub, and hotel fires. The second disaster is an airliner crash in the Florida Everglades in which seventy-three survivors—passengers and flight attendants—looked after themselves until help arrived almost an hour after the crash. In both disasters, the group was composed of couples, small groups of friends, work associates, and unattached individuals. These groups did not constitute organizations or communities in the conventional sense; yet, faced with disaster and the problem of survival, these groups acted with a marked degree of cohesiveness.

Fire and Multifatality Evacuation

Gulliver's Discothèque in Port Chester, New York, was a popular establishment that catered largely to a young adult clientele. Patrons entered Gulliver's on the ground floor, which contained a bar, dining area, and an enclosed kitchen. Just inside the main doors was a narrow flight of stairs that descended into another bar and a dance floor known as the Pit. The split-level layout seemed to add character to the establishment.

A few minutes past midnight on July 1, 1974, more than three hundred people were packed into Gulliver's. The band finished their last set at about 12:50 A.M., when the club manager told the band to ask everyone to leave because a fire had broken out in the building adjoining Gulliver's. The low-key announcement urged everyone to remain calm and leave carefully. Some patrons began to leave the Pit and other areas of Gulliver's and went outside to watch the fire next door. The smell of smoke began to spread throughout Gulliver's, and increasing numbers of people began to leave in an orderly manner. Suggestions were made that people remove their high-platform shoes to avoid ankle injuries on the stairs. Regular patrons began to move toward less direct exits through the basement, guiding others who were unfamiliar with the layout of the building. A majority of those in the Pit, however, remained and continued their conversations and drinking.

Ten minutes later, at least one hundred people remained in Gulliver's, and the band again announced that everyone should leave. Then, dense black smoke erupted from the ceiling and fire exploded across the dance floor and bandstand. Large air-conditioning units tore away from the ceiling and crashed into the crowd below. Orderly dispersal became impossible. Blinded and choking patrons exiting up the stairs began to collide with people leaving the ground floor. Others stumbled and fell on the stairs. People who were moving to the basement or dining room exits became disoriented in the noise and smoke. Unsure of the location and condition of exits, two couples dropped to the dance floor and covered their heads with jackets.

The local volunteer fire department received the call at 1:07 A.M. and responded quickly. When the first units arrived, flames had already broken through the roof of Gulliver's, and most who were to survive had already made their way to safety. Firemen entered the building and rescued a few semiconscious people, including the two couples on the dance floor. The next day, headlines across the nation described terror-stricken crowds and panic stampedes for the exits. In all, twenty-six young people died.

Air Crash: Response of Survivors

Eastern Airlines flight 401, from New York, crashed into the Florida Everglades twenty miles west of Miami International Airport at 11:42 P.M. on December 29, 1972. The jetliner, a Lockheed Tristar, carried 176 passengers and crew and hit the swamp at more than two hundred miles per hour, totally disintegrating as it cartwheeled for almost two thousand feet. Nearly all of the passenger seats ripped loose and, with their occupants, were scattered in a path six hundred feet long. Later, investigators classified the crash as nonsurvivable, yet seventy-three people did survive.

The impact of the crash was sufficient to rip people's clothing from their bodies. Moments after the crash, conscious survivors found themselves injured, completely or nearly naked, wet, cold, and surrounded by darkness and devastation. There was no moonlight and the temperature was in the mid-forties. Deep saw grass, mud, and sharp shredded aluminum made walking difficult and dangerous. It would be almost thirty minutes before the first rescuer located the crash site and an hour before the first survivors would be removed to hospitals.

Survivors reported two major concerns as they waited for help. Their first concern was to give aid and comfort to those near them. One flight attendant began to gather survivors near a prominent chunk of wreckage. She reminded people not to light matches or cigarette lighters in spite of the cold and darkness, then located cushions and placed them to warm and protect the severely injured. In an effort to distract people from their injuries, she led them in singing Christmas carols. Unable to walk because of her severe internal injuries, another attendant took the job of holding and comforting an infant.

The second concern among the survivors was freeing those trapped in the wreckage and locating specific individuals. A New York clothes buyer who had survived uninjured freed two flight attendants trapped in their seats. Then he went through the wreckage and collected cushions and loose clothing and distributed them to the injured. Another passenger who had suffered only a leg wound searched for her husband until she found him alive but trapped in the wreckage. For the next hour she comforted and protected her husband, found clothing and cushions for the injured, and gave directions to the rescuers. At one point she refused to be evacuated and protested loudly that her husband was still trapped. Not until her husband was on his way to the hospital did she agree to be evacuated.

Prominent among the most active survivors were the flight attendants. They gave aid and comfort to the injured and dying, often while they themselves were in great pain. They helped in the early stages of rescue. After receiving treatment in the hospital, some helped console the families of victims. They considered themselves valuable employees of Eastern Airlines, doing a job they had been trained to do, as best they could.

Discussion

These two examples portray the impact of disasters at the interpersonal level of social integration. The evacuation of Gulliver's illustrates people's adaptive responses to a real and immediate threat under rapidly deteriorating conditions. Quite often, the breakdown or failure of adaptive responses is explained in terms of psychological panic. The crash of flight 401 shows the altruistic responses of survivors following a disaster. It is often assumed that survivors suffer from shock following disasters and are unable to help themselves or others. We will examine these assumptions about interpersonal responses in light of the findings obtained by investigators, many of whom worked out of Ohio State University's Disaster Research Center (DRC).

Disasters: Levels of Analysis

We have used the term *disaster* rather freely to this point. Some researchers, such as Dennis E. Wenger (1978), have tried to use the term more precisely, partly in order to provide a means for distinguishing clear levels of analysis in the study of disasters. The first level of analysis is that of *interpersonal* responses, which includes interaction among individuals and small groups. Events such as the evacuation of Gulliver's and the reactions of the survivors of flight 401 are described and analyzed at this level. The next levels of analysis are those of *organizational* and *community* responses to disaster. (We begin Chapter 10 with a description of the 1977 flood of Johnstown, Pennsylvania, and the response of organizations such as police, fire departments, National Guard, and Red Cross to the city's plight. We also present a description of a small rural community's rescue of air crash victims.) Finally, there is the *societal* level of analysis, represented by events such as Ireland's potato famine of the 1840s or the current droughts in eastern Africa (see Chapter 8).

Wenger uses the terms *emergency* and *crisis* for the classification and analysis of disasters. In general terms, *emergency* situations are those in which traditional and existing social arrangements are sufficient to overcome the problems posed by disaster agents. On the other hand, *crisis* situations are those in which new social arrangements must be forged in order to overcome these problems.

At the first level of analysis, that of interpersonal response, emergencies refer to those situations in which group norms and relationships, though perhaps strained, are still able to cope with events. An unexpected death of a family member, for example, usually entails traveling on short notice, arranging temporary lodging, and providing meals. Established family ties as well as the traditional roles of host, hostess, pallbearer, and sympathy giver are called into play. These resources are usually sufficient to carry out a successful funeral.

The term *crisis* refers to those situations in which established group relationships and norms are not sufficient to cope with events, and new roles, relationships, and ways of dealing with the problem must be established immediately. In the case of Gulliver's, band members found themselves playing an unfamiliar but essential role in crowd dispersal. Some people found themselves assisting strangers to exits not normally used in exiting the nightclub. Unable to see or hear, some patrons found themselves groping along crowded halls in a game of blindman's buff in which the stakes were life itself. Some survivors of flight 401 found themselves giving aid and assistance to flight attendants, while others had to make the unsettling decision as to who was alive and most in need of help.

At the level of organizational and community response, the fire at Gulliver's and the crash of flight 401 represent emergencies. In these instances, there were perhaps unusually large numbers of casualties, and, in the case of flight 401, the crash site was quite inaccessible. Still, police and fire departments, hospitals, and the Coast Guard had adequate equipment at their disposal and tactical resources sufficient to the task. Disasters such as the Johnstown flood, on the other hand, usually constitute a crisis for organizations and communities. Police and fire departments are overwhelmed by requests for assistance. Normal communication facilities are knocked out and makeshift arrangements are unreliable. Hospitals are without power and refrigeration. Outside relief agencies converge on the disaster-struck community and initially face problems of coordination of efforts.

At the level of societal response, disasters such as the Johnstown flood represent an emergency but not a crisis. Established federal relief programs are soon brought into operation. Recovery proceeds much as it has with earlier floods throughout the nation. From the standpoint of Wenger's analysis, the United States has faced few if any societal crises because of natural disaster. The Dust Bowl drought of the 1930s perhaps came the closest to being a societal crisis. It produced large-scale economic disruption in the farming sector and migration from the hardest hit regions. Many national agricultural extension services were initiated as a result of the drought. Other nations, however, have not been so lucky. Droughts, floods, famines, plagues, and earthquakes have periodically devastated the nations of Europe, Asia, Africa, and South America. Crises at the level of societal response usually entail crises at all other levels of social integration.

Table 9.1 illustrates Wenger's approach to the classification and analysis of disaster. Dennis E. Wenger (1978) suggests classifying disas-

TABLE 9.1
Disasters and Social Integration

Events	Interpersonal		Organizational		Community		Societal	
	emergency	crisis	emergency	crisis	emergency	crisis	emergency	crisis
Unexpected death of family member	yes	no	no	no	no	no	no	no
Gulliver's fire	yes	yes	yes	no	no	no	no	no
Crash of flight 401	yes	yes	yes	no	no	no	no	no
Farmers' rescue of air crash survivors	yes	yes	yes	no	yes	no	no	no
Johnstown flood	yes	yes	yes	yes	yes	yes	yes	no
Potato famine in Ireland (1840s)	yes	yes	yes	yes	yes	yes	yes	yes

Levels of Integration spans the eight subcolumns above.

ter events in terms of their impact on social integration. Emergencies can be handled within the framework of existing norms, roles, and resources within groups, organizations, communities, and societies. The response to crisis events, on the other hand, involves new, or emergent norms, roles, and alterations in the use and distribution of resources.

This framework is probably of little use to people stacking sandbags during a flood or to community groups planning their disaster preparedness program. However, it can be put to good use in efforts to systematically survey and evaluate the field of disaster theory and research.

Individuals in Disaster

Most theories and research dealing with interpersonal responses to disaster concern the issue of *panic*. Theories of collective behavior differ substantially in their views regarding panic. The mass hysteria and value-added perspectives view panic as a necessary ingredient in situations like the evacuation of Gulliver's

or the reaction of passengers following a devastating air crash. Further, panic is seen as responsible for the sense of confusion and personal helplessness within communities confronted with disaster. On the other hand, the emergent norm perspective minimizes the role of panic in disaster situations. Apparently nonadaptive responses and confusion are not the result of panic but are the properties of emergent groups and definitions of the situation. From the standpoint of the SBI perspective, activities commonly referred to as panic, such as fatal stampedes toward exits, are better understood as behavior organized under adverse and deteriorating sensory conditions.

Disasters and the "Grip of Terror"

The mass hysteria and value-added perspectives consider panic to be a frequent interpersonal response to disaster. The absence of panic in these situations is taken as a stroke of luck. According to the mass hysteria perspective, panic is produced by predisaster anxiety, milling, and circular reaction. From the standpoint of the value-added model, whether one is considering a stampede panic such as Gulliver's evacuation or a financial panic such as the stock market crash of 1929, panic is rooted in hysterical beliefs. Under conditions of structural conduciveness (insufficient exits) and structural strain (strident warnings of danger), hysterical beliefs can arise that restrict people's attentiveness to their environment. People's attention becomes narrowly focused on escape and self-preservation. Thus people shove and trample others in their efforts to get to the main exit while ignoring side exits that are clear. For both the mass hysteria and value-added perspectives, the outward manifestations of panic are *intense personal terror, uncontrolled individualistic flight*, and *emotional shock*.

Intense Personal Terror.   During and shortly following disasters, individuals are seized by terror that strips away their veneer of socialization. People may lose the ability to speak coherently, and their behavior may appear random and ineffective. On the other hand, terror may cause people to act on the basis of naked, short-term self-interest. People may become oblivious to their normal responsibilities to family, friends, jobs, and community. Gripped by such terror, disaster victims have no inclination to cooperate with others or to give aid to those who are suffering.

Uncontrolled Individualistic Flight.   The second manifestation of panic is uncontrolled individualistic flight from real or imagined danger. Panic flight contributes substantially to the death, injury, and disorder that accompany disaster. The uncontrolled and individualistic nature of flight is indicated by such things as movement toward only a few of several possible exits and people being knocked down and trampled. Panic flight may occur as a response to little more than the word *fire* spoken in a crowded auditorium (as described by Klapp—see box, p. 24). The exodus of survivors from Hiroshima and Nagasaki, the movement of people during and shortly following the 1938 broadcast of the "War of the Worlds," and the migration from Ireland during the potato famine are some of the events cited as large-scale panic flights.

The likelihood and extent of flight are increased if people have experienced anxiety or other kinds of emotional strain prior to the disaster. Explicit or strident warnings of impending danger can produce sufficient anxiety to cause terror and panic flight even if the threat fails to materialize. The fear that warnings of danger can produce panic flight in nightclubs, theaters, and hotels has often resulted in the issuing of ambiguous and low-key warnings of fire or, in some cases, no warnings at all.

Postdisaster Emotional Shock.   The final manifestation of panic is the emotional shock that sets in shortly following disaster. Symptoms of this shock include incoherence, spatial and temporal disorientation, and helplessness. Emotional shock significantly reduces the capacity of disaster victims to engage in rescue work, repair damage, or find food and shelter for themselves. Civil and military authorities and disaster assistance organizations expect to encounter helpless and passive people at the scene of disasters.

The "Grip of Terror" Examined

Is panic an essential component of disasters, as the mass hysteria and value-added perspectives suggest? Put another way: Are disaster victims usually gripped by terror that strips away concern for others? Are disaster victims likely to experience shock that severely limits their ability to cope with the aftermath of disaster? In light of much disaster research and consideration of incidents such as those described at the beginning of this chapter, the answer to these questions is a qualified *no*.

Terror Reactions. During disasters, people exhibit a remarkable degree of composure and concern for family, friends, neighbors, and strangers. During the evacuation of Gulliver's, band members remained on the bandstand, urging people to leave and to remove platform shoes to avoid injury. Three of the band members died in the final seconds of orderly dispersal when flames shot across the bandstand. Flight attendants are trained to help passengers from their seats, down escape chutes, and away from the plane in the vital moments following air crashes. Attendants have carried out these activities while injured, being showered by flying glass and metal, and facing the very real danger of violent explosions. Following the 1977 runway collision of two 747s at the Los Rodeos Airport in the Canary Islands, passengers assisted attendants and one another in getting out of and away from the burning planes. A few passengers returned to the flaming wreckage several times to lead others to safety.

Fritz and Marks (1954), in their summary of early disaster research conducted by the National Opinion Research Center (NORC), note that less than 2 percent of disaster victims usually exhibit "highly or mildly agitated states involving uncontrolled behavior" during the time of disaster impact. In addition, the National Opinion Research Center collected data to ascertain if women are more likely than men to exhibit these manifestations of panic. The data show that women are more likely to be perceived and described by men as displaying panic. When self-reports are compared, however, they show that women are no more likely than men to describe themselves as having experienced panic.

Panic Flight. Stampede panics occur very seldom among large numbers of people gathered in nightclubs, theaters, hotels, or auditoriums. As was the case for the fire at Gulliver's, initial reports of these events often mention terror-stricken crowds and death by trampling. Later reports of the same event usually include stories of people maintaining presence of mind and acting with a concern for others. Most apparent trampling deaths later prove to be death by asphyxiation and poisonous fumes in the smoke. This is not to say that no one has ever been trampled when a large number of people evacuated a building; however, injuries and deaths of this sort are far fewer than injuries and deaths from smoke and flames.

It is difficult to find clear, documented instances of panic flight from communities. On the other hand, it is well documented that authorities find it difficult to evacuate communities. Substantial numbers of people refuse to evacuate, evacuate slowly, or leave for locations other than those specified by authorities (Drabek 1969). Often, people attempt to reenter the community before all danger has passed (Fritz and Mathewson 1957). Such behavior was clearly in evidence during recent technological disasters, such as the accident at the Three Mile Island nuclear power plant. These problems have caused many to seriously doubt the adequacy of most community evacuation plans.

Nonflight movement following disasters has often been described as panic flight. For example, Cantril's analysis of the "War of the Worlds" broadcast describes panic flight as part of the hysterical aftermath (see Chapter 5). Cantril (1940) presents interviews wherein people report they were frightened and confused as they moved about on foot or in automobiles during and shortly following the broadcast. These interviews also indicate that people were not fleeing for their lives. Instead, interviewees report they were going to the homes of parents, fiancées, or friends. This concern with contacting others is a common response among disaster-struck populations and should not be equated with panic flight. That same evening, interestingly, the residents of Grovers Mill, New Jersey (the small town where Martians were reported to have landed), claimed that an unusually large number of automobiles drove through their town. This is very similar to the convergence of people on the scene of disasters, which is a frequent component of disasters but can hardly be termed panic flight.

In 1973 similar reports of panic flight followed the broadcast of a fictitious news bulletin announcing a nuclear power station accident in Sweden. Later investigation requested by the Swedish Board of Psychological Defense found that less than 10 percent of the population had misinterpreted the program (Rosengren, Arvidson, and Sturesson 1975). A small number of these people (less than 1 percent of the population) subsequently attempted to contact friends or family. There was no evidence of panic flight.

Emotional Shock.   Postdisaster emotional shock, contrary to the views of the mass hysteria and value-added approaches, occurs rarely, and when it does, it is short lived and affects relatively small portions of the population. For the NORC studies summarized by Fritz and Marks (1954), the largest percentage of a population experiencing postdisaster shock was 14 percent (22 percent of the women and 5 percent of the men). We can state with some assurance that there are no documented instances in which a majority of a population exhibited shock reactions after disaster.

Characteristically, the first rescue and recovery efforts are made by members of disaster-struck communities. These efforts are usually quite direct and effective, partly because of the survivors' familiarity with their community. Neighbors, for instance, are familiar with each other's families and know who is having weekend guests and who is out of town. Consequently, they know better than rescue crews from outside the neighborhood how many people to look for in a collapsed home or who is actually missing. When numbers of homes

are destroyed, survivors construct makeshift shelters or move to the homes of nearby friends and relatives. Communities often underutilize the shelter facilities provided by disaster assistance agencies. The temporarily homeless either avoid the shelters altogether or use them for only a short time. If the option exists, survivors usually prefer to sleep in a real bed and have hot meals at the home of a nearby relative rather than sleep on an army cot and eat peanut butter sandwiches in the high school gym (McLuckie 1970). Civil and military authorities receive complaints from residents who resent the curfews, traffic rerouting, and parking restrictions imposed by authorities to maintain order (Demerath and Wallace 1957).

Disaster investigators note that survivors report experiencing grief, depression, despair, headaches, loss of appetite, sleeplessness, and nightmares in the weeks following disaster. These emotional and physical reactions are not so acute as to be considered postdisaster shock, and they usually do not substantially hinder a community's recovery efforts. Further, the same kinds of reactions follow the death or injury of family members and friends or the loss of property in nondisaster situations.

Rather than giving in to fears, grief, and various manifestations of panic, as the mass hysteria and value-added perspectives suggest, people usually occupy themselves with the problems of rescue and recovery. Some researchers have tried to ascertain the consequences of this denial of emotion in the immediate aftermath of disaster. Findings usually suggest that early denial of emotion may contribute to later feelings of guilt, depression, or neurosis (Kinston and Rosser 1974; Perry and Lindell 1978). Erickson's (1976) study of the Buffalo Creek dam collapse pointed out that severe guilt feelings and depression plagued survivors for several months after the disaster. Silber, Perry, and Bloch (1959) suggest that children are quite susceptible to long-term ad-

justment problems if they become separated
from their parents during the disaster or if they
are not allowed to freely talk about their experiences and fears afterward. Finally, Roth
(1970) suggests that there are cultural differences in the degree to which people express
emotion during disaster. The Greek peasant
women who stand about wailing and crying
following an earthquake are not gripped by
hysteria. Rather, they are giving vent to their
emotion in a culturally prescribed and potentially healthy manner.

Multifatality Evacuations and the SBI Perspective

Decades of disaster research have amassed
considerable evidence suggesting that panic is
an infrequent and quite limited response to disaster. Still, even in recent discussions (Mileti,
Drabek, and Haas 1975), some researchers
maintain that multifatality evacuations represent instances of actual panic. This claim aside,
much of the activity that appears to be panic in
these situations can be better understood as behavior organized under quite adverse and rapidly deteriorating ecological and sensory conditions.

Hardly a week goes by that we do not read
or hear about an emergency evacuation. News
reports of hotel, nightclub, or theater fires in
which everyone escapes are usually quite brief,
while multifatality evacuations are given
lengthy treatment. In nearly all of these latter
descriptions, at least some note is made of successful and initially quite orderly movement
from danger. We'll now turn our attention to
the immediate circumstances that contribute
to the breakdown of this orderly movement.

McPhail states that people do not become
"irrational" during abrupt emergency evacuations. In the case of the 1980 fire at the Las
Vegas MGM Grand Hotel, guests reported get-

ting dressed, finishing baths, notifying roommates and others of the fire, and trying to determine the location and size of the fire, prior
to attempting to leave the hotel (Bryan 1983).
According to McPhail, people initially provide
quite rational instructions for dispersal in the
direction of exits that are either known to them
(people usually leave through the doors they
entered) or suggested to them by the movements of others.

In contrast to the panic image of dispersal,
which suggests that such instructions and cues
can precipitate an immediate stampede, the
SBI perspective maintains that these instructions and cues bring about *orderly movement*.
Movement toward and through exits ranges
from sparse to widespread and from slow to
rapid. Initially, however, such movement is
carried out with a concern for the group and
the overall situation. While preparing to
move, and during movement, people try to remain in contact with friends, relatives, and
others who are accompanying them (Bryan
1983). In the case of the MGM Grand fire,
guests also utilized "survival" information
gained from television, radio, movies, and
periodicals, such as "Do not use the elevators,"
"Use wet towels on face," "Feel doors before
opening," and "Think before acting" (Bryan
1983).

Evacuation is accomplished by additional
instructions that specify orderly movement,
such as "Let's go!" "Don't shove," "Watch your
step, these stairs are steep," "Remain calm," or
"Use the other exit." To varying degrees, people can see one another and monitor the rate,
direction, and progress of movement. In multifatality evacuations, many factors operate to
disrupt and prevent orderly movement.

Overcrowding

Perhaps the most common and immediate
circumstance of multifatality evacuations is
overcrowding. It is difficult to judge the extent

of overcrowding when conditions are initially described as "standing room only," "packed to the rafters," or "overcrowded." In some instances, however, we can assess overcrowding in terms of a building's fire code occupancy limit or licensed seating capacity. When we apply either criterion, it becomes clear that drastic overcrowding precedes most multifatality evacuations.

No specific fire code occupancy limit had been established for Gulliver's Disco. Crowds at Gulliver's were typically described as packed or standing room only. In the case of the Southgate, Kentucky, Beverly Hills Supper Club disaster of 1977, the nightclub had nearly double the number of occupants the building could safely accommodate on the night of the fire (Best 1977). Further, the Cabaret Room, where most of the fatalities occurred, was packed to nearly three times what the room could safely accommodate (Best 1977). One gets a more precise picture of disastrous overcrowding in the case of Boston's Cocoanut Grove fire of 1942. In all, 492 people died, 32 *more* people than the club's licensed seating capacity of 460 (Velfort and Lee 1943). Perhaps as many as 1,200 people—about three times the licensed capacity—were in the nightclub when the fire broke out. It does not seem an exaggeration to suggest that for multifatality evacuations, the numbers of people involved usually far exceed either the common-sense or legal occupancy limit of the facility.

One immediate consequence of extreme overcrowding is the increased potential for breakdown in front-to-rear communication (Quarantelli 1957). When people are standing shoulder to shoulder in large crowds, their straight-ahead and peripheral vision are blocked by those around them. Most people in a densely packed crowd cannot see exits or at least cannot see if known exits are blocked. We all know how difficult it is to carry on conversations in crowded nightclubs, restaurants,

waiting rooms, and theater lobbies. Also, it is very difficult to hear announcements in crowds unless the speaker is using some sort of voice-amplification device. In the absence of audible verbal instructions, such as "Everyone on the west side of the aisle should use exit number four," people receive cues as to the direction of movement from the movements of those directly in front of them. At the center of the crowd, these movement cues can be quite contradictory. People move first in one direction and then in the other, losing their sense of orientation. It is not surprising, then, that some movement in densely packed crowds seems "nonadaptive": toward a single exit, toward closed exits, or toward blind walls.

Another consequence of extreme overcrowding is a corresponding increase in the time necessary for dispersal. Occupancy limits for public buildings are established in part through consideration of the time needed to move a given number of people through available exits. Obviously, dispersal time increases directly with the number of people in the building. In addition, extreme overcrowding, as noted above, can result in slower and less direct movements toward exits than would be the case for smaller numbers of occupants. In this sense, exceeding the legal occupancy limit by 30 percent may actually double or triple the time needed for evacuation.

Limited Time for Dispersal

Under ideal conditions, given the number of occupants and the number and capacity of available exits, it could take at least ten minutes to evacuate a building such as Gulliver's. Fire can spread throughout a building at an even faster rate; multifatality fires often engulf the occupied areas of a building in one to five minutes. These fires often burn for some time prior to their discovery, building up tremendous amounts of heat and smoke in stairwells, within walls, and above suspended ceilings. Contained fires such as these suddenly vent and explode into the oxygen-rich atmosphere of the open spaces of the building. The heat flash can ignite combustible material several yards away, allowing the fire to race down hallways and jump from room to room. Normally, air must contain at least 15 percent oxygen to sustain consciousness. These fires lower the oxygen level inside a building to less than 5 percent almost instantly. The fires that swept Gulliver's and the Beverly Hills Supper Club were of this nature. The fire at the Cocoanut Grove was fed by highly combustible Christmas decorations strung throughout the occupied areas of the nightclub.

Burning plastics, acrylics, and solvents generate extremely toxic fumes. In the Beverly Hills Supper Club, toxic fumes were generated by the burning of carpet padding and wall paneling (Best 1977). Fumes swept through the Cabaret Room so rapidly that patrons died while still seated at their tables. The rapid elimination of breathable air limits the amount of time during which evacuation can occur. Automatic sprinkler systems prevent fires from reaching the venting stage described above, and some sprinkler systems automatically transmit alarms to the fire department. The National Fire Protection Association has noted that there are no recorded instances of fires killing three or more people in buildings equipped with operating sprinkler systems.

The above discussion concerns multifatality evacuations during fires, but similar points could be made about other situations in which the time available for evacuation is limited, such as a sinking ship. Multifatality evacuations occur when the spread of fire, fumes, or some other real threat makes the time available for evacuation appreciably less than the minimum time it would take to evacuate people under ideal conditions.

Instructions for Dispersal

McPhail notes that people provide quite rational instructions for dispersal in the direction of the exits known to them. In the case of Gulliver's, at least three or four minutes elapsed between the band's first announcement of the fire and requests for dispersal and their second set of instructions, given immediately prior to the fire's venting. At least fifteen minutes elapsed between the discovery of the fire in the Beverly Hills Supper Club and the first call to the fire department (Best 1977). It should be noted that club employees had no training or drill in the duties they were to perform in case of fire (Best 1977). Accounts indicate that employees made only one announcement of the fire to patrons during this interim. Dispersal began immediately after this announcement, but it was sparse and relatively slow. From the accounts of these and other multifatality evacuations, it is apparent that the first announcement of the fire and the instructions for movement were low key and somewhat equivocal, such as, "We think there is a fire in the building; maybe everyone should leave." In retrospect, valuable dispersal time was lost because of the delay in announcing the fire to patrons and the use of low-key announcements to avoid panic. Immediate, frequent, and unambiguous announcements—such as, "There is a fire in the building; the fire department will arrive shortly; please leave immediately through the exits to the east parking lot"—would have occasioned earlier and more complete evacuation.

We should not equate prompt notification and the use of clearly audible, direct, and unequivocal instructions with yelling "Fire!" in a crowded theater. Strident instructions are not usually unequivocal instructions. Unequivocal instructions clearly identify the threat, specify immediate movement, identify exits, and, if possible, direct portions of the crowd toward separate exits.

Use of Exits

Descriptions of multifatality evacuations sometimes mention exits that are locked or otherwise unusable. Such instances of entrapment are documented but are certainly not common to most multifatality evacuations. More often, it is simply the case that some exits are not used. Seldom are occupants of a building aware of all exits, particularly in buildings such as restaurants, where patrons are restricted to the public areas. It was noted, for example, that one exit from Gulliver's was from the kitchen. Though five other exits were suggested and used, survivors complained that they had no knowledge of the kitchen exit. Commenting on the exodus from Gulliver's, a fireman pointed out that during such emergencies people usually attempt to leave public buildings through the same doors they entered. When rapid and generally orderly movement is occurring through a known and nearby exit, people are not likely to strike out through an unfamiliar building in search of other exits. Moments later, when dense smoke suddenly obstructs their vision and it becomes difficult to breathe, people are unable to search for other exits.

Another common feature of buildings within which multifatality evacuations have occurred is that many of the exits could not be reached by short-distance, straight-ahead movement. In Gulliver's, for instance, people could exit from the Pit only by moving up a narrow flight of stairs and out the main doors or by going downstairs and out through basement exits. In the Beverly Hills Supper Club, people could only reach some exits by using intersecting hallways (Best 1977). Streams of people met at these intersections, creating traffic jams. In the Cocoanut Grove, the main exit was through revolving doors that became jammed with bodies shortly after people started using them. It is in these places of crowd extrusion that many fatalities occur, including the infamous "trampling deaths." In all likelihood, death by actual trampling is rare; however, people may be knocked down and immobilized in these areas until they are asphyxiated. Occupants' limited knowledge of available exits and exits that can be reached only by negotiating long hallways, stairs, and other obstacles are common circumstances in multifatality evacuations.

Sensory Interference

In order for people to initiate dispersal movement and to successfully negotiate hallways, stairs, and exits, they must be able to provide movement instructions to one another and visually monitor each other's movements. Multifatality evacuations usually entail conditions of sensory interference that severely limit the possibility of providing audible instructions and visually monitoring the movements of others. Human bodies make excellent sound diffusers. Additionally, the shuffle of feet, extraneous conversations, and even the movement of furniture as people initiate movement create substantial background noise. Consequently, once numbers of people initiate movement in overcrowded buildings, it becomes increasingly difficult to provide additional, audible instructions for movement. During the evacuation of Gulliver's, the instructions provided by the band were mentioned by survivors. Standing somewhat above the crowd on an elevated stage and using sound equipment, the band members were in an acoustically advantageous position to make themselves heard above the rising din. In the case of fires, resulting explosions and rumbling flames provide additional background noise with which movement instructions must compete. In the final moments of evacuation from Gulliver's, air conditioners were crashing loudly to the floor and interfering with audible instructions for movement.

Visual monitoring of the movements of others is restricted in crowded areas. Those at the rear of crowds, for example, cannot see that an exit is blocked or that people have fallen on the stairs ahead of them. Consequently, people at the rear keep moving, which results in crushes and pileups near exits and stairways. Streams of people may converge head-on or at right angles in hallways. Again, those farther back in the crowd are unable to see the resulting jam-up and keep moving.

Visual monitoring is often made difficult or impossible by the spread of smoke throughout a building by air-conditioning ducts or other conduits, such as stairwells and suspended ceilings. Even emergency lighting systems are useless in dense smoke. Even if smoke does not create a total blackout within the building, it can be as irritating to the eyes as tear gas, creating blurred vision or temporary blindness. When people are unable to see others or their immediate surroundings, their movement toward exits becomes increasingly disorganized. Careful attention to building design and the selection of building materials, as well as the use of air-conditioning systems that shut down automatically during fires, could do much to alleviate the sensory interference caused by smoke.

Discussion

The social contagion and value-added perspectives cite panic as a fundamental cause of deaths during evacuation disasters. Though recent research casts great doubt on panic as a viable explanation for people's behavior in most disasters, multifatality evacuations are still considered to be instances of true panic. Stampede panics seem to give clear evidence that people lose both their normal attentiveness to the environment and their concern for others. In some instances, people may trample those standing between themselves and safety.

Some writers, such as Strauss (1944), have suggested programs of antipanic training, but for the most part, such programs would be impossible to implement among civilian populations.

The SBI perspective suggests that multifatality evacuations result not from panic but from largely avoidable circumstances, including tremendous and often illegal overcrowding, the unusually rapid spread of fire or other lethal agent (which greatly limits the time for evacuation), and dispersal under severely adverse sensory conditions. Few if any stampede panics have occurred in uncrowded buildings or in buildings where occupants faced a threat that allowed reasonable time for dispersal and otherwise posed little threat to life and limb.

Altruism and Disaster

In contrast to the early "grip of terror" stereotypes, disaster studies frequently document people's high level of concern for and generosity toward disaster victims. Altruism was shown by Iowa farmers who risked their lives to remove survivors from the gasoline-drenched wreckage of an airliner. (We will consider this incident in greater detail in Chapter 10.) Many farm women carried their family's warmest blankets to the crash site with little concern that the blankets would be permanently soiled with bloodstains, mud, and oil. Few blankets in which survivors were sent to hospitals were ever returned. In the days following the crash, warm meals and hot coffee were provided, around the clock, to state police and aviation officials. Finally, farmers provided tractors, loading equipment, and labor during the removal of the wreckage. Families received little reimbursement for their efforts, although reimbursement seemed to be of little concern to these people. They took pride in their generosity.

Altruism may also be reflected in the low incidence of looting during disasters. Disasters present many clear opportunities for looting: homes are broken open, and people's possessions are scattered about streets and fields. But looting during disasters is quite rare (Quarantelli and Dynes 1969). During civil disorders, looters may enjoy a degree of community support, but during disasters, looters are thoroughly condemned by authorities and community members alike. What little looting occurs is usually done by outsiders who converge on the community after the disaster.

In the case of the farmers' rescue of the air crash survivors, the farmers assumed a protective stance with respect to the victims' property. Within an hour, spectators began to converge on the crash site, but the pasture fences made a handy barrier for controlling the crowd. The farmers' concern with crowd control was to keep smokers away from the gasoline in the wreckage and to keep sightseers from picking up the scattered property of the victims. One of the first roles to emerge, aside from rescuer, was that of protector of property. A pile of luggage was started quite a distance from the fences. Later, a cardboard box was kept there for smaller items, such as watches, jewelry, purses and billfolds, and some loose money. Several farmers walked among the rescuers, directing them toward the box of valuables when such items were found. Perhaps the only items of possible value that the farmers removed from the crash site were scraps of aluminum and bolts, which they kept as souvenirs.

Stress Explanations of Altruism

Discussions of disaster-related altruism usually claim that this concern and generosity are seldom shown in nondisaster situations. If this is indeed the case, then what causes disaster-related altruism? Some discussions attribute this altruism to the stress of anxiety and guilt generated by the disaster (Wallace 1957; Martin 1964). Immediately following disaster impact, survivors can look about them and see the capricious nature of what has happened. A tornado, for example, may level homes on one side of a street and inflict little if any damage to homes on the other side. Floods may carry away entire neighborhoods while only flooding basements on the other end of town. Many of the survivors who have been injured can look around and see others in greater pain and, perhaps, the dead. Some disaster studies claim that survivors initially tend to underestimate their personal losses and to feel that others have suffered greater loss (Fritz 1961; Cranshaw 1963). Given this, survivors experience initial feelings of anxiety and guilt as to why God or circumstance has spared them from the greater suffering they perceive others have experienced. Giving assistance to others substantially reduces these stresses. Unfortunately, there have been no real attempts by researchers to systematically study this explanation of disaster-related altruism.

Situational Explanations of Altruism

During the 1960s, there was considerable interest within the field of social psychology in the issue of *bystander intervention*. This research was directed toward ascertaining the conditions under which people would come to the aid of victims of physical assaults, accidents, and seizures. These studies were prompted by the killing of Catherine "Kitty" Genovese in 1964 (Rosenthal 1964). Genovese was knifed by a man as she walked to her apartment building in Kew Gardens, Queens, New York. It was almost 3:30 A.M., the street was deserted, and the neighborhood was asleep. When the attacker struck, Genovese screamed and lights went on in the windows above the street. An onlooker shouted down: "Let that girl alone!" The attacker walked away, only to return as soon as the lights went out. Genovese screamed when he knifed her again, and he left as soon as people came back to their windows. Genovese made her way to the doors of her building, where the attacker found her and stabbed her once more. It was probably not until after the last attack that one of her neighbors called the police. When officers arrived, she was dead and her murderer was gone.

Why didn't any of the thirty-eight witnesses to the killing of Kitty Genovese come to her aid? Why didn't her neighbors call the police immediately instead of nearly thirty minutes after the first attack? Why did only one person call? The bystander intervention research indicates that people usually do render aid in emergency situations but only when certain immediate circumstances are present (Latané and Darley 1968; Wheeler et al. 1978). First, there must be clear and unambiguous distress cues within the situation. Though Genovese screamed and called for help, a number of witnesses interpreted her sounds of distress as a quarrel rather than a murder. Neighbors looking from their windows did not have a clear view of what was going on in the shadows.

Second, witnesses must perceive some responsibility for the victim's fate. This is most likely to occur when the number of witnesses is small or the witnesses constitute a social group, such as a family, work or recreation group, or friendship group. Witnesses are also more likely to assume responsibility if they know the victim. As the number of unassociated witnesses increases, the likelihood of giving assistance to the victim decreases. Latane and Darley describe this as "responsibility diffusion," in which each witness assumes that someone else will come to the aid of the victim or that someone else has already called the police, fire department, or ambulance. In the case

of Kitty Genovese, the person who finally called the police knew her personally.

Third, there is the effect of modeling. If the first bystanders seem to be unconcerned, later bystanders pick up on these cues from those who were there when it started and are less likely to give assistance. Often, the first person to give assistance precipitates helping behavior on the part of a number of bystanders.

Finally, there is the ability to help the victim. Competence based on first-aid training, knowledge of crisis situations, and even martial arts skills increase helping behavior in situations that demand intervention.

Disasters create nearly ideal conditions for eliciting helping behavior. Signs of distress and the need for assistance are obvious and plentiful. Little is ambiguous about shattered homes and open wounds. Those injured, trapped, or missing are known to their neighbors. The role that family, work, neighborhood, and friendship groups play in giving assistance to others is well documented. Often, there is little need to worry about whether someone else has called the police or fire department, as these agencies may have had forewarning, or at least certain knowledge, of the disaster from many sources. Within moments of the disaster's impact, there are numerous models of helping behavior. Finally, the ability to help victims may involve little more than the ability to push aside fallen branches or other debris, give someone a blanket, say a few comforting words, and call for help.

In the later stages of disaster recovery, altruism seems to give way to more selfish concerns (Taylor, Zurcher, and Key 1970). In part, this is because the immediate needs of rescue and assistance have been met, and the more diverse needs of long-range community recovery are emerging. Such needs as home repair financing usually give few outward cues of distress. The altruism of people possessing skills relevant to this kind of assistance, such as local insurance agents and adjusters, comes into play in later stages of disaster. These people may work exceedingly long hours investigating and processing insurance claims so that victims get prompt financial relief.

Summary

Panic is a traditional part of the popular image of people's response to disaster. We need not search too long or too hard to find descriptions of theater, hotel, or nightclub fires that mention human stampedes toward exits and trampled bodies in hallways and stairwells. Panic is an almost instantaneous response to both real and imaginary threats. Part of American folklore includes the panic that resulted from the 1938 "War of the Worlds" broadcast. Even today, descriptions of this event mention suicides and terrorized flight from New Jersey and New York. This popular imagery has led to the refusal to give warnings in emergency situations in an effort to prevent panic.

The panic image of individual responses to disaster is central to the mass hysteria and value-added perspectives of collective behavior. Panic is caused by circular reaction or hysterical beliefs that restrict people's attention to their environment. These theories present a "grip of terror" image of disaster response. That is, during disaster impact, people's attention focuses on their own survival, and they lose all concern for the well-being of family, friends, and neighbors. Panic flight is instantaneous, and people are trampled or roads and highways become clogged by traffic as a result. Finally, emotional shock sets in following disaster, and people become unable to carry out rescue and recovery work.

Even the early disaster response survey by the National Opinion Research Center (NORC) indicated that panic as depicted in the "grip of terror" image was a poor representation of people's actual response to disaster. Later research by the Disaster Research Center (DRC) showed that victims of disaster retain their presence of mind during disaster, retain concern for family, friends, neighbors, and community, and are very active during the rescue and recovery phase of disaster.

This research-based view of individual responses to disaster is reflected in both the emergent norm and SBI approaches to disaster response. The emergent norm view, for example, characterizes disaster response as highly normative in character and suggests that people become more rather than less responsive to the needs of friends, family, neighbors, and their community. The SBI perspective clearly applies to the classic stampede panic situation. In multifatality disasters, deaths and injury seldom if ever are a direct result of panic. Instead, deaths and injury are an unavoidable outcome of evacuation under unusually adverse conditions. Adverse conditions include extreme overcrowding, very limited time for dispersal because of the rapid spread of fire or deadly fumes, sensory interference caused by overcrowding, noise, and smoke, late and/or ambiguous warnings of danger and inadequate dispersal instructions, and, finally, poorly accessible exits. The panic explanation blames the victims for the unfortunate outcome of multifatality evacuations. The SBI perspective, on the other hand, points out preventive measures that can be implemented through building codes, fire code regulations, and emergency procedures for management and staff of hotels, restaurants, nightclubs, and other enclosed facilities that accommodate large gatherings.

Contrary to the assumptions of the "grip of terror" explanation, a close examination of people's response to disaster reveals that people usually show high levels of concern and generosity toward disaster victims. One explanation of disaster-related altruism emphasizes the anxiety-reducing effect of this altruism, but this would be very difficult to test in the field. Studies of bystander intervention, on the other hand, suggest some rather specific factors that probably promote disaster-related altruism. During disaster, there are numerous and obvious distress cues. People often face disasters with their relatives, friends, and neighbors in the community. These social groups are more likely to render assistance to people in distress than groups composed of mutual strangers. Disaster presents opportunities for meaningful assistance to people possessing even limited helping skills. Finally, during disaster, there are usually numerous models for rendering assistance to those in need.

The bulk of early disaster research examined interpersonal responses to disaster. More recently, research efforts have turned to the analysis of organizational and community responses to disaster. Much of this research has occurred through the efforts of Ohio State University's Disaster Research Center and the Research Program on Technology, Environment and Man at the Institute of Behavioral Science, University of Colorado. In Chapter 10 we will look at the disaster responses of organizations, communities, and societies.

Organizations, Communities, and Societies in Disaster

When disaster strikes, individuals usually look first to the safety of themselves and those around them. Soon, however, people become aware that they are also members of organizations, communities, and societies and that these relationships have an impact on their activities. For instance, people often must try to get time off from work to clean up their houses. People also experience a heightened community spirit as they pitch in to restore their neighborhoods, and they become aware of how much they take community-based services such as clean water and emergency health care for granted. Finally, people find that they must comply with bureaucratic demands and seemingly unnecessary red tape to obtain federal disaster relief funds.

Two Disasters

In this chapter we examine organizations, communities, and societies in disaster. We will begin by considering two examples of disaster. First, there is the Johnstown, Pennsylvania, flood of 1977 and the recovery efforts that emerged in the weeks following the flood. These efforts involved the coordination of the resources of many volunteer, private, and governmental organizations into an effective as-

sault on the damage caused by the disaster. In the second instance, a farming community quickly organized an effective rescue of the survivors of an airline crash. For some farmers, this rescue involved placing their own lives on the line to save people they did not know and would likely never see again. In the days that followed, the community assisted state police and aviation investigators working at the crash site.

Organizations in Disaster: The Johnstown Flood

At about 7:30 P.M. on Tuesday, July 19, 1977, it started to rain throughout the Conemaugh Valley of Pennsylvania. In Johnstown, residents welcomed the thunderstorms as relief from a week-long heat wave. By 5:00 A.M., however, 11.8 inches of rain had fallen. According to the National Weather Service, a rainfall of this magnitude had never been recorded on the North American continent and was likely to occur only once in ten thousand years. During the night, six dams in the Conemaugh Valley had burst or been topped by floodwaters. The death toll was alarming: seventy-three known dead and eighteen missing. More than a thousand homes were damaged or destroyed. Stores and other businesses were heavily damaged. Public buildings such as Johnstown's David A. Glosser Memorial Library and the War Memorial Arena were flooded. Highways, bridges, and railroad lines were washed out. The official property damage estimate was nearly $250 million.

During the first hours of the rain, people's main concern was with the blockage of storm sewers and basement flooding. By midnight, however, people's concerns turned to sheer survival. Water entered the ground floors of homes, and people moved to attics and rooftops. At about 1:00 A.M., dams began to burst and walls of water swept through the already flooded communities of the Conemaugh Valley. In the steel mills, anxious workers tried to call their homes, but telephone lines had been washed out. Widespread power outages occurred. In Johnstown, residents of the Grand Hotel moved to the upper floors as water rose in the streets outside. Throughout Johnstown, more than three thousand automobiles floated down streets and into rivers. Some cars were occupied, and people died attempting to wade from their cars to higher ground. Thousands of accounts could be given of people spending a frightening night without light, transportation, or telephone. Lightning flashes showed people eerie glimpses of rising, rushing water filled with debris from shattered homes, uprooted trees, and, occasionally, bodies. Throughout the night, people were concerned with their immediate safety, but they could do little about the deteriorating conditions around them.

The rain stopped about dawn, which also revealed a scene of unbelievable destruction. Distant communities were just becoming aware of the disaster, and assistance was rendered rapidly and generously. Those arriving to help, however, found that the residents of Johnstown and nearby communities had already begun recovery efforts. Ham radio operators were functioning as dispatchers for the many recently formed work and rescue crews,

and they continued to play a critical role by coordinating recovery efforts until telephone service was partially restored, days later. Small boats and large trucks were being used to move those stranded by the water to safety. Throughout the morning of the flood, National Guard helicopters transferred blood and medical supplies from the disabled refrigeration units of the Johnstown Red Cross center to a milk warehouse outside the city.

By noon, three thousand hot meals were being trucked from Pittsburgh to Johnstown by the Salvation Army. Throughout the next nineteen days, the Salvation Army operated twenty-five emergency vans, distributing sandwiches and coffee to work crews. The Salvation Army also sponsored chicken barbecues and provided hot meals at refugee centers. During this period, other groups, such as the Mennonite Disaster Service, Catholic church groups, and even a Baptist choir from Birmingham, Alabama, provided assistance. Some groups limited their assistance to a particular segment of the disaster-struck population or to a particular task. For example, some groups sought out and assisted the elderly or invalids who could do little heavy cleanup work. Groups from Penn State University helped with the salvage efforts at the library.

Refugee centers were quickly set up in schools, churches, and even a convent, and they also functioned as daycare centers for children when parents returned to the family homes to assess damage and start the cleanup. Volunteers took children to playgrounds and also provided entertainment for them in the refugee centers. Despite the many refugee centers available, many people elected to stay in the upstairs of their homes without electricity or telephone while they cleaned out the ground floors and basements.

In the days following the disaster, the chief concern of most people was the cleanup, work that was made even more tedious by the oppressive heat and humidity that continued across the Conemaugh Valley. Furnaces, washers, dryers, and freezers were ruined and had to be removed from basements. Basements and ground floors had several inches of mud in them and furniture was ruined. Removing mud-soaked sofas, rugs, and mattresses was heavy, hot, and depressing work. Time after time, people would pause and look sadly at a mud-drenched memento such as a family photo album or a souvenir from a summer vacation. The loss of mementos was perhaps more depressing than the loss of less personal but more expensive items such as autos or furniture. Many people and groups from the Wilkes-Barre community offered informal assistance and advice gathered from their experiences with recent floods. They told residents of Johnstown, for example, not to immediately repaint walls, because mud would continue to seep from them for months afterward. They informed residents which kinds of furniture could be successfully dried out and restored and what items should be discarded.

In retrospect, some recovery efforts were ill advised and ineffective. Perhaps people tried to resume normal activity too soon—five days after the flood, gasoline fumes in the storm sewers exploded, destroying a store, killing one person, and injuring six others. Following the flood, there was a persistent but probably unfounded fear of looters. In general, however, the effectiveness of the recovery efforts in Johnstown was comparable to that of formal and more structured organizations that respond to unusual but less devastating situations.

Communities in Disaster: Rescue of Air Crash Victims

Sunday, August 24, 1954, had been an unusually stormy day across northern Iowa. The farming community ten miles south of Mason City had been receiving thunderstorms throughout the afternoon; finally, at about 4:45 P.M., a very brief but violent thunderstorm struck, dropping at least an inch of rain in ten minutes. As this last storm rapidly subsided, one farm family sat down to supper. They had just begun to eat when they heard their dogs barking and then a knock at their door. When they went to the door, the family was surprised to see a drenched and mud-spattered young woman standing on their porch. The woman looked at them and stammered, "We crashed . . . we need help," and then collapsed. Going to her aid, the family noticed the wreckage of an airliner strewn across their nearby pasture. The crash of Braniff flight 152, carrying nineteen passengers and crew, was the worst domestic airline crash of 1954. For this farming community, the next few hours would be remembered and discussed for years to come.

The young woman, who had walked nearly a quarter of a mile with a compound fracture of the ankle, was the flight attendant and the only crew member to survive. As soon as she had been moved to a couch, the farm wife telephoned the hospital in Mason City, informing them that an airplane had crashed and that ambulances were needed immediately. She then called other neighbors and the state police.

The first farmer to arrive at the crash site could hear crying and talking inside the crushed fuselage, but he was unable to find a way inside the wreck. Another farmer soon arrived and was immediately sent to bring heavy jacks and chains to the crash. The third farmer to arrive was a rather small man, and he located a hole in the fuselage and was able to squeeze inside. He shouted to the others who were arriving to keep all cars, trucks, and tractors up on the road and not to smoke because the fuselage was filled with several inches of gasoline. One semiconscious woman was pinned in the wreckage in such a way that her face was partially immersed in the gasoline, and she was in immediate danger of drowning. Almost all of the remaining passengers had been jammed into a heap in the front of the fuselage by the impact. Another rescuer was able to squeeze into the wreck and together the two men began to reposition the survivors.

Numbers of rescuers were now arriving with jacks, chains, ropes, and pry bars to separate the wreckage enough to begin removing survivors. As they set about this task, other farmers drove back to the nearest farms and removed barn doors and wooden gates to serve as improvised stretchers. Farm wives had set up a collection center for blankets, pillows, bandages, and hot water and were bringing these to the crash site. Less than fifteen minutes had elapsed since the flight attendant had knocked on a stranger's door for help.

As the first survivor was being removed, a state police car and an ambulance arrived. The trooper and ambulance crew expressed surprise and regret as they told those at the crash site that they had interpreted the emergency call as the crash of a light plane and not an airliner. Immediately, calls were sent out for more ambulances and state police.

In the meantime, farmers continued their rescue efforts. Many farmers and their wives had taken first-aid classes at one time or another and were also knowledgeable about back injuries. Consequently, survivors were moved carefully after being secured to barn doors and gates. The survivors were gathered together a safe distance from the gasoline-soaked wreckage and were cared for and comforted by their rescuers. Ten people were taken from the wreckage alive, but two died before reaching the hospital. Another victim, a sixty-eight-year-old man, died two days later.

By 7:00 P.M., all survivors and bodies had been transported to surrounding hospitals. Throughout that night and the next week, many of the farm families provided meeting places, coffee, and food for state police, firemen, reporters, and aviation officials. Farmers assisted in removing the wreckage from the field after the crash investigation was completed. Finally, for years afterward, some farm families and survivors exchanged letters, cards, and even Christmas gifts.

Organizations in Disaster

The emergent norm perspective emphasizes that people become acutely aware of their social ties and commitments to others during disaster. Much disaster research documents this characterization. With heightened salience of interpersonal ties, many people are confronted by the dilemma of having to choose among the various roles they occupy. Lewis Killian (1952) was the first to discuss the more common dilemmas in his analysis of multiple-group membership during disaster. Perhaps the most common conflict encountered is between the demands of primary groups such as family, friends, and neighbors and the more instrumental and impersonal demands that are part of one's association with most formal organizations. Put in less abstract terms, people must choose between their loyalty to family and friends and, usually, loyalty to their jobs. Disaster research shows that people usually give priority to the needs of family, friends, and neighbors (Killian 1954; Barton 1969). Such actions clearly create problems for organizations, particularly if the majority of workers leave factories, offices, and stores unattended while they check on the whereabouts and safety of their family and friends. Further, effective disaster responses depend on at least some people, such as police, fire, and hospital personnel, giving priority to their formal roles within organizations.

Organizations and Personnel Allegiance

Problems of personnel allegiance are minimized for those organizations with clearly defined roles in areas of community protection and disaster response. These organizations include police and fire departments, utility companies, and hospitals (Dynes 1970). Occupants of roles in these organizations have a clear perception of the necessity for continued operation of the organization during disaster. Many members of these organizations receive training that specifically emphasizes job priority during disaster. Sometimes this training includes family disaster planning. Knowing that their families have first-aid kits, stockpiles of food and water, emergency shelters, and agreed-upon evacuation plans, police, fire, and hospital workers have some assurance that their families can cope with disaster in their absence. Community members may also pressure members of relevant emergency organizations to stay on the job (Dynes 1970). Implicit pressure is exerted when community members approach these people for assistance. Failure to give assistance is likely to be interpreted as cowardice, laziness, insensitivity, lack of professionalism, or an attempt to "cheat the taxpayer."

Problems of personnel allegiance are much greater for organizations with no clear potential for disaster assistance, such as factories, department stores, or entertainment and recreational facilities. People who work in such organizations are seldom given disaster-related training. In some factories, emergency shutdown procedures may be ignored as workers rush home to be with their families during a disaster (Killian 1952). Many organizations of this type may simply cease operation during the initial stages of a disaster (Dynes 1978).

Personnel allegiance may not pose such extreme problems when workers and supervisors receive early and unequivocal notice that their families and neighborhoods are in no immediate danger. Sometimes this can be inferred simply by knowing the nature and location of the disaster (Killian 1952). When disaster strikes the workplace and nearby communities, personnel allegiance is more likely if workers have close personal ties with one another. In these instances, people are more likely to give assistance to their friends and relatives at the workplace before leaving for home. At the same time, workers are more likely to be concerned about the well-being of the workplace, at least as far as it concerns the safety of the trapped and injured. Efforts to extinguish fires, secure dangerous industrial chemicals, and properly shut down machinery are more likely in these situations.

Sometimes problems of personnel allegiance are aggravated by the actions of supervisors. Supervisors with close personal ties to their subordinates are more likely to give priority to workers' concerns than to the interests of the organization (Killian 1952; Haas and Drabek 1973). Often, supervisors have received little instruction as to organizational priorities in the event of disaster. Confronted with the choice between the oftentimes implicit and unstated demands of the organization and the immediate and unequivocal demands of their subordinates, it is not surprising that supervisors fail to enforce organizational interests. New supervisors or those with few personal ties to their subordinates are more likely to enforce their perception of organizational interests (Killian 1952).

Organizational Responses to Disaster

In an ideal sense, formal organizations have rather clear-cut boundaries in terms of the tasks they usually perform, definite membership, formal roles, and established lines of authority. Disasters may distort the form and operation of organizations from this ideal. Organizations often confront tasks far different from those they usually carry out. During disaster, the membership of organizations may change. Some members are injured or dead, while others have temporarily defected to aid their families. Occasionally, disaster may actually increase organization membership, as auxiliary personnel are activated or people volunteer their services. Formal roles and lines of authority are altered as organization members are faced with the necessity of making decisions normally made by others.

The range of documented organizational responses to disaster is enormous. Russell R. Dynes (1970, 1978) has done much in the way of condensing these findings into an "ideal type" description of organizational response to disaster. Much of the following discussion is based on this work.

Dynes (1970) develops a convenient four-fold typology of organizational response to disaster. One dimension of this typology is the nature of the *tasks carried out by organizations* in the wake of disaster. Some organizations respond to disaster by carrying out many of those *regular tasks* that the organization frequently and routinely performs in nondisaster situations. For police departments, regular tasks revolve around the protection of life and property and maintaining order. During disaster, police still maintain a direct role in carrying out these tasks. They aid the injured, watch for looters, and direct traffic around or through the disaster area. Some organizations respond to disaster by carrying out *nonregular tasks*. During the Johnstown flood, operators of a milk warehouse were called upon to store blood and perishable medical supplies. Schools were temporarily turned into shelters for the homeless.

The second dimension of Dynes's typology is the nature of *organizational structure* utilized in disaster, that is, whether organizations use their *old and established* structure or develop *new and untried* structures. For police and fire departments, disasters may involve little if any change in organizational structure. Fire officers may work double shifts, and such routine tasks as making fire safety inspections may be discontinued; overall, however, the authority structure of the department and role

expectations remain the same. Other organizations may experience substantial alterations in their structure as they respond to disaster. Utility companies, for instance, may shift a large portion of their organizational resources to the task of restoring water, gas, electric, and telephone service. Supervisory personnel may be temporarily transferred from the office to the field, and clerical staff may be asked to help load utility vehicles. Organizations such as the Red Cross may undergo substantial transformations as they coordinate their efforts with state and national Red Cross offices. Finally, there are the many emergent organizations, such as neighborhood cleanup crews and temporary communication centers. These groups do not constitute formal organizations. Still, they must resolve the problems of task priority, command and authority, communication, and resource allocation in order to mount effective rescue and recovery efforts.

Established Organizations. Dynes's typology of organizational responses to disaster is presented in Table 10.1. There are four types of organizational responses. Type I groups, or *established organizations*, respond to disaster by performing familiar tasks and utilizing old and established structure. Typically, these organizations, such as police and fire departments, hospitals, and the National Guard, are clearly expected to play a primary role in disaster response and recovery.

Expanding Organizations. Type II groups, or *expanding organizations*, also have a traditional role in disaster response. These organizations expand or otherwise alter their structure while carrying out regular tasks during disaster recovery. The American Red Cross is a good example of an expanding organization. The Red Cross maintains a stance of disaster readiness. Its day-to-day activities, however, are typically carried out by a core of volunteers who maintain training programs in the

TABLE 10.1
Organizational Responses to Disaster

Type of organization	Disaster-related task performance	Disaster-related structural alterations	Example
Type I: Established organizations	Performance of many familiar tasks; demand for service is greatly increased	Few structural changes; changes that occur are largely the result of increased demand for organization's services; tasks carried out by existing personnel	Police, Fire departments, National Guard
Type II: Expanding organizations	Performance of familiar tasks; prepared to carry out disaster-related tasks	Major structural changes due to disaster-related tasks and integration with other groups and volunteer or auxiliary personnel	Red Cross, utility companies
Type III: Extending organizations	Performance of largely unfamiliar disaster-related tasks	Major structural changes due to disaster-related tasks; existing personnel carry out tasks	Local construction company, student organizations help salvage library
Type IV: Emergent organizations	Performance of unfamiliar disaster-related tasks; emergent definition of tasks to be carried out	Emergent structure; shifting and temporary membership	Neighborhood rescue and cleanup crews

areas of first aid, water safety, and accident prevention. When the Red Cross swings into action during disaster, the active core is joined by numbers of less active members and volunteers. Further, in large-scale disasters, national officers and personnel may arrive at the scene and oversee the local chapter. Other types of expanding organizations include CB and ham radio clubs, boat clubs, and four-wheel-drive vehicle clubs.

Most expanding organizations are voluntary associations, and problems of membership discipline may be greater than for organizations consisting of paid workers. In addition, there is the problem of coordinating and reconciling the different aims of local, regional, and national levels of association in these organizations.

In large-scale disaster, established organizations may take on some of the characteristics of expanding organizations. Utility companies, for example, may be overwhelmed by tasks that they routinely perform on a much smaller scale. These tasks include debris removal, major repairs, and transportation of supplies. To meet this unusual volume of familiar tasks, substantial shifts in work duties and authority are necessary.

Extending Organizations. Type III groups, or *extending organizations*, extend their activities to include nonregular tasks while retaining much of their predisaster structure. Examples of extending organizations include voluntary groups such as local Boy Scout troops who serve coffee, run errands, and perhaps heft sandbags during disaster. Student organizations from Penn State University worked to salvage books at the Glosser Memorial Library following the Johnstown flood. In early stages of disaster recovery, construction companies frequently make their equipment and personnel available to those searching the debris for survivors. While extending organizations retain much of their predisaster structure, decision making tends to occur at lower levels of organizational authority than is the case in day-to-day operations (Quarantelli 1970).

Emergent Organizations. Type IV groups, or *emergent organizations*, are typified by the neighborhood rescue and recovery teams that form almost immediately following disaster impact. Occasionally, these groups assume the qualities of formal organizations, with definite task specialization, definite membership, and clearly defined roles and authority relationships. Typically, these emergent groups are built around interpersonal relationships that are part of preexisting work groups, families, and neighborhood association patterns.

Turner and Killian (1972) point out that an "ephemeral and temporary" division of labor emerges among community members following disaster. This division of labor arises with respect to tasks such as rescue and transporting survivors to hospitals and, later, to tasks such as removing fallen trees, mud, broken glass, and wreckage of buildings. Volunteer work crews are also formed to transport and distribute fresh water, food, and clothing and to provide transportation for community members.

Louis A. Zurcher (1968) participated in and studied such work crews following a Kansas tornado. Zurcher notes that some work crews emerged from preformed groups such as the Mennonite Disaster Services and civic clubs such as the Veterans of Foreign Wars. Other work crews consisted of residents who were strangers to one another prior to the disaster. These work crews emerged about thirty-six hours after the tornado struck and were relatively small, usually consisting of fewer than fifteen people. Zurcher described those who joined as people who had no "preempting obligations to help specific relatives, friends, or neighbors" and had found "appropriate channels for their motives to volunteer." One might speculate that in addition to the obvious opportunity to help one's neighbors and community, disasters give some people an opportunity to dramatically justify their earlier purchase of four-wheel-drive vehicles, chain saws, and CB radios.

Discussion

Turner and Killian make frequent use of disaster-related examples when they present the emergent norm perspective of collective behavior. For Turner and Killian, disaster turns people's concerns to the repairing and maintaining of personal ties and organizational relationships. Dynes's typology of organizational response summarizes the kinds of changes that have been observed among different organizations as they work to meet the challenges imposed by disaster. In brief, the organizational changes that occur during disaster are related to the tasks the organization regularly performs, or is prepared to perform, as well as to the organization's structure prior to disaster.

Established organizations carry out familiar tasks and undergo minimal restructuring during disaster. These groups have clear and traditional roles in disaster recovery. Expanding organizations are prepared to carry out familiar tasks but must expand or alter their structure to do so. Expanding organizations, such as the

American Red Cross, often have traditional roles in disaster recovery. Extending organizations accomplish nonregular tasks during disaster with essentially the same structure used in their day-to-day operations. Extending groups generally have no traditional role in disaster recovery. Finally, emergent groups form at the scene of disaster to meet the most immediate demands of rescue and, later, to play an active role in neighborhood cleanup and recovery. These groups emerge out of family, work, and neighborhood networks of interpersonal association. Typically, these groups last only a short time and dissolve toward the end of the disaster recovery period.

Interorganizational Responses to Disaster

Disaster brings about temporary changes within organizations; it also brings about many changes among organizations. Before disaster, the relationship between the police department and the local Red Cross chapter may be quite indirect. For example, some police officers may take first-aid refresher courses offered by the Red Cross. During disaster, however, the relationship between the police department and the Red Cross chapter may be more immediate and direct. Police officers and Red Cross volunteers may work side by side while rescuing people. These organizations will probably see the need to exchange information with one another. Police may be asked to provide vehicles and officers to assist in Red Cross efforts to distribute food and clothing. Police concerns for security and traffic control may directly conflict with Red Cross volunteers' desire to have free access to the disaster site. A wide range of interorganizational changes have been documented. Dynes (1978) has condensed these findings into an overall summary of interorganizational responses to disaster.

Communication.   The first interorganizational response to occur following disaster is usually the joining together of organizations for the purpose of communication. Immediately following disasters, survivors gather together and exchange information about injuries and property damage. Often, they gather near prominent landmarks or places offering shelter or adjacent to areas accessible to emergency vehicles. Many of the injured are brought to this gathering place for aid and transportation to hospitals. Others gather here to inquire about the missing and injured. This site emerges as the operations center for further rescue and recovery work. Representatives of various organizations converge on this site and expand the scope of its operations. Probably the first organization to be represented is the police, followed by hospital personnel. Short-wave and CB radio clubs may also set up equipment at this location, further enlarging the communications link to the outside. Later, the Red Cross, Boy Scouts, church groups, and private vendors may also converge to provide food and coffee to those in the operations center and to neighborhood work crews.

Recovery Task Coordination and Resource Allocation.   Another interorganizational response emerges to deal with the substantial problems of recovery task coordination and resource allocation. Looking after the injured is usually given clear priority in disasters. Once this task is in hand, however, there is often considerably less consensus regarding the next priority. Should city work crews, for example, be assigned to help utilities restore electrical and telephone service, or should they help the municipal water department? Representatives of the organizations involved in disaster-related activities meet and reach a working consensus regarding community priorities. Temporary lines of authority are established among representatives of city work crews, utilities, and groups under contract to provide cleanup services. Representatives of voluntary organizations and emergent work crews may also seek or be requested to provide input into these decisions. This group functions around-the-clock to settle procedural problems as they arise.

Disaster-Related Scarcity.   A third type of interorganizational response arises to deal with disaster-related scarcity. Hospitals may trade thermometers for antibiotics in an effort to meet immediate postdisaster medical needs. Suppliers may be asked to make special deliveries of surgical equipment. Private pilots and corporations may be asked to make their aircraft available for transporting medical supplies and personnel. City governments may approach county agencies and private contractors for the use of heavy equipment. In disaster, organizations unfamiliar with one another tend to avoid communication. Usually, organizations see if they can obtain assistance from their old suppliers and clients before initiating new relationships. As each organization restores contacts with its suppliers and clients, a web of functional integration is established that facilitates disaster response.

Excess Resources.   Interorganizational responses also arise to deal with the surprising problem of excess resources. Following many disasters, communities have been swamped with unsolicited aid in the form of food, clothing, and various other tangible items (Fritz and Mathewson 1957). Some of this aid can be of immediate use to disaster victims. Much, however, is not. Donated goods arrive in amounts far greater than what is needed. Some items are either not needed at all or are unusable. There are instances in which disaster victims have been shipped truckloads of unlabeled and damaged canned goods, gigantic tennis shoes, used magazines, defective electric fans, and lice-infested used clothing. In some cases, disaster

victims were asked to pay shipping costs. Perhaps some of these gift givers view disasters as an opportunity for tax deductions or as a dumping ground for unwanted items. Even if they are given an opportunity to refuse these gifts, disaster victims frequently accept them in an effort not to appear ungrateful. In any event, unsolicited goods add to disaster site congestion and may disrupt the local economy. More important, from the standpoint of organizations, the storage, sorting, and distribution of unsolicited goods absorb the services of people and material resources that could be used for more essential tasks. The distribution of donated items, whether they are critically needed or not, can cause conflict between organizations, as well as between organizations and the general populace.

Means of Interorganizational Response

Interorganizational responses occur with respect to problems of restoring communication, task coordination and resource allocation, disaster-related scarcity, and control of excess resources. How do organizations get together in the wake of disaster to solve these problems?

Prior Planning.   One means of interorganizational response is through prior planning. Some communities maintain disaster preparedness and evacuation programs that specify the roles that many community-based organizations will play in disaster response. Often, police are assigned primary responsibility for sounding warnings, making evacuation decisions, and establishing postdisaster communication with organizations outside the affected area. Firefighting priorities are established for the fire department. Some city governments have standing contracts with private construction firms for the temporary use of heavy equipment in the event of disaster. Church and civic groups may make their own plans for distributing donated goods.

Planning for disaster does not guarantee that all problems of interorganizational coordination can be eliminated. As communities grow and change, these programs can quickly become obsolete. Further, planners of disaster preparedness programs cannot anticipate all community needs created by disaster; nor can they know the capabilities of emergent groups. Some community organizations will be totally unaware of disaster plans. Finally, many communities have no disaster plans at all. Fortunately, there are other means of interorganizational response.

The Emergency Domain. In addition to prior planning, organizations get together by way of organizational goals and leadership decisions. Dynes refers to this as association on the basis of legitimate claims on the emergency domain. Established groups such as police and fire departments, hospitals, and utility companies, as well as many expanding groups such as the Red Cross and Salvation Army, have clear and undisputed claims on the emergency domain. These organizations will be among the first to contact one another in the event of a disaster.

Extending and emergent organizations have a less clear claim to the emergency domain. Their role in disaster response may be dictated by circumstance rather than by any generally recognized claim to the emergency domain. For example, because their refrigeration units were still working, milk warehouses were used to store blood following the Johnstown flood. Fast-food outlets may extend their hours as the demand for quick meals increases. Boat clubs and four-wheel-drive clubs may provide rescue and transportation services during floods and blizzards.

The degree to which the leadership of these groups can integrate their activities with those of police, hospitals, and other organizations with clear claim on the emergency domain will determine the success of these groups' claim to legitimacy. They may be viewed as providing a valuable service, or they may be seen as a nuisance. Even emergent cleanup crews are occasionally seen as an annoyance by police and National Guard who try to control movement within the disaster area.

Finally, some organizations make no claim on the emergency domain. High schools cancel athletic events, theaters and department stores close, and bridge, garden, and literary clubs cancel their meetings. In part, these organizations cease operation because of personnel defection to organizations with greater claim on the emergency domain. When these organizations once again begin to operate, it usually denotes the end of the disaster period.

Supplier-Client Relationships. Another means of interorganizational response is by way of previously established supplier-client relationships. These relationships provide a network of association that can be partially or totally activated following disaster. This usually occurs in response to problems of disaster-related scarcity. Dynes suggests that there is a tendency to initiate few new supplier-client relationships for the purpose of disaster response. In part, this may be due to the difficulties that organizations have in judging one another's reliability and competence during disaster. Further, disaster frequently creates the need for special orders, processing, delivery, and means of payment. Shipments of items needed at the scene of the disaster must be given priority, while shipments of unneeded items must be postponed until clients are ready to receive them. Such special needs are best met through long-established supplier-client relationships.

Personal Contact. Finally, interorganizational response is carried out through personal

tions, such as drug and alcohol rehabilitation programs or church programs that provide counsel to troubled teenagers, also meet this function. Families and friendship groups also meet needs in this area, particularly at times of childbirth, illness, or death.

Community Structure

Community structure provides the means through which the above functions are carried out in a regular and predictable fashion. Wenger identifies four important features of community structure.

Cultural Values and Beliefs.   Values are collective definitions of what is good, just, and worthy of achieving. In modern, ethnically and occupationally diverse communities, there is a minimal consensus of values; many divergent values are pursued simultaneously within the community. Despite this marked diversity of values, however, beliefs in modern communities tend to reflect an "individualistic-activistic" stance toward life. That is, individual efforts on one's own behalf are seen as the best way of relating to the world. Further, it is believed that the individual pursuit of self-interest and personal gain generally contributes to the overall good of the community.

Normative Structure. Normative structure refers to the explicit and implicit guidelines for behavior that exists within a community. As is the case with values, normative consensus is relatively low in communities with high ethnic and occupational diversity. Still, some general normative guidelines exist, the most important of which are the traditional rights and concerns that accompany property ownership. There is also a tendency to judge collective decisions in terms of long-range consequences and cost effectiveness. There are also those norms that constitute distinctions of

status. These norms regulate interaction between the rich and the poor and between men and women, and they usually tend to establish nonegalitarian patterns of interaction between these groups.

Organizational Structure.   The formal ties among organizations whose primary activities are carried out within and for the community are part of community organizational structure. These include the organizational ties between the police and fire departments or between hospitals, patients, and local sources of medical supplies and other services.

Another element of community organizational structure is the extent of ties to organizations outside the community, many of which are hierarchical in nature, such as the relationship between local welfare agencies and state departments of welfare. In these types of relationships, the local community organization is in a subordinate position.

Modern communities have extensive ties with nonlocal organizations. To the extent that these ties predominate, those between local organizations are less central to the overall functioning of the community. Further, extensive ties between local subordinate organizations and distant superordinate organizations reduce community autonomy.

Power Relationships.   According to many sociologists, power relationships in modern communities typically follow the pluralist pattern. That is, there are several sources of power within any community, and there are many conflicting interests among people and organizations with power. Consequently, the power relationships within a community are seldom directed toward a common objective. Some sources of power, such as police, fire, and welfare departments, operate in clearly defined areas. Other sources of power, including property ownership, possession of scarce skills and

knowledge, interpersonal influence, and political parties, operate in less clearly defined
areas. Power derived from these sources is often exercised indirectly and intermittently.

Response to Disaster and Alterations in Community Functions

The functional and structural components
of community life discussed above are generally taken for granted within the communities in
which they operate. That is, community functions are carried out concurrently, with little
concern for overall priorities. The elements of
community structure order activity in such a
manner that community functions are carried
out on a continuing basis. Disasters disrupt
this fluid nature of community life. In disaster,
people must immediately consider the priority
of community functions, and they must alter
community structure accordingly.

*Production, Distribution, and Consump-
tion.* Following disasters, normal production, distribution, and consumption activities
are typically given low priority. Factories and
many retail stores cease operation during the
early stages of disaster recovery, while facilities with clear relevance to the immediate crisis
are given priority. As the earlier discussion of
extending organizations indicates, disaster-
related operations are usually quite different
from normal operations. Disasters overload
and often cripple transportation facilities, so
trucks, buses, vans, and autos are pressed into
emergency service to take the injured to hospitals or transport the dead to morgues. Police
may allow only emergency-related traffic into
the disaster area while halting or rerouting
normal commercial traffic. The reopening of
factories, stores, offices, and normal traffic
routes usually denotes the end of the initial recovery period.

Socialization. Socialization functions are
also given low priority during early stages of
disaster recovery. Schools are often turned
into emergency shelters and distribution centers. In some cases, schools are unable to function normally because area transportation
facilities are in shambles. The reopening of
schools also signals the end of the initial recovery period.

Participation. The social participation
function of community life takes on increased
visibility and priority in disaster. This is the
case even though conventional forms of community participation such as work and school
have been temporarily suspended. Disaster
fosters social participation in other ways. Immediate demands are created by the tasks of
rescuing and transporting the injured. Cleanup
crews emerge, and volunteer groups, such as the
Red Cross or Salvation Army, are activated.

There are also some less obvious channels
of social participation. The elderly, for example, may be drawn into more intense community involvement as their neighbors, at least
for a time, show greater concern for their
physical and emotional welfare. Older people
may also be requested to look after children
during later recovery efforts. Teenagers, who
occupy many marginal roles in community
life, often find opportunities in disaster to fill
more central roles in emergency social systems. Form and Nosow (1958) note that teenagers ran errands, carried emergency supplies,
and even transported the dead and injured to
hospitals following a Michigan tornado. Teenagers often constitute a major portion of the
work force recruited to heft sandbags during
floods.

Finally, in the days following disaster,
neighborhood groups and organizations spon-
sor fish frys, chicken barbecues, and other
communal functions that sometimes impart a
festivallike atmosphere and help to dispel the
depression that accompanies cleanup efforts.

Social Control. Community social control functions are given greater priority during disaster. This is the case even though some social control activities may be relaxed during disaster; specifically, some research suggests that police assign lower priority to making arrests for traffic offenses, drunkenness, and disturbing the peace (Wenger 1978). In part, this may be due to a lower incidence of these offenses during disaster recovery. In any event, police priorities shift to the prevention of looting. The generally recognized low incidence of looting during disaster may be due to these efforts, although some suggest that police are overly concerned with looting and could better serve their communities by giving more attention to other functions.

A major social control function for police, and other groups as well, is dealing with the convergence of people and donated goods to the disaster site. Traffic control problems are often aggravated by sightseers and outsiders who have come to the community to volunteer their labor. Church groups usually take an active role in storing, sorting, distributing, and, in some cases, disposing of donated goods.

Mutual Support. The social support function of community life emerges as a clear priority during the early stages of disaster recovery. For a time, life in the community becomes emotionally and physically intimate. Neighbors who may have hardly spoken to one another now share fears, hurts, and hopes. Outward signs of support and caring, such as pats on the back, hand holding, and hugging, are more frequent than usual.

Perhaps this intimacy arises because there is an increased reliance on face-to-face communication in the emergency social system. Further, there are fewer social barriers to communication in the emergency social system. Damaged houses, for example, no longer provide seclusion for their occupants. Clothing that is borrowed, torn, or mud stained is unlikely to convey social standing. The elderly who seldom venture from their homes may be quite literally thrust into the social life of their neighborhood by disaster. Community response to disaster takes on an intimate and supportive character in part because many of the facades and tactics we use to isolate ourselves from others no longer operate.

A major mutual support concern within a community is sheltering the homeless. Communities provide temporary shelter in gymnasiums, auditoriums, and church basements. These public shelters are almost always more than sufficient to meet the needs of the homeless, because many people make their homes available to relatives and friends who need shelter (Dacy and Kunreuther 1969). Social relationships established in public shelters are likely to reflect mutual support, even between ethnic groups who have previously experienced mutual antagonism (Fritz, Rayner, and Guskin 1958). However, research also suggests that the longer these temporary living arrangements are maintained, the greater the likelihood that disharmony will develop.

Another mutual support function to emerge during disaster is that of victim-advocate. After disaster, many victims must deal with insurance companies, find sources of credit, perhaps seek public aid, and, in general, deal with a number of private and governmental agencies. For many, this is an unfamiliar, first-time experience. Though most disaster victims can handle these difficulties by themselves, some cannot. Increasingly, church groups are recognizing this need and including victim-advocate programs as part of their disaster assistance planning (Bush 1979). Victim-advocates help people deal with private and governmental agencies in the aftermath of disaster. In particular, victim-advocate programs target the elderly, the non-English-speaking, the poor, and small businesses for their services. A few victim-advocate programs provide volunteers to assist in the repairing and rebuilding of homes and businesses.

Finally, some mutual support efforts take the form of programs that provide long-term counseling to disaster victims. Months after a disaster, some people still need to ventilate their fears and feelings about what happened. Often, these people were injured, had family members killed, or sustained major property losses. Also, some parents may need to discuss the adjustment problems of their children in the wake of disaster. These programs pull together volunteers with skills in the areas of personal and family counseling, such as clergy and social work students (Bush 1979).

Response to Disaster and Alterations in Community Structure

The alterations in community functions summarized by Wenger entail corresponding alterations in community structure. When there are forewarnings of danger, as with hurricanes, some structural changes may occur before disaster strikes.

Values and Beliefs. Disaster brings about a temporary consensus of values and a change in beliefs. Disaster focuses community concerns on humanitarian values of care for the injured, aid for the homeless; and the protection of life over property. Diverse materialistic values, for the moment, are of secondary importance. At hardly any other time are people in a community as united in their concerns for the well-being of others.

Beliefs in the utility of self-interest shift to beliefs in the benefits of working for the common good. Beliefs about self-reliance become tempered with the recognition that some needs are best met through the generosity and cooperation of others. In later stages of disaster recovery, beliefs about the cause of disaster may become important. This is particularly true for

such technological disasters as mine explosions, refinery fires, or hazardous chemical spills. In these instances, much postdisaster concern centers on the assignment of blame. Those deemed responsible may escape censure if they can clearly demonstrate predisaster competence and concern for safety. If not, these people are likely to be charged with incompetence and greed (Drabek and Quarantelli 1967). Such charges may permanently alter the relationship between organizations and the community.

Normative Structure. Most changes in the normative structure are related to the use of property. Emergent norms often override the traditional rights and concerns that accompany property ownership. Immediately following disaster impact, all kinds of goods are appropriated for the use of rescuing and transporting the injured. People who own tractors, trucks, boats, and airplanes are often confronted with demands to assist in rescue efforts. Few owners deny these requests, even though the wear and tear on their equipment may be substantial. Other goods and equipment are pressed into service in a manner that would constitute theft in nondisaster situations. For example, people may break locks of company equipment sheds in the early stages of disaster response. Later, most if not all items commandeered in this fashion are returned.

Another type of norm to emerge in the early stages of disaster response is that of immediacy: disaster victims want action, the sooner the better (Bruning 1964). During this stage of disaster response, relatively few decisions are made in terms of long-range consequences or overall cost effectiveness. Rather, decisions are made and judged in terms of immediate effectiveness. Sometimes, for example, casualties are brought to hospitals in subcompact cars, while four-wheel-drive trucks are being used to carry a few pints of blood to aid stations near the disaster site. This is certainly not a cost-effective or even convenient use of resources. But in terms of immediate effectiveness, it works: casualties are getting to the hospital, and blood is getting to the disaster site.

Disaster responses may alter norms that regulate interpersonal relationships. Emergent norms in this area tend to be more egalitarian than those prior to disaster. Patterns of association based on distinctions of high and low social status are temporarily abandoned; that is, the rich and the poor are more likely to treat each other as equals during disaster. Further, norms that regulate relationships between ethnic groups are much less salient. Finally, women may temporarily have access to roles normally carried out by men.

Organizational Structure. During disaster response, alterations in organizational structure usually take the form of an overall strengthening of a community's internal and external organizational ties; that is, the number and intensity of contacts between organizations substantially increase. Dormant ties are reactivated and new ones are sometimes initiated.

The strengthening of organizational ties is quite obvious when communities have some forewarning of disaster, as when a community braces itself for a hurricane. This preimpact stage is characterized by intense interorganizational contact within a community. Local hospitals take stock of their supplies and contact each other regarding last-minute needs. Police departments issue statements to radio and television stations, while factory and business personnel contact police and radio stations to inquire about the severity of winds and danger of flooding.

The preimpact stage is also characterized by greater contact with organizations outside the community. Police and fire departments maintain closer contact with the National Weather Service. Hospitals reaffirm mutual aid agreements with hospitals outside the community.

Local Red Cross chapters contact state organizations to discuss impending needs, and National Guard units are placed on standby alert.

Interorganizational ties within a community remain strong during and immediately following disaster impact. However, ties to organizations outside the community may be temporarily weakened or broken. This may be due to temporary isolation caused by damage to telephone lines, collapsed bridges, or flooded highways. To the degree that external ties are broken, community autonomy is increased. This temporary isolation and autonomy can be a positive factor in early disaster response. Community needs are more easily given priority over the interests or policies of distant superordinate organizations. For instance, it is easier for extending organizations to loan personnel and equipment when the home office is unable to voice objections. It may even be possible to conceal the extent of this community assistance.

In the later stages of disaster recovery, external ties are once again intensified. This is particularly true for expanding organizations such as the Red Cross, which receives money, supplies, supervisory personnel, and volunteers from regional headquarters. On the other hand, the added presence of outside organizational personnel increases the likelihood that the needs of these organizations will take precedence over local interests. That is why the later stages of disaster response are often marked by greater amounts of dispute and bad feelings.

Power Relationships. Community disaster response usually involves a temporary alteration in power relationships. The pluralistic pattern of power relationships is replaced by a more centralized and authoritarian power structure. Following disaster, an ad hoc group of representatives from city government, police, volunteer organizations, and private business is formed to deal with the problems of recovery task coordination and resource allocation. For a time, this group occupies a central authority role within the community. Typically, this group is quite unified in terms of recovery goals. Such centralized authority and goal consensus seldom exist in everyday situations.

Power is also used in a more authoritarian fashion in the disaster-struck community. Given the sense of urgency in the early stages of disaster response, few people object to the orders they receive from the police. Authoritarian structure is most clearly seen when military organizations such as the National Guard are used in disaster recovery. Community members may be required to get travel permits in order to go to their homes in the disaster area. Curfews are imposed as a precaution against looters or as a means to discourage sightseeing. Initially, community members view these authoritarian measures as necessary or at least tolerable. In the later stages of disaster recovery, however, travel permits, roadblocks, and curfews may actually impede recovery efforts. Consequently, community members come to regard authoritarian measures as disagreeable and voice their objections.

Finally, there is the issue of emergent leadership during disaster. What are the personal characteristics of those who assume unusually active roles in disaster situations? According to the findings of disaster research, the effective community leader usually possesses disaster-related skills and has previous experience with disaster. In addition, these leaders have limited ego involvement in the situation. This means that people who know that their families and property are safe are more likely than others to tend to the larger needs of the community. Research also suggests that those who already occupy leadership positions are likely to extend their leadership functions during disaster. For example, business leaders, chiefs of police and fire departments, and hospital ad-

ministrators are more likely than others to assume major leadership roles in disaster recovery. In part, this may be because community members demand that people in these roles play a major role in disaster recovery.

Discussion

Much of our discussion so far would lead us to believe that disasters bring out the best in people. People do not panic but respond effectively to even the most terrifying situations; people tend to be altruistic in disaster; organizational priorities can quickly shift to meeting the immediate needs of the community; communities display a degree of harmony seldom seen in everyday situations. All these statements are supported by disaster research. However, the above statements apply mainly to the early stages of disaster recovery.

As communities enter the later stages of disaster recovery, we see a different picture. Once again, people begin to give priority to even minor individual and family needs and show less concern for the lingering problems of others. Invariably, stories circulate about people who lost nothing but received large amounts of aid and others who lost everything and received no aid. Relief agencies are charged with inefficiency and callousness. As organizations resume their normal operations, the full cost of the disaster comes into focus. City governments look at budgets that have been severely depleted or totally overrun. Earlier antagonisms that had been set aside emerge again. Political opponents charge one another with using the disaster situation for political gain. Groups within the community may object to proposed reconstruction plans.

Fortunately, disaster research shows that this period of disharmony also passes. Disaster nostalgia replaces emotional intensity. People tell their children how they survived the winter of 1977, how they cleaned up the house after the flood, and how they were never so frightened as when they saw the tornado coming. Within a few years, lives will have been resumed, organizations restored, and the rubble of disaster cleared. By then it will be difficult to detect any lasting effects of the disaster (Wright et al. 1979).

Societies in Disaster

Compared to what we know about individuals, organizations, and communities in disaster, we have relatively little specific knowledge about societies in disaster. Perhaps this is because we use a number of terms other than *disaster* to refer to calamitous events of sufficient scale that they produce noticeable changes in the operation of an entire society. Instead of calling these events disasters, we call them droughts, famines, plagues, and wars. Dynes (1975) has offered a classification of societies in terms of their vulnerability to disaster.

Dynes's Typology

In quite general terms, Dynes views the societal response to disaster as a result of population size, economic base, and the extent of coordination between organizational levels in the society. Taking these factors into account, Dynes identifies three types of societies with characteristic patterns of response to disaster.

Type I Societies. Type I societies have small populations and are organized in terms of family, kin, and clan or tribal relationships. The economic base of these societies is food gathering. Dynes characterizes these societies as having a tenuous ecological base, which makes them quite fragile and lacking in resources for adapting to disastrous situations. Consequently, disaster can produce considerable disruption and social change in these societies. In the most extreme cases, disaster can totally destroy these small, fragile societies.

Type II Societies. Type II societies have larger populations than Type I societies. Their economies are based on some sort of farming that regularly generates economic surplus. Consequently, Type II societies have some, though limited, ability to replace resources lost through disaster. Social organization is somewhat more complex in Type II societies and is based on villages that are integrated into regional forms of association, such as kingdoms and empires. Disasters produce moderate amounts of disruption and social change in Type II societies.

Type III Societies. These societies have large populations and highly complex and integrated social structures, such as nation states. They have considerable physical resources and surplus to replace what is lost through disaster. Type III societies also have agencies that are directly concerned with disaster response. Consequently, disaster produces relatively little social change and disruption in Type III societies.

Societal Consequences of Disaster. Dynes's threefold typology roughly follows the distinctions usually made between hunting and gathering, farming, and industrial societies. For Dynes, the impact of disasters is inversely related to the degree of modernity and technological development within a society. The "primitive" hunting and gathering societies are much less capable of coping with disaster than more "advanced" societies.

Dynes's view is clearly in keeping with conventional ideas regarding the relative capabilities of these societies. In the following sections, we will reexamine this view and present some alternate ideas.

Hunting and Gathering Societies

The species *Homo sapiens* emerged some fifty thousand years ago. Since then, more than 90 percent of human social experience has transpired within hunting and gathering societies. Although this way of life has often been characterized as fragile and ecologically tenuous, the hunting and gathering form of association has endured nearly five hundred centuries. Only in about the past ten thousand years have other forms of human association emerged to challenge this way of life (Fagan 1976).

Clan and tribal associations among hunting and gathering groups temporarily brought sizable populations together for the purposes of hunting, butchering, and drying meat, as well as trade (Wormington 1957). The primary structural unit of day-to-day association, however, was the family band. These microsocieties usually consisted of fifteen to forty people and seldom had more than one hundred members. As groups approached this upper limit of size, they broke into smaller groups and went their separate ways. When the first farming groups emerged, about ten thousand years ago, the world's population stood somewhere between 5 and 10 million people. This sparse population, however, was divided into more than one hundred thousand small hunting and gathering societies (Lenski and Lenski 1978).

The way of life in these small societies was characterized by almost continuous travel as they followed the seasons and herds of migrating animals. These groups did not build permanent dwellings. Igloos, yurts, tipis, and huts were either abandoned or dismantled and carried with them when the group moved on. It is quite likely that all the clothing, tools, and weapons that any one of these groups possessed could be packed into a small trailer.

How did disaster agents such as storms, droughts, fires, floods, and diseases affect these societies? Quite likely, hunting and gathering groups had no clear perception of disaster apart from their daily problems in living. What little evidence there is to support this assertion comes from studies of hunting and gathering groups that survived into the twentieth century. These include Eskimo groups, the !Kung bushmen of Africa, Indians of Central and South America, and some groups of the South Pacific Islands. Though these groups have words to refer to storms, floods, epidemics, and misfortune, they have no words that have an equivalent meaning to *disaster* (Jones 1971). Obviously, individual hunting and gathering groups were annihilated by flood, fire, volcanic explosions, and disease. This does not mean, however, that disaster agents usually caused widespread and substantial alterations in these societies. Rather, the mode of existence of hunting and gathering groups, in many respects, minimized the impact of these disaster agents.

In an economy based on hunting and gathering, every unit of energy put into the system in the form of hunting and gathering activity yields about 1.5 units of energy output in the form of food calories. Therefore, a hunt that yielded meat with a caloric value of 15,000 units involved the expenditure of 10,000 calories by the hunter, for a net gain of only 5,000 calories (Kemp 1971). Further, in a band of twenty people, there were probably no more than five prime hunters. Under these conditions, hunting and gathering groups lived with the constant peril of starvation. The injury of a hunter, or the failure of a hunt, could represent a disaster for the group. The way of life in hunting and gathering groups was structured in such a way as to eliminate, as much as possible, this potential for disaster.

Most hunting and gathering groups are perhaps better described as gathering and hunting groups. That is, gathering was usually their primary and most constant source of food. All members of the band helped in the gathering of vegetables, grains, bird eggs, fruits, nuts, and berries. Insects, rodents, and reptiles were also part of the diet of hunters and gatherers. This wide range of food items better ensured that people would not go hungry too often.

As noted above, the injury or death of a hunter could severely reduce a group's food supply. Consequently, the hunting methods used by these groups were quite unlike the techniques used by today's sportsmen. Hunters rarely engaged dangerous game in mortal combat, and when they did, it usually had ceremonial overtones. (Today's African bushmen, for example, occasionally hunt lion to prove their courage, and so they use only a single spear.) Everyday hunting methods for early hunters and gatherers relied heavily on the use of entrapment, poison, and the taking of small, young, or disabled animals. In Europe, hunters stampeded mammoths, bison, and wild horses into bogs where the animals became trapped in the mud. In North America, hunters stampeded large game over cliffs or into gullies (Wormington 1957). In Africa and the jungles of Central America, hunters developed a variety of poisons for use in the hunt. Eskimos used whalebone blades embedded in frozen meat to rupture the stomachs of polar bear. Many of these techniques resulted in substantial overkill, which may have contributed to the extinction of several animal species. However, these techniques ensured that the hunter would live to hunt another day.

Hunting and gathering societies were constantly on the move, following animal herds and gathering seasonal plant life along traditional migration routes. Their high mobility served to reduce the impact of localized weather conditions, such as floods and drought. These groups were often able to travel up to thirty miles in a single day and more than two hundred miles in a week. With their high degree of mobility, hunting and gathering groups could easily flee from immediate dangers or leave regions that were not to their liking.

It is easy to visualize a situation, such as a flash flood, in which a hunting and gathering group could lose most of its material possessions. This loss would not create as severe a hardship for hunters and gatherers as it would for people in other kinds of societies. Almost every member of a hunting and gathering band possessed basic survival skills. In a short period of time, nearly all the material goods necessary for the group's well-being could be fashioned from raw materials immediately at hand. Once they reached a place of comparative safety, the hunting and gathering band would quickly turn to the tasks of building fires, shelters, and tools. Within hours, the group would be warm and dry and have serviceable spears, bows, and arrows.

The hunting and gathering way of life served to keep human populations dispersed. Even in the most favorable environments, population density rarely exceeded three people per square mile. Not only were hunting and gathering populations sparse, contact between groups was infrequent. These ecological conditions inhibited the spread of contagious diseases such as smallpox, cholera, and plague.

The hunting and gathering way of life was ecologically suited to the environments in which it flourished, much more so than the ways of life that were to follow. Even so, hunting and gathering groups often faced severe hardship, and few of us today could successfully adapt to this way of life.

The most disastrous occurrence for hunters and gatherers was contact with other social forms. Hunters and gatherers have seldom been able to compete effectively for territory and other resources used by farming and industrial societies. Most often, hunters and gatherers retreated into lands that other societies considered worthless. With decreased mobility and increased population density, hunters and gatherers often fell victim to starvation and disease. The most obvious instance of this process was the concentration of the native American populations onto reservations, which began shortly after European colonies were established in the New World. Throughout the world, the process of concentration was often accompanied by vicious exterminations (Jones 1971). Even benevolent gestures such as introducing modern tools into their material culture often resulted in the destruction of hunting and gathering groups (Sharp 1952). Of the thousands of hunting and gathering groups that once existed, fewer than three hundred survived into this century. The destruction of these groups and their habitats has accelerated. In all likelihood, no hunting and gathering groups will survive into the next century (Lenski and Lenski 1978).

Farming Societies

The first farming societies emerged about ten thousand years ago in various parts of the world. Horticultural societies farmed the jungles, tilling small garden plots with digging sticks and hoes. Agricultural societies farmed the open lands, using plows and draft animals. Both types of farming societies sometimes used irrigation systems. Farming represented a tremendous shift in the energy flow within societies. Every unit of energy put into farming yields about fifteen or twenty units of energy output in the form of food calories (Rappaport 1971). Compared to hunting and gathering societies, farming societies generated economic surplus. Both horticultural and agricultural farming were accompanied by the growth of permanent settlements—villages, towns, and cities—and drastic increases in population density. Farming was also accompanied by the emergence of larger political units, such as city states, empires, and nations.

Although this way of life produced surplus, it also increased the potential for disasters, particularly those associated with crop failure.

In farming societies we see the expansion and formalization of religion. Asking the gods to deliver a good harvest was a central theme in early religions. In the Mayan and Aztec empires of Central America, human sacrifice was used to coax the gods into cooperation. The Mayans also took some matters into their own hands by constructing an elaborate system of wells and cisterns to carry the empire through the dry season. These wells and cisterns took on religious significance. Human sacrifices were carried out at the wells, and some of the Mayans' finest architecture and art was devoted to the construction and decoration of wells and cisterns. Activities such as these, carried out in farming societies, can be viewed as structural responses to disaster.

Unlike the temporary camps of the hunters and gatherers, permanent settlements are vulnerable to a number of disaster agents. Archaeological excavations reveal that many ancient villages were destroyed by earthquakes and floods. The majority, however, were destroyed by fire. In some cases, new villages were built upon the ashes of the old, only to be destroyed by fire once again. Whether by wind, fire, or water, the archaeological record offers ample evidence that the end of most ancient villages was disastrous.

Occasionally, archaeological digs reveal that settlements were abandoned while still intact. This and the predominance of burned villages suggests that epidemics may have been responsible for the extinction of many ancient villages. Early farming settlements were so spatially compact that, even though they seldom contained more than one hundred residents, the population *density* usually exceeded that of the worst slums of modern cities. This very high population density, coupled with a near total lack of sewage facilities, created ideal conditions for the spread of plague, cholera, and smallpox. Surviving descriptions of Europe's plague years often mention that villages were burned and abandoned when they were struck by disease.

Compared to hunting and gathering societies or industrial societies, early farming societies were probably the least able to respond to disaster. To a large degree, early political systems, particularly empires, were systems designed to systematically exploit and drain the resources within a given region for the benefit of the central authority. When outlying towns were struck by disaster, they could expect little organized assistance from the central authority. Even if the central authority sought to provide assistance, it was severely hindered in its efforts by slow and unreliable transportation systems. There are places in the world today where material and political conditions are hardly better than those confronting ancient farming societies. It is in these areas that the impact of disaster is most keenly felt.

Industrial Societies

A number of definitions of an industrial society are available. According to their common elements, an industrial society is one in which (1) less than half of the population is directly engaged in farming, (2) most wealth is generated through industrial production, and (3) more than 2,000 kg of coal-equivalent energy is consumed annually per person. According to this definition, Japan, Taiwan, Mexico, Canada, the United States, and nearly all the nations of Europe are industrial societies.

Early industrial societies continued the trend of growth and population concentration found in farming societies, and their cities were as unsanitary and disease ridden as the towns in farming societies. Today, the urban centers of industrial societies are considerably cleaner and safer than they once were. People no longer live in constant fear of mass epidemics of deadly contagious diseases. This relative safety depends upon complex and expensive systems of sewage disposal and carefully monitored programs of inoculation and public health measures. Were these complex systems to break down, as would likely be the case in the event of nuclear war, survivors would soon experience firsthand the horrors of the epidemics of the past.

In industrial societies, certain agencies have direct roles in disaster response and recovery. In part, this is the result of increased awareness of industrial societies' tremendous structural interdependence of regions, organizations, and functions, and the need for some mechanism to quickly repair breaks in this social fabric. The existence of disaster-related agencies also presupposes that industrial societies anticipate a given amount of disruption from disaster agents. These disruptions can be anticipated because of the demographic characteristics of industrial societies.

Industrial societies increasingly press into disaster-prone areas. For millions of years, hurricanes have battered the Eastern Seaboard of the United States, the Gulf of Mexico, and the eastern coast of Central and South America, all now heavily populated. The ancient Mayans in the Yucatan adapted to this feature of the environment by building villages and cities well inland or on high ground (Kurjack 1974; Sanders and Marino 1970). Even today, those who live near these sites are seldom harmed by hurricanes. Recent settlement patterns in this area, however, clearly favor beachfront development. Resorts, hotels, and private homes—as well as the people in them—now fall victim to disaster.

Similar things can be said about modern settlement patterns on the Gulf of Mexico. Nearly 6 million people now live in southern Florida, once the home of a few hunting and gathering bands.

The city of San Francisco is built over the San Andreas fault line, another disaster-prone area. In 1906, San Francisco was heavily damaged by earthquake and resulting fires. Much additional damage occurred when dynamite was used to blast a firebreak across the city because water lines were ruptured by the quake. The effects of the disaster resulted from the combined effects of the disaster agent and the lack of disaster preparedness in the community.

The growth of industrial societies has also increased the likelihood of technological disasters, the potential scope of which is limited only by our imaginations (Vacca 1974). Some immediate concerns are worth mentioning. The transportation of poisonous or explosive chemicals has resulted in many fatal disasters and emergency evacuations, while the transportation of liquified natural gas (LNG) poses a disaster threat of incredible magnitude. Ships carrying thousands of tons of LNG routinely enter New York Harbor and the East River. Though it is claimed that the explosion of a fully laden LNG tanker is unlikely (but not impossible), the explosion—if it did occur—would be larger than the atomic explosion over Hiroshima. Some have even speculated that an unexpected explosion of an LNG tanker in New York Harbor might be mistaken for a nuclear explosion and accidentally trigger a nuclear war. Contingency plans call for firefighters to abandon the harbor area and begin fighting fires four miles inland (Mostert 1974). In the past fifteen years, large oil tankers have exploded in various oceans of the world. These explosions have been less powerful than the explosion of an LNG tanker would be. Still, had one of these explosions occurred in a populous area instead of in a remote loading terminal or at sea, it would have constituted one of the largest disasters to befall an industrial society.

There are also silent disasters posed by the disposal of dangerous chemicals. The Love Canal disaster illustrates this problem. The scale of contamination was sufficient that hundreds of people lost their homes as a result of careless but common chemical disposal procedures. Recent attempts to reclaim some of the homes

at the edge of the contaminated area have fostered considerable debate. In any event, it is unlikely that people who move back to Love Canal will ever be completely at ease with their decision. One outcome of this disaster is that it dramatically calls attention to the fact that industrial societies have little control over the amount of lethal industrial byproducts they generate. Love Canal has also shown that we have virtually no social mechanism, apart from the profit motive, to substantially reduce the amount of chemical dumping. Finally, Love Canal has shown us that the costs of cleaning up even small chemical dumps are well beyond the budgets of most local governments. Undoubtedly, a large portion of these costs will have to be shared by the federal government or directly assessed to the industries that did the dumping. Even then, the cleanup costs may equal or surpass the $90 billion that were spent to put men on the moon. Ultimately, we may find that some dumps cannot be cleaned up, and communities will have suffered irreparable damage. As with Love Canal, the dump area will be paved over and surrounded by chain link fences. Even then, underground water supplies will be highly contaminated.

Finally, there is the slow disaster. For decades scientists have warned of ocean pollution, but little general concern has been shown, in part because it is difficult to "show" people clear evidence of damage to the oceans. Even major oil spills can be cleaned up, and later studies show that the oil has little lasting impact on ocean life. At least this is the case where oil spills occur infrequently. In areas where oil and other chemical dumping is routine, the surrounding ocean areas are dead. The degree to which the oceans can sustain this present burden is debatable. The problem with slow disasters is that when the first dramatic signs of danger appear, it may be too late to prevent disaster. Those who study the ocean ecological system fear that by the time they convince nations that the oceans are dying, it will no longer be possible to save the oceans.

Other slow disasters include air pollution and the accompanying acid rains and climatic alterations. There is also concern with the degree of genetic standardization of world food crops. Each of these slow disasters could inflict damage on the world food supply beyond the range of human experience. In the last twenty years, for example, nations have come to rely on fewer genetic varieties of rice, soybeans, wheat, and corn. As food crops become more standardized, the possibility arises that a few crop diseases could spread worldwide and destroy a large portion of the food supply.

We have seen how difficult it is to get families to evacuate their communities in the face of such obvious threats as flood and fire. How then can we get people to take seriously those threats that manifest only subtle and conflicting signs of danger? These "disasters in disguise" have been created almost exclusively by the industrial social order.

In some respects, industrial societies are well equipped to respond to and recover from disaster. They have rapid and reliable systems of communication and transportation, as well as economic surplus that can be used to tide people over while disaster recovery efforts are underway. Industrialized nations have many organizations with a clear responsibility for disaster response and recovery. In the United States we have the Red Cross, Salvation Army, and the Mennonite Disaster Service. The National Weather Service monitors and reports on dangerous storms. The National Guard and U.S. Army Corps of Engineers restore essential services and clear debris. Financial assistance for disaster victims is made available through the Federal Disaster Assistance Administration and the Small Business Administration. The Farmers' Home Administration provides disaster relief loans to farmers.

However, industrial societies have created new kinds of disasters with air and water pol-

lution and the disposal of hazardous wastes. They have not adapted to this type of disaster as well as they have to natural disasters. Had Love Canal been hit by a tornado, for example, residents would have received all sorts of immediate and long-term aid from a number of sources. As it was, however, it took years of petition and protest before government agencies would acknowledge the existence of a problem. Even then, some public officials stoutly denied that the high rate of miscarriages, birth defects, cancer, lung diseases, and genetic abnormalities were the results of the chemicals buried under Love Canal. It took nearly five years of agitation before the president of the United States declared Love Canal a Federal Disaster Area, and it took an act of Congress before the government agreed to buy up the homes. It is too soon to tell whether industrial societies possess the adaptability and resources to prevent or recover from these disasters of their own making.

Summary

In this chapter we have examined disasters from the standpoint of responses made by organizations, communities, and societies. From the standpoint of organizational responses to disaster, such efforts involve varying degrees of change in organizational structure. Many of these changes can be understood in terms of an organization's expected and official role in disaster reponse. Organizations with a clearly defined and immediate role in disaster response undergo fewer internal changes than other organizations. Supplier-client and interpersonal contacts between organizations are of immediate importance in establishing interorganizational responses to disaster.

At the community level of analysis, social participation, social control, and mutual support functions predominate in community responses to disaster. Disaster response also produces a temporary but obvious convergence of community values, beliefs, norms, and power structure. Organizational ties within a community are strengthened through intense interaction. For a short period of time, communities enjoy greater autonomy because of weakened ties to external organizations. Finally, communities usually demonstrate remarkably rapid and complete recovery from disaster.

At the societal level, different types of societies have experienced and responded to disasters in different ways, according to their population size, economic base, and extent of coordination between organizational levels. In all likelihood, hunting and gathering societies of the past had no conception of disaster apart from the problems they faced on a daily basis. The small size, great mobility, and sparse distribution of these groups greatly alleviated the effects of most natural disaster agents, such as hurricanes, floods, droughts, earthquakes, and disease. Most members of hunting and gathering societies possessed essential survival skills. Further, these groups could make nearly all their material possessions from raw materials near at hand. Consequently, these groups were able to quickly replace much of what was lost through accident or disaster.

Farming societies historically contained densely populated permanent settlements. These villages and towns seem to have been quite prone to destruction by earthquakes, floods, and fire. They were also subject to fatal epidemics. The regional coordination within early political systems was often ineffective, and as a result, disaster-struck areas received little if any assistance from central authorities. Farming societies have historically been the least able to cope with disaster.

Industrial societies have largely eliminated epidemics as a disaster agent. However, populations of industrial societies have increasingly pressed into disaster-prone areas, including coastal areas battered by hurricanes, floodplains, and geological fault zones. Most industrial societies possess disaster response organizations that mobilize rapid and effective assistance. It is too soon to tell whether these organizations will be able to cope as readily with large-scale technological disasters.

CHAPTER 11

Individuals and Riots

Many of the hostilities that led to the American Revolution were riots. Further, a major riot has probably occurred in the United States during every decade since our nation was founded. Riots and their effects on people and institutions have been a longstanding concern in the field of collective behavior.

Most people agree that riots involve crowds and injury or the threat of injury to people or property. Beyond this, there is little agreement. Civil and military authorities in the United States must act on the basis of legal definitions of riots. To authorities, riots are a form of collective behavior that is by definition against the law. In Chapter 12 we will briefly consider some of the legal definitions of riots used in the United States. Sociological characterizations, however, are more elaborate, divergent, and certainly less exact than legal definitions. We will discuss how the mass hysteria, emergent norm, value-added, and SBI perspectives characterize riots.

Between 1965 and 1972, several hundred riots occurred in the United States. Most occurred in our major cities. In 1967 alone, eighty-three people were killed, nearly two thousand were injured, and nearly $100 million worth of property was destroyed. In the aftermath of this horrendous loss of life and property, governmental and private agencies tried to find out why the riots were occurring.

Consequently, a very large volume of riot-related research was accumulated during the late 1960s and early 1970s. Even today, sociologists often return to this data with new questions and ideas. In order to systematically explore this large body of research, we will examine riots from the standpoint of individual participation and, in Chapter 12, from the levels of organizational, community, and societal responses to riots.

Sociologists frequently refer to three types of riots: communal riots, political riots, and commodity riots. *Communal riots* are characterized by collective violence between opposing racial or religious groups; they are also commonly referred to as "race riots." The antagonists are usually civilians, and conflict starts over some contested area, such as a neighborhood, beach, or factory (Janowitz 1968). Police may inflict casualties as they attempt to keep opposing groups apart, but most injuries and deaths result from attacks by civilians on one another.

In *political riots*, violence centers on a specific government policy. England's Gordon Riots of 1780, America's antidraft riots during the Civil War, and some anti–Vietnam War disorders fall within this category. Generally, the contending groups in a political riot are civilians and the police or military who are attempting to quell the disorder. The actions of citizens usually take the form of rowdy disobedience of government representatives. Occasionally, citizens attack police with clubs, rocks, bricks, or other projectiles. Sometimes civilians attack government property that symbolizes the issues involved. Rarely do civilians use firearms or such weapons as Molotov cocktails. Nearly all casualties and injuries in political riots are inflicted by authorities as they attempt to restore order.

In *commodity riots*, the object of attack is more clearly the property rather than the people of another racial or religious group. In commodity riots, violence is directed primarily at the buildings, merchandise, and equipment of another group. In the 1700s, workers who smashed the machinery being brought into factories to replace them and housewives who overturned grocery stalls during the "bread riots," or blacks who looted and burned white-owned businesses in the ghetto in the 1960s were involved in commodity riots. Though commodity riots do involve isolated attacks by civilians on one another, most violence occurs between civilians who are attacking or looting property and the authorities who are trying to stop them.

Two Riots

We begin this chapter with a description of a communal riot and a political riot. We will then consider riots from the standpoint of each of the general theories of collective behavior. Each presents a different view of the nature of riots and the activities of which they are composed. We will review and discuss research that was conducted to test the value-added theory of hostile outbursts. Finally we will review the riot participation literature that was designed to find out who riots.

Communal Riot: Detroit, 1943

During the 1920s, Detroit was the fastest-growing metropolitan area in the United States. In 1928 nearly 90 percent of Detroit's blacks and more than half of the whites were newcomers. The majority of those moving to Detroit were from the South. Leaving the traditionally white-dominated social order of the South, whites and blacks moved into a new social order in which they competed, on much more equal terms, for jobs and housing. The first racial conflicts occurred in the mid-1920s when black families moved into all-white neighborhoods. In a few instances, terrified blacks shot at the crowds that taunted them and threw bricks, rocks, and coal into their homes (Levine 1976). In 1941 racial clashes occurred in Detroit when blacks were used as strikebreakers at the Ford River Rouge Plant. Racial clashes occurred at Northwestern High School later that year. Early in 1942, there were racial disturbances at the Sojourner Truth housing project.

As our nation's war effort strengthened and Detroit became known as the "arsenal of democracy," many hoped that these ugly events were a thing of the past. For a time, it seemed that the war had drawn the races together. Everyone working together—that was what democracy was all about.

The racial truce was broken Sunday evening, June 20, 1943. Like the Los Angeles "zoot-suit" riots a month earlier, the Detroit riot began with fights between white sailors and nonwhite civilians (Turner and Surace 1956). Fighting started at about 10:30 P.M. at Belle Isle Park, a public beach. Sailors from the naval armory and young black men were the first to land punches on one another. Large numbers of people were on Belle Isle at the time. The weather was fine, and for many it was the weekend before high school graduation. Within ten minutes, hundreds of people were involved in the fighting. From the beginning, it was whites against blacks. Those who tried to leave Belle Isle had to pass over Belle Isle Bridge, and white youths and sailors turned the bridge into a gauntlet for escaping blacks. Many of the first casualties to be brought to hospitals were injured on or near the bridge.

Just what happened in these early moments of the disorder is unclear. Some reports indicate that police did little to disperse crowds or break up fights, particularly when blacks were getting beaten. Blacks who ran to police for protection often received none. This display of police indifference may have contributed to the spread of the disorder. Within an hour, fighting between wandering groups of whites and blacks was occurring over a wide area beyond Belle Isle Park (Lee and Humphrey 1968:72–79).

Both whites and blacks repeated accounts of how the fighting started. For the whites, fighting started "because Negroes had raped and killed a white woman on the Belle Isle Bridge, . . . because Negroes had attacked some white girls while they were swimming at Belle Isle, and . . . because the Negroes tried to throw the whites off Belle Isle." For blacks, fighting started "because a bunch of white guys killed a Negro woman and her baby at Belle Isle Park, . . . because the whites threw a Negro woman and her baby off the Belle Isle Bridge, and . . . because the whites tried to throw the Negroes off Belle Isle." These stories of where and why fighting was occurring were disseminated widely by word-of-mouth and public announcements in nightclubs and at the gates of factories (Lee and Humphrey 1968:27).

The fighting increased in intensity when the factory shifts changed. Between midnight and 2:00 A.M., blacks going to or returning from work were attacked. In some areas, whites systematically stopped streetcars to search for black targets. Likewise, at least one streetcar

loaded with white workers was stopped by a group of blacks, who then severely beat some passengers. Groups of whites formed outside two all-night theaters and beat blacks who attempted to leave. Police watched passively for some time before they attempted to disperse the crowd or warn blacks inside the theaters (Lee and Humphrey 1968:28).

At about 3:00 A.M., groups of blacks began to vandalize and loot white-owned stores in the predominantly black Paradise Valley area near Belle Isle. In retaliation, whites began to overturn and burn autos driven by blacks. Many of the occupants were beaten before they could escape.

At 4:00 A.M., the Detroit police commissioner held a meeting with the mayor, the U.S. Army commander of the Detroit area, the FBI agent in charge of the Detroit area, a captain from the state police, and the Wayne County sheriff. At this meeting, the army commander informed everyone that troops could be on patrol within an hour of their callup. When the meeting ended at 6:30 A.M., however, it had been decided that the rioting was slowing and federal troops would not be needed.

Had the police commissioner received better information, he would have known that the rioting had not slowed. Looting and car burnings continued. Hospitals contained growing waiting lines of injured, and at 6:15 A.M., the first death was recorded: a black man bled to death; the source of his wounds was unknown.

By 9:00 A.M., a black delegation from the Detroit Citizens' Committee met with the mayor of Detroit and urged him to use federal troops to stop the rioting. A prominent black minister began to tour the Paradise Valley area with a sound truck, urging people to return home. The governor arrived in Detroit at 11:00 A.M. and called for federal troops, but he was told that troops could not be used unless he declared martial law. The governor felt that the declaration of martial law was an extreme step, and he declined the offer of federal troops. During this time, blacks continued to loot, whites continued to overturn and burn cars, and blacks and whites were attacked and beaten.

At noon, the mayor attended the Detroit Citizens' Committee meeting. The president of the United Automobile Workers' Union spoke out strongly against the rioting. Later in the day, the union would call an emergency meeting of shop stewards to "intensify the Union's educational program for building labor unity between men and women of all races." Some committee members suggested that they urge the governor to declare martial law and send in the troops. Others suggested, instead, that a black auxiliary be formed to assist police in stopping the riot (Lee and Humphrey 1968:32).

About 1:30 P.M., high schools began to dismiss their students for the day. Some students converged on Woodward Avenue, the area of heaviest violence. Other students simply tried to make it home without injury. Finally, white and black youth, quite peacefully, watched the Metropolitan League baseball championship at Briggs Stadium (Lee and Humphrey 1968:35).

At 3:00 P.M., a civilian peace patrol was established under the authority of the Office of Civil Defense. The patrol was composed of about 250 volunteers, black and white. The patrol had no power of arrest and was instructed to confine itself to monitoring activities, giving assistance, and offering persuasion. Even though the rioting was still very intense and attacks frequent, more individuals were beginning to act as "counterrioters." A white minister and his son drove around confronting groups of whites who were stalking blacks. He quoted scripture and argued with the crowd while his son escorted blacks to their cars. Likewise, blacks helped whites get out of dangerous areas. A group of church, labor, and youth leaders met and issued a joint statement urging the use of federal troops, requesting that radio broadcasts ask people to stay off the streets, and appealing to the newspapers to avoid inflammatory stories (Lee and Humphrey 1968:35–37).

Despite the efforts of counterrioters, violence continued, and as late afternoon approached, it accelerated. A crowd of nearly ten thousand people gathered near city hall on Woodward Avenue. Several attacks occurred as blacks were taken off buses and streetcars that passed through the area. Anti-Jewish hate literature was being passed about. Unsubstantiated but inflammatory statements were broadcast over the radio. It was announced, for example, that state police were watching for carloads of "armed Negroes headed for Detroit from Chicago" (Lee and Humphrey 1968: 38).

At about 6:30 P.M., the governor declared a state of "modified" martial law in the counties of Wayne, Oakland, and Macomb. His order also banned the sale of alcoholic beverages and closed all amusement places at 9:00 P.M. until "further notice." A curfew was imposed from 10:00 P.M. until 6:00 A.M. for people "not going to or coming from work." Finally, the governor's order prohibited the carrying of arms "of any sort" by anyone other than police.

While the paperwork to implement the governor's declaration was being completed, rioting continued. At about 8:30 P.M., police and residents of a mission hotel exchanged gunfire for several minutes while a crowd of nearly one thousand spectators watched. As white crowds moved into the black residential section of Paradise Valley, they were met with volleys of rocks and an occasional shotgun blast. A black man was attacked and beaten unconscious near the federal building. The U.S. Army commander for the Detroit area witnessed the beating from his office window and sent officers to rescue the victim (Lee and Humphrey 1968:41).

Federal troops did not move into the streets until nearly 9:00 P.M. Within an hour, however, two full battalions of military police patrolled the streets of Detroit. By 10:30 P.M., almost everywhere, the rioting had stopped. It wasn't until nearly midnight that President Roosevelt signed the form authorizing the use of federal troops in Detroit! For the most part, the Detroit riot of 1943 was over.

Compared to many urban disorders, the Detroit riot of 1943 was a very short riot—violence lasted little more than twenty-four hours. The intensity of the violence, however, has seldom been witnessed: thirty-four people died (twenty-five blacks and nine whites), and more than one thousand people received injuries at the hands of others. More than eighteen hundred people were arrested and charged with offenses ranging from manslaughter to traffic violations. Absenteeism from work during the riot decreased wartime productivity by nearly half. About $2 million worth of property damage occurred: buildings were damaged, stores looted, and cars were destroyed. Finally and interestingly, in the factories of the "arsenal of democracy," whites and blacks continued to work side by side and without incident as violence carried the day outside. A month later, the U.S. Attorney General attributed this to effective union discipline.

Political Riot: Kent State University, 1970

On May 4, 1970, after three days of disorder, Ohio National Guard troops fired on students at Kent State University. The shooting lasted for about ten seconds. Thirteen of the sixty-seven rounds fired hit people: four students were killed, and nine were wounded. As the news of the killings spread across the nation, disorders intensified on other campuses.

The disorder at Kent State was part of a nationwide protest that began on Thursday,

April 30. That morning President Nixon announced that American and South Vietnamese troops were entering Cambodia to destroy enemy sanctuaries. The decision to invade Cambodia was one of the best-kept secrets of the war. There were none of the usual rumors, leaks, denials, or discussions that made many events of the war "old news" by the time they finally happened. For several months, Nixon had also publicly pursued a policy of "winding down" the Vietnam War. The news of the Cambodian invasion came as a tremendous shock and disappointment to people who were hoping for smaller combat losses and American troop withdrawals. Consequently, protest of the invasion came quickly. Thursday evening protest rallies were held at Princeton, Rutgers, and Oberlin College. Within days, some form of protest had occurred on almost two-thirds of the colleges and universities in the United States. Most protest was peaceful. At more than one hundred universities, however, protest turned disorderly and violent, severely hindering university functioning. Dozens of universities were either closed temporarily or dismissed early (Peterson and Bilorusky 1971: 15-69).

At Kent State, a brief, peaceful protest rally was held on the commons—a field near large dormitories and major pedestrian walkways—at noon on Friday. The ROTC building was located on the northwest edge of the commons. The presence of large gatherings of students on or near the commons was not unusual. This ecological feature of the Kent State campus was critical to what followed (Lewis 1972:66).

It is unlikely that the Kent State administration anticipated further rallies or disorders. On Friday afternoon, the president of Kent State left for Mason City, Iowa. The first disorder started Friday evening, near the campus. At about 11:00 A.M., students barricaded a street on which several bars were located. Soon, a bonfire was started in the street, and students began to harass passing motorists. Initially, city police did not interfere. As complaints mounted, however, the city police decided to close the bars, hoping that students would return to campus. Instead, angry patrons left the bars and began to mill in the streets. Soon antiwar chants were raised, and students threw rocks and bottles at one another and at police. Some in the crowd of about twelve hundred people broke store and office windows. The police chased the crowd toward the campus and, at about 2:00 A.M., finally dispersed it with tear gas. The crowd did about $30,000 damage, and sixty arrests were made.

All day Saturday the campus was calm. Rumors circulated that Weathermen radicals, Hell's Angels, and Black Panthers were headed to Kent State to help battle police. Local merchants claimed they received threats. At about 8:00 P.M. a crowd began to gather on the commons, and within an hour, more than one thousand students and others were present. Observers, including Jerry M. Lewis (1972), indicate that no violent plans were openly proposed. Still, people began to throw rocks at the ROTC building. After several windows were broken out, burning trash was thrown inside. At 9:00 P.M., the fire department arrived. Students cut the fire hoses and threw rocks at the fire crew. The fire trucks retreated, and at 9:30 P.M., campus police dispersed the crowd with tear gas. Shortly, the Ohio National Guard arrived on the commons under orders to protect property. At this point, they could do little more than watch the ROTC building burn.

Throughout the remainder of the disorder, communication between the guard and university officials was meager. Officials were frequently indecisive and offered the guard few guidelines as to what they expected from them. In turn, the guard seemed to take actions that seemed arbitrary and unilateral. In a sense, university officials took a hands off policy once nearly two thousand guard troops entered the campus. The only mediators between students and the guard were the unofficial student and faculty monitors.

Once the crowd had been dispersed from the commons, there were no further confrontations on Saturday night. On Sunday morning, Governor Rhodes arrived at Kent State. After a brief tour and an inspection of the ruins of the ROTC building, he denounced the students as "the strongest, well trained, militant group ever assembled in America." The university president returned to Kent and met briefly with the governor at the airport. At 4:00 P.M., the university issued orders prohibiting all forms of demonstration, "peaceful or otherwise."

On Sunday afternoon, the guard used tear gas to scatter a crowd near the president's house. On Sunday evening, a few hundred students marched down Main Street toward the center of Kent. They were stopped at the northwest corner of the campus by a line of guard. Students sat down in the street and asked to meet with the mayor and university president. While they waited, they chanted vulgar and familiar protest chants: "One-two-three-four: we don't want your fucking war," "Hell no, we won't go," "Fuck Nixon," "Pigs off campus, pigs off campus," and "Strike, strike, strike." After an hour and a half, the guard told students they were in violation of the curfew and then used tear gas. The noise of helicopters, the flash of searchlights, and general commotion continued nearly all night.

On Monday morning, students returned to classes, and it seemed as if the university might return to normal. The university president left campus at about 11:45 A.M. to dine with four university vice-presidents. At about the same time, a crowd began to gather on the commons. No organized protest or demonstration was attempted, though some students began to taunt the guardsmen who were posted around the shell of the ROTC building. Shortly, students were told they were in violation of Sunday's order prohibiting demonstrations, and the riot act was read. Tear gas was then used to disperse the crowd.

One group of students descended a shallow hill that led to a nearby football practice field. They were followed by about seventy National Guard troops wearing gas masks. Other students remained in the general area of the commons. Students on the field began to throw rocks and chunks of dirt at the guard, who responded with tear gas canisters. In the open space of the football field, the gas was ineffective. Soon students were throwing the canisters back at the guard. Students who had gathered in a parking lot north of the field and on a veranda of a campus building west of the field watched and cheered. After tossing tear gas canisters back and forth, the guard reformed their lines, kneeled, and leveled their rifles at the students. Students responded with taunts and the chant "Shoot, shoot, shoot." The guard abruptly turned and marched off the field and back up the shallow hill. When they reached the top, near the veranda, they turned and fired.

When the shooting started, people scattered, fell to the ground, and hid behind trees, buildings, or parked cars. When the shooting stopped, few students ran from the area. Instead, people began to cluster around the fallen. Other students began to group together and move slowly toward the guard. Shouts of "Murderers! Murderers!" were raised. The troops who fired were immediately ordered from the area, and the remaining troops assumed a formation to move against the crowd. For a moment, it looked as if another clash was about to occur. Then faculty marshals moved between students and the guard. Faculty pleaded with students to remain calm or leave the area and with the guard officers not to charge the students. There was a standoff situation until ambulances started to arrive. After the dead and injured were removed, the size of the crowd diminished. Shortly, Kent State University was closed by order of its president and the Common Pleas Court of Ohio.

Levels of Analysis

Riots can be studied and analyzed in terms of individual activity as well as organizational, community, and societal responses. Each level of analysis poses different problems and questions. At the individual level of analysis, many questions revolve around the issue of riot participation. McPhail notes that at this level of analysis, most explanations of riot participation have been couched in terms of "individual predispositions," or attitudes, motives, and beliefs that lead people to participate in a riot.

Attitudes, motives, and beliefs have traditionally been measured by questionnaires containing attitude scales administered to arrestees or residents of riot communities. In some studies, attitudes, motives, and beliefs have been inferred from the socioeconomic characteristics of arrestees and residents without the use of attitude scales. It is assumed, for example, that unemployed persons are more likely to feel deprived and frustrated and are therefore more likely to participate in riots than others. Finally, riot participation has been examined in terms of demographic attributes (and attitudes and motives inferred from them). Young men, for example, are considered to be more impulsive and daring than others and hence more likely to participate in riots. In the case of the urban riots of the 1960s, blacks were considered to be more deprived and frustrated than other groups and thus more likely to participate in these riots.

The study of riots can be approached from the standpoint of organizational responses. How, for example, do police departments mobilize for riot control? What are some of the common riot control tactics of police, and what are the outcomes of these tactics? What roles do civilian organizations play in riots?

Some militant black organizations have been suspected of starting urban disorders during the 1960s. Are such suspicions warranted? The role of black organizations, particularly of civil rights and church groups in efforts to limit and calm disorder, are much more apparent. We must also consider the media. How does the media report disorder? Does, as some critics claim, media coverage facilitate the spread of disorder from one community to another? Does media coverage intensify violence? How does the picture of disorder presented by the media influence decisions made by other organizations, such as the police and legislative bodies? Finally, did the experiences of the 1960s and 1970s with student and urban disorders alter organizational responses to these types of events?

Examining riots from the standpoint of communities raises other kinds of questions. Much attention has been given to the question of whether we can ascertain a community's potential for disorder. In other words, are there "riot-prone" communities? Sociologists have attempted to find out what particular blend of community socioeconomic and demographic characteristics are related to the occurrence of riots (Spilerman 1976). There is also the "pressure cooker" characterization of communities and riots. Does the occurrence of a riot relieve social pressures in a community and thereafter decrease the probability of further riots and other forms of social protest or political violence?

Finally, there is the issue of societal responses to riots. Are there meaningful differences between societies in the manner in which they respond to riots? Some have suggested, for example, that there are major differences between police responses to riots in the United States and Great Britain. Similar differences have been suggested between the responses of "modern" and "developing" nations. What, if any, are these differences? We must also consider other, more general responses to riots.

One response to the riots of the 1960s was the establishment of the National Advisory Commission on Civil Disorder. President Lyndon B. Johnson appointed this commission, composed of governors, mayors, lawyers, and even a couple of sociologists, to study the riots. The commission was charged to determine the causes of urban riots and suggest ways to prevent further riots. When confronted by riots, other countries have established similar commissions to study and recommend responses to riots. Still other societies have shown little interest in studying riots. Instead, they have established special police units to suppress rioting, have formed secret police units to infiltrate civilian organizations, or have relied on martial law to keep order. What leads one society to study riots and another to turn to violent suppression and the suspension of civil liberties?

There are a number of levels of analysis from which we can examine riots. This chapter focuses on individual participation in riot activity. In Chapter 12, we will consider organizational, community, and societal responses to riots.

Riots as Collective Behavior

Each of the general theories presents a different image of individual participation in riots, and each presents a different explanation for participation. Many of our stereotypes regarding people's behavior during riots comes from the mass hysteria perspective. We will begin by examining this perspective and riot stereotypes.

The Mass Hysteria Perspective

Descriptions of riots and mob action are frequently used to illustrate the mass hysteria perspective of collective behavior (LeBon [1895] 1960; Blumer 1957; Myers 1948; Klapp 1972).

During the riot, we supposedly witness the most extreme instances of contagious mental unity. Normally law-abiding people are stripped of their veneer of socialization: rioters are extremely suggestible; they are irrational and destructive. Even sociologists who otherwise find the mass hysteria perspective of little utility often use such terms to describe rioters and rioting behavior.

Stereotypes. Such characterizations are indeed tempting, particularly when we are describing the actions of those with whom we disagree politically or do not share social and ethnic heritage. Rudé's study of the riots of the industrial and French revolutions does much to dispel the mass hysteria characterization of riots. These crowds did not act without provocation; their destructiveness was not indiscriminate or uncontrolled; their acts were not totally devoid of political and economic purpose (see Chapter 3). Certainly, these riots are not representative of all riots, but Rudé's work does point out the futility of trying to match any extreme characterization with riots in general.

Carl Couch (1968) examined some of the common stereotypes of crowd behavior, most of which originate in the mass hysteria characterization of riots. Couch argues that if crowds are as suggestible as claimed, authorities could control riots simply by suggesting that rioters disperse and go for a cold swim. During riots, including those described at the beginning of this chapter, a number of responses occur when police order crowds to disperse. Contrary to the unruly image of riotous behavior, some people do in fact disperse or at least move away from the police. Some in the crowd may be unable to leave the area because others are blocking their way or because no escape routes are available. Some fail to hear or otherwise take note of the dispersal orders. Finally, some people in the crowd may taunt authorities or openly defy the dispersal order.

Occasionally, some in the crowd may even order the police to go away and leave them alone! Conformity with the instructions of authorities and one's colleagues is more likely in socially structured environments, such as bureaucracies and primary groups. In crowds, whether it be a riot or an audience, compliance with instructions will usually be less complete. Couch (1970) suggests that this is because there are greater difficulties in monitoring the behavior of others, gaining attention and acknowledgment of others, and acting together in the crowd.

The Emergent Norm Perspective

Turner and Killian (1972) discuss many processes that occur within riots. For them, a riot is not something that "just happens" because of internalized hatreds, excitement, or suggestibility. Turner and Killian (1972:154–158) discuss the manipulation of crowds in a variety of situations. Riots, or a collective attack against people or property, are developed through emergent definitions of what is appropriate behavior. Thus the people being attacked must be vilified and shown to be deserving of whatever they get. During the Detroit riot, for example, the Ku Klux Klan distributed antiblack and anti-Jewish hate literature. Once the scope of the violence had spread far beyond that of punishing any particular individuals who may have started trouble on Belle Isle, new justifications for violence emerged. In the later stages of the riot, violence was justified as a rightful way to "show the niggers their place." At this stage, violence was being defined as a means of intimidating and controlling an entire group of people.

The emergent norm perspective suggests that within the mob there is a degree of structure. This structure is usually not rigid, nor does it necessarily exist prior to the crowd. We will discuss emergent organization within riot crowds in greater detail in Chapter 12. Here, it is sufficient to note that descriptions of the Detroit riot concluded that the groups of whites and blacks who roamed around the city searching for victims had their origins in neighborhood gangs. These gangs were mobilized and expanded to include new people during the riot. Some gangs appeared to be content with harassing or roughing up their victims, while others seemed to adopt a pattern of administering severe beatings or openly attempting to kill their victims.

As we shall see in Chapter 12, the emergent norm perspective of Turner and Killian emphasizes the definitions that groups develop and apply to one another. Within riots and other conflict situations, standards of behavior develop that serve to limit or increase the level of violence. Finally, Turner and Killian emphasize the emergent character of conflicting groups within the riot situation.

The Value-Added Perspective

Smelser breaks down the field of collective behavior into the craze, the panic, the hostile outburst, the norm-oriented social movement, and the value-oriented social movement. Crazes and panics are often followed by hostility, which in turn can provide the starting point for more general norm- and value-oriented social movements (Smelser 1962:271–274).

The Hostile Outburst.   Smelser defines the *hostile outburst* as "mobilization for action under a hostile belief" (1962:226). His concept of the hostile outburst encompasses most riots (1962:101), but not all hostile outbursts take the form of rioting. For Smelser (1962:222), hostile outbursts can take the form of widespread public outcry for the punishment of offenders, petitions to governments, demands for impeachment, the distribution of scathing pamphlets, and the threat of rioting. Further,

there has been some difficulty in distinguishing a genuine hostile outburst from what Smelser calls a "mere disturbance of the peace" (Quarantelli and Hundley 1975:382–384). For Smelser, hostile outbursts manifest all five value-added components: structural conduciveness, structural strain, generalized hostile belief, mobilization for action, and action of social control. Each component contributes to the overall nature and outcome of the hostile outburst.

Structural Conduciveness.   Structural conduciveness refers to the most general social boundaries within which collective behavior operates. Structural conduciveness that facilitates hostile outbursts includes (1) the structure of responsibility during conditions of strain, (2) the presence of channels for expressing grievances, and (3) the possibility of communication among the aggrieved (Smelser 1962:227).

Prior to a hostile outburst, a structure of responsibility must exist that allows people to identify a clear target for their hostility. Hostilities may often appear to focus on an arbitrary target but seldom on an ambiguous one. In some situations, there are obvious targets for hostility, such as elected officials who have clear authority and responsibility within a particular area of social concern. President Hoover was the target of much blame and outcry at the beginning of the Great Depression. He had inherited what seemed to be a vigorous national economy, and he appeared to take a laissez-faire attitude as the Depression grew. Sometimes an accused criminal becomes the target of hostility, as in the case of lynchings. This is particularly true when the accused had a prior reputation as a dangerous person or a troublemaker. People who have firsthand familiarity with the accused's reputation are likely to be among the most immediately involved in the lynching. Finally, a structure of responsibility exists in communities having longstanding racial or ethnic cleavages. Almost anything can be readily blamed on minority groups.

Hostile outbursts are made more likely by the presence of channels for expressing hostility. Opportunities to openly express hostility arise when authorities are unable or unwilling to prevent hostile outbursts (Smelser 1962:231–236). Retreat or hesitation by police in the early stages of disorder is likely to increase disorder. At times, the knowledge that police and other authorities are sympathetic to their aims can encourage people to express hostility. The knowledge that local police wouldn't shoot whites contributed to the incidence of lynching of blacks (Cantril 1941).

Opportunities to express grievances and anger, short of open violence, can preclude hostile outbursts. Even token concessions to petition and protest can give the aggrieved a sense that they can achieve their ends through institutionalized channels. Token concessions can also function to divide an otherwise united opposition. The abrupt closing of channels for protest and the elimination of other means of handling dissatisfaction often precede outbreaks of collective violence (Smelser 1962:236–240).

Finally, hostile outbursts are facilitated by communication among the aggrieved and immediate accessibility to objects of attack. The areas of cities in which urban riots occur provide nearly optimum conduciveness to hostile outbursts. Population density, coupled with an almost around-the-clock continuous street life, greatly facilitates face-to-face communication and assembling. Residential dwellings interspersed with or very near to commercial buildings present immediate opportunities for looting and destruction of commercial property. The destruction of usually white-owned property has characterized most urban disorders since the 1960s.

Structural Strain.   The next value-added determinant is structural strain. The most fre-

quent source of strain in the origin of hostile outbursts is deprivation, which, for Smelser (1962:245), can be "real or threatened, absolute or relative." Deprivation is most likely to be a source of structural strain when it can be easily attributed to the actions of a definite person or group, a change in organizational policy, or other definite normative changes. Historically, either the imposition of new taxes or the withdrawal of longstanding or promised privileges has often preceded collective violence. The raise in oil prices by OPEC nations in 1972, for example, triggered angry protest throughout the United States. Not all student protest in the 1960s and early 1970s was directed against the Vietnam War. Other protest, such as the free speech movement and protest against dress codes, restrictive dormitory rules, and job recruiting on campus, reflected a substantial shift in the lifestyles of young people. Conflicts of values are an enduring source of structural strain within communities having clear economic, ethnic, and political cleavages. Value conflicts between Catholics and Protestants, for example, have been a longstanding source of collective violence in Ireland. Finally, Smelser identifies the lack of information as a source of structural strain. Inadequate communication contributes to the strains that lead to scapegoating and the spread of outlandish rumors. Misinformation or the lack of information has preceded many types of collective violence, such as lynchings, violent labor disorders, and rebellions.

Generalized Hostile Belief.   The next value-added component of hostile outbursts is a generalized hostile belief. The conditions of structural conduciveness and structural strain are usually sufficient to create a level of "free-floating or broadly focused" aggression within society (Smelser 1962:249). We see this type of aggression in the vague fears and intolerance that often exist between religious, racial, or ethnic groups. Protestants, for example, fear and resent the supposed political power of Catholics, while Christians resent the economic power of Jews. Whites maintain negative stereotypes about the lifestyles of blacks.

This aggression is aggravated and thrown into sharper focus by precipitating events that confirm or justify existing hatreds and fears. The Gordon Riots of 1780, for example, were sparked by a Parliamentary measure extending the rights of Catholics. For weeks, London was torn by rioting as Protestants demanded a rescinding of these rights (Rudé 1964:57–59). Smelser (1962:249–252) also notes that sharp new deprivations, the sudden closing of an opportunity for peaceful protest, and rumors can also serve as precipitating events. Finally, a precipitating event may include·some obvious "failure" that demands an explanation and assignment of responsibility. The aftermath of the Cocoanut Grove fire included a hostile outburst of editorials, accusations, and inquiries in an attempt to assign responsibility for the tragedy (Velfort and Lee 1943).

Though the precipitating event sharpens the focus of aggression, a generalized hostile belief is necessary for a hostile outburst. The generalized hostile belief assigns blame to a specific agent, group, or person; further, it includes a desire to punish or remove the responsible agent. Finally, the generalized hostile belief includes a sense of omnipotence—the actual feeling on the part of the aggrieved that they have the power to accomplish their aims (Smelser 1962:101–109). Smelser points out that this feeling of omnipotence is usually quite unjustified, though it may be fostered when authorities refrain from the use of force or act indecisively in the early stages of an incident. For Smelser, the feeling of omnipotence accounts for those situations in which unarmed civilians attack armed police. This feeling can be at considerable variance with the realities of the situation.

Mobilization for Action.   Given an aroused and angry group, the next value-added component in a hostile outburst is the mobilization for action, in which Smelser (1962:253–254) emphasizes the role of leadership. Leadership may simply consist of a model—the person who strikes the first blow, throws the first rock, or fires the first shot. Or the leader may be a person who deliberately urges others to hostile action. Finally, groups and organizations may assume a leadership role in the developing conflict. This includes groups such as the Weathermen, who organized war protests on American campuses.

Another factor in the mobilization for a hostile outburst is preexisting structures that provide channels for action. Simply put, Smelser (1962:255–256) argues that casual gatherings of pedestrians or tavern customers are likely to exhibit hostility in the form of an "uncoordinated brawl." The form of hostility is likely to be more structured when it is based on preexisting organizational relationships, such as the authority and committee structure of a trade union. Factories may be surrounded, picket lines maintained, and food and entertainment provided to workers standing picket duty. The outbreak and carrying out of hostilities will usually follow a "hostility curve" (Smelser 1962:257–261).

Smelser divides hostile outbursts into a real and a derived phase. In the initial or real phase, hostilities focus quite narrowly on the precipitating event and the specific conditions of social strain. Initial hostilities, however, may create conditions of structural conduciveness for the expression of additional hostilities. Hostilities then broaden in scope, taking in many issues besides the precipitating event, and other groups and people are drawn into the conflict. This is the derived phase of the hostile outburst. In this sense, the Watts riot of 1965 was but a preliminary phase in the more general wave of hostility that swept the United States in the 1960s.

Action of Social Control. The final value-added component is the action of social control. The response of authorities to hostilities is a determinant not only of the intensity and duration of disorder but also of its content and character. Police can create a false sense of power, or feeling of omnipotence, in the crowd if they are indecisive in the first stages of disorder. In addition to conventional crowd control responses, authorities can plant counterrumors to dissipate generalized hostile beliefs. Legal and economic concessions can be made that reduce structural strain. Polish authorities exercised greater surveillance and control over Solidarity leaders in an effort to bring the outlawed labor union into line.

Evaluating the Value-Added Approach to Riots

Smelser (1962:385–386) describes the value-added components as creating the necessary conditions for the occurrence of collective behavior. This means that when we observe collective behavior, we should also be able to find evidence of each of the value-added components. If we observed collective behavior and could not find evidence of a generalized belief, for example, then we would know that this component is not necessary for the occurrence of collective behavior. Such evidence would lead us to reject or at least modify the value-added explanation of collective behavior.

There is disagreement among sociologists as to whether the value-added components create the necessary conditions for collective behavior. This is particularly true when we consider hostile outbursts, or riots. There are two studies, for example, that apply the value-added model to the analysis of campus riots. The first

TABLE 11.1
Hostile Outbursts: Tests of the Value-Added Components

Value-added component	Study	
	Lewis	Quarantelli and Hundley
Structural conduciveness	Yes	Yes
Structural strain	Yes	Yes
Generalized hostile belief	Yes*	No
Mobilization	Yes	No
Action of social control	Yes	Yes

*See Table 11.2.

disorder, which was studied by Quarantelli and Hundley (1975), followed the arrest of a female student for jaywalking. It lasted for about six hours and included substantial property damage, civil disobedience, the harassment of police, and a protest march. Jerry M. Lewis (1972) studied the Kent State disorder, described at the beginning of this chapter. These two studies reached quite different conclusions regarding the adequacy of the value-added explanation of hostile outbursts.

Table 11.1 summarizes and compares the findings of these two studies. Both studies found evidence for structural conduciveness, structural strain, and action of social control. But Quarantelli and Hundley did not find evidence of a hostile belief; further, the mobilization process that occurred during the disorder did not develop in the manner described by Smelser (Quarantelli and Hundley 1975:374–381). Lewis did find evidence of a hostile belief, and he agreed with Smelser's description of mobilization. These inconsistent findings and conclusions merit further discussion.

TABLE 11.2

Two Interpretations of Generalized Hostile Belief Data

A. *Data as Presented by Lewis (1972)* *

Did you think that the National Guard would fire on students?

	Participants	Observers	Nonattenders
Yes	5	129	513
No	509	1,746	2,346
Uncertain	27	280	807

B. *Lewis Data Collapsed to Show Relationship between Attenders and Nonattenders* **

Did you think that the National Guard would fire on students?

	Attenders	Nonattenders
Yes and uncertain	441	1,320
No	2,255	2,346

*This relationship is statistically significant (p < .001) but weak (Cramer's V = .16).

**This relationship is statistically significant (p < .001) but weak (ϕ = .22).

Quarantelli and Hundley note that while some students taunted police, there was little indication that they felt omnipotent or felt that they had the power to "remove or punish" city police. In fact, a wide diversity of beliefs was in evidence. Some students were at the scene to "be with friends," to "see what was happening," or to "make observations for a collective behavior course." A few students indicated that the protest might serve to air grievances and eventually improve relations between students and police. Finally, some students expressed concern that nothing would come out of the protest except "trouble for students." Such a diversity of views is indeed contrary to Smelser's description of a generalized belief.

Much of Lewis's support for the existence of a generalized hostile belief came from a survey conducted among Kent State students weeks after the disorder and killings (1972:64). The survey classified respondents as nonattenders, observers, and participants (see Table 11.2A). Nonattenders—those who were absent from the scene of the shootings—were more likely

than others to think that the National Guard would fire on students. Those who participated seemed to be convinced that the guard wouldn't fire. There were many more observers at the scene of the shootings than participants. On the basis that bullets do not discriminate between observers and participants, these two categories could be combined into the category of attenders. When the Lewis data is examined in this fashion, as it is in Table 11.2B, the difference between attenders and nonattenders is not as great. Further, the data did not include nearly six hundred respondents who were at the scene of the shootings but were classified as "counterdemonstrators" and "others." Given this possible alternate interpretation of the data and this omission of respondents, one cannot say that thinking the guard would fire on students kept students away from the scene of the shooting. Finally, even if this relationship were more distinct than it is, it tells us little about generalized hostile beliefs. Thinking that the guard would not fire as it attempted to control unarmed students seems quite reasonable; it can hardly be described as a feeling of omnipotence.

Quarantelli and Hundley (1975:377–381) note that mobilization during the campus disorder involved more than modeling, or the deliberate agitation of students by radicals. Much mobilization seemed to occur through friendship channels, while other mobilization was simply the result of passersby stopping to talk with others in the gathering. The activities within the gathering did not correspond to what Smelser terms the *real* and *derived* phases of mobilization during disorder. During the last three and a half hours that the gathering was assembled, people did little more than stand around a bonfire. Police and university officials in and around the crowd were generally ignored.

Smelser takes a very broad view of structural strain: real or threatened, absolute or relative material deprivation; norm and value conflict; and inadequate communication. Conceptualized so broadly, it seems that almost any circumstance can be interpreted as causing some type of structural strain. Not surprisingly, then, both studies found evidence for structural strain prior to and during the disorders. Quarantelli and Hundley (1975:373–374) inferred structural strain from the long-standing opinion among students that police were negatively biased in their dealings with them. Lewis (1972:61–62) argued that the simple presence of National Guard on the Kent State campus represented the primary source of structural strain for students. Likewise, the students' open defiance of the university's ban on rallies was a source of structural strain for the guard. Beyond these few inferences, none of these researchers attempted to develop or empirically test Smelser's ideas about structural strain; they did not, for example, attempt to find out whether there had been a rising level of structural strain prior to these disorders. Smelser also claims that collective behavior is in part an effort to reduce conditions of strain

within the social system. But these researchers did not try to determine if strain was lower after the hostilities than it had been at the beginning. In short, the researchers simply assumed that structural strain was present during the disorder. They did not attempt to develop or test specific propositions about the role (if any) of structural strain in the playing out of these hostile outbursts.

These two studies highlight some of the major problems with the value-added approach to hostile outbursts, or riots. In particular, there is difficulty with the generalized hostile belief component. Smelser (1962:226) states that "participants in an outburst must be bent on attacking someone considered responsible for a disturbing state of affairs." What can be said, then, of counterrioters, many looters, or those whose participation is brief and perhaps largely due to their proximity to the disorder? In riots we encounter hostile beliefs and behavior, but these are intermingled with and often subordinate to other kinds of quite different attitudes and actions (Quarantelli and Hundley 1975:384).

Smelser views mobilization primarily in terms of actions taken to excite the emotions of the aggrieved. He devotes relatively little attention to how these social relationships and activities actually bring people together and are used to carry out a course of action.

Finally, there is structural strain, which Smelser defines so broadly that virtually anything can be taken as an indication of structural strain. More recently, several attempts have been made to better define and empirically study structural strain. Tilly (1975) summarizes these efforts and concludes that existing models of structural strain tell us little about the occurrence of disorder and political violence. Gamson, Fireman, and Rytina (1982:8) argue that violence is not an eruption of latent tensions and frustrations; rather, it is an outcome of a more or less continuous process of mobilization and conflictive interaction.

The SBI Perspective

The SBI perspective emphasizes that people engage in a wide variety of activities during riots, none of which is inherently "riotous." The central task in explaining people's involvement in riots is to account for variations in individual activity while at or near the scene of the disorder.

The Monolithic Conception of Riots.   McPhail (1971) uses the phrase "monolithic conception of riots" to describe the way in which sociologists often approach the study of riots and riot participation. Sociologists (as well as journalists, politicians, and anyone else with an opinion on the subject) frequently describe riots as if they consist of a unitary type of human action such as running or swimming. To say that someone is running or swimming conveys a specific image and meaning that we all recognize. The monolithic conception uses the term *rioting* as if it conveyed a similar unitary meaning. We talk about people who are rioting much as we talk about people who are running or swimming—as if rioters were carrying out a unitary activity called rioting. Orders are given to "stop the rioting," "rioters" are to be arrested, and sociologists study "riot participation."

The Differentiated Approach to Riots. Rioting is not a unitary action. Both McPhail (1971) and Wohlstein (McPhail and Wohlstein 1983) suggest that we approach the study and explanation of riots by viewing them as "complex and differentiated phenomena." In fact, the behavior of a person during a riot may consist of a wide variety of both violent and nonviolent activity. A person may throw rocks at police at one intersection and help police aid an injured person at another. People who engage in violent, destructive, or antisocial acts do not do so continuously during their presence at a disorder. Further, many conventional and routine activities are considered to be antisocial when they occur during a riot. In many communities, for example, people routinely loiter on street corners, in front of taverns, and in parks. During riots, such gatherings are usually forbidden and are broken up by police. The massive amounts of property damage that occur during many riots may result from relatively few violent acts on the part of relatively few people. Once a firebomb has been lobbed into a building, for example, flames spread quite rapidly without any further attendance from rioters. Many people in the riot area may do little more than walk around and look at the damage that has occurred. Finally, some people's activities may revolve around protecting their property or some types of community property, such as recreation centers, and urging other people to "go home and calm down." In short, people engage in a wide variety of activities during a "riot," none of which are inherently "rioting" behavior.

The monolithic conception of riots has also been part of the discussion of riots as a collective social phenomenon. Riots have been discussed as if they have discrete starting and ending points, much like a game of football. We read or hear about the event that triggered the riot. Likewise, riots are described as ending on certain days. Between the time that the riot starts and ends, many discussions seem to imply that rioting is more or less continuous. These discussions fail to acknowledge that the starting point of a riot is often quite arbitrary. Descriptions of riots provided by the National Advisory Commission on Civil Disorders, for example, note that most of the riots were preceded by many abrasive confrontations between police and residents of riot areas in the months and weeks before the riot. The confrontations identified as the "precipitating events" of many riots appear to be very similar to these earlier incidents. The media has often described disorders as riots before police and other officials have designated them as such. In some instances, the police have had difficulty contacting mayors and governors to inform them that a situation was out of control and that additional assistance was needed. The "beginning" of a riot involves not only disorder but also an emergence of consensus among police, mayors, governors, and usually the media.

Such consensus is not automatic, nor does it necessarily occur given a specific amount of violent or disruptive behavior. During the 1960s, people were quite sensitized to the issue of riots. The National Advisory Commission noted that many of the events that were then being called riots would have probably been considered simple disturbances of the peace years earlier. On the other hand, many of us can recall instances, such as the celebrations that usually follow World Series victories, in which people were injured, looting occurred, and property damage was considerable. When these events are described as riots, city officials quickly deny the charge. These are not riots; they are enthusiastic displays of civic pride! Finally, there are instances in which strikers or war protesters demonstrate their views in a rowdy or aggressive manner. Few injuries result, and little property damage occurs. Many of these events are considered to be riots, however, as legal interest is shown in the violent intent of those taking part in demonstrations.

The monolithic conception characterizes riots as events with discrete starting and ending points, but this view fails to acknowledge the consensual nature of identifying events as riots. Ideas about the attitudes, hostile beliefs, and other social pressures that are claimed to produce riots must be reconciled with the problem of defining a given event as a riot.

Further, the monolithic conception of riots fails to acknowledge that the many and diverse activities that constitute rioting are not continuous. During the Watts riot of 1965, the 1967 riot in Detroit, and the 1968 riot in Washington, D.C., activities such as looting, arson, and rock throwing peaked during the hours of 10:00 P.M. and midnight. These activities steadily declined through the early morning hours, until noon, then again gradually built up through the afternoon and early evening (McPhail and Wohlstein 1983). Crowds are not continuously present, and such violent acts as assault occur sporadically. Looting usually occurs in the first hours of the disorder and is often quite selective: appliance and liquor stores may be hit, while pawn shops may be left alone. National Advisory Commission data indicate that most property damage and attacks against police or troops occur during evening hours. In the mid-morning hours, the streets in the riot area may be nearly deserted. Such dramatic fluctuations in the kind and amount of activity in communities during riots are not recognized within the monolithic conception of riots.

Noting these problems with the monolithic conception of riots, McPhail suggests that we no longer view riots as the outcome of individual motives and beliefs or the socioeconomic attributes of the communities in which riots occur. Instead, he suggests that we examine assembling and dispersal processes and the communication processes that make them possible. Riot participation studies have told us very little about the sequence of interpersonal exchanges that are part of riot mobilization. We must examine the wide variety of activities individuals carry out during the course of a disorder. Such inquiries can tell us, for example, which activities are violent and antisocial and which ones are not. A greater appreciation of the relative prevalence of truly destructive and dangerous behavior can have important implications for the way in which police, city and state officials, politicians, and the media respond to civil disorder.

Individual Participation in Riots

Few events of recent years have inspired as much sociological research as the urban disorders of the 1960s. It was assumed that a careful comparison of rioters and nonrioters would tell us what attitudes, beliefs, and tensions led people to riot. Some people thought that this research would allow us to predict when riots were likely to occur and, perhaps, provide the means for preventing riots. In general, riot research fell far short of these goals. Although riot research provides answers to some rather important questions, it does not answer the questions researchers set out to answer.

Riot Participation

McPhail (1971) reviewed ten studies of major urban disorders occurring between 1965 and 1967. The riot participation studies were carried out following riots in Watts (1965), Omaha (1966), Detroit (1967), Milwaukee (1967), and Newark (1967). The first task in these studies was to determine who had actually taken part in the riot. Classifying people as participants and nonparticipants in a riot is not as simple as classifying people as male and female or as young and old.

As we noted earlier, people's involvement in riot-related activities is not continuous, and these activities are not necessarily violent or even antisocial. Consequently, each study developed one or more measures of riot participation, of which the most frequently used was arrestee status. Six of the studies compared a sample of respondents arrested on riot charges with a control sample of people from the community in which the riot occurred. This type of comparison is not entirely satisfactory. Some sociologists have suggested that people who commit the most violent acts are also the most likely to evade police, while many of those arrested, such as female looters, are probably the least wary and experienced at evading apprehension. In short, arrestees are not a representative sample of those who participated in the riot in one manner or another. Because of this problem, researchers developed other measures of riot participation that did not rely on arrestee status. These measures were based on self-reports. Respondents selected from neighborhoods in which riots occurred were asked what they did, what they saw, and whether they considered themselves to be riot participants. On the basis of these self-reports, comparisons could be made among people the researchers classified as rioters, nonrioters, and, in some instances, counterrioters.

Many sociological discussions of hostility, rebellions, and riots, such as Smelser's value-added model or Davies' J-curve of rising expectations, suggest that social deprivation leads to frustrations that are vented in acts of aggression. Variants of this idea, at least in the 1960s, were part of the "common knowledge" within the behavioral sciences. Consequently, almost all riot investigators sought to ascertain the hostile beliefs, negative attitudes, and frustrations that led to riot participation. Some of these psychological attributes were measured directly with attitude/opinion questionnaires. In other instances, individual tendencies to riot were inferred from people's socioeconomic attributes, such as income and education levels, and demographic characteristics, such as age, sex, and ethnicity. These various measures of people's predispositions to participate in riots are summarized in Table 11.3.

Altogether, these ten studies tested 287 separate relationships between some predisposition to riot and a measure of riot participation. Of the 287 relationships, 268 (93 percent) were either not statistically significant or were of weak magnitude. This means that nearly all of the predispositions to riot turned out to have little if any association with riot participation! Even the associations with the most immediate bearing on the deprivation-frustration-aggression explanation of riots showed a similar pat-

TABLE 11.3

Riot Participation Studies: Independent Variables and Their Strength of Association with Riot Participation Measures

	Strength of Association				
Independent Variables	*Not Significant*	*Weak*	*Moderate*	*High*	*Total*
Attitude statements	18	55	6	0	79
Social relationships and interaction	26	31	1	0	58
Socioeconomic attributes	22	34	1	0	57
Experiences and opinions of discrimination	15	30	5	0	50
Demographic attributes	5	18	4	2	29
Political participation	5	9	0	0	14
Totals	91	177	17	2	287

SOURCE: Adapted from Clark McPhail, "Civil Disorder Participation: A Critical Examination of Recent Research," *American Sociological Review* 36:1062.

tern of weak relationship (McPhail 1971: 1063–1065).

Only seventeen relationships were of moderate strength, and most of these were between opinions that police frequently mistreat blacks and arrestee status. These relationships held for both black and white arrestees. Such findings seem to suggest that negative opinions about police lead to riot participation, but McPhail cautions that this interpretation may be incorrect. It seems likely that many of the negative opinions about police were generated when people were arrested, held in jail, and charged with crimes. In other words, negative opinions about police may have been a result rather than a cause of riot participation. This interpretation seems likely because lower associations were obtained between negative opinions and the self-report measures of riot participation that did not include arrestee status.

The only independent variables to show a fairly consistent and strong association with riot participation were age, sex, ethnicity, and education level. Young black males who had not completed high school were more likely than others to participate in riots. These rela-

tionships are open to two quite different interpretations. We might immediately assume that young people are more daring than older people and that blacks are more disenchanted than whites with the political climate. We might also assume that males are more daring and aggressive than females and that greater educational attainment makes people more rational and less likely to riot. McPhail suggests an alternate interpretation that is not based on these stereotypes. He suggests, simply, that these people are more available for riot participation by virtue of the large amount of uncommitted time that results from "being young, black, male, and without educational credentials" (1971:1069).

Future Studies

Given the meager findings of the riot participation studies, we need not conclude that they were a waste of time and money. If nothing else, these studies strongly suggest that in the future we must attempt to explain riot participation in terms other than individual attributes. One alternate approach is suggested by

McPhail's differentiated view of riots, which is discussed above. Taking this point of view, Wohlstein (1982) suggests aims for future riot participation research. New research should examine the assembling processes that are part of the disorder. Researchers should determine how people first hear of the disorder, what they are doing at the time, and their location. Such information can tell us the sources and sequences of assembling instructions that route people to the scene of the disorder. It can also tell us what types of activities compete with or preclude riot participation. Finally, this type of information is necessary in order to determine what role, if any, proximity plays in riot participation.

Rather than trying to classify people into general categories of participants and nonparticipants, future research should try to obtain detailed, hour-by-hour accounts of what people actually did during the time frame of the riot. We already know that people defy and attack police, destroy property, and loot during riots. Earlier riot participation research has told us little about the immediate circumstances that bring people to carry out such activities. We know even less about people's activities when they are not confronting police, destroying property, or looting. In order to fully account for what people do during riots, we need to know how people become involved in competing activities that may take them from the scene of the disorder.

The type of research suggested by Wohlstein goes far beyond earlier riot participation research. Much of this research will have to rely on self-report information. One hopes that some of this research can be augmented and verified by firsthand observation.

From the standpoint of the mass hysteria perspective, riots result from underlying hatreds, aroused emotion, and suggestibility. During riots people are "out of control" and largely unresponsive to normal social influences. The emergent norm perspective stresses that collective definitions, normative constraint, and emergent interpersonal relationships continue to guide behavior during riots. The value-added perspective casts riots within the framework of the hostile outburst. Structural strain and generalized hostile belief components of riots, however, were found to obtain little clear support in riot participation studies. Finally, the SBI perspective develops a differentiated view of riots. Riots can be analyzed from the standpoint of such generic processes as assembling, behavior within gatherings, and dispersal.

Finally, we examined riot participation studies, which take riot participation as the product of individual psychological and socioeconomic characteristics. The capability of explaining individual riot participation from such independent variables is minimal. We suggested that in the future more firsthand attention be given to the processes through which people become involved in wide varieties of riot-related activities.

Summary

We began this chapter with a description of two riots, a communal riot and a political riot.

CHAPTER 12

Organizational, Community, and Societal Responses to Riots

During August 1965, the Watts area of Los Angeles was torn by nearly a week and a half of rioting that began on Wednesday evening, August 11. Most of the violence and destruction occurred during the next five days, but the police curfew was not lifted until August 22. By then, thirty-four people were dead and hundreds were injured. Nearly four thousand people had been arrested in connection with the rioting. Hundreds of businesses in Watts had been burned or looted. It had taken a massive police response to end the rioting. Almost the entire Los Angeles police force, hundreds of state police, and more than thirteen thousand California National Guard had been used in Watts.

Watts is often thought of as the prototype of the hundreds of urban riots that occurred in cities across the United States during 1965–1972. These riots can be classified as *commodity riots*. Relatively little violence occurred between black and white civilians. Instead, blacks attacked and looted white-owned property in their neighborhoods. Most of the violent conflict occurred between black civilians and police, National Guard, and, occasionally, federal troops.

In this chapter we will examine how social control organizations respond to riots. The disorderly and violent acts that later become identified as the start of a riot may be very

similar to many other events that routinely occur within a community. As the number of violent acts escalates and the number of people involved increases, police and other public officials come to the consensus that things have gotten out of control or that a riot is occurring. We will examine the legal definitions used by authorities to distinguish rioting from other kinds of activity. We will then briefly consider the kinds of changes that occur within police departments as these organizations take action to stop the rioting. We will also consider the kind of organization that emerges among community members. Some of this emergent organization is *antisocial*, as people work together to thwart police and carry out looting. Other emergent organization is *prosocial*, as groups go into their community to urge calm, care for the injured, locate the missing, and monitor police-civilian contacts. We will also consider the kinds of crowd control tactics that are used by police and National Guard during riots.

What kinds of communities are likely to have riots? During the 1960s, it seemed that rioting was epidemic and that no ethnically mixed community would escape such violence. Sociologists have examined the city-to-city spread of disorders to see if certain community characteristics contributed to the outbreak of violence. We will examine the research that was designed to measure the "riot proneness" of communities.

What kinds of changes occur within communities during and following riots? Interestingly, there are some striking similarities between community responses to riots and community responses to disaster. There are some important differences as well. In this chapter we will look at community responses to riots within the framework developed by Wenger (1978) for the analysis of community responses to disaster.

Are there important societal or cultural differences in the ways nations respond to riots? In some nations, rioting is routinely quelled by the use of lethal fire, while other nations use lethal force only as a last resort. Some governments respond to widespread rioting by suspending all civil liberties and instituting martial law, while other governments try to muddle through, leaving civil liberties intact. Some governments, such as Great Britain and the United States, have spent considerable amounts of money to study the problem. We will examine some of the sociological explanations of these differences in societal response.

First, we will consider the Watts riot of 1965. As noted above, it was the first large-scale riot of the 1960s and is seen by many as the prototype of what was to follow. Every summer during the next seven years found areas of major cities in flames. The chant of "Burn, baby, burn!" was first raised in Watts and was raised again and again in the later riots. The Watts riot was typical in another way. Police, plagued with communication problems, had great difficulty in mounting effective riot control in the first hours of the disorder. Public officials who were needed to make important decisions were unavailable at critical times. Finally, police and National Guard decided to use high-powered weapons in Watts, which greatly added to the death toll.

The Watts Riot: August 11–22, 1965

Descriptions of the Watts riot generally agree that the event that triggered the first violence was the traffic arrest early Wednesday evening, August 11, of a young black man, Marquette Frye (Cohen and Murphy 1966; Conot 1967). From the moment a California Highway Patrol motorcycle officer pulled Frye over, only a block from his home, the arrest had gone wrong. To begin with, the arrest attracted an unusually large number of spectators. It had been a very hot afternoon, and people were enjoying the coolness of the evening on the sidewalks, streets, and front porches of Watts.

At first, the spectators were quite passive. When Frye began to verbally resist arrest, he was shoved by police; then Frye's brother and mother loudly intervened. By now, other officers had arrived at the scene of the arrest, and their vehicles added to the congestion. Night sticks were used on the Frye brothers, and their mother was manhandled into a police car. Spectators began to jeer the police. When police attempted to leave, they were spat upon. An officer waded into the spectators to apprehend the spitter. He struggled with a young woman wearing a beautician's smock that unfortunately looked like a maternity dress. The sight of a police officer manhandling a pregnant woman infuriated the crowd. Police called for additional assistance, and soon there was a large tangle of police vehicles and angry civilians. Finally, forty-five minutes after Frye had been pulled over, the police attempted to leave the area. Retreating police vehicles were sent on their way with a barrage of rocks, bottles, and obscenities. Shortly thereafter, the crowd broke into several smaller groups and dispersed.

By 9:00 P.M., large but casual crowds had gathered at nearby intersections with Imperial

Highway. People stood in groups on the sidewalks; others loitered in front of stores and filling stations. Children darted about and threw rocks at one another. Soon, police began to patrol these crowds, and by 10:00 P.M., nearly one hundred officers were on hand. Obscenities and insults were directed at police as they stood about near the crowds. Shortly, people started to throw rocks at police and passing cars. Police then attacked with night sticks in an effort to clear the crowds from the south side of the highway. Again and again, police charged, people scattered, and crowds reformed some distance from the police and resumed their taunts and rock throwing.

Soon, the violence escalated. At the intersection of Avalon Boulevard and Imperial Highway, crowds began to smash windows of cars. A station wagon, used by a television crew, was overturned and set on fire. Residents of Watts who were trying to restore calm suggested that traffic be stopped. Police refused, claiming that they lacked authority to close the highway. Shortly after midnight, traffic increased as factory shifts ended. Crowds began to surround cars and pound on them after breaking their windows. Some white motorists jumped from their cars and fled toward police. A few of the whites were beaten, but others were helped out of the area by blacks. The abandoned cars were overturned and set on fire.

During this first evening of violence, at least two dozen black and white civilians were injured, seventeen police received hospital treatment, and twenty-nine people were arrested. By 2:30 A.M., Thursday, police had dispersed the crowds and assumed that the disturbance was all over.

On Thursday morning, welfare workers called clients and urged them to keep their children off the streets. It turned out to be another hot day, however, and by noon crowds had begun to gather in Watts. Thursday evening started out much like the night before, with rock throwing and attacks on vehicles. Police attempted to disperse crowds, while refusing to halt traffic along Imperial Highway. Crowds attacked both police and firemen. Looting began, and on Thursday evening one store was set on fire. After a night during which scores were injured and arrested, police again assumed that it was all over. The worst had yet to come.

Friday was even hotter than the days before. Looting began early in the morning and at about 1:30 P.M., the first firebombing occurred. Soon, because of the firebombs and brisk winds, entire blocks of Watts were burning. The primary targets of firebombs were white-owned businesses; residences and black-owned businesses were usually spared. Fire department crews were unable to check the flames, in part because they were often attacked by crowds. Looting continued as buildings burned.

Late in the afternoon, police began to fire over the heads of crowds. The shooting soon became lethal. The first person to die was a black man, standing in front of a barber shop. He was killed by a stray bullet, fired a block away. The next person to die was a police officer, killed by the accidental discharge of another officer's shotgun. By 9:00 A.M. on Saturday, eighteen people had died in Watts.

The California National Guard was officially called up Friday afternoon, but the first thousand-man contingent did not move onto the streets of Watts until 11:00 P.M. This was not nearly enough manpower to contain the rioting. The guard could do little more than scatter looters and set up roadblocks. The darkness and lack of familiarity with Watts further hindered their efforts. As dawn approached, however, the rioting quieted.

All day Saturday, National Guard continued to arrive, until maximum strength was reached Saturday evening. Firebombings and skirmishes continued throughout the early afternoon and into the night. National Guard fired on looters and autos at roadblocks. By late Saturday night, another twelve people had been killed.

Sunday was quiet. Some looting continued as people sifted through the burned-out shells of buildings. In the stores that had received little damage, proprietors and their help remained to discourage looters. Sunday evening was also quiet. Now, it seemed, the worst really was over.

On Monday, arrests continued, and a young looter was killed, but for the most part, Watts remained quiet and few crowds gathered anywhere. Tuesday, August 17, was quiet as well. That evening at 10:00 P.M., the first National Guard units were withdrawn from Watts, and on Sunday evening, August 22, the last guard left Watts. Monday, eleven days after the arrest of Marquette Frye, the evening curfew was lifted. The Watts riot was officially over.

Legal Definitions of Riots

Mobs, *mob action*, *unlawful assembly*, and *routs* are terms that in federal, state, and municipal criminal law have the same or nearly the same meaning as *riot* (Williams 1962). In general, all these terms refer to gatherings of three or more people who share a clear intent to do violence, to terrorize, and otherwise disturb the peace to achieve their ends. The ends may be unlawful, as is the case with looting, destroying property, or interfering with the working of city government. In some instances, the ends may be lawful, as is the case with a political rally. If, however, the rally is staged in a "violent and tumultuous" manner, it can legally constitute a riot.

In some instances, riot and mob action statutes include reference to the unlawful and violent "exercise of correctional or regulative power" by assemblages of people. The actions of vigilante groups and lynch mobs fall within this category.

Some statutes attempt to define *riot participation*. In general, riot participants are those who remain at the scene of a disorder following an official "reading of the riot act," or orders to disperse. Under some statutes, remaining at the scene of a riot does not make a person a rioter. Some word or gesture, even if the language is not violent, that indicates a willingness to assist the rioters must be manifested before the person can be declared a rioter. Under a few statutes, people who remain at the scene and act to suppress or calm the rioting are considered to be nonrioters.

Compared to other areas of American criminal law, riot and unlawful assembly statutes are quite vague and subject to wide interpretations. A few clarifications, however, are worth noting. In some towns having ordinances against Sunday movies, theater owners and patrons have been prosecuted under unlawful assembly statutes, but these cases were dismissed because the patrons did not display "violence, terror, or tumult." Likewise, peaceful marches usually do not constitute unlawful assembly. Finally, some towns have attempted to prosecute groups of street-corner loiterers as unlawful assemblies. These cases were also dismissed due to a lack of "violence, terror, and tumult," even though loiterers occasionally hindered other pedestrian traffic.

Some of the riot participation studies discussed in Chapter 11 equated riot participation with being arrested and charged as a rioter. Though these people may be considered rioters in the legal sense, they may not be rioters in a sociological sense. When police use mass arrests in dealing with disorder, many of those arrested have engaged in no violent acts or, at least initially, have no negative attitudes toward police and other authorities. Some of those arrested were simply in the wrong place at the wrong time.

Organizations and Riots

Once police and other public officials have reached a consensus that "things have gotten out of control" or that a "riot" is occurring, several kinds of organizational changes occur, many of which are similar to changes that occur during disasters. Some sociologists have even suggested that riots are a type of disaster (Form and Nosow 1958). This approach has some merit when one considers the similarity of organizational responses to both riots and disasters.

Social Control Organizations

Though crowd control is a routine task for police, the control of violent or openly hostile crowds is not. Hence police departments take on many features of expanding organizations under these conditions (see Chapter 10, pp. 193–194). Like expanding organizations during disasters, police departments undergo organizational changes as they extend shifts and, in some cases, activate auxiliary police units. As is the case during disasters, police departments may also strengthen their ties to other police departments in nearby areas. This strengthening of ties occurs as other police departments initiate contacts to find out what is happening in the riot area or as police departments anticipate the exchange of personnel or equipment. Local departments may initiate contact with state police in the early stages of the riot, informing them of the status of the situation. State police may then take officers off routine patrols and assign them to the riot area as observers or advisers. If state police are fully activated for riot duty, substantial organizational changes occur in local and state organizations as these two agencies coordinate their efforts. The riot-related changes that occur within police departments are probably not as makeshift as those that occur in other expand-

ing organizations during disaster, because police departments usually have clearly specified contingency plans for riot control.

These organizational changes are important to an understanding of how and when a given type of disorder becomes defined as a riot. In the Watts riot, for example, coordinated and extensive organizational responses were delayed for several hours, while arson and looting continued. A major reason for this delay was the difficulty encountered in reaching the governor's office for the purpose of activating the California National Guard. The police and mayor of Los Angeles decided that the rioting could no longer be controlled during the second day of the disorder, but Governor Edmund G. Brown, Sr., was on a European trip and did not return to Los Angeles until the fifth day of the riot. Officials contacted Lieutenant Governor Glen Anderson, who insisted on personally visiting the riot area before calling up the guard. It wasn't until 5:00 P.M. on Friday, August 13, the third day of the disorder, that the guard was officially called out. Prior to the official callup, however, the guard had been assembling in various armories. Still, they did not arrive in Watts until after 10:00 P.M. Initially, about 1,200 troops were used. But in the darkness and on unfamiliar streets, the guard could do little more than chase looters away from stores. More troops were brought in, until nearly 60 percent (or 13,500 troops) of the California National Guard patrolled the riot zone (California Governor's Commission Report on the Los Angeles Riots 1965).

Delay in appropriate police response was also noted by the National Advisory Commission as a contributing factor in the growth of many other riots during the 1960s. Delays were attributed to many causes. One frequently mentioned cause was the inability of police officers to recognize "precipitating incidents." As we noted earlier, most precipitating incidents are discovered after the fact—in the weeks and months following the disorder—as police, city officials, media, citizen groups, and sometimes sociologists try to figure out what "really" happened. This "Monday morning quarterbacking" is perhaps thought-provoking but is of little utility to the police units in the field. Most precipitating events had little to set them apart from other routine events in the community. Here it is suggested that the delay of appropriate police response in the case of riots is a feature of organizations and the relationships between them rather than the result of "poor judgment" or "lack of sensitivity" on the part of individual police officers.

The response of organizations other than police and National Guard also warrants some note. Fire departments were overwhelmed with calls during many of these disorders, and crews who answered alarms were often attacked by crowds at the scene of the fire. In some instances, fire departments refused to answer calls in the riot area unless they were escorted in by the police or the guard. At times, police gave priority to protecting fire crews over making arrests or breaking up looting crowds. During some of the major disorders, hospitals near the riot zone were overwhelmed with injuries, and ambulance service was difficult and at times impossible. As in disasters, many of the injured arrived in private vehicles or on foot. The riot-related overload produced organizational changes within hospitals quite similar to the ones that accompany natural disasters. Finally, the breakdown of usual transportation facilities often accompanies both disaster and disorder. Bus and taxi service within the riot area were usually discontinued in the first hours of the disorder, often at the order of police. Sometimes, however, bus and taxi companies made this decision on their own, after vehicles were damaged or drivers refused to enter the riot area. Bus and taxi service were often not restored until weeks after the riot, and their absence may have actually prolonged the disorders, because many residents of the riot area could not get to work (Lee and Humphrey 1968; Bullock 1969).

Emergent Organizations

Looting crowds have been characterized as "individualistic" (Turner and Killian 1972). That is, in the looting crowd there is little cooperation among members, and there is a sense of urgent individual competition as people try to grab the most valuable items and escape with as much as they can carry. Contrary to this characterization, however, there appears to have been a considerable amount of emergent organization among looters during the urban disorders of the 1960s. Some people, for example, told others where various types of goods were available for the taking. Looters often exchanged goods, trading beer and wine for shoes or small appliances for clothing, and some looted items appear to have been stockpiled for later redistribution (Cohen and Murphy 1966).

In some of the riots, police and fire department personnel were fired on by civilians, which led some to portray sniping as a "new pattern of violence" that characterized the riots of the 1960s (Janowitz 1968; Masotti and Corsi 1969). McPhail and Wohlstein (1983) note that other research ran counter to this characterization. For example, Knoph (1969a) found that in only two of the twenty-five reported incidents of sniping during July and August of 1968 were police killed. In nearly half the reported incidents, police later denied that sniping had occurred, and in other incidents snipers missed police or only inflicted minor injuries. In these incidents, civilians used low-powered weapons, and the shootings appear to have been individual impulsive acts rather than well thought out plans to pin down or kill police. The National Advisory Commission also concluded that most of the incidents thought to be "sniping" were actually city and state police forces shooting at each other.

Emergent organization among looters and the fear of snipers led the National Advisory Commission to investigate charges that large-scale riots were carefully planned uprisings or conspiracies. The commission (1968:89) concluded that "the urban disorders . . . were not caused by, nor were they the consequence of, any organized plan or 'conspiracy.'" This conclusion does not mean, however, that there was an absence of emergent organization within communities during the riots.

Riots, like disasters, confront people with many problems. Some people probably discuss what they would do if a riot starts in much the same way that they discuss what they would do if disaster strikes. Emergent organizations frequently solve anticipated and unanticipated problems very effectively. Though previous planning is only one component of their actual response to these problems, the effectiveness of emergent organization gives the appearance of careful prior planning. We are most tempted to assume prior planning when an emergent organization temporarily foils the objectives of formally organized groups, such as the police, or accomplishes ends that are usually viewed as antisocial.

Ironically, the most obvious emergent organization among people in riot areas was directed toward prosocial ends. There may be fundamental similarities between the crowds that roam the streets during riots and the groups that carry out rescue and recovery activities during disaster. Both types of groups appear to form through the use of preexisting family and friendship ties and residential patterns. During the riots, emergent organization was evident among those who transported the injured to hospitals and among those who worked to locate the missing at hospitals, jails, and morgues.

The National Advisory Commission found that positive civilian social control efforts developed in eighteen of the twenty-four disorders they examined. In these and other disorders, counterriot groups were usually composed of ministers and church members, city employees, and members of youth gangs (cf. Knoph 1969b). The efforts of these groups were similar to those of the Watts Non-Violent Action Committee, which worked to calm the violence in the later stages of the riot (Cohen and Murphy 1966:130). The committee also distributed leaflets during the disorder, urging residents to report to them any instance of police brutality (Cohen and Murphy 1966:112–113). In several disorders, emergent groups took up weapons to protect fire department crews and ward off looters. Finally, people established rumor control centers that functioned to provide accurate information during the disorders (Knoph 1975).

Crowd Control Tactics

Several "how-to" books set forth principles and tactics of crowd and riot control. In a manual prepared in 1947, Joseph P. Lohman presented six general principles of crowd control. These principles raise issues and advocate methods that are clearly reflected in more recent crowd control manuals used by police and military personnel. Some critics of police action during the urban and student riots of the 1960s argue that police failed to follow generally recognized principles of crowd control (Hundley 1968). Although this criticism has some merit, the failure to follow established crowd control principles may have resulted partly from problems with the principles rather than from police malpractice.

Assumptions

The generally advocated principles of crowd control are based on at least three assumptions. First, it is assumed that police have a sufficient number of officers at hand to carry out crowd control tactics. Second, it is assumed that the officers present can act as a coordinated unit. These first two assumptions are problematic. In the early stages of many riots, a major problem confronting police is getting sufficient numbers of officers to the scene of disorder. It may take large police departments several hours to become fully activated for riot duty. The first officers to arrive at the scene of a developing disorder may have little advance information as to the nature of the situation. As was the case in the Watts riot, officers may arrive in an uncoordinated fashion, from many directions, thereby adding to the congestion and confusion at the scene.

The third assumption on which common crowd control principles are based is that police are able to foretell the future. That is, some crowd control principles instruct police on ways to respond to milling crowds and precipitating events. Milling crowds may be breaking no laws, and they do not necessarily constitute an overt threat to life or property. Quite simply, a milling crowd may not be a matter of police concern. We have noted above that a precipitating event may initially appear no different from other routine events in a community. It would indeed be helpful if police could tell beforehand which types of crowds and events would eventually turn into riots. Almost always, however, such insight is gained after the fact.

Principle One

Lohman's first principle of crowd control embodies all three of the above assumptions. The first principle is the *removal or isolation of the individuals involved in the precipitating incident before the crowd has begun to achieve substantial unity*. The removal of individuals from crowds increases in difficulty with the size of the gathering and the number of people to be removed. Those involved in the precipitating event are most likely to be at the focal

point of the crowd—in the center. At times, these people will resist removal or at least chant, sing, or be verbally abusive as they are being removed. In turn, these activities are very likely to increase the focus of the crowd. The verbal gestures of those being removed provide cues to others in the gathering, and chants, jeers, and obscenities may be shouted by a majority of the onlookers. The removal of persons from the crowd may in fact produce the "substantial unity" Lohman describes.

In practice, Lohman's first principle of crowd control suggests that police should use care in the location and circumstances in which they detain citizens in public places. If the option exists, police should carry out these contacts away from pedestrian flow or gatherings that could become focused on them. If arrests are necessary, they should be carried out quickly and with minimal displays of force. Police should operate on the assumption that once a crowd begins to gather, it will continue to increase in size, at least until the arrest is completed and police have left the area. They should try to develop a sense of how fast the crowd is growing and use this awareness when they make decisions in the field. The use of computers to check drivers' licenses, vehicle registrations, and outstanding warrants has shortened the time needed to make a routine traffic arrest. Priority codes, to be used when rapid assembling is occurring, could further shorten this response time.

Police may be able to anticipate the kind of responses arrestees will make in the event they are removed from the gathering. If highly visible and vocal responses are likely, this will probably produce greater focus within the gathering. At this point, alternatives to arrest and removal should be considered. A verbal warning or a ticket to appear in court may be a prudent substitute for a street arrest. In any event, police should be aware that their calls for additional assistance are likely to produce additional assembling by civilians. A few extra officers may be of little help in controlling a gathering of greatly increased size.

Principle Two

Lohman's second principle of crowd control is the *interruption of communication during the milling process by dividing the crowd into smaller units.* This principle can be carried out only with a sufficient number of police officers at the scene. Further, unless these officers can act as a coordinated team, attempts to divide the crowd will probably result in further disorder. James Hundley (1968) noted that police in riot situations usually failed to divide the crowd; instead, they usually attacked along a frontal line in an attempt to push the entire crowd out of a contested area. In an open area such as a park or a university mall, breaking a gathering into smaller groups may be difficult if not impossible. In an open area, the crowd simply parts in front of the police units, envelops them, and regroups behind them. This situation existed immediately prior to the National Guard's shooting of students at Kent State (Lewis 1972). Lohman's second tactic is more workable in an enclosed area with several narrow exits, such as a street. Police units can approach the gathering from opposite ends of the street. As the police units draw together, people can disperse through divergent side streets, alleys, and across yards. Dispersed in this fashion, people are less likely to immediately regroup and confront police (Momboisse 1967:428–435).

Principle Three

Lohman's third principle of crowd control is the *removal of the crowd leaders, if it can be done without the use of force.* Before crowd leaders can be removed, they must be identified. In some instances, this can be quite a simple matter. Leaders may be well-known personalities, as when Dr. Martin Luther King led protest marches, or they may carry bullhorns and wear armbands, special hats, or clothing that sets them apart from the rest of the crowd.

Often, however, the identification of crowd leaders is not so simple. In crowds that confront police during riots, leadership is often emergent and transitory, provided by people who give instructions that others near them follow (Turner and Killian, 1972:80–95). Such leaders are often people with the loudest voices or people who are at some prominent location in the crowd where they can be seen and heard by many others. Their influence on the activity of the people near them is often incomplete and of momentary duration. During the Watts riot, for example, the movement of crowds from one location to another was preceded by shouts of street addresses or store names.

Identifying leaders (or shouters) in this type of situation is quite difficult, and arresting and removing an individual considered to be a leader is not likely to halt such activity. Momboisse suggests that when it is not advisable to remove emergent leaders, police can sometimes limit their influence. In some situations, for instance, prepared scripts or music played over loudspeakers can jam the internal communication upon which emergent leadership is based. Also, if police know some of the people within the crowd, they can call upon them to help control it. If members of the gathering are unknown, individuals can be appointed or called upon to assist police. Occasionally, police can circulate through the gathering, saying things to individuals that counter the suggestions being made by other crowd members. Momboisse refers to this type of activity as rumor control. Also, police can provide instructions for immediate activity that can counter the instructions of emergent leadership. During one of the last great "panty raids" at the University of Iowa, in 1967 (see Chapter 7, pp. 152–153), state police circulated through the crowds who roamed the streets near the women's dorms. They urged young men to "have fun" but "stay off fire escapes" and "don't damage property."

The removal of a boisterous and prominent member of a gathering often produces a temporary focus within the gathering and creates further crowd control difficulties. Momboisse refers to particularly conspicuous emergent leaders as "agitators." If these agitators cannot be removed from the gathering, police can, without being verbally abusive, say things to deflate them in the eyes of the crowd. Pointing out an obviously inaccurate statement made by agitators, or questioning their motives, can accomplish this objective.

Principle Four

Lohman's fourth principle of crowd control is *distracting the attention of the crowd from its focal point by creating diversions at other points*. This tactic is particularly effective if the gathering loses membership as it moves from one location to another.

This principle can be illustrated by an event that occurred during Hiroshima Days, a week of antinuclear protest in New York City, in August 1970. Several hundred protesters marched to a bandshell in Central Park for a rally. The rally did not start promptly, however, because two competing antinuclear groups began a strident debate onstage to determine which group should be first on the program. As the debate wore on, a few who had marched to the park left the rally. This movement accelerated when a Trinidad steel band began to play within earshot of the bandshell. Thirty minutes later, many more than half of those who had first gathered at the rally were assembled around the steel band. The steel band ended their set with a very upbeat number; then the musicians abruptly grabbed their instruments, dashed to

an old station wagon, and sped out of the park.

Many in the audience were surprised by the band's rapid departure. As this gathering broke into small conversation groups, dispersal began. Only a small portion of the audience returned to the rally. Whether the presence of the band was a coincidence or simply clever crowd control by the New York Police Department is not known. In either case, it illustrates Lohman's fourth principle of crowd control.

Principle Five

Lohman's fifth principle of crowd control is *preventing the spread and reinforcement of the crowd by isolating it*. To begin with, police can advise people to stay away from the riot area through public announcements and news coverage. When police attempt to physically isolate a crowd, much depends on where the crowd is located. A university administration building occupied by a few dozen students protesting dormitory rules can be isolated rather easily. Likewise, small mining towns can be isolated by police during labor disorders.

On the other hand, the Los Angeles Police Department and nearly 13,500 California National Guard were not able to totally isolate Watts. The street pattern of Los Angeles is based on the grid pattern, typical of most American cities. The Watts area probably has more than thirty thousand possible entry and exit points, such as major highways, streets, alleys, and yards (California Governor's Commission Report 1965). Likewise, movement in and out of the Detroit riot area, though difficult, was not impossible (Stone 1969).

Much of Momboisse's discussion of riot control details effective tactics for isolating riot zones in the urban area. Momboisse (1967:401–402) views containment as a defensive tactic, however, and cautions that containment must not become the sole objective of riot control. Efforts to encircle a large area can greatly disperse police forces and leave them vulnerable to attack. Often, encirclement will fail because of the great mobility of rioters. Even when near total isolation can be achieved, it can have a negative effect. People in the riot area may be reluctant to leave if they think that all routes in and out of the riot area are being guarded by police. Ultimately, the successful isolation of large urban areas depends on the cooperation of the majority of the citizenry.

Principle Six

Finally, Lohman suggests the *show of force* as a principle of crowd control. Large numbers of police, who display weapons with a clear readiness to use them when disorder is imminent can intimidate potential rioters. The show of force can make the actual use of force unnecessary.

Momboisse (1967:326) points out the show of force is likely to succeed when the number of potential rioters is small and police have greater numbers. It is most effective when dealing with people who have had little previous contact with police or experience with disorder. In general, however, Momboisse cautions against the use of the show of force. The show of force is usually carried out by police making a grand entry into the scene of the disturbance. The movement of large numbers of police, accompanied by sirens, flashing lights, and police vehicles, can provide a focal point for and initiate assembling processes. Quite simply, the show of force can increase the size of gatherings as it is carried out.

Further, the show of force can infuriate rather than intimidate. Those in an "angry and unruly" crowd can easily interpret the show of force as police overreaction and brutality. The show of force by police can provide cues for a show of force by those in the gathering. There are many instances in which the arrival of police reinforcements apparently triggered, or renewed, violence. In Boston, on September 8, 1975, loud and unruly crowds had gathered at public schools during the first week of a newly instituted racial busing plan. The "grand entry" of eighty National Guard troops produced further assembling at one school. Shortly, the cursing crowd started to throw rocks at the guard and began to damage buses. Dozens of arrests followed. It is difficult to determine the amount and type of force that must be displayed in order to intimidate people and not infuriate them. History gives us many examples of people attacking tanks with sticks and bricks or taunting ranks of soldiers armed with fixed bayonets. Momboisse suggests that police should, as a rule, display no more force than they are authorized and prepared to use in any particular situation.

Some Additional Insights

In light of past experiences with these crowd control principles, we have gained some additional insights. For example, the use of large stationary formations of police are to be avoided when possible. Often, such formations provide focal points for assembling processes, particularly when formations block normal routes of travel or are used to secure buildings. Crowd control options are greatly reduced in the dense and focused gatherings that are produced. Instead, if possible, small mobile teams of officers should be used to patrol these areas. Volumes of traffic, which can be monitored by police, should be allowed to move through these areas.

Rather than the show of force, Momboisse suggests a strategy of force in reserve. This may have been part of the Iowa Highway Patrol's planning in dealing with the University of Iowa disorder that followed the killing of students at Kent State in May 1970. When the

Highway Patrol arrived in Iowa City, there had already been two days of disorder. One campus building had been burned, the ROTC building had been heavily damaged, and about three hundred students had been arrested. Across the campus, students speculated as to when the state police would arrive. Beginning at about noon on the second day of the disorder, individual patrol cars, carrying two officers each, began to cruise the streets near the center of campus. The police cars evoked stares from students but little else. By midafternoon, however, there were at least three state police cars per block in the campus area. Had the Highway Patrol used the grand entry, students who had been awaiting their arrival would probably have assembled at the center of campus. Instead, the patrol had, without flashing lights and blaring sirens, slowly saturated the campus area with a considerable number of state police. They had not created a focal point for assembling by students.

A few days earlier, students had established a protest-command center in an apartment building near campus. Here, students compiled information regarding the movement of campus and city police. Student protest marshals were dispatched from their command center to locations where police-student confrontations were occurring. The student marshals attempted to maintain order by urging students to be calm and police to refrain from the use of force. The command center also provided a place for student leaders to meet with one another and to plan organized protest activities. The field commander of the Highway Patrol visited the student command center on the afternoon of the patrol's arrival. He informed students of the patrol's objectives and gave them some advice on how to better carry out their marshaling efforts. Finally, he told students that he would be at the patrol's command center, at a motor inn on the outskirts of Iowa City. He told students they were welcome

to visit the patrol's command center and that he would be available for consultation.

When students arrived at the motor inn, they saw a parking lot full of state police cars, buses, communication trailers, and a large number of officers. Though few of the officers who patrolled the campus were wearing riot helmets or carrying riot batons, the students could see rows of helmets and batons on display at the control center. Momboisse would describe this tactic as force in reserve. At the scene of disorder, police and riot control equipment are not displayed in a manner likely to produce a focal point for assembly or needlessly antagonize civilians. Procedures are established, however, that make it clear to civilians that considerably greater force is near at hand.

Momboisse emphasizes the importance of maintaining communication between police and civilians during disorder. Even during the most severe disorders described in this chapter, authorities were able to recruit assistance from civilians in the riot area. Recognized community leaders, as well as members of youth gangs, put forth great effort urging people to return to their homes (National Advisory Commission 1968:177–178). By maintaining communication with civilians, police gather valuable information that can be used to evaluate rumors. The Iowa Highway Patrol initiated and then maintained communication with students at the University of Iowa during the disorder described above. At this time, there were frequent reports that the Black Panthers and the Hell's Angels would soon arrive in Iowa City to help students battle police. The Iowa Highway Patrol was able to quickly dismiss this information as "rumor and fancy" because of their ongoing communication with students and student leaders. The Highway Patrol was also able to inform student organizations of the guidelines governing street crowds, rallies, and arrests during the period of disorder. Likewise, student protest leaders were able to inform the Highway Patrol of their plans for pending rallies and demonstrations. Many misunderstandings were worked out in conferences rather than in street battles.

Finally, Momboisse frequently suggests that police must be sensitive to the level of conflict in which they are involved, and they must respond in a manner that communicates police readiness without unnecessarily raising the level of conflict. Police control the use of many different "symbols of conflict," including riot helmets and face shields, riot sticks, various types of firearms, and even armored personnel carriers. Certain types of activities also symbolize conflict. The wedge formations police use to break compact gatherings into smaller groups and lines of troops in kneeling positions, with rifles leveled and aimed, are symbols of conflict. How these symbols are selected and used by police can play an important role in the development of conflict.

At times, police can reduce the level of conflict by refraining from the use of symbols of conflict. Prior to the Iowa Highway Patrol's arrival on the campus of the University of Iowa, there had been an increasing spiral of conflict. Communication between students and campus and city police had broken down entirely. The local police patrolled the county courthouse lawn with automatic weapons. Tear gas had been used against crowds of students, and more than $100,000 worth of property had been destroyed. Across campus, students spoke of the pending arrival of the state police. It was said that they would enter the city in armored personnel carriers and use 50-caliber machine guns against students. Some students collected rocks for throwing and bottles for Molotov cocktails and even discussed ways of obtaining firearms and gas masks.

The Highway Patrol failed to validate the dramatic spirit of conflict that was emerging. Their entry into the campus was unobtrusive, and they did not wear riot gear when they were on campus. Seeing the state police in regular uniforms and patrolling the campus with two-man teams was a marked contrast to what most students had expected. After their arrival on campus, little property damage occurred and mass arrests ceased. The Highway Patrol's crowd control tactics were in sharp contrast to those used at Kent State. From their first movement onto Kent State campus, National Guard troops wore full riot gear and carried rifles. They repeatedly used riot formations in their confrontations with students. Finally, even if by accident, the ultimate symbol of conflict was utilized—lethal gunfire.

Communities and Riots

Sociologists have attempted to answer two kinds of questions about communities and riots. The first question is that of "riot proneness" and whether some cities are more likely than others to experience riots. The second question is that of determining the kinds of changes that occur within communities during and following riots.

Riot Proneness

One of the first studies to empirically examine the question of riot proneness was that of Lieberson and Silverman (1965). These researchers compared seventy-six cities that experienced race riots between 1913 and 1963 with a matched sample of seventy-six nonriot cities for that same time period. They selected nonriot cities for their size and proximity to the riot city. Lieberson and Silverman concluded that riot cities were more likely to have a high level of economic competition between the races and municipal governments that were unsympathetic and unresponsive to black problems.

This type of paired comparison analysis was not possible for the decade of the 1960s, when at least 820 racial incidents were recorded by various sources. Of these incidents, 341 disorders were described as involving "significant instances of black aggression" or "riots." Simply put, there were not enough nonriot cities to construct a matching sample for riot cities!

Faced with this difficulty, Seymour Spilerman (1970) developed a different kind of analysis. Instead of comparing riot and nonriot cities, he compared the actual distribution of riots with hypothetical distributions generated by mathematical models. Spilerman began his analysis by noting that there were 673 cities with populations greater than twenty-five thousand in 1960. Then Spilerman identified the way in which 341 riots would be distributed among these 673 cities, assuming that riots were random events and each city had an equal probability for disorder. Under these hypothetical conditions, 405 cities should have no disorders, 206 cities should have only 1 disorder, 52 cities should have 2 disorders, 9 cities should have 3 disorders, and 1 city should have 4 disorders.

The actual distribution of riots was significantly different from this hypothetical distribution. In fact, 504 cities had no disorders, 93 cities had one disorder, 36 cities had two disorders, 19 cities had three disorders, and 21 cities had four or more disorders. This comparison shows that despite the greatly increased number of riots in the 1960s, they were not random occurrences.

Using more elaborate mathematical procedures, Spilerman created other hypothetical distributions. He constructed a hypothetical "riot reinforcement" distribution in which the occurrence of a riot in a city would make it more likely that the city would experience further riots. The riot reinforcement model suggests that the initial disorder would generate interracial hatreds and mutual preparations for further violence. Spilerman also created a "negative reinforcement" distribution in which the occurrence of a riot would decrease the likelihood of further riots in that city. The negative reinforcement model assumes that a riot would result in the release of accumulated tensions and provide evidence of the futility of violence. Finally, Spilerman created a "geographic contagion" distribution in which the occurrence of riots in nearby communities would contribute to a city's riot proneness. None of these hypothetical distributions matched the actual distribution of riots.

The hypothetical distribution that most closely matched the actual distribution of riots was based on the assumption that communities have different underlying disorder propensities. In one sense, this was the same conclusion that was reached earlier by Lieberson and Silverman (1965). However, Spilerman rejected their conclusion that the important differences between communities were black-white economic competition and unresponsive city government.

Spilerman (1970:642) examined eighteen community attributes and their relation to the number of disorders within the community. He used, for example, the percent of dilapidated housing as a measure of social disorganization and the size of the city council as a measure of effective political structure. He also examined income, unemployment, and median levels of education as indicators of absolute and relative deprivation. Low correlations were obtained between these measures and the number of disorders in a city. The only measure that was strongly associated with the number of disorders was the absolute number of black residents in a city. Spilerman (1970:645) concluded that "the larger the Negro population, the greater the likelihood of a disorder. Little else appears to matter."

Spilerman explains this conclusion in terms of a nationwide pattern of black discontent sufficient to overwhelm the impact of local conditions (Spilerman 1970; 1971; 1976). The number of blacks in a city increases until a "critical mass" is reached, and disorder follows.

The Differentiated View.   Spilerman's findings run largely counter to McPhail's differentiated view of riots. The differentiated view clearly suggests that some city environments provide greater likelihood than others for assembling processes and, in turn, disorders (McPhail 1971). The age structure of a population and unemployment rates are crude indicators of people's relative availability for involvement in disorder. The character of residential patterns and patterns of traffic flow create conditions of greater or lesser proximity among available people. The availability and proximity of persons create a favorable precondition for assembling processes. Street arrests are one source of assembling cues that often denote hostility. Face-to-face communication networks within the community transmit and augment these cues. Spilerman did not examine such factors as these in his analysis.

Factors in the differentiated view of riots are important because they constitute an "immediate interactional environment" for people (McPhail 1971:1072). The immediate interactional environment for the urban disorders of the 1960s was typically a mixed residential and commercial area of a city. Most riot areas were more densely populated than the rest of the city, and more than 80 percent of the residents were black. In these areas, the greatest number of people were killed, injured, or arrested, almost all property damage occurred, and police concentrated their greatest control efforts. Outside the riot areas, little damage occurred, and few arrests were made. It follows from the differentiated view, therefore, that the riot area, not the entire city, is the proper unit of analysis.

Spilerman, however, used the riot city as his unit of analysis. Granted, when comparing cities, there seems to be little besides the size of the black population that distinguishes one riot city from another. Comparing riot areas, however, may reveal substantial differences in, for example, age structure and unemployment rates. Likewise, street arrests may be considerably more frequent in some riot areas than in others. Street patterns and residential patterns may create quite different degrees of conduciveness for assembling among riot areas.

David Snyder (1979) conducted a study of the urban riots between 1961 and 1969 that used the predominantly black census tract area, or "ghetto," as the unit of analysis. Further, Snyder attempted to examine variables suggested by the differentiated view of riots. He assumed that the likelihood for instructions to assemble was a function of the number of police-resident contacts within the ghetto, and he created a variable that would reflect the probable number of these contacts. The "area-contact-interaction" variable was based on the number of police, the number of blacks in the ghetto, and the size of the ghetto relative to the rest of the city.

Instructions to assemble are more likely to result in assembling if many people hear or see them. Snyder constructed a "spatial availability" variable, which was the number of street intersections within the ghetto. The greater the number of street intersections in the ghetto, the greater the likelihood that people will see and hear assembling cues. Snyder also suggested that further studies include the density and type of residential dwellings in the ghetto. Widely dispersed housing and high-rise housing are relatively less conducive to assembling than dwellings clustered close together.

People are likely to assemble when they have few or no competing commitments. Consequently, Snyder constructed a "temporal availability" variable, which consisted of the number of ghetto residents between the ages of fifteen and thirty-four, the number of unemployed residents, and the number of people who recently moved into the ghetto. These people are generally assumed to have greater amounts of unstructured or uncommitted time at their disposal than others.

Finally, assembling is more likely to be extensive when face-to-face communication links spread assembling cues throughout the ghetto area. Snyder used the population density of the census tract as a crude indicator of these communication links, and he suggested that future studies take into account communication barriers, such as rivers, highways, or railways that intersect many ghetto areas.

Snyder admits that his measures of ghetto characteristics are nearly as crude as Spilerman's citywide measures. Further, information about predominantly black census tracts was available for only 244 of the 341 disorders included in Spilerman's study. Even so, Snyder's differentiated variables are more closely associated than Spilerman's with the number of disorders occurring in ghettos. The differentiated view of riots, according to Snyder, clearly shows that some ghettos are more riot prone than others. This is not because some ghettos have greater levels of discontent than others. Rather, some ghettos have significantly greater numbers of police-citizen contacts that can be easily observed by ghetto residents. Further, Snyder's analysis suggests that ghettos with younger populations, high unemployment, and many new residents are more likely than others to experience disorder. These people are more likely than others to be "on the streets" with "nothing to do."

Finally, Snyder's analysis confirms the idea that assembling and resulting disorders are likely to occur in ghettos where news can be transmitted rapidly among the residents. High population density, large numbers of people on porches and sidewalks and in the streets and parks, and few ecological barriers to face-to-face communication seem to be clearly associated with a ghetto's riot proneness.

Community Responses to Riots

Riots and people's response to them produce a number of functional and structural changes within communities. Many of these changes are documented in the riot studies conducted during the 1960s. In order to systematically present these findings, we will use Dennis E. Wenger's (1978) framework for analyzing disaster-related community changes.

Functional Changes. Wenger identifies four community functions in his discussion of community responses to disaster (see Chapter 10, pp. 199–207). The first function is the wide range of activities that constitute the production, distribution, and consumption patterns of community life. The second function includes the activities and organizations that carry out child and adult socialization. The third community function is participation. Work, school, and voluntary service organizations, kin, and friendship groups provide opportunities for instrumental and noninstrumental participation in community life. Finally, there is the mutual support function. Families, as well as formal organizations, provide psychological and material support during times of stress.

Riots, like disasters, produce important and noticeable changes in these normal community functions. Wenger notes that the type of production facilities in a community is related to possible disaster outcomes; similarly, the proximity of residences to streets, stores, and factories is a major factor in a community's conduciveness to riot (Snyder 1979; McPhail 1971). Further, the timing of production, distribution, and consumption functions determines the tempo of community life. Work hours and vacation schedules determine when substantial portions of a population have free time at their disposal. The majority of urban riots began or reached their peak during evenings and on weekends (National Advisory Commission 1968:71 and 360–406). During the "long, hot summers" of the 1960s, riots most frequently occurred during the vacation months of July and August.

After disasters, communities often face the problem of distributing unsolicited gifts of food, clothing, and other useful items. No such generosity is shown to riot communities. In fact, some resources, such as bus and taxi service, may be withheld from the riot area for some time after order is restored.

The restoring of production, distribution, and consumption functions signifies the end of the disaster period and is often accomplished within a surprisingly short period of time (Wright et al. 1979). In contrast, community functions are restored slowly following riots. In some riot areas, such as Newark, New Jersey, and Watts, the burned-out shells of buildings still stand, years after the disorder. The rebuilding of riot communities is often hindered by a serious lack of property insurance in the areas where riots occurred. The National Advisory Commission (1968:305–312) noted that in some areas nearly half of the commercial businesses had neither fire nor theft insurance prior to the disorder. Unlike the case with disasters, no direct federal "riot assistance" was immediately available to finance reconstruction. After the riots, residential and commercial insurance rates often tripled. The high cost or total unavailability of insurance decreases the rate at which commercial property within the ghetto can be bought and sold, greatly hindering the ghetto's recovery. Finally, some commercial properties in the ghetto may, for all practical purposes, be abandoned after riots.

Socialization functions are of secondary importance to community life during disasters. Schools may be dismissed in advance of hurricanes or blizzards. Similarly, some schools were dismissed when "a riot was likely." Although this precaution was well intentioned, many of the children and teenagers who were released from school eventually became involved in disorders. Schools, daycare, and recreation centers were seldom looted or vandalized, even though they contained valuable items (Berk and Aldrich 1972; Quarantelli and Dynes 1968).

During disasters, the participation and support functions of community life are heightened. There is some evidence that similar things happen during riots. Quarantelli and Dynes (1968) point out that the looting that occurred during the urban disorders of the 1960s was carried out by residents of the community. Further, their actions received a great deal of community support. This is in sharp contrast to the looting that occasionally accompanies disaster. Disaster-related looting is usually carried out by outsiders, and their actions are condemned by community members. Some suggest that during riots looting is often initiated by local criminal gangs. In the later stages of a riot, it is clear that looting is carried out by people from all age and income segments of the riot area, with little competition or conflict. Looting is carried out quite openly by small groups and families, often with the encouragement of bystanders. Surveys conducted after riots indicate a substantial support for these activities, even among nonparticipants (Thomlinson, 1968; Oberschall, 1968).

Riot-related opportunities for participation in community life were increased where youth patrols were organized by police, city officials, churches, members of local antipoverty agencies, and autonomous Black Power groups (Knoph 1969b). Sanctioned youth patrols were used in at least eighteen major cities during 1967 and 1968, and their size ranged from twenty (Pittsburgh) to nearly five hundred (Newark). They assumed a variety of official and unofficial names, including White Hats (Tampa), Peace Monitors (San Francisco), Youth Alliance Security Patrol (Boston), and the "soul patrol" (Providence, Rhode Island). These groups provided a "socially approved" activist role for many youth gangs. Patrols guarded against vandalism, tried to calm crowds, monitored police activity, and offered general assistance, such as providing coffee for police, aiding Red Cross workers, and evacuating people from burning buildings (Knoph 1969b:18).

The National Advisory Commission took a largely negative view of the youth patrols, noting that they had no "clear and legitimate authority" and therefore contributed to the confusion during riots. Further, the commission characterized the youth patrols as "ineffective" in preventing violence. Knoph (1969b), who studied the youth patrols in great detail, came to the opposite conclusion, stating that "In the . . . cases where information is available, youth patrols were extremely effective in handling crowds and reducing tensions."

In most cities, following a major riot, job training programs, neighborhood improvement associations, and youth-oriented programs were initiated (Bullock 1969:51–103). Most of these organizations were short lived, and few are active today. For many people, however, a riot provided a stimulus for a few months of increased community participation.

We know relatively little about the degree of personal support shown toward residents who suffered as a result of a riot. Quite likely, friends and neighbors offered sympathy to the injured and even to those who were arrested. Quite likely, looted food and clothing was offered to people in need. Little compassion was shown, however, to the merchants who were burned out or looted. In fact, some stores that had been looted were burglarized shortly after they reopened (Cohen and Murphy 1966).

Structural Changes.   Wenger (1978) identifies four structural elements of community life in his discussion of community responses to disaster. These structural elements are the community's value and belief system, social norms,

organizational structure, and power relationships. Disasters usually produce an increased consensus of values and beliefs within a community. For a brief period of time, humanitarian values and beliefs in the effectiveness of cooperation become central to community life.

There appears to be a similar growth of consensus and alteration of community values and beliefs during riots. For a brief period of time, activist values and beliefs become central to community life. From the end of World War I until the 1960s, riots of a racial character in the United States had value and belief overtones of race warfare (Grimshaw 1968). During these riots, inaccurate rumors of cross-racial assaults upon women and children were used to justify attacks on members of the other race. For the most part, groups of white civilians hunted down and attacked blacks who were outside "their area of the city." Sometimes, whites actually invaded the black areas of the city, attacking people and property (Grimshaw 1960).

This pattern of conflict was not typical of the disorders during the 1960s. The antagonists were largely residents of black communities and the police and National Guard. Rumors of cross-racial assault of women and children were not a substantial ingredient of these disorders. Blacks concentrated their attacks primarily on property rather than on people. There were no attempts to invade white communities.

Grimshaw attributes these marked differences to the ideology that inspired the riots. While the overwhelming majority of blacks expressed fear and dismay at the burning, destruction, and loss of life during the riots, they did not see the riots as purposeless, nor were they unsympathetic to the rioters (Thomlinson 1968). The majority of a national sample of blacks saw the riots as a way to call attention to their problems, express their discontent to whites, improve their conditions, and end discrimination (Thomlinson 1968). Many blacks viewed the riots of the 1960s as a black revolt against intolerable conditions.

Following disasters, most changes in the normative structure are related to the use of property. Heavy equipment may be appropriated to rescue and transport the injured. Under other circumstances, this might well be considered theft. Quarantelli and Dynes (1968) point out that a similar normative transition took place during riots of the 1960s. A very broad cross section of community residents, not just the "criminal element," took part in looting. Further, the looting was carried out openly and with enthusiasm. Looters were also rather selective: their most frequent targets were grocery stores, followed by furniture, clothing, and liquor stores. Banks, schools, manufacturing plants, and private residences were largely ignored.

Because of this open, enthusiastic, and selective character of looting, Quarantelli and Dynes concluded that it was normatively regulated. They suggest that this looting represented "situations of temporary and localized redefinitions of property rights" (1968:8). This means that few looters and bystanders viewed the ransacking of local stores as simple theft. Instead, they saw their actions as a type of "justice" in which today's looting equalized years of mistreatment by white merchants. Looting was seen as a means of communicating to the broader society that something was fundamentally wrong about the marked inequality of the American economic system.

Disasters produce a temporary weakening and then a strengthening of ties between the community and outside organizations. A similar pattern occurs for riots. Initially, the riot community may be isolated by police and National Guard from surrounding areas, although this isolation is usually not complete. Many goods and services provided by outside organizations may be withheld from a community during and for a time following the riot. After order is restored in a riot community, ties to organizations providing social services may

be increased. The National Advisory Commission recommended a marked upgrading of job training, remedial education, and community development programs within riot areas in an effort to "prevent further riots."

Finally, power relationships become more authoritarian during disasters. Similarly, authoritarian patterns of power use occur in riots, most obviously in the riot control efforts of police and National Guard. Moderate black organizations, such as the NAACP, were able to wield power in a more authoritarian fashion following riots, in part because more of the white community felt that moderate organizations represented the "responsible leadership" of the black community.

Societies and Riots

Napoleon claimed that the most effective means of stopping riots was a "whiff of grapeshot." Contrary to Napoleon's view, however, having access to lethal force does not solve all the problems of crowd control in riot situations. Turner and Killian (1972:160–161) note that even in totalitarian regimes, some police and soldiers may feel a sense of sympathy for those they must suppress. In these extreme instances of totalitarian control, ethnic, religious, or regional identities may inhibit the unrestrained use of force against rioters.

Other factors also operate to restrain police in their use of force in riots and uprisings. In the later stages of revolutions, for example, police may refuse to fire on or otherwise suppress crowds in the name of an authority that may soon be deposed. Such defections and mutinies of the military and police have signaled the end for many governments throughout history (Rudé 1964; Tilly 1975).

Sometimes authorities may hesitate in using wholesale lethal force out of fear of sanctions from other governments. The United States has threatened to withhold and has at times withheld foreign aid out of concern for violations of human rights. Likewise, the World Bank shows concern for political stability in making and extending loans to nations.

In some instances, the use of force may be curtailed by the simple realization that it may enlarge the scope and intensity of disorder. The unrestrained use of force against one group may bring other groups into the conflict. This can happen, for example, in labor disputes. The violent suppression of workers in one industry can bring about sympathy strikes by workers in other industries.

The use of lethal force by authorities has often served as a justification for the use of lethal force by their victims. The blatant use of force on street crowds can also change the nature of conflict. Open, relatively unorganized, and isolated defiance can give way to more broadly based and organized resistance. Further, the aims of this resistance may change from relatively nonviolent reform to violent, total revolution. Stalin, for example, pointed out how the whips and saber blades of the czar's cossacks served to infuriate and radicalize the pre-revolutionary street crowds of Russia (Stalin 1953).

The use of force may also be ruled out because of its cost. The cost and difficulties in using the latest weapons to quell their own citizenry may give some governments pause. These resources of terror can be put to better use (such as intimidating nearby nations), particularly when less forceful means of crowd control offer promise of success.

Finally, the use of force may be restrained when authorities are dealing with disorders involving high-status or popular groups within the society. Students were shot and killed on at least three separate occasions during the student disorders of the 1960s and 1970s. In two instances—those at Jackson State, Mississippi, and Orangeburg State, South Carolina—the student body was composed almost totally of blacks. The other incident, of course, was at Kent State, Ohio, a predominantly white university. Though there were numerous demonstrations at Ivy League and Big Ten universities, lethal force was not used at these schools, and on the whole, student riots were treated in a much more restrained fashion than the urban riots of the time or the labor riots of earlier decades.

Cultural Differences

It has often been suggested that there are cultural differences in the ways that societies view the use of harsh tactics of crowd control. It is noted, for example, that English bobbies seldom use firearms in crowd control, in part because they are dealing with a more "civilized" or "reserved" populace. In recent years, however, urban disorders in England have usually occurred in areas where recent, often non-English-speaking immigrants have settled. In London's Brixton riots of 1981, violence occurred for nearly a week, with much arson and looting. Only one casualty occurred, however—a boy who was struck and killed by a police vehicle. The Brixton riots present a sharp contrast to the thirty-five deaths that occurred during the Watts riot or the thirty-nine fatalities of the Detroit riot of 1967.

Such differences, however, can only be attributed to cultural factors in the most general sense, if at all. There are more immediate considerations. First, it must be noted that a fair number of the casualties that occurred during riots in the United States were not the result of direct police action. For example, two civilians died in Detroit when they walked into downed power lines (National Advisory Commission 1968). In Watts, some people died in fires, and the only police officer to die was killed by the accidental discharge of his partner's shotgun (Conot 1967).

Not all civilians who were injured or killed by police gunfire were deliberately shot while committing crimes. Numbers of people died simply because high-powered weapons were often used in densely populated urban areas. Police frequently fired over the heads of looters without taking direct aim. Sometimes, police shot in the general direction of buildings that they suspected to contain snipers (National Advisory Commission 1968). Some National Guard and police units had little riot training or experience, and at times, these units discharged their weapons without orders to do so. In Detroit, troops fired 201 rounds, and in Newark, National Guard and police fired 13,326 rounds, including 50-caliber tracer bullets (National Advisory Commission 1968). Many of those who fell were not intentional police targets. Rather, they were hit by bullets and ricochets hundreds of yards from where the weapons were fired. Perhaps the development of more precise and less lethal weapons is in order.

In recent English riots, the majority of injuries were inflicted upon the police, while in the United States during the disorders of the 1960s, police sustained only about 10 percent of the fatalities and less than 30 percent of the injuries (National Advisory Commission 1968:66–67). It seems that the English are willing to tolerate injured police more readily than dead civilians.

Finally, it should be noted that English crowd control tactics have not always been so refined. Rudé, for example, documents the brutal character of riot control tactics used in England during the industrial riots of the eighteenth and nineteenth centuries (Rudé 1964). The vicious response of British authorities to the naval mutinies of the eighteenth century are also well documented. It seems, therefore, that no group is "culturally immune" from the use of harsh riot control tactics.

Normative Constraint

The reliance on harsh and brutal riot control tactics seems to occur when neither side feels a normative constraint on its actions toward the other party (Turner and Killian 1972:161–162). These conditions may be approached within political systems that deny fundamental rights of property or dissent to groups within their midst. Such disenfranchised groups are usually held in low regard throughout the society. The use of violent suppression is likely to occur at the slightest provocation on the part of the low-status group. Further, this suppression will probably be approved of or at least not objected to by the dominant groups in the society. In fact, the brutal actions of authorities may simply be a "legal" form of the same suppression used by the dominant groups in their normal dealings with the outcast group.

The responses of authorities to many Indian uprisings on the American frontier exemplify this type of situation, which still exists in those parts of the world where some industrializing societies confront hunting and gathering or horticultural groups. These small groups are being exterminated at the slightest provocation, and in extreme instances, those being attacked may not even be considered to be part of the human race. The nineteenth-century extermination of native Tasmanians by European colonists is one such example. Some of the victims were used for dog food.

This lack of restraint is also seen in those settings where longstanding or traditional antagonisms exist between control agents and crowd members. Thus we see many instances where brutal suppression is directed against the members of religious and racial minorities. Often the most brutal actions are taken by auxiliary police or militia composed of local residents. The massacre of Muslim civilians by local Christian militia in Beirut, Lebanon, in October of 1982 is an example of this situation.

Finally, restraint is less likely to be shown in regions that are isolated from the public eye. Some discussions of riot control claim that the presence of the media contributes to the intensity and spread of violence. To a limited extent, this may be the case. However, media coverage can also serve to limit disorder. Several studies of the urban disorders of the 1960s and 1970s show that about half of those people who eventually became involved in the disorder in some manner either heard their first news of the disorder by word-of-mouth or were at the scene of some of the earliest confrontations (National Advisory Commission 1968). They were not brought to the event on the basis of news coverage. Further, most news coverage contained appeals to people to remain calm and stay out of the riot areas.

Both authorities and civilians are likely to show restraint in the presence of the media. During the expulsion of demonstrators from the steps of the Pentagon in October 1967, for example, federal troops repeatedly ceased clubbing demonstrators, and demonstrators stopped throwing trash at the soldiers, when the television cameras were turned in their direction. The most ugly and brutal suppression of humans usually occurs far from the eye of the media. The death squads of authoritarian regimes carry out their atrocities on country roads and in isolated jungle clearings. News teams from the United States and other countries have often been attacked by local authorities while covering these conflicts. Their news reports have also been closely censored. The most bloody labor confrontations in the United States occurred deep in the mountains of Appalachia or in the small mining towns of the West and received little media coverage.

Summary

Riots, like disasters, produce a number of changes within and among community organizations. When faced with the problem of controlling hostile crowds, police departments, fire departments, hospitals, and public transportation lines take on many features of expanding organizations. Counterrioters, looting crowds, and crowds opposing or assisting police are similar in process and structure to the emergent groups in disaster.

We considered six principles of crowd control used by police organizations. Many of these principles assume that police have sufficient numbers of officers at hand and that these officers can be deployed in the field in a coordinated fashion. Crowd control principles also assume that police will be able to identify incidents that are likely to precipitate riots and take action before crowds achieve unity. These assumptions are often the most problematic aspects of crowd control. We used the differentiated view of riot behavior to evaluate these crowd control tactics.

Community-wide, riots produce a number of changes that are similar to those produced by disaster. During and after riots, such community functions as production and socialization are given less priority, while social control, participation, and mutual support may be strengthened in ways similar to those of communities coping with disaster. We noted some exceptions to this pattern. Following riots, for example, there is little evidence of convergence of unsolicited goods into the impact area. Also, the restoring of preriot production, distribution, and consumption functions is slow compared to the recovery of communities after disasters.

Finally, we gave some consideration to the ways in which societies respond to riots. Some societies respond with severe repression, while others are much more accommodating or at least far less violent in their responses to riots. Perhaps this is due to the level of threat that leaders perceive in the actions of rioters. Sometimes societies can accommodate a considerable level of domestic violence without destroying the social fabric. Sometimes, however, riots are but an initial phase in a process that drastically transforms institutions, governments, and even societies.

CHAPTER 13

Protest

Two Protests

We begin this chapter with a description of two instances of *social protest*. The first was a protest mounted by parents to resist the transfer of teachers within their school system. Fifth- and sixth-grade students held an orderly noon-hour demonstration to protest the transfer of their favorite teacher. Parents circulated a petition and collected more than one hundred signatures asking that the transfers be rescinded. They sent a spokesperson to confer with the district superintendent, who bluntly told them that the transfers would stand. Finally, more than two hundred parents attended a meeting of the school board to voice their objections and to present an alternate transfer plan. The board took little formal notice of the protest, and the transfers were carried out.

The second instance of protest was a twelve-year struggle to obtain recognition of a coal miners' union. Protest took several forms during this struggle. The miners' first protest was a poorly organized, fifty-six-day strike that failed to win them any concessions. The next time the miners struck, it was as a local of the newly formed United Mine Workers of America. Their employer refused to deal with the union in any fashion, then fortified the mine and brought in strikebreakers from out of state. Striking miners spent the winter in tents near the mine, picketing and occasionally blocking roads to the mine. Finally, miners fired upon a train carrying strikebreakers to the mine, killing one passenger and wounding twenty others. Strikers, strikebreakers, and mine guards battled one another until the state militia arrived to restore order. Three months later, when the militia left, fighting again broke out and five strikebreakers were killed. The militia returned, and several strikers were tried for murder and acquitted. Finally, after twelve years of conflict, the mine was sold, and the new owners immediately recognized the union.

These two examples represent the extremes in a continuum of protest. At one end of this continuum is the highly *localized protest* that focuses on a specific grievance. This type of protest often receives little attention outside the community in which it occurs. It is also short lived, lasting but weeks from beginning to end. Participants generally avoid disruptive tactics, relying instead on petition and persuasion.

At the other end of the continuum is *protracted protest*. Though the miners' protest started with specific grievances at the coal mine, it came to embody the nationwide conflict between employers and organized labor. This type of protest is waged for very high stakes, which is perhaps why such protest is often marred by extreme hatreds and bloodshed. It is fairly easy to see how protest at this end of the continuum can be viewed as a component of social movements.

In general, protest leaders are neither professional agitators nor people greatly skilled in the political process. At least this is the case at the outset. Protest is carried out by those who have little recourse to more effective means of influencing the political process. Protest often fails, and when it succeeds, it often does so in terms other than the initial goals. Occasionally, however, protest can result in the acquisition of considerable influence in the political process.

In much of this chapter, we will focus on protest at the "modest" end of the continuum. In Chapters 14 and 15, we will consider more extensive instances of protest from the perspective of social movements.

Public School Protest

In May of 1983, during the last week of school, seven teachers in Campus, Illinois, were abruptly informed that they would be transferred to other district schools in the fall. The teachers had not been consulted beforehand, nor were they given reasons for the transfers. The reassignments posed hardships for the teachers and angered many students and parents.

Much of what followed revolved around the transfer of a very popular sixth-grade teacher, Mary Sidmore, from Washington School. Shortly after the school board's plans were announced, townspeople were surprised to see a noon-hour demonstration by Washington School students, protesting Sidmore's transfer.

A concerned parent, Joan Wallace, presented a petition to the president of the Campus school board on May 27. The petition carried the signatures of more than one hundred Washington School parents, and it requested a special meeting to consider the transfer of Mary Sidmore. The petition was denied the same day it was presented. The president agreed, however, to put the matter on the agenda of the board's regular meeting, a month later, if officially requested to do so.

Joan Wallace then called a parents' meeting to discuss the transfers. Washington parents were notified by phone and others by radio announcements. The meeting was well attended by Washington School parents, but few attended from other schools. At the meeting, Wallace was appointed spokesperson for the group, which decided to take the transfer issue before the June school board meeting. A number of parents also agreed to write letters to the editor of the local newspaper in an effort to widen community opposition to the transfers. Others agreed to personally contact board members and express their dissatisfaction with the reassignments. Finally, the group decided to contact parents at other district schools and try to persuade them to speak out against the transfers.

While preparing for the board meeting, Joan Wallace discovered that according to Board Policy 1069, the transfers were the responsibility of the district superintendent, not the board. The board president told Wallace that little could be accomplished at an open board meeting and suggested that she talk with the superintendent of schools behind closed doors. In the conference with the superintendent, Wallace was told that his decision to transfer teachers was based on administrative considerations and that the reasons for specific transfers were confidential. When Wallace said that this was not a satisfactory explanation, the superintendent stated calmly that Mary Sidmore and the other teachers should consider themselves lucky to still have jobs. The closed door meeting ended on this discordant note, and it was agreed that the matter would be taken before the board.

While they prepared for the board meeting, the parents' group decided to point out that the unilateral transfer of teachers for "administra-tive" rather than academic reasons was inap-propriate. They also decided to request that Board Policy 1069 be amended to include input from the board members, teachers, and con-cerned parents when transfers were being con-sidered. Finally, they suggested an alternative plan that involved only two transfers rather than seven.

On June 20, the board of education held their monthly meeting, and more than two hundred parents attended. Shortly before the meeting, Joan Wallace learned that the trans-fers were not on the agenda; instead, she was scheduled to speak as a "visitor" to the meet-ing. Wallace was one of the first speakers. After she delivered her statement, the board referred Policy 1069 to their policy committee, which was scheduled to meet a month later. The board did not discuss the transfers or so-licit questions from the audience; it simply moved on to other business. While the con-cerned parents looked on, the board discussed and approved a raise in administrative salaries and the renewal of a food contract. The board also discussed energy conservation measures, admission prices to athletic events, and re-quests for leaves of absence. Finally, near the end of the meeting, a disgruntled parent, Law-rence Tanner, spoke from the floor. He pointed out that the board was acting in an extremely arrogant manner by not even discussing the is-sue of teacher transfers, even though two hun-dred people had come to the meeting for that purpose. The meeting was then adjourned.

After the meeting, it was clear that little had changed. The board had referred one of its policies to a committee that would meet in three weeks, but it had not explained the rea-sons for the transfers or taken notice of the parents' alternate plan, and, obviously, the transfers would be carried out in the fall. As Joan Wallace observed later, "The board's best weapon was absolute silence."

Three weeks later, the policy committee met and discussed Policy 1069. Nothing was changed. Mary Sidmore asked to appear be-fore the board for an explanation of her trans-fer. Her request was denied. In the fall of 1983, four people ran for the school board with the support of many Washington School parents. Two of them were elected.

Industrial Protest

In the spring of 1890, representatives of the American Miners' Association, the Miners' Na-tional Association, and the National Federation of Miners and Mine Laborers held a conven-tion. In the days that followed, the three un-ions decided to merge and the United Mine Workers of America was founded under the leadership of John McBride. Ironically, at about the same time, Samuel T. Brush of Carbon-dale, Illinois, was organizing the St. Louis and Big Muddy Coal Company, which sank its first shaft into the rich coal fields near Carter-ville, Illinois. At the very outset, Brush stood firm: there would be no unions at his mine. Soon, the St. Louis and Big Muddy would be the most productive underground coal mine in Illinois. A clash between Brush and the Unit-ed Mine Workers was inevitable (Angle 1975:89–116).

Sam Brush was not an outgoing man, and he was quite puritanical in his personal con-duct. Though he was often described as a tact-ful manager who was always "ready to remedy any grievance" of those who worked for him, he did not pay his employees well. St. Louis and Big Muddy Coal Company miners were paid subsistence wages of about $20 a month, and most of them rented company houses for $5 a month. The miners also worked under rules specifying that they would forfeit all pay due them and be evicted from company houses if they joined a union or went on strike.

In April 1894, John McBride declared that wages in the nation's mines had "sunk below the limit of human endurance" and called a nationwide strike. At that time, the United Mine Workers had fewer than 11,000 members and only 300 members in Illinois. Still, 130,000 unorganized miners, including those at the St. Louis and Big Muddy mine, joined the strike. The mine owners held firm. The strike collapsed two months later, and miners returned to work across the nation. Those at the St. Louis and Big Muddy mine held out to the end, returning to work after fifty-six days at their previous wages (Angle 1975:93–97).

Though the strike did little to increase the wages of miners, it brought many new members to the United Mine Workers. The St. Louis and Big Muddy miners, however, remained unorganized. In May 1897, new wage reductions were announced by Illinois mine operators, and another strike seemed imminent. The United Mine Workers called the strike for July 4. Workers at the St. Louis and Big Muddy mine ignored the strike call. On July 15, Sam Brush announced that he would raise wages if workers would stay on the job. Workers agreed, and they kept their promise, even though they received heavy pressure from strikers in nearby counties. That year, the St. Louis and Big Muddy Coal Company mine produced more coal than any other mine in Illinois (Angle 1975:95).

The strike of 1897 was a success. In October, mine operators yielded and promised wage increases, the first in nearly ten years. During January 1898, workers at the St. Louis and Big Muddy Coal Company were able to form a United Mine Workers local without Sam Brush's knowledge. In March, Illinois mine operators and the United Mine Workers announced their agreed-upon wage increases. They were substantially higher than what Brush was paying, and he refused to meet them. Eighty percent of his miners struck.

For six weeks, Sam Brush ran the mine with a reduced work force. Finally, he called the union's strike committee and delivered an ultimatum: unless they returned to work within five days, he would bring in black miners he had recruited in Tennessee. Preparing for trouble, Brush hired more mine guards and stockpiled arms and ammunition. He even mounted a gatling gun near the mine entrance. The strikers held firm, and on May 20, about 150 black miners and their families arrived by train. Nearby mines soon announced wage cuts and plans to import black miners. The strike spread.

Strikers picketed and sometimes blocked roads leading to the mines. Numerous attempts were made to persuade the strikebreakers to walk out. A few defected and joined the strikers; others simply left the area. Brush continued to import blacks for replacements rather than hire back his former workers. Many strikers spent the winter of 1898 living in tents. A new union local was established at the St.Louis and Big Muddy mine, again without the owner's knowledge.

The St. Louis and Big Muddy Coal Company continued to operate, but output was way down from the previous year. The company was near bankruptcy and receivership when Brush announced that he would pay his workers more than the Illinois union-operator scale and institute an eight-hour workday but would not recognize the union.

For nearly a year, there had been little violence in the St. Louis and Big Muddy Coal Company strike. Then, Sam Brush discovered that a new union had been organized among the nonstriking workers, and he summarily fired three of its leaders. Others in the union demanded that the three be rehired, and Brush refused. On May 15, 1899, half of the miners walked out.

On June 30, a small crowd of strikers met the train bringing in thirty more black miners to replace strikers and deserters. Quite likely, a striker fired the first shot, and guards, mine officials, and passengers immediately returned fire. Within seconds, about twenty people were wounded, and one passenger was killed.

Brush was also on the train; he shot at the strikers and escaped uninjured. The train pulled out of the station under fire and made it to the mine.

Later in the day, several hundred men surrounded the mine, and shooting continued through that afternoon and into the night. Toward morning, the mine guards and strikebreakers counterattacked. Strikers obtained more weapons and ammunition during the day, and it looked as if a major battle was about to occur. Shacks that had been hastily built for the blacks who had joined the strike were burned. The Williamson County sheriff managed to keep the opposing forces apart until two hundred state militia arrived in Carterville on July 2 and restored order.

The St. Louis and Big Muddy mine continued to operate through the summer, and the militia left Carterville on September 11. The next day, Sam Brush was attacked and beaten. A week later, fighting broke out between black strikebreakers and white strikers at a tavern in Carterville. The fight escalated into shooting, and five strikebreakers were killed.

The militia returned to Carterville and were kept there until trials were held for those accused of the murders of June 30 and September 15. Much in the trials focused on the conflict between mine operators and the union rather than on the guilt or innocence of the accused. The juries returned not guilty verdicts in all the trials. The last trial ended on March 4, 1900, and at its conclusion, the judge admonished those in the crowded courtroom to forget the hatreds that had led to the Carterville tragedies (Angle 1975:102–115).

The judge's hopes came to pass. Sam Brush and his sons operated the St. Louis and Big Muddy Coal Company mine with nonunion blacks for another six years without major incident. Still, turnover was high, security costs were high, and output was uncertain. Finally, in 1906, the mine was sold to the Madison Coal Company, which renamed it, simply, the

Madison Number 8. The gatling gun was removed, and Madison Number 8 was worked from then on under contract with the United Mine Workers of America.

Protest as Collective Behavior

The mass hysteria, emergent norm, and value-added theories of collective behavior describe and explain protest in much the same way. In describing protest, each emphasizes that protest is an expression of localized grievances, such as dissatisfaction with the actions of a local school board or an employer's intransigence. Protest is carried out by small homogeneous groups trying to accomplish seemingly modest and definite aims or goals. When protest moves beyond clearly local concerns, draws upon a more diverse constituency, and seeks broad or multiple goals, it is transformed into a social movement.

In explaining protest, the general theories view protest as a result of some sort of social unrest or social strain. These theories acknowledge that resistance by authorities can crush protest, but they emphasize that such resistance is more likely to transform protest. Resistance can draw other dissatisfied groups into the conflict, make protest more disruptive and violent, and broaden the goals of protest.

The Mass Hysteria Perspective

Herbert Blumer (1957:24) briefly notes that protest is a form of social unrest that is characterized by "feelings of frustration . . . over an existing mode of life and a consequent readiness to lash out in violent forms of attack on targets symbolizing that mode of life." Orrin E. Klapp (1972:206) defines *protest* as a more or less rational, verbalized expression of grievances, usually in terms of injustice. Protest aims at telling what is wrong and finding means to remedy a problem, and it brings the pressure of public opinion upon the existing system and its officials. If a clear and immediate remedy is lacking, protest becomes the early stage of a social movement.

For Klapp, the public perception of protest is an important determinant in its outcome. If protest takes the form of orderly petition and patient willingness to accept compromise solutions, public opinion is likely to be favorable. The more protest is recognized as legitimate, the more quickly are the grievances of the protest group set right.

Protest can be perceived as an illegitimate threat to the social system, particularly when it takes the form of disruptive demonstrations, strikes, boycotts, name-calling, and/or violence. Public opinion then pressures authorities to make no concessions and to deal severely with the protest groups. Such harsh control responses by authorities are likely to channel protest into more general social movements.

In Klapp's view, protest is an outgrowth of social strain and accompanying tensions. Consequently, other opportunites for expressing tensions serve as a safety valve that can reduce the incidence of protest. Institutionalized opportunities for tension release accompany such violent sports as boxing, wrestling, hockey, and football. Other institutionalized opportunities include holidays, national celebrations, and religious services. Klapp suggests the establishment of a national "tension monitoring agency." He also suggests building more safety valve institutions through greater investment in leisure and religious institutions.

The Emergent Norm Perspective

Turner and Killian (1972:420) make a distinction between "primitive" and "modern" protest. Primitive forms of protest do not actually bring about changes in the organization of society; they merely exact concessions within the existing structure. This type of protest is characterized by Robin Hood groups and by the localized disputes over the ownership of livestock and farm produce that characterized medieval society (Hobsbaum 1959). These primitive forms of protest pitted one local communal group against another (Tilly 1969).

Modern protest is characterized by the linkage of groups beyond the boundaries of local communities into classes, ethnic groups, age groups, and other broad constituencies. Unlike participants in primitive protest, participants in modern protest can generate a shared conception of changing the structure of society. Modern protest, therefore, can be transformed into general social movements.

The Value-Added Perspective

Protest is not one of the collective episodes identified by Smelser. Instead, he encompasses protest within hostile outbursts and norm- and value-oriented social movements. Hostile outbursts such as riots may be preceded and followed by the expression of specific community grievances. Protest is also the incipient phase of social movements.

Lack of opportunity for protest is one condition of structural conduciveness that conributes to hostile outbursts, while opportunity for protest is one condition of structural conduciveness that contributes to the development of social movements.

Often, generalized beliefs develop in the context of protest. In the case of blocked protest, generalized hostile beliefs are formed that later lead to attacks on authorities or other groups within the community. In the case of social movements, protest experiences can lead to beliefs that much greater changes in the social order are necessary to accomplish group ends.

Some hostile outbursts grow out of confrontations between authorities and people already mobilized for protest. Mobilizing people for localized protest is often but a dress rehearsal for the massive mobilizations that are part of norm- and value-oriented social movements.

The action of social control is often constrained by public opinion. Nonviolent forms of protest are likely to create favorable public opinion. Social control is then inclined to take the form of redressing grievances and other kinds of accommodation. Further, discontent is also likely to remain narrowly focused on specific grievances, a characteristic of norm-oriented social movements. Disruptive or violent protest, however, often engenders negative public opinion that in turn encourages suppression by authorities. As we will explain in Chapters 14 and 15, suppression is likely to move the discontented in the direction of value-oriented social movements.

The SBI Perspective

Unlike the other general theories, the SBI perspective takes a microapproach to protest. Specifically, this perspective examines how demonstrations, marches, and rallies are organized, how these are controlled by their leaders and civil authorities, and how they are terminated. McPhail has conducted extensive firsthand studies of demonstrations, marches, and rallies in Washington, D.C., and other major eastern cities. He has also made an extensive review of published studies that focused on individual participation in civil rights, student, antiwar, and antinuclear protests as well as religious rallies. (We will discuss McPhail's work in the context of social movements in Chapter 15.)

Findings about demonstrations, marches, and rallies can be generalized to other forms of protest, such as petition campaigns, boycotts, strikes, and even violent confrontations. To date, however, few attempts have been made to do so.

The Origins of Protest

Anger and indignation do not automatically translate into social protest. People often become upset by the actions (or inaction) of public officials and government agencies, businesses, and employers. They may complain to their families, friends, neighbors, and/or work associates, and some may write sharply worded letters to their local newspaper, congressional representative, or Better Business Bureau. Though people often talk of confronting employers, government agencies, and other authorities, collective protests such as petition campaigns, demonstrations, marches, picket lines, strikes, and boycotts seldom materialize.

William Gamson, Bruce Fireman, and Stephen Rytina (1982) devised an experiment wherein thirty-three groups confronted a situation in which collective protest was an appropriate response. (Details of the experiment are presented in Chapter 3.) Though all the groups took issue with the conditions facing them, only sixteen groups succeeded in drawing together and offering unanimous collective resistance. Gamson's study provides important insights into the origins of social protest.

Confrontations with Unjust Authority

In Gamson's experiment, people volunteered for what was described as a survey of community values being conducted by an organization called Manufacturers' Human Relations Consultants (MHRC). At the beginning of the experiment, subjects were paid $10 by the MHRC representative and asked to sign a participation agreement in which they were informed that their responses would be videotaped for later use in a trial. They were then asked to give their opinions about unmarried couples living together. In none of the groups were strong objections to unmarried cohabitation expressed. Then the MHRC representative asked members of the group to act as if they were "very offended" by cohabitation. The MHRC representative was asking people to commit perjury! At the conclusion of what was usually a stormy and abrasive encounter, the MHRC representative attempted to get group members to sign affidavits stating that they were aware that the videotapes would be used in court.

All thirty-three groups started the experiment in a *compliant* manner. That is, the participants attempted to carry out the requests of the MHRC representative to the best of their abilities and in a cheerful and enthusiastic manner. In all the groups, the tone of the interaction changed substantially when the subjects were instructed to act as if they were offended.

An early and common response was *evasion*. Participants did not confront the MHRC representative directly but instead failed to perform in the correct or desired manner. Participants acted as if they were offended but used very sarcastic tones, talked with obviously fake accents, or talked in the third person. Others claimed that they were "poor actors" and remained silent when it was their turn to speak.

Another common response was to *challenge the context* of the encounter. Participants questioned the representative's conduct and attempted to renegotiate the conditions of compliance. Participants often asked the representative to explain why they were being asked to act offended. They asked questions about the MHRC and its relationship to the defendant in the trial, a large oil company. Some participants asked if they would get to view the tapes later or be able to state on camera that they were not giving their true opinions.

Challenging the context usually merged into *dissent*. Participants loudly rejected the representative's justifications and criticized the MHRC. A few participants stated that the rep-

resentative was asking them to commit perjury, and some compared the encounter to Watergate. In general, dissent represented a clear shift in the direction of the encounter.

All but four of the groups reached the stage of open and loud dissent. In many respects, however, dissent is but a simple outcry against the directives of authority. When they were presented with the final affidavits, dissent subsided in thirteen groups. In four of these groups, a majority signed the affidavits, and in nine groups, a minority signed. To successfully challenge authority, groups had to turn the unorganized babble of dissent into collective protest.

Gamson and his colleagues observed three types of protest in this experiment, the most elementary of which was collective *resistance*. Resistance involves not the concealed intent of evasion but the open and stated refusal to perform as authorities command. In the MHRC encounter, resistance took the form of a group's unanimous refusal to sign the final affidavits. Sixteen of the groups passed the threshold of boisterous dissent and openly and unanimously refused to sign the affidavits.

A more developed form of resistance to authority is *preparation for future action*, in which participants attempt to do more than openly disobey authority; they make plans to act against the authority. Nine of the sixteen groups exchanged names and phone numbers and agreed to meet after the MHRC session. When asked later, they stated that their intent was to collectively contact the Better Business Bureau, judges, lawyers, and newspapers to "blow the whistle" on the MHRC.

For five of these groups, refusal to sign the affidavits and plans for future action did not seem sufficient, so they took *direct action*. Direct action involves attempts to immediately sabotage and destroy the authority system. In these five groups, members seized the original participation agreements and the final affidavits, and members of one group threatened to seize the video equipment as well!

From the results of their experiment, Gamson and his colleagues have developed an explanation of how groups are able to successfully draw together and launch protest against authority. The protest may well fail to better the plight of the group, but at least it has been launched.

Kinds of People Who Protest

Many sociologists explain collective behavior phenomena in terms of kinds of people and the attitudes they carry with them. Gamson and his colleagues, however, found little relationship between people's successful protest in the MHRC encounter and their attitudes toward government, big business, or protest in general. But they did find some differences in terms of the previous experiences of people within the groups. A number of people had previous organizational experience as officers in voluntary associations. Many of the participants were college educated, and some stated that they had taken part in political demonstrations and strikes. Individuals with these previous experiences were not evenly distributed throughout the groups. Eleven groups had deficits in one or more of these areas. Four of those groups failed to voice dissent, and none of them managed to successfully mount protest, while about half of the groups with full assets failed to collectively resist the MHRC representative.

Groups composed of people who have had few previous experiences that contribute to the organization of protest seem to have great difficulty in translating dissent into collective resistance. On the other hand, having access to these resources is certainly no guarantee that protest will materialize. The necessary ingredients for group protest seem to be kinds of acts that severely challenge authority, free the

group from fears of "making a scene," and increase the group's capacity to act as a unit.

Kinds of Protest Activities

At the beginning of their encounter with the MHRC, participants had no reason to suspect that the MHRC was something other than what it appeared to be. They thought that the MHRC was a legitimate business enterprise that was following standard professional procedures and paid above-average compensation. As the encounter unfolded, however, it became apparent to many that their initial impressions were in error. As Gamson and his colleagues described it, it became apparent that the MHRC was working on behalf of its oil company client to suborn purjury. It was collecting material that could distort the true nature of community standards in a trial.

Reframing. In the descriptions of encounters provided by Gamson and his colleagues, it appears that in nearly all of the groups, participants sensed that something was wrong as soon as the MHRC representative asked them to act offended. Almost immediately, people began to act evasively and to question the representative about his instructions. What did not happen immediately in some groups, and what failed to occur at all in others, was a clear verbalization of just what was wrong with the representative's request. Gamson and his colleagues refer to such verbalizations as *reframing.*

Reframing involves *attention calling*—words and deeds that clearly point out what the authority is doing or about to do in the encounter. Attention calling keeps the authority's actions from passing unnoticed. In many of the groups, people called attention to the fact that the MHRC representative was asking people to act as opposed to expressing their true feelings. Some drew attention to this when they expressed concern that these instructions were not on the videotape. Others drew attention to the representative's request by claiming that they were not good actors or by deliberately overacting. Participants made this seem like a great departure from their initial understanding of what they were to do in the encounter.

Reframing also involves *altering context* through acts that apply the injustice frame to what is happening. In the MHRC encounter, people pointed out that the representative was asking them to distort community standards. Others made reference to Watergate, and in a few encounters, participants forcefully informed the group that they were being asked to commit perjury. Reframing acts, which break down an encounter's sense of legitimacy and replace it with a sense of injustice, usually occurred within the context-altering and dissent phases of confronting authority. Groups in which reframing acts occurred early were much more likely to translate reframing into successful protests than groups in which reframing occurred later or not at all.

Divesting Acts.   Another important class of activities, *divesting acts*, typically follow or occur with reframing acts. Divesting acts are "declarations of independence" that sever people's obligation to authority. Groups in which such acts occurred early were more likely to launch unanimous protest than those in which these acts occurred later or not at all.

In the MHRC encounter, divesting took the form of *contract voiding*. Participants challenged the representative by noting that his requests violated the terms of the participation agreement. In some groups, these claims were reinforced by offers to return the MHRC money and by threats to walk out.

Divesting acts also *negate fear of making a scene.* In many groups, one or more participants suggested "going along" with the MHRC and then forgetting the whole thing. These suggestions were quickly countered in some

groups by reminders that the MHRC requests were unethical if not illegal. In several instances, fears of making a scene were reduced by a general spirit of rowdiness that developed in a group.

Working Together.   In addition to reframing and divesting acts, most of the sixteen successful groups showed an early and clear internal rapport that allowed them to work together nearly as a team. This rapport consisted of *loyalty building* and internal *conflict managing*.

An act that contributes to loyalty building is *consensus calling*. Participants can say things that make the group aware of its shared outlook. Because the issues were so blatant in the MHRC encounter, the discovery that everyone agreed did not provide a great boost to group solidarity. Nonetheless, in most of the unsuccessful groups, the possibility of collective resistance was not even discussed. People seemed to decide individually whether to obey or disobey the representative. In successful groups, the issue of collective disobedience was often raised early and discussed openly.

Another contributing factor to group loyalty is *protest humor*. In the MHRC encounter, humor, sarcasm, and irony were a means by which the group created its own solidarity in opposing the representative. In addition, humor also served a divesting function by contributing to the rowdy atmosphere of some groups. Once a wide-open atmosphere was established, there was little decorum left to lose in scenes created by open defiance of the representative.

Shared collective orientations toward protest were created most openly and directly by people *speaking for the group*. In the MHRC encounter, a number of people adopted the role of spokesperson. Often these people were the most straightforward with their comments to the representative. The spokespersons took the initiative in using the words *we, our,* and *us* when talking to the representative; they were also the initiators of many reframing and divesting acts. Successful groups often had more than one spokesperson. Without a spokesperson, few groups succeeded in unanimously opposing the representative.

Managing Conflict. In many of the groups, some people openly disagreed about how to interpret the representative's actions and explanations. In other groups, people advocated compliance with the representative. In most of the successful groups, disagreements were resolved early and compliance suggestions were countered right after they occurred. These groups contained unofficial diplomats who not only recognized and quelled disagreements quickly but strengthened group solidarity in the process. Groups that failed to unanimously oppose the representative also failed to recognize and resolve disagreements in the early stages of the encounter.

Discussion

At the beginning of this section, we noted that anger and indignation do not automatically lead to protest. Gamson, Fireman, and Rytina's study of protest under controlled conditions shows that a number of acts must occur together in order for protest to occur. Anger and indignation, if they are necessary for protest at all, must occur in the form of evasion, challenges to the context of authority, and open criticism and disapproval of authority. Even these are not guarantees that sustained protest in the form of resistance, preparation for future action, or direct action will develop.

Participants in protest must engage in reframing acts that focus attention on the conduct of authorities, removing the acts of authorities from the part of social life that is taken for granted. Reframing also includes identifying the acts of authorities as a violation of the shared moral principles of the participants.

Participants in protest must also engage in divesting acts that in one way or another declare them free from further obligations to obey authority. Divesting acts also free participants from the fear of bringing their discontent into the open and creating a public scene.

Participants in protest must build loyalty to their group. Rowdiness and protest humor provide a means of creating such solidarity by strengthening group determination and giving courage to those who publicly challenge authority. Articulate spokespersons can promote unity by making the group aware of its shared outlook.

In the MHRC encounters, the representative did nothing to directly hinder the development of protest. He did not threaten or cajole. In real life, authorities are seldom so passive, and they can do much to hinder the development of protest. In the following sections we will look at protest as it is developed and used in the real world.

Views of the Political Process

In any community, state, or nation, a number of groups contend for power, privileges, and material resources. Describing how these contests are carried out has fostered considerable debate among sociologists. The debate can be characterized by comparing two views of the political process—the *elitist* view and the *pluralist* view.

The Elitist View

In some instances, the struggle over power, privileges, and material resources is a lopsided struggle, with a few powerful groups, or elites, usually getting their way while other groups get little. Elite groups are often able to ignore public opinion if it exists at all. When the stakes are high or differences in power are great, contending groups may use coercion and even terror tactics against one another to achieve their ends. Contention often degenerates into pitched battles in which contending groups try to crush or eliminate one another. Victory goes to the powerful, even if their aims are frivolous, vindictive, or blatantly selfish.

The elitist style of contention for power, privileges, and material resources is a no-holds-barred contest in which ruthless tactics usually bring success. New groups must do battle to gain recognition and admittance into the political arena. This means that those who use protest as a way of achieving their ends are constrained from the outset to use violent and disruptive tactics. Further, they must expect harsh treatment from the authorities and the groups they challenge. Public opinion counts for little, and it is unlikely that protest groups will find eager allies.

The Pluralist View

In contrast, the contention for power, privileges, and material resources in some communities, states, and nations is much more balanced and peaceful. Most contending groups are quite evenly matched in terms of resources, so no single group gets its way all the time. In the pluralist system, favorable public opinion is a valuable resource that must be nurtured. Even the most powerful groups are unable to achieve lasting gains in the face of negative public opinion. On the other hand, the weakest groups, if they ride favorable public opinion, can make enormous gains.

The pluralist system encourages and thrives on coalitions based on mutual self-interest. The aims of the most powerful groups are frequently thwarted by temporary coalitions of less powerful groups, and the weakest groups can make headway through coalitions with other groups. Coalitions usually last as long as

the interests of groups coincide, and they are seldom so long lasting that they come to constitute an elitist threat to the pluralist order.

The pluralist style of contention for power, privileges, and material resources is based on implicit but nonetheless powerful rules that govern political conduct. The most important rule is that contending groups must leave intact the pluralist value structure, even if the stakes are high. This means that new groups are free to enter into the arena of contention whenever they obtain sufficient political skill, resources, and popular support. Likewise, new groups that pursue political aims through legitimate means must be acknowledged and allowed to flourish. Groups that try to crush or eliminate other groups pose a clear threat to the pluralist system. "Battles to the death" are to be strongly condemned.

Another important rule is that only those groups that use the institutionalized means of contention may succeed. Groups attempt to influence one another through persuasion, bargaining, coalitions, lobbying, and the ballot box. Groups that depart from this norm and use disruptive tactics—ranging from peaceful demonstrations to terrorism—must be barred from success, even if their aims are worthy.

Theories of Collective Behavior and Pluralism

As described above, the elitist and pluralist views represent "ideal type" characterizations of the political process. In many respects, the mass hysteria, emergent norm, and value-added theories of collective behavior assume that modern Western democracies operate much more along pluralist lines than along elitist lines. This assumption is clearly reflected in these theories' characterization of protest. In modern Western democracies, according to these theories, any group can become an accepted contender for power, privileges, and/or material resources, as long as it plays by the pluralist rules. For protest groups, success lies in the direction of accommodation and a willingness to compromise and form coalitions.

Protest groups are constrained to nurture favorable public opinion. Groups that use disruption and violence instead of petition and persuasion invariably create negative public opinion, which drives away potential allies and coalition partners. Negative public opinion also allows authorities to use more repressive measures in dealing with protest groups.

A Study of Pluralism and Protest

If tactics of disruption are doomed to failure in a pluralist system, why do protest groups so often utilize these tactics? William Gamson's (1975) study of social protest provides some partial answers to this question. Gamson developed a technique of systematic historical analysis of protest in the United States from the early 1800s to 1945. His research methods, which are described in detail in Chapter 3, involved a systematic search of selected history books for mention of what Gamson terms *challenging groups*.

Challenging Groups

Challenging groups organize around specific grievances, and they attempt to gain concessions from other groups, such as legislators, employers, or police. Challenging groups begin their careers outside the pluralist system; they are newly formed and have no institutionalized base of support or history of recognized accomplishments.

Gamson selected a sample of sixty-four challenging groups that ranged in size from several hundred to more than a million members. Some of these groups were organized along bureaucratic lines and gave formal sta-

tus and duties to their members. Challenging groups used a wide range of tactics to accomplish their aims, ranging from pluralistically acceptable tactics of petition and formation of new political parties to the unacceptable tactics of disruption and violence. Some challenging groups initiated violence, attacking authorities or other groups, while others resorted to violence only when attacked by authorities. Some challenging groups were the passive recipients of violence. Finally, a number of challenging groups managed to avoid violent confrontations altogether.

Successful Protest

Gamson used two criteria to assess the degree to which challenging groups were successful. His first criterion was *acceptance into the pluralist arena of contending groups*. Some challengers were eventually asked to appear before governing bodies as a legitimate representative of a constituency. Others entered formal negotiations with government or employers. Sometimes, governing bodies and businesses formally recognized, in writing, that challengers were legitimate representatives of a constituency. Finally, challengers were sometimes offered formal membership and positions of status in the organizational structure of government or business.

Gamson's other criterion of success was *obtaining new advantages for the challenging group and its constituency*. Some challenging groups sought the passage of legislative packages. Some of these packages, such as income maintenance plans, would have benefited people other than members of the challenging group, while other packages would have benefited only the challenging group. Some groups sought concessions from business, such as hiring agreements, wages, and prices paid for farm products.

Some challenging groups succeeded in terms of both acceptance into the pluralist arena and obtaining new advantages. Other groups succeeded in terms of only one criterion. For example, some groups were granted acceptance but were unable to convert their newfound role into tangible gains for the constituency. Other groups simply did not seek acceptance themselves but were able get significant parts of their goals enacted. Finally, some challenging groups failed totally. Gamson examined a number of factors associated with success and failure. These factors can be divided into three categories: (1) the structure of challenging groups, (2) the goals of challenging groups, and (3) the tactics of challenging groups.

Structure. Gamson found that bureaucratically organized groups with centralized authority were more likely to succeed in terms of acceptance and winning new advantages than other groups. Some challenging groups were hindered by factionalism; that is, early in a group's development, internal dissension developed over goals and strategies for attaining them. Some disputes were so severe that members left the original group and set up a splinter group. Splinter groups were typically smaller than the original group but nonetheless managed to effectively compete for members and the public eye. Factionalism, however, greatly decreased the chances of success for both the original group and the splinter group. Nonbureaucratic and decentralized groups seldom succeeded in gaining acceptance or new advantages. If these groups were also factional, complete failure was certain.

Gamson also found that large group size helped to obtain acceptance, although group size had little relationship to gaining new advantages. Small groups were as likely to achieve new advantages as were larger groups.

Challengers obtained resources to support their campaigns in various ways. Some groups were *solidaristic*; they had minimal criteria for membership and allowed nearly anyone to join. Because solidaristic groups depended on voluntary contributions from members, many of them were rich in membership but poor in financial resources. *Privileged* groups obtained most or all of their financial support from philanthropists, often also utilizing other resources of the philanthropist, such as newspapers, housing, or land. Finally, *selective incentive* groups offered some tangible benefit for contributions or imposed an effective dues structure on members. These groups also tended to be bureaucratically structured and have centralized authority.

Solidaristic groups were the least likely to gain acceptance or new advantages. Privileged groups were slightly more likely to achieve success than solidaristic groups. Selective incentive groups were much more likely to achieve success than either solidaristic or privileged groups.

Goals. A goal of some challenging groups was to displace members of the pluralist community; that is, they sought to replace public officials, government agencies, and employers. Though none of the challenging groups had displacement as their only goal, those that included displacement seldom succeeded in obtaining acceptance or new advantages.

Some groups focused their efforts on a single goal, while others sought several goals simultaneously. One might expect that highly focused groups would succeed more often than groups that divided their efforts among objectives. One might also expect that groups that pursued several goals might obtain some of them, while groups that pursued only one risked total failure. Surprisingly, Gamson found little difference in success for groups that pursued a single goal and those that pursued several.

Tactics. Most challenging groups attempted to make use of the peaceful (and pluralistically acceptable) tactics of persuasion and petition. Some groups relied on these tactics exclusively. Other groups used nonviolent but disruptive tactics of name-calling, marches, demonstrations, and boycotts. Though no group relied exclusively on violence, a number of groups either initiated violence on their own or responded violently when attacked by police or employers. Some groups responded passively when arrested or attacked.

Challenging groups that used pluralistically acceptable means to achieve their ends had few successes. Groups that used disruptive tactics achieved greater successes, and those that used violence were the most likely to succeed. Groups that responded passively when violence was used against them had the fewest successes.

Pluralism Reconsidered

The results of Gamson's study show that well-organized and authoritarian groups that are not reluctant to use disruption or violence are the challengers most likely to be accepted as legitimate representatives of and win new advantages for their constituencies. This historical pattern strongly suggests that most pluralist assumptions about orderly social contention must be reevaluated and perhaps even set aside in the analysis of social protest.

A few of the pluralist assumptions do seem to hold. Challenging groups that seek to eliminate or displace established groups almost always do fail. Also, the pluralist view does acknowledge the importance of political skill and effective organization in attaining success. Beyond this, little of the history of protest in the United States seems consistent with the pluralist view.

Admittance into the pluralist arena of contention is not as easy as the pluralist assumptions suggest. Groups that have relied on persuasion, petition, and patience have seldom been recognized as legitimate representatives of constituencies by legislators or employers.

As the elitist view suggests, new groups must do battle to gain recognition and admittance into the political arena.

The pluralist assumptions of orderly contention seem to apply rather well to groups already in the pluralist arena. However, authorities, legislators, and employers do not extend these rules to their dealings with challenging groups. Fights to the death are to be avoided in the pluralist arena, but challenging groups are fair game. In the past, tactics of infiltration, provocation, deceit, entrapment, and discreditation were freely used against challengers. Spies and agent provocateurs were sent into challenging groups, and both police and private security forces were used to harass and intimidate them (Marx 1974). Barefaced lies were used to discredit challengers in the public eye. Authorities paid little attention to violent attacks on challenging groups yet arrested challengers for the slightest of infractions. The use of underhanded and even brutal tactics against passive challengers posed little risk. Challengers who did not fight back obtained no sympathy, particularly within the pluralist arena. These challengers eventually faded away, failing to gain acceptance or new advantages.

Perhaps because they understood what was in store for them, some challengers initiated violence. Other groups used disruptive tactics and responded with violence when arrested or otherwise provoked by authorities or employers. Not all these combative groups gained acceptance or new advantages, but most did. In particular, the groups that were well organized, had clear authority structures, and had strong member discipline were the most likely to succeed.

Gamson notes that the pluralistic virtues of petition, persuasion, and patience have little instrumental value for challenging groups. Though it is not clear that violence and disruption necessarily led to success, it is certain that they do not inevitably lead to failure, as the pluralist view suggests. When challenging groups use disorderly tactics, there is no historical evidence that they generate sufficient public indignation to ruin their opportunities for success. When violence is used against challengers, there is no compelling evidence that it brings allies and sympathetic third parties to the aid of the victim. When we examine the history and dynamics of protest in the United States, it becomes clear that restraint is not rewarded by success.

Protest as a Political Resource

In this chapter we have characterized protest as a localized event that is focused on concerns of the immediate community. Protest leaders are seldom professional agitators or people greatly skilled in the political process. Protest is carried out by groups who have little recourse to other, potentially more effective means of influencing the political process. The typical lifespan of a protest group may be measured in months, from the first enthusiastic organizational meeting to the time when a meeting is called and no one comes.

In large measure, this view is derived from Michael Lipsky's (1968) description of protest. Lipsky defines *protest* as *activity by relatively powerless groups, directed against a target group, characterized by showmanship, and calculated to bring third parties into the arena of conflict in a manner beneficial to the protest group.* The character and outcome of protest is determined by interaction among relatively powerless (protest) groups, target groups, and third parties.

Relatively Powerless Groups

Membership in a relatively powerless, or protest, group is usually small and drawn from a narrow, or localized, constituency—parents in a school district, members of a neighborhood, students of a university, or employees of a business enterprise. Seldom is membership in a protest group national or even statewide in scope, and only occasionally is a sizable majority of the potential constituency active in the group. Given that protest groups are typically formed from very narrow and small constituencies, few members of the group have had any previous experience with protest.

Money. The financial resources of a protest group are usually very limited. Some constituencies can use personal savings or take out loans to support their protest efforts, but other constituencies, such as unemployed workers, may be financially destitute. This means that protest groups are limited in terms of their ability to afford mailings, telephone calls, and reimbursements for travel, meals, and hotel bills. Often, they cannot afford offices. Thus many protests are organized out of basements, garages, and living rooms. Finally, protest groups often cannot pay for legal assistance and technical advice.

Access to Power Brokers. Protest groups have limited access to such power brokers as mayors, members of Congress, corporate leaders, university presidents, and heads of federal and state agencies, although occupants of these positions play important third-party roles in the resolution of protest. Power brokers often have no prior dealings with protest leaders or their constituencies, and protest leaders are rarely at liberty to casually call or obtain appointments with power brokers. Members of protest groups seldom have informal relationships with power brokers.

Access to Media. Protest groups typically have difficulty in getting media coverage for their side of the story. Reporters may have little interest in getting the background of a protest; instead they are at hand during the crisis phase of protest, when leaders are the busiest. The leader must often meet with the press with

FIGURE 13.1 *Protest*

Protest is characterized by showmanship. University professors do not usually think of themselves as members of a relatively powerless group. When faced with declining enrollments, shrinking budgets, and threats of layoffs in recent years, however, faculty members found they had very little influence with university governing bodies. On some campuses, faculty groups turned to protest in an effort to press their concerns. Many of these groups soon affiliated with national organizations such as the American Federation of Teachers and the National Education Association. (Photo by Grant Bogue.)

little preparation, and in order to maintain the interest of the press, leaders may need to make more radical statements than they would like.

Target Groups

Protest activity is directed toward target groups. According to Lipsky, the identifying characteristic of a target group is that it has the capacity to grant most or all of the protest group's demands. Target groups include numerous federal and state agencies, city governments, police departments, utility companies, school boards, local welfare offices, and university administrations. Lipsky argues that target groups are usually in a position to grant substantial concessions to protest groups, but he notes that target groups frequently claim to lack the authority or resources to meet protest groups' demands. This claim is one of several tactics calculated to thwart protest; if compelled to do so by third parties, target groups can usually grant substantial concessions to protest groups.

Access to Power Brokers.   In comparison with protest groups, target groups are likely to have far greater access to power brokers. Target groups often have institutionalized ties to power brokers. For instance, university presidents have institutionalized access to the business and civic leaders on the university's board of governors, while utility companies have institutionalized relationships with state legislatures and numerous large businesses. Target groups are also likely to enjoy less formal contacts with power brokers, including association through business, community service organizations, country clubs, and churches. Target groups are, therefore, better able than protest groups to communicate their side of the dispute to powerful third parties.

Access to Media.   Target groups often enjoy institutionalized access to the media. These groups may have a communications staff and may hold regularly scheduled press conferences. Even at impromptu conferences, the communications staff can present well-designed and edited statements to reporters. Consequently, target groups usually have considerable opportunity and likelihood of getting their side of the story to the press.

Third Parties

Lipsky defines third parties as groups that can greatly influence the decisions of target groups with respect to protest. In protest, the main power linkage is between target groups

and third parties, and a list of third parties would be nearly identical to a list of target groups. In practice, the difference between third parties and target groups is determined by the context of the conflict. For example, a school board might be a target group in one conflict and a third party in another.

Though target groups can essentially ignore protest groups, they cannot ignore the requests of third parties; often, this is because the third party stands in institutionalized relationship to the target group. If a city council is beseiged by protest, the police department may function as a third party.

The Dynamics of Protest

For Lipsky, protest is the political resource of the powerless. Protest groups are severely limited in their capacity to bargain with or coerce target groups, which means that protest groups have no tangible resources to exchange for concessions from target groups. They cannot promise substantial numbers of votes or contributions; nor can they carry out successful strikes or boycotts.

The only immediate alternative open to protest groups is what Turner and Killian (1972:293) call *persuasion*—the use of symbolic manipulation without substantial rewards or punishments. Some types of persuasive protest tactics are designed to appeal to the good nature of target groups and third parties. These include the presentation of petitions, peaceful and orderly presence at meetings, and requests to third parties for assistance.

Other protest tactics, such as picketing, sit-ins, and the disruption of meetings, are designed to harass or embarrass a target group. These tactics usually call protest to the attention of third parties and the general public. It is the publicity and notoriety brought about by these tactics, not the tactics themselves, that are most distressing to a target group.

FIGURE 13.2   *The Dynamics of Protest*

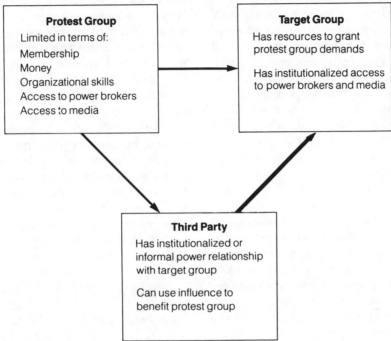

By identifying protest as an activity of relatively powerless groups, Lipsky poses a fundamental distinction. Protest cannot be identified simply by actions such as picketing, sit-ins, or disrupting of public meetings; only when these activities are carried out by relatively powerless groups does protest occur. These tactics are the most important and perhaps the only way that protest groups can influence target groups and third parties.

However, when the United Auto Workers picket an assembly plant, it is to maintain morale and discipline among the strikers. It is the activities at the bargaining table that are the most important influence on management. Behind the United Auto Workers' bargaining team stand thousands of dues-paying members, a staff of lawyers, testimony of economists, and a political organization. Picketing

has little influence at the bargaining table. This is *power politics.*

In Lipsky's model of protest, the main power linkage is between the target group and third parties, and as we noted above, these two groups usually share both institutionalized and casual relationships with one another. In order for protest to succeed, protest groups must get third parties to urge concessions by target groups through these channels (see Figure 13.2).

Third parties might urge target groups to make concessions for a number of reasons. Perhaps the most obvious reason is genuine sympathy for the protest group. Protest by handicapped or elderly groups is likely to generate considerable community support. Third parties may also urge concessions in order to create difficulties for a target group. For instance, protest groups may be demanding the release of information concerning health hazards in a particular factory. Competitors may use their influence to obtain this information, knowing that it may prove damaging and will be difficult and costly to provide. Finally, third parties may urge concessions to gain material advantages for themselves. Builders' associations and labor councils urge city governments to undertake the remodeling of public housing in anticipation of contracts and jobs.

The Failure of Protest

As the political resource of the powerless, protest is not particularly valuable, because it often fails. According to Lipsky, protest seldom succeeds because many external constraints operate against those who attempt to lead protest. Further, target groups have an impressive arsenal of tactics to use against protest leaders and groups.

External Constraints on Leaders

Those who organize and lead protest confront a number of external constraints that operate against the successful outcome of protest. The demands of family life and work limit the time leaders can devote to organizing protest, yet protest leaders must take the time to become familiar with the grievances of their followers. The meager resources of the constituency usually place severe limits on available protest tactics. Much of a leader's time and energy is spent in finding volunteers to perform essential tasks. Finally, protest leaders seldom have reliable access to the media. These constraints merit further discussion.

Strain of Competing Commitments. Competing commitments posed by family and jobs are perhaps the most immediate constraint

upon protest leaders. These commitments limit the time that leaders can devote to protest. Full-time jobs typically leave only nights and weekends free to organize protest, and part of this time is absorbed by commitments to family. Consequently, protest leaders can seldom devote full time to their protest efforts.

Indeed, much of the time used by protest must be "appropriated" from time usually devoted to family and job. Leaders shirk their share of household chores, miss family meals, and attend meetings that last into the early morning hours. Weekends are taken up by travel and more meetings, with little time left for family activities. At work, protest leaders may arrive late and leave early. It is not surprising that leading protest can precipitate problems at home and at work.

Familiarity with Constituency and Their Problems. In the early 1960s, the Students for a Democratic Society (SDS) failed to organize protest among the urban poor near their campuses. The SDS was unsuccessful in part because, as affluent, upper-middle-class students, they did not correctly perceive the needs of those they were trying to help. The poor were interested in immediate problems, such as food, rent, and medical care, while the SDS was interested in more abstract objectives, such as building a nationwide political alliance between students and workers.

The poor were also familiar with the unpleasant outcomes of confrontations with authority, such as arrest, police harassment, and losing jobs and welfare benefits. The poor feared that they and not the students would bear the brunt of the consequences if protest led to trouble.

Not just anyone can lead and sustain protest. A leader must develop a clear understanding of the likes, dislikes, talents, and weaknesses of the constituency in order to plan protest strategy. Successful leaders have considerable firsthand experience with the problem they are protesting and may have a personal stake in the outcome. Thus, those who lead protest against racial discrimination have themselves experienced discrimination, and those whose neighborhoods have been contaminated by toxic wastes lead protests demanding cleanups and/or financial restitution.

Resources of the Constituency. The lower the socioeconomic status (SES) of the constituency, the fewer resources there are available for travel, postage, telephone calls, and office space. Low SES groups are also more subject than others to reprisals for protest activity. They have less job security and may be vulnerable to the loss of welfare benefits. Some constituencies may be hampered by the inability to speak English.

From the standpoint of leadership, the higher the socioeconomic status of the constituency, the greater are the options for protest tactics. Having money to charter buses and even airplanes gives leaders access to an increased number of demonstration sites. Middle- and upper-income groups have greater job security than low-income groups as well as more opportunities to take time off from work. These groups also have greater access to good typewriters, duplicating equipment, and sophisticated computers.

In general, the higher the SES of the constituency, the greater the resources available and the lower the vulnerability to reprisals. On the other hand, the higher the SES of the constituency, the lower is the likelihood that they will need to resort to protest in order to make their needs and interests felt and heard.

Volunteers. Protest leaders are dependent on the availability and good will of many volunteers. Volunteers provide secretarial services, canvass neighborhoods to distribute leaflets, solicit donations, and seek potential members. Leaders may also have to depend on others to volunteer the use of trucks, vans, automobiles, office space, and equipment.

Protest leaders usually find it difficult to maintain a full-time office staff. It is also difficult to carry out tasks requiring more or less continuous effort, such as putting out newsletters on a fixed schedule. But volunteers are often unavailable when they are needed and much of a protest leader's efforts are devoted to rounding up sufficient numbers of volunteers to carry out essential tasks.

Access to Media. As noted above, protest groups do not have institutionalized access to the media. Seldom can protest leaders devote full attention to the media, and they often use bizarre protest tactics to obtain attention. At times, protest leaders must make extreme statements, outlandish promises, and threats to the target group in order to maintain media coverage. In turn, this type of activity is often described in negative terms by the media (Blanchard 1968).

Time. Time also works against the protest effort. Often, protest fails to halt such target group projects as building hazardous waste dumps or reorganizing school districts. As these projects move to completion, protest is likely to be considered moot. Protest can become old news within weeks, and media coverage becomes increasingly tenuous. Further, as protest drags on, it is difficult to maintain the commitment and efforts of volunteers.

Target Group Tactics

Target groups are usually in a position to anticipate protest. This is particularly true when target groups attempt to construct nuclear power plants, dams, airports, highways, hazardous waste dumps, or prisons. If protest is anticipated, the early work on these projects is likely to be done in secret. Land purchases, for example, are made as inconspicuously as possible. Only when the project is well underway do target groups go public and file for building permits and zoning changes or seek bond referendums.

Target groups may also seek to activate community support before protest develops. This includes making speeches to chambers of commerce and building trade councils that emphasize the sales revenues and jobs the project will generate. Finally, target groups may attempt to co-opt those in the community who might be likely to initiate protest.

If protest does develop, target groups have a number of effective tactics to use against protest. In general, these tactics are calculated to give the appearance of change and concern, while simply wasting time.

Granting Symbolic Satisfactions. Target groups may grant symbolic satisfactions to protest groups in an effort to create an image of change and concern in the eyes of third parties. Such gestures include naming dams or airports after the heroes of the protest group. Pledges to carefully manage and monitor toxic waste dumps or to plant trees to improve the appearances of prisons may calm protest. Sometimes, a target group may create its own commisson to study the protest group's grievances. These symbolic satisfactions are granted using generous and tactful rhetoric, with full media coverage.

Claims of Constraint. A target group may also claim that it lacks the money to meet the protest group's demands. This is a particularly persuasive tactic when budgets are notoriously tight. It is quite likely, however, that the target group's estimate of what it would cost to meet the demands is greatly exaggerated. Lipsky notes that if they are sufficiently pressed to do so, target groups can meet demands by restructuring their budget.

A target group may also claim that it lacks the authority to grant the protest group's demands. This is a particularly effective tactic if the protest group can be persuaded to take its grievances elsewhere. It is in the protest group's interest, however, to keep its efforts focused at the local level. When a group attempts to take its protest to the state legislature, for example, its effort will probably have much less impact than at the local level. This is because state legislative bodies routinely hear protest from all corners. A small protest group is likely to be ignored in the clamor for attention of the legislature. Also, it will be difficult for a protest group to carry on a lengthy protest if its members must commute great distances.

Response to the Worst. A target group can disrupt protest by responding to the worst or most visible instance of the problem faced by the protest group. For example, if a group is protesting the poor condition of public housing, the housing agency might repair a few severely deteriorated apartments, using funds from the budget for routine maintenance. Of course, these projects would be given as much publicity as possible. Though a few apartments might be repaired, the overall condition of public housing would not be much improved.

Sometimes, a target group may establish a "crisis program" to thwart protest. Crisis programs cover a wide range of grievances, and they include telephone "hotline" programs to report crimes or obtain psychological counseling, as well as rape counseling and drug rehabilitation programs. A crisis program gives the appearance of change and concern, but the intent is more to disrupt protest than to render a genuine service. Further, crisis programs are often funded by cutting the budget of less visible but more effective programs that benefit the protest group. Finally, crisis programs are far less expensive than comprehensive efforts to improve the quality of community life. Once they have created a crisis program, the target group can claim that the protest group is ungrateful or greedy if it asks for more.

Fear of Bad Precedents.   Target groups can often thwart protest by forcefully arguing that granting protest demands will set a bad precedent. Target groups argue that "if we give in to one protest group, we will have to give in to all of them." In general, this argument is well received by third parties. In practice, however, it is obvious that if a target group gives concessions to one protest group, it need *not* give concessions to other groups. The political process is not characterized by distributive fairness but by groups competing for scarce resources. When faced with this tactic, a protest group must be quick to counter with the argument that its demands are legitimate. What the target group does for other groups in the future is not the question.

The Search for Alternatives.   When a target group builds an airport or a hazardous waste dump or proposes to cut school budgets, it can disrupt protest by demanding that the protest group present an "alternative" to the target group's plan. This tactic immediately casts the protest group as a "bunch of complainers." At best, it can totally reorient the efforts of the protest group. Instead of maintaining pressure on the target group, protesters try to become amateur ecologists, engineers, city planners, and economists. While the protesters are trying to come up with an alternative plan, the target group's plan is moving forward. If the protest group actually succeeds in presenting an alternative plan, it can usually be dismissed as too costly, incomplete, or simply impractical.

An astute protest group can respond to this tactic by loudly noting that it is not its responsibility to come up with comprehensive plans. The group must point out that it is the target group's responsibility to come up with plans that are acceptable to concerned groups within the community.

Temporary Concessions.   A target group can often grant substantial portions of a protest group's demands and then phase the changes out once the protest group ceases to exist. During the 1960s, for example, protesting university students demanded a voice in such academic matters as course offerings and content, faculty retention, and grading policy. Students demanded to attend departmental faculty meetings to press these demands, and some departments allowed student representatives to do so. After several noisy meetings at which little real business was conducted, students failed to show up. In other departments, however, constitutions and official procedures were altered to include student representation on departmental committees. This represented an *institutionalization* of student demands. Today, in these departments, faculty members seek student votes on pending matters. Early in each academic year, the faculty urges students to elect their representatives so that departmental business can get underway.

Measures of Success

In the most obvious sense, protest is successful when the target group capitulates and grants most or all of the protest group's demands. In real life, this seldom occurs. Target groups have a wide range of tactics they can employ to waste time while projecting the appearance of change and concern. For protest groups, success must often be judged in terms other than immediate concessions from the target group.

Group Transformation.   For some protest groups, success is achieved by abandoning the arena of protest and transforming the protest group into a more powerful organization. Often this occurs when protest groups affiliate with larger, well-established organizations. For instance, after failing to achieve gains on their own, dissatisfied employees may join labor unions and work for change through the mechanism of collective bargaining. Groups protesting hazardous waste pollution in their community may affiliate with nationally organized environmental groups. When a protest group affiliates with an established organization, it may obtain resources such as financing, legal assistance, information, and the help of professional organizers. On the other hand, the protest group may lose a great deal of autonomy. The larger organization may insist that the protest group moderate its demands and alter its tactics. Further, the protest group must divert effort from its own concerns to the broader objectives of the larger group. Though substantial gains may be achieved through affiliation, the protest group, as such, ceases to exist.

Taking Credit for Changes. Piven and Cloward (1979:36) argue that protest groups usually win only what "historical circumstances has already made ready to be conceded." In recent years, for example, utility companies across the United States have shelved plans to build nuclear-powered generating stations. A number of nuclear power plants have been abandoned while under construction. It is difficult to attribute these developments solely to the "No Nukes" protests that plagued these projects, even though protest groups have taken or been given credit for this change in policy. Rather, it is quite clear that utility companies have found nuclear power plants to be more expensive to build, less reliable, and more expensive to maintain than was previously thought.

Target groups may cite protest as the reason for scrapping projects or policies they have already found to be unsound, too costly, or obsolete. Attributing change to protest is one

way that target groups can eliminate the necessity of acknowledging their own mistakes. This stance can also foster the image that the target group is responsive and people oriented. The media may also identify protest as a major cause of change while ignoring underlying causes, and protest groups are usually willing to take credit for changes that would have occurred in the absence of protest. When protest challenges important policies and high-priority projects, it usually fails. When protest challenges policies or projects that target groups find burdensome, protest often succeeds.

Target Group Awareness. At times, success must be defined simply in terms of compelling the target group to take the protest group into account. Protest may bring valid issues to the public eye that would have otherwise passed unnoticed. This does not mean that the protest group wins concessions; it may win little more than the target group's recognition that a problem actually exists. The target group may be able to explain its programs and objectives to the satisfaction of the protest group. In either event, the protest group has made an accounting of itself; it has not been ignored.

Summary

In this chapter we have focused on protest—attempts by relatively powerless groups to influence the political process through pressure of petition, demonstrations, strikes, boycotts, and, occasionally, violence. Those who lead protest are seldom professional agitators or people skilled in the operation of politics.

The mass hysteria, emergent norm, and value-added perspectives view successful protest as highly dependent upon favorable public opinion, which they suggest can be achieved by adhering to the pluralist rules of political moderation. Success is gained through petition, the formation of coalitions, and a willingness to compromise.

Anger and indignation do not automatically translate into protest. Participants in protest must engage in reframing acts that focus attention on the conduct of authorities and identify their acts as a violation of the shared moral principles of the community. Protesters must also engage in divesting acts that declare them free to challenge and disobey authorities. Finally, participants must build loyalty to the protest group through shared acts of commitment, including protest humor.

Once initiated, protest may well fail to achieve the ends sought, because target groups and authorities have an impressive arsenal of tactics to use against protest. The findings of Gamson run counter to the assumptions about the dynamics of protest contained in general theories of collective behavior. Gamson finds little historical support for the assumption that moderate protest tactics are the most likely to bring success. Instead, those groups that used tactics of disruption and were willing to use violence if provoked were more likely than others to gain recognition as legitimate representatives of constituencies and to make tangible gains. This is not a call to violence but an acknowledgment that the pluralist tactics of moderation do not serve protest as well as is suggested by general theories of collective behavior.

Lipsky discusses the constraints that operate against successful protest. In general, protest groups are hindered by a lack of money and a lack of access to power brokers and the media. Leading protest is often a thankless and exhausting task, and protest leaders are hindered by competing demands on their time and the availability of volunteers to assist them.

Target groups are in a much more enviable position. They can readily use tactics that waste time while giving the appearance of change and concern. Target groups often have considerable organizational and financial resources that they can use to thwart protest.

When protest groups do make tangible gains, it is often by way of group transformation. Through affiliation with national groups, local protest groups can acquire sufficient financial and organizational resources to enter the arena of "power politics." Sometimes protest groups succeed by taking credit for changes that were near at hand, before their protest began. Finally, there is some merit to viewing success simply in terms of compelling the target group to take the protest group into account, even if gains are not realized.

In this chapter we have primarily discussed protest that revolves around localized concerns and grievances. Sometimes people use protest in an attempt to change conditions that are of much greater scope. This is when protest and social movements merge. In the next chapters we will examine the dynamics of social movements.

CHAPTER 14

Social Movements: Origins, Character, and Member Commitment and Control

Social movements are the most encompassing and the largest-scale events included within the field of collective behavior, and they contain many other kinds of collective behavior, such as that of newly formed groups, crowd behavior, innovative behavior, protest, and collective violence. The term *social movement* has also been applied to such large-scale events as the French, American, Mexican, and Russian revolutions (Wood and Jackson 1982).

In this chapter we will examine the mass hysteria, emergent norm, and valued-added perspectives on social movements, each of which offers an explanation of the patterns of growth and decline of social movements. These traditional approaches focus on the issues of movement origins, movement character, and membership commitment and control. Though there are some fundamental differences among the perspectives in their approaches to these issues, there are also a number of important similarities.

The traditional perspectives characterize social movements as arising within groups facing some sort of social hardship, such as material deprivation, political oppression, and threats to ethnic survival. Social movements arise among groups that long for the renewal of cherished values; they seldom arise among contented or complacent groups.

Social movements are usually spoken of as pursuing goals, which broadly include seeking or preventing change in society. Specifically, movement goals include reform and revolution, ethnic betterment or suppression, withdrawal from society, personal enrichment or transformation, and various forms of religious salvation. Movement ideology sets forth movement goals in dramatic terms and specifies broad strategies for attaining them.

Goals are pursued through uninstitutionalized and unconventional means. That is, much of the important work of social movements occurs outside established political parties and the legislative process, and social movements attempt to bring about change through such unconventional means as personal conversion, agitation, protest, force of example, force of numbers, and force of arms.

At some point in their development, nearly all social movements are opposed by established authorities. This opposition can take the form of attempts to co-opt or discredit leaders or their followers, subtle intimidation, and violent suppression. From the standpoint of the dominant society, social movements appear to be a source of unjustified and potentially dangerous disruption. Only occasionally do dominant groups perceive a social movement as an ally or a bringer of welcome change (Wood and Jackson 1982).

Finally, it is traditionally held that social movements seldom achieve the goals they initially set forth. During the course of a movement there may be changes in leadership personnel, and external conditions may bring about changes in movement membership and interests. The reactions of authorities may necessitate revisions of movement goals. If a movement is to make gains, goals must be altered and sometimes abandoned. In those instances where social movements are part of dramatic alterations in society, such as the Great Revolutions, actual changes may have little resemblance to the changes first sought by the movement.

We begin this chapter with a description of the spread of Ghost dancing among the American Indians. In Chapter 15 we will examine the formation of the Solidarity Union by Polish workers. Although these movements occurred nearly a century apart and within different cultures, they illustrate many of the characterizations of social movements mentioned above. The Ghost Dance and Poland's Solidarity movement both arose among people facing daily hardships. These two movements used greatly dissimilar tactics, but both sought to better the lot of their constituency, and both were altered by movement growth and changes in leadership. Finally, both movements encountered increasingly harsh responses from authorities.

The Ghost Dance Movement

The first Ghost Dance took place among the Paiute Indians on the Walker Lake, Nevada, Indian Reservation in January 1889. The Ghost Dance was organized by a Paiute shaman, or medicine man, named Wovoka. In his early teens, Wovoka was orphaned and was cared for by a white family who named him Jack Wilson. When he was about thirty years old, Wovoka was struck down by a severe fever, during which he had mystical visions. Afterward, Wovoka claimed that he was Christ. He had been instructed by God to lead his people in the Ghost Dance in order to usher in a new era of peace and harmony between Indians and whites.

The Ghost Dance actually consisted of five all-night dances performed on consecutive evenings. A large dancing circle was prepared and temporary shelters built nearby. The Indians danced and sang both old songs and songs composed for the Ghost Dance. In some tribes, dancers often trembled violently and fainted. Among the Arapaho, some dancers would stand rigidly for hours in a trancelike state. During their faints or trances, dancers said they were transported to the happy hunting ground, where they visited with their dead ancestors. Occasionally, those who fainted claimed to have been cured of diseases. On the morning of the fifth day, the dancing ended with a vigorous shaking of all the blankets brought to the dancing circle, a bath in nearby streams, and a feast. The series of five dances was then repeated at intervals.

Wovoka never left his reservation to spread the Ghost Dance. Arapaho and Cheyenne medicine men and chiefs visited Wovoka, who provided them with written instuctions on how to perform the Ghost Dance. Mooney (1896) has preserved Wovoka's instructions to the Arapaho and Cheyenne:

When you get home you must make a dance to continue five days. Dance four successive nights, and the last night keep up the dance until the morning of the fifth day, when all must bathe in the river and then disperse to their homes. You must all do this in the same way.

I, Jack Wilson, love you all, and my heart is full of gladness for the gifts you have brought me. When you go home I shall give you a good rain which will make you feel good. I will give you a good spirit and give you all good paint. I want you to come again in three months, some from each tribe in Indian Territory.

There will be a good deal of snow this year and some rain. In the fall there will be such rain as I have never given you before.

Grandfather says, when your friends die you must not cry. You must not hurt anybody or harm anyone. You must not fight. Do right always. It will give you satisfaction in life. The bearer of this letter has a good father and mother.

Do not tell the whites about this. Jesus is now upon the earth. He appears like a cloud. The dead are all alive again. I do not know when they will be here; maybe this fall or in the spring. When the time comes there will be no more sickness and everyone will be young again.

Do not refuse to work for the whites and do not make any trouble with them until you leave them. When the earth shakes do not be afraid. It will not hurt you.

I want you to dance every six weeks. Make a feast at the dance and have food that everybody may eat. Then bathe in the water. That is all. You will receive good words again from me some time. Do not tell lies.

The Ghost Dance also spread by word-of-mouth from reservation to reservation. Within two years, the Ghost Dance spread among nearly all of the Indian tribes west of the Mississippi. The dance was modified in its transmission among the many tribes, but wherever it occurred, it was misunderstood and usually feared by whites (Mooney 1896).

The Ghost Dance movement lasted less than three years. It occurred at a time when the policy of the United States government was to force the Plains Indians onto reservations. Even if they had been inclined to do so, it was difficult for the Indians to establish an emotional bond with the reservation. Federal administration of the reservations was notoriously corrupt and insensitive to Indian ways, and the reservations were often located in areas far from the Indians' traditional homes and hunting grounds. It was army policy to move Indians during the winter months, when miserable weather made it difficult for Indians

to flee in large numbers. When they arrived on the reservation, food rations and blankets were usually in short supply, shelter often consisted of drafty sheds with straw on the floor for bedding, and medical care and sanitation were minimal. Indians were often moved from one reservation to another with little forewarning or explanation (Brown 1971).

By 1890 the power of the great Indian leaders was broken. Ironically, only a few of the chiefs had died in battle. Many had simply surrendered or had been arrested by the U.S. Army. Crazy Horse was assassinated after he surrendered to military authorities. Geronimo was sentenced to a long prison term and died in captivity, while some of the war chiefs, such as Satanata, killed themselves rather than submit to the indignity of prison (Brown 1971). Chief Joseph (see Chapter 8) was separated from the Nez Percés and exiled to Colville Reservation in Washington. Among the great leaders, only Red Cloud and Sitting Bull remained with their people, the Cheyenne and the Sioux.

The placing of Indians on the reservations gave many whites their first close look at the remnants of Indian life. By the whites' standards, Indians seemed lazy, unclean, vicious, and superstitious. One goal of the Bureau of Indian Affairs was to "civilize" and Christianize the Indians. Consequently, when whites saw the Ghost Dance, they interpreted it as a threat. The Indians seemed to lose all interest in schools, church, and farming during the Ghost Dance, and in some instances, outbreaks of violence occurred between Indians and whites during the dance. In fact, the reasons for these outbreaks had little to do with the Ghost Dance. Still, whites perceived the Ghost Dance as a preparation for war, failing to see that it was a blending of Indian and white cultures. The Ghost Dance was similar to many other Indian ceremonies and beliefs, but it also had its origins in the Christian beliefs that whites were imposing on the Indians. No agents from the Bureau of Indian Affairs or army officers ever questioned Wovoka about the Ghost Dance or the beliefs it embodied.

The Ghost Dance had perhaps its greatest impact among the Sioux. In 1890 the Sioux had only recently been driven onto reservations in the Dakota Territory (what is today North and South Dakota). The boundaries of these reservations were constantly renegotiated, and Indians lost more and more land to white settlers. Sitting Bull strongly advocated keeping Sioux land intact, and the renegotiations became increasingly bitter.

In the spring of 1890, the Ghost Dance was introduced by a Sioux medicine man, Kicking Bear, who had personally visited Wovoka. Kicking Bear considerably altered the Ghost Dance. He claimed that the ancestors visited during fainting and trances would soon return to the living world; further, the earth would be transformed—the buffalo would return and the whites would be swept away. Still, Kicking Bear did not call for violence by the Indians— all they had to do was dance and sing. The coming messiah would take care of the whites. Among the first to perform the dance were the many Sioux women who had lost husbands in battles with the army; they eagerly awaited the return of their warrior husbands.

By fall, the Ghost Dance was disrupting reservation life. Many children stayed away from school, little work was being done on the farms, and trading post business had declined. The bureau and the army began to intimidate the Indians in an effort to halt the Ghost Dance. At this time Kicking Bear introduced the idea of the Ghost shirt, which had the magical property of stopping bullets. Indians wearing a Ghost shirt could continue the dance without fearing the soldiers. Almost immediately, the belief arose that a Ghost shirt would make a person invincible in battle. Whites sensed the potential for trouble in the Ghost shirt belief, and on November 20, the bureau issued the order to "stop the dancing."

Various forms of intimidation were used on the many reservations where Ghost dancing was occurring. Some reservation officials cut rations, while others promised more rations if Ghost dancing ceased. On the Sioux reservation, the Ghost Dance was being carried out during snowstorms and freezing weather. Although Sitting Bull probably viewed the Ghost Dance as a waste of time, it was decided that arresting Sitting Bull would halt the Ghost dancing among the Sioux. On December 15, 1890, an attempt to arrest Sitting Bull ended tragically. Sitting Bull and his son were killed, as were six of Sitting Bull's followers and six Indian policemen.

As word of Sitting Bull's death spread, hundreds of Sioux, including Kicking Bear, fled the reservation. Some rode into the Badlands to hide, while others tried to get to the Cheyenne reservation to seek the protection of Red Cloud. The army pursued those who had fled and captured a band of about 370 Indians on December 28. The next morning, near Wounded Knee Creek, shooting broke out while the army was disarming their prisoners. Light artillery raked the camp, and inexperienced and angry soldiers slaughtered the Indians. Within minutes, nearly 300 Indians, over half of them women and children, and 60 U.S. soldiers had been killed or wounded.

During the following year, 1891, the Ghost Dance seemed to fade as rapidly as it had appeared. It returned among the Kiowa about four years later and then among the Arapaho and Cheyenne. By then, Wovoka had returned to the obscurity from which he came, and he played no role in the revival of Ghost dancing. In their second encounter with Ghost dancing, authorities were much more accommodating than before. Today, the Ghost Dance is part of the cultural heritage of many tribes.

Ghost dancing did not occur among the Apache and Navaho people. In these cultures, ghosts were feared much as they are in most white cultures, and the idea of calling ghosts

FIGURE 14.1   *The Ghost Dance Movement*

One of the beliefs in the Ghost Dance movement was that shirts and robes could be given the magical property of turning aside bullets. In this drawing made by Standing Bear, a Ghost Shirt is being tested. According to the artist, many witnessed this test. The Ghost Shirt became popular after the U.S. Army threatened the use of force to stop the Ghost Dance movement. (Photo courtesy of Milwaukee Public Museum.)

back to the living world held no appeal. Few Comanches practiced the dance. Even among the Sioux, where the dance had such disastrous consequences, only about half the Indians participated. Often the dance created friction between progressive and traditional Indian factions (Mooney 1896).

The suppression of the dance by authorities probably led to more problems than the dance itself. Whites who had little understanding of the origins or nature of the dance concluded that it was "heathenistic" and fostered Indian violence. The violence, however, was largely a continuation of conflict patterns established well before the Ghost Dance era. Whites who feared the Ghost Dance failed to see the similarities between the dance and their own fundamentalist Christian revivals.

The Mass Hysteria Perspective and Social Movements

Blumer (1946) defines *social movements*, quite simply, as "collective enterprises to establish a new order of life." He breaks them into the categories of general and specific movements. By general social movements, Blumer is referring to the "gradual and pervasive changes

in the values of people," such as those embodied in the labor movement, women's movement, and peace movement. General social
movements have an unfocused character, with
shifting leadership and informal membership.
Their history is characterized by periods of intense activity and periods of relative calm or
decline. A specific movement often arises out
of a general social movement. A specific social
movement has clearly defined goals, definite
leadership, and, at times, formal membership.
Reform and revolutionary movements typify
the specific social movement.

Patterns of Social Unrest

Social movements and other forms of collective behavior arise out of conditions of *social unrest*—a generalized condition of
aroused emotion and unease in society. During
social unrest, people's behavior takes on a random or aimless character, and the source of
this restlessness is only vaguely perceived.
People experience excited feelings of apprehension, insecurity, and eagerness. During social
unrest, people are easily irritated and more
suggestible than usual; their attention spans
are shortened, and they approach states of
psychological instability.

Blumer identifies five types of social unrest.
First, there is unrest characterized by collective
insecurity and wariness of the future. This fear
is unfocused, and people may simultaneously
fear several threats to the future. Rapid social
and technological change can foster this type
of unrest. A second type of unrest is composed
of general feelings of frustration and protest
over the present way of life. Though the frustration is general, people share a willingness to
violently attack prominent symbols of the dis-
pleasing way of life at the slightest provocation. Political oppression is likely to foster this
type of unrest. Social unrest may also take the
form of flight from the present life. This type
of unrest is marked by the rise of new philos-

ophies and yearnings for utopian existence,
and it is likely to occur when conventional phi-
losophies no longer seem to speak to individual needs. A fourth type of social unrest is
characterized by those periods when strong
feelings of happy anticipation and a desire to
"do things" sweep across society. The early
stages of economic recoveries and the first
months of new political leadership may take
on such characteristics. Finally, there is the unrest of despair, which takes the form of open
and deep lamentation or fatalistic withdrawal
from society. National failures or severe economic deprivation may lead to such unrest.

The Life Cycle of Social Movements

Blumer suggests that there is a natural life
cycle for social movements. In many respects,
the life cycle is tied to the rise and decline of
aroused emotion. Social movements have
their beginnings in social unrest and collective
excitement. Leaders channel this aroused emotion in the direction of institutional change. If
movements are to succeed, aroused emotion
must eventually be dampened and people's en-
ergies turned to the systematic pursuit of movement goals. Finally, enthusiasm for change
must be transformed into discipline to maintain the gains of the movement.

The Preliminary Stage.   The preliminary
stage of social movements is characterized by
social unrest. The masses are restless and express vague feelings of uneasiness or unhappi-
ness with existing social conditions. Their unease may be heightened by agitators who
instigate brief and localized outbursts of violence, revelry, or religious revival. In the preliminary stage, movement organizations either
have yet to form or consist of small, isolated
groups of misfits.

The Popular Stage.   In the popular stage,
social unrest is transformed into intense collective excitement, in part because people are in-

creasingly certain about the cause of their discontent. Prophets play a central role in the development of this certainty. Prophets are intellectuals or others with a talent for creating a social myth to account for discontent. They develop ideas and images to account for present conditions and suggest ways to collectively establish a new way of life. The social myth may be simplistic and have no direct bearing on the actual causes of discontent, but due to heightened suggestibility, the social myth becomes the rallying cry and ideology of the movement.

Growth is rapid during the popular stage. Membership is drawn from idealists who are strongly committed to the movement's ideology, leadership, and goals. Leadership is provided by prophets and reformers whose source of power is the intense personal devotion of their followers. During the popular stage, formal structure is largely mitigated against by rapidly changing circumstances.

The Formal Organization Stage.   As movements develop, they may be hindered, challenged, or attacked by established authorities. Consequently, if it is to survive, the movement must be transformed into a disciplined organization capable of securing member commitment and pursuing effective strategies. Aroused emotion and ideological enthusiasm may actually hinder movement development at this stage. Aroused emotion weakens discipline, while zealous commitment to movement ideals precludes compromise. During the formal organization stage, idealists may well leave the movement. In any event, there is growth in the number of members who chiefly identify with the movement as an organization rather than as an ideology.

Prophets and reformers are replaced by strategists whose talents lie in the areas of long-range planning and compromise. During this stage, the movement adopts a formal structure. Critical positions are staffed by paid employees, although the majority of the work is still done by volunteers. Established authorities may recognize the movement as a potential ally in the pursuit of their particular aims. It is during the formal organization stage that movements make their greatest and most lasting gains.

The Institutional Stage.   The final stage of development begins when the movement becomes recognized as a more or less permanent and integral feature of society. In the case of reform movements, the central concern is to maintain hard-won gains. Leadership is now provided by adminstrators whose skills lie in routinizing the movement's day-to-day activities. Membership views the movement as a means of livelihood or as an official agency that is especially considerate of their needs.

In the case of revolutionary movements, this stage begins shortly before the taking of power. No longer the enemy of the state, the movement now *is* the state. Even greater discipline is required of members, who must now guard against the undermining of their gains. The complete institutionalization of the movement may well mean the elimination of earlier institutions and, perhaps, the people in them. Ironically, the movement may have to purge itself of the idealists who have stuck with the movement from the beginning. These people are likely to be displeased with the compromises that have been made along the way to power, and their criticisms may be very sure sources of trouble as the movement consolidates its power. If they survive their purge, however, idealists may well furnish the active core for the next round of social movement activity.

Meaning-Seeking Movements: The Hippies

Not all movements that we normally think of as social movements follow the life cycle described by Blumer. Some movements seem to generate tremendous enthusiasm and depart from traditional lifestyles but do little else. The hippie movement of the late 1960s and early 1970s was such a movement.

The hippies should not be confused with student radicals or motorcycle gangs. Nor should the hippie movement be confused with the student protest or antiwar movements. If there was any particular ideology of the movement, it could be summarized by the slogans of "dropping out" and "doing your own thing." Almost by definition, the hippie movement precluded institutionalization of these aims. There was very little formal organization within the movement. A few hippie communes assigned those present to tasks of cleaning and cooking but little else. For a time, the most active center of hippiedom was the Haight-Ashbury district of San Francisco. Here, nearly continuous rock concerts, drug sales, and open street life gave the impression that one had truly escaped from the conventional world. To be considered a "true" hippie, one had to make at least one pilgrimage to the Haight-Ashbury.

Hippies wore long hair and dressed in clothes of their own design. They often wore military clothing embroidered with flowers and peace emblems. The preferred mode of transportation was a van, equipped for camping and painted in psychedelic patterns. Otherwise, hippies hitchhiked.

The lifestyle of hippies included free and open sex and the frequent use of drugs, principally marijuana and LSD. Hippies tended to shun hard liquor, drinking mostly beer and wine. It was considered improper for a hippie to refuse to share food with another hippie. They felt that sleep was a waste of time. Hippies would often go on sprees of drugs, sex, music, and carousing that would last for days; then, when total exhaustion set in, they would "crash," or sleep for a few days, "get their shit together," and start over again. Hippies often staged love-ins—open-air rock concerts with

displays of affection, some nudity, the use of drugs, and general revelry. Hippies tried to live a life of nonviolence and love for humanity. They often attended antiwar rallies and honored labor boycotts, and they tried to ignore race as a social distinction.

The parents of hippies usually hated this lifestyle. Their children seemed to have no desire to achieve material success or settle down to any semblance of a conventional lifestyle. Parents worried for the safety of their children. Many stories circulated of hippies being killed while hitchhiking or making drug deals. Parents also worried that their children were scrambling their brains with too many drugs.

The hippie movement began to fade in the early 1970s. This decline was foretold when many hippies "got clean for Gene" and worked for Senator Eugene McCarthy's bid for the Democratic presidential nomination in 1968. When Nixon was elected, hippies started to turn to other pursuits. Many became active in the ecology movement and attended the first Earth Day celebrations. Others "found Jesus" or joined the Moonies. Finally, many hippies finished college, married, and took jobs. A few of them established businesses that catered to their earlier lifestyle: organic foods, music, and clothing stores.

What types of social change did the hippie movement bring about? Some have argued that the change was decidedly negative, exemplified by the loosening of society's sexual mores. Still, as one commentator noted, as much as the hippies would like to think otherwise, they did *not* invent sex. Would drugs be a problem in society today if it had not been for the hippies? Certainly today's style of drug use is far removed from the "peace-love" and "consciousness-expanding" drug use of the hippies. The hippies were the first to suggest the legalization of marijuana, although that seems as remote today as it did in 1970. Even the hippies' eccentric and casual style of dress soon gave way to the expensive chic of designer clothing. If any social changes can be directly attributed to the hippies, they were inadvertent rather than planned.

Orrin E. Klapp (1972) identified the hippie movement as a movement oriented toward "meaning seeking." Such movements arise when people's social experiences generate intense boredom; they are a search for meaning as well as an emotional catharsis. According to Klapp, only modern and affluent societies are capable of generating such boredom. Boredom is increased in a society in which nearly everything is artificially packaged and prefabricated. Hippies preferred their communes to the "ticky-tacky" suburbs where all the houses and people were the same. Even in cities, hippies tried to grow some of their own food. Hippies often built their own houses, and they pioneered in the construction of geodesic dome structures. Finally, boredom is increased in societies that are low in personal input and require little involvement. Perhaps the wildest political convention in our nation's history was the 1968 Democratic Convention in Chicago—the one the hippies crashed.

Features of meaning-seeking movements include the revelrous expansion of sensory horizons. Hippies did not use drugs for just another thrill; instead, they developed elaborate justifications for drug use, including the "expansion of consciousness" and "heightened creativity." Many terms used to describe drug-induced states, such as *spaced-out, freaking, bad trip*, and *psychedelic*, were coined or popularized by the hippies. Sock hops in the high school gym and jazz festivals gave way to the total sensory immersion of the rock concert–light shows of the Doors and the Grateful Dead.

Creativity is another characteristic of the meaning-seeking movement. The music, clothing, and art of the hippies clearly broke with tradition. Hippies enlivened the tradition of the street musician and personalized clothing design. Many elements of today's commercial

art can be traced back to the psychedelic art of the hippies.

Finally, meaning-seeking movements are characterized by primitive romanticism, which includes freedom from external obligations. The philosophy of the hippies captured this ideal in two words: *dropping out*. Primitive romanticism includes roving and vagabondage, something the hippies developed to a science, and also includes a sense of wild naturalness, clearly signified by the hippies' long hair and beards. Finally, primitive romanticism is based on a life of immediate action. For the hippies, life was simply a matter of "*doing your own thing.*"

In many respects, Klapp's description of meaning-seeking movements and how they arise seems more an attempt to account for the hippie movement than it is a general theory of social movements. Still, Klapp maintains that meaning seeking is found in nearly all social movements and is found in its purest form in movements such as the hippie movement. Meaning seeking is an important component of the civil rights, women's rights, antiwar, and ecology movements. According to Klapp, these movements are collective attempts to both redress social grievances and escape the boredom of life in modern society.

The Emergent Norm Perspective and Social Movements

Turner and Killian define a *social movement* as a collectivity acting with some continuity to promote or resist a change in the society or group of which it is a part. Social movement collectivities differ from formal organizations in that leadership is determined more by the informal response of members than by formal procedures for legitimizing authority. Further, social movement collectivities are more structured than *mass movements*, such as people caught up in clothing fads, and *followings,* such as those parents who raise their children according to the suggestions of Dr. Benjamin Spock.

Social Movements: Character and Process

For Turner and Killian, there are four important points regarding the character and process of social movements. First, unlike that of formal organizations, the character of movements changes from day to day. At one time, movement activities may center on clarifying and articulating objectives, while at another time, movement activities may center on recruiting new members. At still other times, movement activities may center on planning and carrying out demonstrations. Finally, some movements may successfully implement their goals and become an integral part of society.

These observations might suggest that movements change through a life cycle process, as suggested by the mass hysteria approach. For Turner and Killian, however, the life cycle view better accounts for the way in which social movements like to portray their history rather than for the true sequence of events. Though social movements are continuously in flux, the nature of this change is such that no typical sequence is generally valid.

The second important point is that the course and character of social movements are shaped by the interplay between value, power, and participation orientations within the movement (see Chapter 2). At times, movement activity is characterized by the structuring of beliefs, the articulation of grievances, and the thought of solutions (value orientations). Such activities must at times compete with or be replaced by considerations for implementing solutions or reaching accommodations with groups and interests external to the movement (power orientations). Finally, at times, movements focus on meeting needs that arise because of participation in the movement.

Members must obtain minimal levels of gratification in order to remain with the movement (participation orientations).

The third important point is that social movements are shaped by external relations. These relations include the ways in which external publics define movements and the kinds of support and opposition that movements encounter. These external relations can either strengthen or hinder and weaken social movements.

Finally, social movements bring about normative transformations in society. They propose new views of the world and new social arrangements based on these views. Sometimes the normative transformations that occur are not those originally envisioned or intended by the movement.

The Role of Emergent Norms

Widely held views regarding social movements include the ideas that social movements arise among groups experiencing severe deprivation and that movement goals are generally aimed at removing the source of discontent. Turner and Killian take issue with these ideas. They note that it is not necessarily the most deprived groups, or their most deprived members, that form social movements. Further, movement goals do not necessarily correspond to the source of discontent. These anomalies can be explained in part by the *emergent norms* that guide social movements.

The Sense of Injustice. For Turner and Killian, the common element in the norms of nearly all social movements is a sense of injustice—a clear conviction that existing conditions are wrong and must be changed. In the initial stages of the movement, this sense of injustice is expressed in the words of the agitator; later, it comes to be embodied in the jargon and songs of the movement. Satire of the values and behavior of groups that the movement opposes expresses the sense of injustice. Finally, the sense of injustice may even be reflected in styles of dress adopted by the movement. In the 1960s, for example, radical college students pointedly abandoned Ivy League styles to wear the denims and boots of the working class. The jargon, songs, satire, and fashion of a movement all serve as a constant reminder that existing standards of what is necessary or desirable are in need of change.

For people in the movement and many outside the movement, the sense of what is just and unjust seems self-evident once it is established. Often, the most enduring product of a movement is the revised conception of justice, reflected in the powerful statements of leaders, in songs, and in styles of dress.

The sense of injustice is not an automatic outgrowth of deprivation. For a disadvantage to be considered an injustice, it must be shared by a group possessing its own internal communication network, sense of group identity, and subculture. These conditions are not met within many highly deprived groups: internal communication is sporadic or absent; the group is fragmented by divergent interests and needs; and its subculture is damaged or destroyed through contacts with dominant groups.

Charges of injustice are always based on unfavorable comparison with the wealth, freedom, or power possessed by another group. The sense of injustice is not likely to develop among groups with little knowledge of the lifestyles of others. People frequently counter charges of injustice by pointing out that others have a worse lot than the movement group. Thus minority groups are pitted against one another and people who protest the draft are told to "go to Russia."

Intellectuals often play a central role in articulating the sense of injustice. For Turner and Killian, the strains of the intellectual role and the diversity of positions occupied by intellectuals ensure that they will always be concerned with uncovering social injustice. Their views are likely to serve any group that gains access to them and is ready to see its situation in terms of injustice.

Turner and Killian note that coming to view one's own lot as unjust requires some daring and confidence in being able to play a more important role than at present. Pariah groups and outcasts are slow to question their lot. People totally dependent on a dominant group are the least likely to challenge the propriety of their situation. In order to mobilize stigmatized groups, it is essential to arouse their sense of self-worth and confidence that they can better their lives.

Movement Goals. Movement goals do not necessarily follow from the sense of injustice, nor do they always strike directly at the source of discontent. Causes of discontent are rarely so immediate and self-evident that collective discussion and definition are unnecessary. According to Turner and Killian, people identify the source of their discontent on the basis of ideas presented to them with authority and clarity. Individuals' belief that they have correctly identified the cause of their discontent is based on their particular knowledge of external conditions, their views of human motivation, and social support for their emerging views.

Widely dissimilar goals can arise from nearly identical dissatisfying situations. Movement goals may take two general directions—societal manipulation and personal transformation. If changing society seems an appropriate response to the situation, movement goals may take the form of programs of reform, the elimination of "scapegoats" and their evil "conspiracies," or total revolution. If personal transformation seems an appropriate response, movement goals might be a particular type of personal religious conversion, the establishment of schools to teach language and job skills, or the establishment of separate communities.

For Turner and Killian, goals are the tangible accomplishments sought by the movement. They must be credible to the constituency; esoteric or idiosyncratic goals appeal to narrow audiences and serve to limit membership. Goals must unite rather than divide important constituencies within the movement. The movement must present a hierarchy of goals, including those that are immediately attainable. Achieving stated goals is one standard by which the movement's success or failure is judged.

Movement Ideology. Movement norms are embodied in movement ideologies that offer simplifying perspectives through which people can make sense out of overwhelmingly complex events and find certainty in otherwise vague and ambiguous situations. Ideologies are normative world views that provide people with a simplified frame of reference for understanding events and people. Often, ideologies are portrayed as scientific views of the world. But such ideologies differ from scientific theories in that they are based on unfounded assumptions and use paranoid rather than scientific logic. These ideologies can attribute virtually any social ill to capitalism, imperialism, communism, or conspiracy.

Ideologies place the movement and its goals in a moving time perspective. They detail past injustices and mistakes, present a simplified view of the present, and predict an inevitable future utopia.

Ideologies closely identify the movement's goals and interests with the general welfare: ultimately, the movement represents what is best for society and the world. Quite often, movement ideology supports this view by laying claim to the virtues of the downtrodden, the patience and wisdom of the silent majority, or the superior contributions of a particular group.

Finally, ideologies create villains who conspire against the general good for their own sinister interests. Labor unrest is caused by "communist agitators," pollution is caused by "greedy corporations," and moral decay is caused by "atheists and secular humanists." For Turner and Killian, villain ideology keeps people from acknowledging that the evil may have complex causes well outside the scope of movement goals.

Membership Commitment

For many social movements, members need be committed only to the extent that they are willing to attend occasional meetings, sign petitions, and donate moderate amounts of money. Membership in a "respectable" social movement can be scheduled into a normal life pattern with little difficulty. For these movements, securing commitment from members centers on coordinating roles inside and outside the movement. For example, meetings are scheduled so that they do not conflict with work. Movements such as these frequently plan activities such as picnics or carnivals for the entire family. Finally, some movements may provide such benefits as food co-ops or low-cost vacation plans for their members.

In some social movements, members must be committed to the extent that they will give nearly all their time and worldly goods to the movement, allow the movement to educate their children, and face physical dangers or even death. Rarely is membership commitment and control as total as that found within the People's Temple of the Disciples of Jesus Christ, led by Jim Jones. On Saturday, November 18, 1978, 913 members of this cult committed suicide at their jungle commune in Jonestown, Guyana. The suicides followed the murder of California Congressman Leo Ryan, members of his staff, and reporters who had visited the cult to investigate charges of mistreatment of cult members. Jim Jones had prepared his following for mass suicide for at least two years. They often practiced a communionlike ceremony in which members drank

Kool-Aid. Jim Jones told his followers that someday the Kool-Aid would contain cyanide.

Jack Douglas (1967) notes that there are several reasons why *individuals* may wish to commit suicide. Some people commit suicide for revenge—to embarrass or hurt those that they leave behind. Others commit suicide to change their identity in the eyes of others—to show that they are braver and better people than others realized. Some people commit suicide to gain the sympathy in death that was denied in life. Finally, some people may commit suicide to leave a troubled or meaningless life and find a better existence.

Jim Jones made all these motives personally meaningful to the members of his group, and the group practiced the suicide ceremony almost daily in the months preceding the actual suicides. After Ryan's death, when the group felt that they would soon be attacked by the Guyanese Army, the suicide ceremony began. Jones again reminded the members how their suicides would embarrass the United States in the eyes of the world. He said that everyone would come to realize that their group was composed of brave and principled people rather than social misfits. As they drank the poison, Jones assured members that they were "dying with dignity" and that others would soon feel sympathy and sadness for the cult. Finally, Jones assured the members that they were going on a final happy journey and would soon be reunited in "another life" (Cahill 1979; Winfrey 1979).

Jim Jones used tactics of persuasion that clearly spoke to common individual motives for suicide. By itself, however, such persuasion is not likely to produce the mass suicides witnessed in Jonestown, Guyana. In addition, Jones created a communal environment in which he could exercise very tight control over the day-to-day activities of the People's Temple group. This context of social control, built up over several months, greatly augmented Jones's tactics of persuasion.

Turner and Killian note that membership in a "peculiar" or revolutionary movement requires that the member make a choice between the movement and a normal lifestyle. Securing commitment, in this instance, centers on encouraging a clear choice to join the movement and making that choice irrevocable. Soon after arriving in Jonestown, People's Temple members found that this decision was irrevocable. Members who wanted to leave found that their passports and money were being kept under lock and key by Jones. He also had an elite security guard that kept close watch over the commune. Dissatisfied members were publicly chastised for their lack of enthusiasm and adherence to temple principles. Simply running away was not an attractive alternative because of the dense and deadly jungle that surrounded the commune for miles. Finally, Guyanese authorities were likely to return to the commune any runaways who managed to escape through the jungle.

For Turner and Killian, intense commitment to a movement is achieved through (1) conversion, (2) esprit de corps, (3) rewards for participation, (4) personal identification with the movement, and (5) breaking ties to conventional life. In the following section, we will discuss these elements of commitment separately. In practice, these elements often mesh with one another.

Conversion. Turner and Killian define *conversion* as a fundamental and wholehearted reversal of former values, attitudes, and beliefs. Conversion is manifested in the drastic repudiation of conventional patterns of speech, dress, living arrangements, and occupation. For those who have undergone conversions, the experience is usually described mystically as "seeing the light," "getting the spirit," or "finding oneself." Conversion is usually described as a short-lived, intense, and singular experience that occurs at some important juncture in one's life.

Though conversion is usually described in highly personal terms, Turner and Killian note that many social factors operate to bring about these experiences. They draw heavily on Lofland's study of the Doomsday Cult in their characterization of conversion. Converts to the Doomsday Cult had usually reached a turning point in life when their conversion experience occurred. Turning points included divorce, a second failure in college, failure in business, and a career disrupted by illness. People were at a point in life when most major previous commitments had been fulfilled or abandoned. Conversion occurred when these people found companionship and social support in a movement promoting interesting views. Many similar things can be said of the converts to the People's Temple.

Esprit de Corps.   Esprit de corps is a sense of enthusiasm for and pride in the movement. Esprit de corps thrives on victory and often disappears quickly in the face of adversity. Therefore, one ingredient in member commitment is movement success, which is sometimes fabricated to create esprit de corps. Rallies are purposely planned for small halls to ensure "capacity crowds," and attacks are made on weak opponents to ensure victory.

Movements also maintain esprit de corps by establishing rigid standards for membership, thereby creating clear in-group and out-group relationships. Members share a sense of belonging to a group that excludes those who are not "good enough," "smart enough," or "strong enough" to belong. Movements in which membership status is unclear or open to virtually anyone cannot establish such sharp in-group–out-group distinctions.

Participation in rituals and ceremonies also creates esprit de corps. Turner and Killian note, for example, how the mass rallies of the Nazi party generated movement spirit. The rallies brought together and offered something for every contingent of the movement, from the elite S.S. troops to the Hitler youth groups. Songs written especially for the movement were sung, honors were publicly bestowed, and new plans and programs were unveiled. Major rallies were yearly affairs, and at their completion, planning started for the following year's rally. At Jonestown there were daily meetings, rallies, group prayers and songs, and chastisement sessions.

Rewards for Participation.   Turner and Killian suggest that material rewards such as money and property seldom accrue to movement leaders or members in sufficient abundance to make participation lucrative. Occasionally, however, movement leaders may become public figures of sufficient stature that they are sought as highly paid lecturers. Some activists achieve enough notice that they are approached by established groups to serve as consultants or liaisons. However, nonmaterial rewards, such as status, companionship, and a sense of accomplishment, are usually more important than material rewards in maintaining movement commitment. The People's Temple was based on a hierarchical system of authority; members could advance into positions closer to Jim Jones.

Turner and Killian note that "license" may be a nonmaterial benefit of participation in some kinds of movements. For many people, a temporary escape from conventionality, boredom, and depression is a valuable commodity—a chance to create some memories to savor in later years. The wide-open lifestyle of the hippies of the 1960s is a case in point. Free sex, recreational drug use, frequent travel, and the general attitude of "doing your own thing" provided a very exciting episode in many people's lives.

Personal Identification with Movements. Loyalty to a movement is likely to be greatest among people who personally identify with the movement by thinking of themselves first and foremost as civil rights workers, born-again Christians, feminists, and so on. Turner and Killian identify several ways in which such intense personal identification can be created. The most intense personal identification is probably created by movements that demand that people change their names upon entering. Militant, separatist, or fiercely religious organizations utilize this form of commitment. In accepting new names, the members literally accept the identity that the movement has prepared for them.

Some movements foster commitment by refusing to acknowledge members' previous life experiences in the outside world. Thus people who have held high-status jobs before entering the movement will be ritualistically humiliated by being required to perform menial tasks. People possessing skills will be trained in new skills. In extreme instances, the movement will not even acknowledge marriages performed outside the movement. Some groups, such as the Unification Church, arrange marriages among the members.

Movements that demand extreme levels of personal commitment usually foster this by also demanding that members adhere to particular dietary rules, such as eating no pork, practicing vegetarianism, or only eating communally. Some movements enforce rules of dress that clearly set members apart from the rest of society.

Breaking Ties to Conventional Life. Member commitment may be inadvertently strengthened by negative community responses to the movement. Even if negative reactions eventually destroy the movement, their immediate effect is to brand the members or make former membership a stigma. It then becomes difficult if not impossible for members to ever be fully reintegrated into the community.

Millennial movements usually demand a severance of ties to the outside world. This isolation seems quite reasonable in terms of the movement's ideology: the outside world will soon be destroyed or drastically altered. Maintaining interest in the outside world can only jeopardize one's future status in the new order.

Millennial and other social movements often demand that members turn over a large share of their income. In extreme cases, members may be required to turn over all their worldly goods, including land, businesses, houses, stocks and bonds, autos, social security checks, and credit cards. In return, the movement may provide them with food, shelter, and medical care. These practices create a strong incentive to stay with the movement: those who leave are virtually destitute.

Turner and Killian suggest that involvement in some social movements exposes people to intense and repeated damnation of conventional life. These experiences can render people incapable of rejoining and performing competently in conventional society. Many recent efforts at deprogramming members of religious cults fail, in part because former members encounter intense difficulties in coping with family, neighbors, friends, and jobs.

Members of the People's Temple had limited ties to outside groups, and moving to Guyana usually severed any remaining nongroup ties. One indication of the limited ties to outside groups is that four months after the bodies had been returned to the United States, only about one third of them had been claimed by family or friends (Winfrey 1979).

Member Control

Committed members are not necessarily disciplined and obedient members. For many respectable movements, a highly disciplined constituency is not necessary or even desired. For peculiar or revolutionary movements, member control is of more vital concern. Overall movement success depends on maintaining strict control over members' actions.

These movements are more likely than others to be threatened with sanctions or attacked by outside groups. Unless member control can be maintained at such times, the movement may well collapse.

Much of what Turner and Killian say about maintaining membership control can be summarized as *intensive interaction*. Lofland (1966) also used this term to describe how the Doomsday Cult maintained control over its members. In its most extreme form, intensive interaction is found within communes, such as the People's Temple settlement in Jonestown. Typically, commune members sleep together in dormitories, eat together in large dining halls, and work together in fields, kitchens, and laundries. There are almost daily meetings of the entire commune to pray, conduct business, or engage in recreation.

Movements foster intensive interaction in other ways. A meeting hall or headquarters can provide a place where members can gather for meetings or just "hang around." Weekends can be reserved for prayer meetings, picnics, or excursions for members. Movements typically maintain mailing lists and telephone directories of members. The mailing of announcements, minutes of meetings, or newsletters can provide frequent contact between the leaders and members.

Intensive interaction also means that movements try to promote a sense of urgency among the members. In many instances, the need for urgent action in pursuit of movement goals is fairly self-evident. At other times, movements become intensely involved in activities that seem only vaguely related to their stated goals. In either event, movements typically lose ground if they fail to keep their members busy.

For militant groups, intensive interaction centers on preparing for conflict. Day-to-day activity centers on learning how to use weapons and on martial arts drills. Members may practice mock attacks and stage war games.

For millennial movements, intensive interaction centers on making preparations for the day of judgment. For nearly all social movements, intensive interaction develops around recruiting new members and planning demonstrations.

Lofland (1966) noted that Doomsday Cult recruitment setbacks were immediately followed by periods of intense activity to achieve ends that usually had little relationship to movement goals. These activities included moving their headquarters or initiating remodeling projects. When these undertakings were completed, the movement turned again to recruiting new members. Though intensive interaction may involve the entire membership, it usually serves to maintain control over the central core of the movement.

Movement leaders can sometimes generate conformity among the members by threatening to leave the movement. This tactic was frequently employed by Jim Jones. Other leaders have impressed conformity on the movement by fasting or by doing some other penance for the errors of the followers. These tactics work only for leaders who enjoy nearly unanimous support within their movement. Without such support, these tactics can ruin a movement by destroying the leader's credibility or breaking the movement into factions.

Finally, movements maintain discipline by screening the membership. Days before many sit-in demonstrations, civil rights groups held workshops to train members in the tactics of nonviolence. Those who planned to take part in the sit-ins were insulted, jeered, spat upon, slapped, punched, and kicked. Those who were unable to remain passive in the face of such abuse were not allowed to demonstrate (Belfrage 1965; Peck 1962). Organizers of protest against the Vietnam War tried to exclude "crazies" from their demonstrations. Crazies often disrupted otherwise peaceful demonstrations by attacking police and spectators, damaging property, interrupting speeches, or acting bizarre in front of the television cameras. Attempts were made to exclude the crazies because they were unpredictable and the antiwar movement was often judged on the basis of its most visible elements, such as the crazies. Finally, many felt that the crazies were actually police agents sent to incite violence and thereby discredit the antiwar movement (Marx 1974).

Movement Decline

Turner and Killian note that both success and failure can lead to movement decline. For the relatively few social movements that achieve their goal of societal reform, success removes the reason for the movement's existence. Millennial movements usually disintegrate after their prophecy of doomsday fails to materialize.

Most movements, however, decline without obtaining clear success or having decisive failures. They just wither away. Many movements fail when major political parties adopt their rhetoric and, sometimes, their causes. The "Tax Rebellion" of the late 1970s consisted of numerous local movements to cut taxes. The rebellion floundered as tax cutting became a constant theme of the Republican and Democratic parties.

Movements that are clearly centered on a particular leader fail if the leader dies or is discredited. The Black Muslim movement fell into confusion and decline after the assassination of Malcolm X, and the anti-Communist movement of Senator Joseph McCarthy lost considerable headway following his congressional censure.

Finally, movements decline from what Turner and Killian describe as "combat fatigue." For many, intense involvement in a social movement places severe strain on their relationships with family, friends, neighbors, and their careers. Movement activities are often emotionally and physically exhausting. People are drawn to social movements in part by the discovery of new, interesting, and rewarding interpersonal relationships. Over time, as with most social relationships, these ties lose some of their appeal. Indeed, though members may achieve considerable gratification while participating in social movements, for most people, other stresses also accumulate as a result of participation, and the stresses eventually outweigh the gratifications.

The Value-Added Perspective and Social Movements

Neil J. Smelser distinguishes social movements from *general movements*. General movements are shifts in societal norms and values that occur sporadically and without unity or focus. These include the labor movement, the peace movement, secular humanism, and feminism. For Smelser, these movements are composed of many groups often working at cross purposes with one another and clearly lacking a sense of shared purpose. Such movements are characterized by periods of intense activity and periods of inaction. General movements represent a type of "cultural drift" and are not sufficiently crystallized to be considered collective episodes.

A social movement has a clear focus and a sense of direction and is likely to be composed of fewer groups than general movements. Participants in a social movement have a clear awareness of common identity, direction, and shared interests. Finally, a social movement is sufficiently coherent and concentrated in time and social strata that it constitutes a collective episode. For Smelser, there are two categories of social movements. Depending on their focus and the social conditions under which they develop, social movements are classified as either norm oriented or value oriented.

Norm-Oriented Social Movements

For Smelser, a norm-oriented movement is a "collective attempt to restore, protect, modify, or create norms in the name of a generalized belief." This definition means that participants in the movement are trying to change particular norms, or ways of doing things, in a society. The movement's focus is on the behavior of people either within the movement or outside the movement. Behavior may be changed directly, such as when a religious cult prescribes a certain lifestyle for its members, or indirectly, such as when a group works to get a particular law enacted. Any kind of norm—economic, political, educational, religious, or lifestyle—may become the focus of a movement. The result of a successful norm-oriented movement is usually a new lifestyle, custom, government agency, interest group, or political party.

The vanguard of a social movement is often a single group or organization. The Chicago Women's Club, for example, was the driving force behind the "child-saving" movement of the 1890s (Platt 1969), which culminated in the establishment of the juvenile justice system in the United States. The Chicago Women's Club operated a coordinated campaign of public speaking and private lobbying that resulted in the Illinois Legislature passing, with little alteration, the club's plan for the treatment of young criminal offenders in the jails and courts. Within months, the Illinois plan had been adopted in five other states.

Sometimes the same norm-oriented movement works through one group and then another. Smelser notes that in the 1880s, grievances of Midwest farmers were first voiced through the Farmers' Alliance, an independent association. Grievances were later articulated through a rurally based political party, the People's Party. Finally, the Democratic party became the channel for the expression of grievances.

Occasionally, the norm-oriented movement will work through several groups simultaneously. The movement against the Vietnam War operated through numerous groups, ranging from newly emerged militant groups such as the Weathermen to long-established pacifist groups such as the American Friends Service Committee (the Quakers).

The Value-Added Sequence of a Norm-Oriented Movement

In order to understand how the value-added process works to produce norm-oriented social movements, we must comment briefly on the nature of value-oriented social movements. As we shall see, norm-oriented and value-oriented social movements differ in scope. Norm-oriented movements seek to change a part of the society, while value-oriented movements frequently seek to change the entire society. The value-added process functions to keep a norm-oriented movement focused on a particular problem or issue.

Structural Conduciveness. Norm-oriented movements are likely when social conditions encourage the expression of limited demands rather than demands for fundamental changes in society. Demands are more likely to remain narrowly focused in societies where there is a clear separation between political, military, economic, and religious authorities, as in many Western democracies. Also, demands are more likely to remain narrowly focused when no single ethnic group monopolizes a particular sphere of authority. Under these conditions, movement demands tend to be formulated more in terms of specific programs for normative regulation than in terms of sweeping changes.

In societies in which religious and political authorities are one and the same, demands for change inevitably tend to be defined as "crusades" or "heresies." In societies in which political and military authorities are closely tied, demands for change are likely to become defined as "subversion" or "treason." When political power is monopolized by a single ethnic group, demands are couched in terms of the "moral rights" of the conflicting groups. Under such conditions, nearly any demand for change comes to be generalized into a conflict over fundamental values.

Norm-oriented movements are also encouraged by decentralized authority structures in which discontented groups can bypass the authorities and directly implement change. Thus, in the United States, newly formed religious groups are free to start their own private schools, segregationists are free to establish private playgrounds and pools, and natural food enthusiasts are free to start food cooperatives. Avenues for change, however, are never completely free of obstacles. If they were, change would occur without the need for joining together in a social movement.

Finally, norm-oriented movements are likely when there is a lack of opportunity for individual adaptive responses. Social movements among American farmers began to flourish in the 1880s because the frontier had disappeared, and farmers who experienced difficulties no longer had the option of moving westward and starting over.

Structural Strain. According to Smelser, collective behavior of any kind is an effort to reduce structural strain, which can arise in a number of ways. The most obvious and direct source of structural strain is a sudden decline in the availability of material rewards within a society. Economic recessions and depressions cause such declines. Lowered profits, unemployment, and inflation create conditions such that people's earlier standards of consumption are no longer attainable. Marked shifts in the distribution of material rewards can also produce strain. Distribution strains are produced by disasters, the relocation of factories and jobs, and the obsolescence of trades and skills.

Shifts in the definitions of major roles can produce conditions of strain. Changes in role definitions of women, for example, have brought about collective demands by women for equal job opportunities and pay, daycare programs, and, recently, equal insurance and retirement benefits.

The rise of new values can create strain with respect to social conditions that were previously taken for granted. The rise of "quality of life" values has led environmental groups to challenge longstanding industrial practices, such as the casual disposal of hazardous wastes. Campaigns to ban smoking in public places have replaced ad campaigns to encourage smoking. Christian fundamentalists advocate the banning of rock and roll.

For Smelser, all forms of collective behavior are an effort to reduce structural strain. To become a determinant of a norm-oriented social movement, structural strain must combine with conditions of structural conduciveness that narrow the focus of grievances.

Generalized Belief. Generalized beliefs place blame on specific groups and their policies for the conditions of strain. For example, early-parole programs or judges who are "soft" on crime are frequently blamed for rising crime rates by people who believe strongly in law and order. In the case of norm-oriented movements, generalized beliefs identify a rather clear and definite object of blame. More generalized objects of blame, such as the "evils of capitalism," "secular humanism," or "the workings of Satan," are part of value-oriented movements.

Generalized beliefs go beyond merely casting blame. The generalized belief also offers a solution to the dissatisfying situation, such as passing a law, creating a regulatory agency, or scrapping an antiquated custom. Those committed to the belief feel strongly that adoption of the program will remove the source of the strain.

A generalized belief may be precipitated by the sudden symbolization of the conditions of strain. Such precipitating events include the arrest of a leader or a vicious act by a suspected agent. The clear refusal of authorities to take remedial action toward the dissatisfying conditions or the appointment of unpopular officials can also precipitate generalized beliefs. Finally, the threat of success by a counter-movement can promote a generalized belief. Events such as these focus attention and beliefs on a particular person, agency, event, or situation. In addition, precipitating events create a sense of urgency.

Mobilization for Action. Mobilization for norm-oriented movements occurs in three stages. First, there is the incipient phase of slow, searching activity. Typically, generalized beliefs have yet to become sharply focused, and a sense of urgency is absent. Movement followers are relatively few in number and are often people directly affected by the conditions of conduciveness and strain.

The real phase of mobilization occurs following sudden increases in conduciveness and strain and the full development of a generalized belief. Membership increases sharply among those experiencing strain. In the real phase of mobilization, the movement's program is discussed throughout the society, and speculation occurs as to the likelihood of movement success.

In the final, or derived, phase, members are attracted from more diverse groups than was initially the case. These new members often contribute to a widening or shift in movement aims. Once the movement's program has been implemented and its effects seen, changes in movement structure occur. Membership may be lost among initial followers because the program does not turn out to be as effective as envisioned in the generalized belief.

Changes in movement leadership usually occur during the derived phase. Leaders whose skills lie in the areas of stating grievances and developing campaign strategies are replaced by leaders with skills in seeking power and prestige for the movement. Leadership shifts during the derived phase contribute to changes in movement direction and membership.

Ironically, success can often lead to the disappearance of a movement because its reason for existence becomes moot. Failure leads either to the disappearance of the movement or to shifts in membership and goals. In the latter case, failed movements often leave behind small, highly cohesive, interest groups.

Action of Social Control. Authorities have the power to encourage, redirect, or suppress norm-oriented social movements. They may wish to encourage these movements in order to avoid the more sweeping challenges posed by value-oriented movements. For example, authorities may insist that movement expression remain within the bounds of law while also introducing bills requested by the movement. Further, authorities may give public hearing to complaints, even if there is no intention of acting on them.

Authorities may wish to redirect norm-oriented movements, again to avoid the more fundamental challenges posed by value-oriented movements. Authorities can redirect movements by encouraging particular kinds of programs or solutions and discouraging others. They can also redirect movements by co-opting the movement leadership through the manipulation of power and prestige rewards. Appointing leaders to commissions or agencies or granting them personal channels of communication with authorities can serve to re-direct norm-oriented movements.

Authorities suppress norm-oriented movements in the hope that more general movements will not arise. Suppression may be blatant, as when authorities attempt to arrest or, in extreme instances, deport or kill movement followers. Under such conditions, a militant underground movement is usually created. Most suppression is less blatant.

Authorities who suppress norm-oriented movements may feel that they are being "quite reasonable" and may be unaware that they are encouraging less desirable collective expressions. This type of suppression includes the refusal to recognize the movement and its demands, as well as suggestions that the movement represents only a small and "noisy" or "uninformed" minority. Authorities can also suppress norm-oriented movements by taking sides with countermovement groups. Such acts arise from authorities' negative stereotypes of the movement and their sympathies for those who voice opposition to the movement. This lack of impartiality by authorities may channel norm-oriented movements into other types of collective behavior, such as hostile outbursts or value-oriented movements.

Value-Oriented Social Movements

A value-oriented social movement works toward a much larger and more general change in society than does a norm-oriented movement. Smelser defines the *value-oriented movement* as a "collective attempt to restore, protect, modify, or create values in the name of a generalized belief." The generalized belief is often so elaborate that it takes the form of a complex world view, or ideology. The belief sets forth new values or revives old values, and it views social relationships based on present values as evil, destructive, or in a state of decay. The rewards for complying with societal norms and conscientiously fulfilling statuses and roles are seen as worthless or unfair. In short, the generalized belief upon which a value-oriented movement is based portrays present social conditions as hopelessly beyond repair. Only a far-reaching and fundamental change can set things right.

For Smelser, in the most elementary form of the value-oriented movement, adherents see themselves not as agents of change but as beneficiaries of change. This is particularly true with *nativistic*, *messianic*, and *millennial* movements, which are dominated by mystical or religious beliefs. Nativistic movements occur among defeated and oppressed people who still retain remnants of their own culture. Though these people lack the means to overthrow their oppressor, they can envision a swift and imminent return to old and better ways. Smelser identifies the Ghost Dance movement among the Sioux as a nativistic movement.

Messianic movements envision a similar transformation of the present order. The transformation is at the command of the savior or messiah, and followers of the messiah will be rewarded for their faith and loyalty by receiving preferred statuses in the new order. Perhaps the most successful messianic movement was the early Christian movement. Millennial movements are similar to messianic movements in that they envision the return of the savior on a day of judgment. The faithful will be rewarded and the unfaithful punished at the millennium.

Other value-oriented movements include sect formation. Sects are commonly defined as splinter groups from larger, established religions. The sect usually splits from the larger church because of differences over the interpretation of scripture or religious experiences. Thus, beliefs are the central focus of the sect at the time of its formation and departure from the parent church.

Utopian movements center on a unique lifestyle derived from the values of the group. Often, utopian movements rely on recruitment by example. The Utopian Socialists of the 1870s, for example, felt that their communes would be such models of order and prosperity that others would imitate them and voluntarily cast capitalism aside. Utopian movements, if they survive, usually evolve into small, exclusive, and self-contained groups with little interest in transforming the rest of society.

Finally, value-oriented movements include large-scale political revolutions that fundamentally transform or destroy the social institutions of the old order. The American Revolution overthrew the institutions of colonialism. The French Revolution ushered in a modern industrial order by demolishing the institutional base of the older agrarian society—the monarchy and the Church. Finally, the Russian Revolution swept away an unwieldly mixture of monarchy, feudalism, and capitalism to establish the basis of a socialist society.

The Value-Added Sequence of a Value-Oriented Movement

In the case of value-oriented movements, the value-added determinants function to keep the movement oriented toward producing a fundamental transformation of society.

Structural Conduciveness. As noted earlier, value-oriented social movements are most likely in societies in which there is little if any separation between political, military, economic, and religious authorities. Under such conditions, any demand for normative change is likely to immediately generalize into value conflict.

Value-oriented movements are more likely than norm-oriented movements among groups with severely restricted access to legitimate channels for expressing grievances. Such groups include colonized peoples, slaves, native populations suppressed by foreigners, outcasts, and the extremely poor. Nativistic, messianic, and millennial movements are the most likely value-oriented movements to develop among these people.

Structural Strain. Strain arises when people lack the knowledge and skills to successfully cope with problematic situations. When conditions producing strain are seemingly far beyond people's capacity to explain in ordinary terms, mystical explanations suggest themselves. Nativistic and millennial movements flourished during the plagues of the Middle Ages. Nativistic movements occur among colonial peoples who have not assimilated knowledge of the technology, economy, and customs of their masters.

Generalized Belief. A value-oriented belief sets forth the role of the movement in the coming transformation of the social order. If members perceive that the means of bringing about change are closed to them, as is often the case among subjugated and demoralized people, then the movement is likely to assume a passive role in this transformation. The most passive form of a value-oriented movement is a collective retreat from everyday life into intoxicating activity. Peyote cults among Indians of the Southwest exemplify this extreme form of a value-oriented movement. A less passive movement relies on the hope that rituals and supplication will bring forth the millennium of an avenging messiah or cultural hero. The Ghost Dance is an example of this form of movement.

Movements develop an activist orientation when members perceive the possibility of causing change themselves. The simplest form of activism is found in movements that try to achieve separation of the tormented from their tormentors. Such movements take the form of a migration in search of the "promised land" to establish a utopian community. A stronger activist orientation is found in evangelical movements, such as the born-again movement among fundamentalist Christians. Evangelism is partly based on the belief that mass conversions will change society in the desired ways. In extreme instances, conversion can be forced on others. Finally, the most developed sense of activism is found in movements that seek the outright destruction of the old order. Revolutionary movements fall within this category.

Mobilization for Action. Value-oriented movements are almost always initiated by charismatic leaders—people whose authority resides primarily in their personal manner, the force of their convictions, and their ability to convince others to follow them. Smelser notes that charismatic leadership is particularly valuable in the incipient phase of movement growth.

Value-oriented movements are more prone to the divisive effects of accommodation than are norm-oriented movements. Norm-oriented movements usually pursue definite and well-defined aims, and accommodations to achieve these aims can readily be evaluated in terms of their results. Value-oriented movements pursue much broader aims. After prolonged effort, idealists begin to feel that these aims cannot be realized, and they lose hope for the movement. Committed members begin to feel that practical compromises represent backsliding and degeneration of the movement. These concerns are likely to generate internal conflict that results in movement fragmentation or collapse.

Nearly all value-oriented movements fail to bring about the changes they envisioned. In the face of this failure, some movements fade away totally, though a few condense into closely knit and exclusive groups. Some movements, such as the Communist party of the Soviet Union, live on in institutionalized form to oversee the changes they produced.

Action of Social Control. Smelser sets forth a model for peacefully containing value-oriented movements. First, authorities must clearly rule out the expression of hostility through violence by the movement. This is accomplished by the quick, decisive, and impartial use of force in response to the very first violent outbursts by the movement.

Second, authorities must rule out direct challenges to the legitimacy of the government. This is accomplished by clearly identifying those governmental activities that are not open to challenge. Any change in the scope of legitimacy must be clearly restricted and implemented by defined procedures, such as constitutional amendment.

Third, authorities must open manageable channels for peaceful agitation for change. They must permit a meaningful and public airing of grievances. They must at least accommodate and perhaps even encourage peaceful demonstration.

Finally, authorities must make meaningful attempts to reduce the source of strain that initiated the movement. In fact, it may be difficult for authorities to take such a stance in those instances in which the strain derives from the status of colonial subject, slave, or outcast groups.

If authorities behave in this fashion, Smelser argues, then the value-oriented movement should make accommodations to the larger society or disappear altogether. In some instances, the value-oriented movement may be transformed into a less threatening, norm-oriented movement.

Summary

Social movements represent the most encompassing and largest-scale phenomena included in the field of collective behavior. In this chapter we have presented the traditional approaches to social movements embodied in the mass hysteria, emergent norm, and value-added perspectives.

From the standpoint of the mass hysteria perspective, Blumer defines social movements as "collective enterprises to establish a new order of life." Social movements arise from a number of patterns of social unrest that make people psychologically receptive to movement ideologies that "explain" and offer "solutions" to their difficulties. A social movement follows a life cycle of increasing formalization until it comes to constitute a social institution. Klapp notes that some social movements lack the coherence of the life cycle suggested by Blumer. He refers to such movements as "meaning-seeking" movements, which arise from patterns of social unrest characterized by "boredom" with the established order. Klapp uses this line of analysis to explain the hippie movement of the 1960s.

From the standpoint of the emergent norm approach to social movements, Turner and Killian define social movements as a collectivity acting with some continuity to promote or resist social change. They suggest that social movements develop through the interplay of value, power, and participation orientations rather than through a definite life cycle. Underlying nearly all social movements are norms that reflect a sense of injustice or the conviction that existing conditions are wrong and in need of change. Movement goals and ideology are not necessarily logically derived from the material conditions that give rise to the sense of injustice. Movement goals and ideology frequently take the form of scapegoating and simplified world views.

For Turner and Killian, the commitment of members to a social movement does not arise from their aroused emotion. Instead, membership commitment is maintained through processes of conversion, esprit de corps, rewards for participation, personal ties to the movement, and the breaking of ties with conventional life. Leaders of social movements maintain control over committed members by creating a siege atmosphere, or a constant fear of external attack, and maintaining what Lofland refers to as intensive interaction within the movement. Leaders may also exercise control by threatening to leave the movement and by excluding members who fail to live up to

the standards of movement discipline. Finally, a social movement experiences decline when established groups adopt some of its rhetoric and causes, when movement leaders die or are discredited, and/or when members become exhausted and bored.

Smelser's value-added perspective defines social movements as uninstitutionalized efforts to alter the determinants of social action. Norm-oriented social movements are efforts to alter the normative structure of society and are characterized by reform movements. Norm-oriented movements are likely to arise in societies in which there is a clear separation between the economic, religious, and political spheres. Ample opportunities for the expression of dissent and the implementation of change without the approval of authorities also contribute to the formation of norm-oriented social movements. In the absence of such conditions, dissent is quickly labeled by authorities as heresy or treason. Under these conditions, social movements tend to pursue much larger social transformations. Smelser refers to these as value-oriented movements, which include nativistic, messianic, millennial, and revolutionary movements. These movements usually arise among the most severely oppressed people. Authorities are seldom able to make lasting, mutually agreeable accommodations with such movements.

CHAPTER 15

Social Movements and Mobilization

Sociologists have recently given attention to how social movements mobilize or otherwise obtain resources to support their efforts. These resources include a sizable and active membership, well-attended demonstrations and rallies, and the ability to turn out votes for political candidates and referendums. Resources also include such material goods as money, cars, and buses; buildings for headquarters, meetings, and housing; and even businesses. Movements mobilize material resources by way of donations or by accumulating enough cash to buy needed items.

We begin this chapter with a consideration of Poland's Solidarity movement. We will then use the SBI perspective to examine the processes involved in mobilizing people for demonstrations and rallies. Well-attended and organized demonstrations and rallies not only contribute to movement credibility, they also contribute to membership discipline and enthusiasm and help press movement demands.

The mobilization of people and other resources is facilitated when movements adopt formal structures similar to those found in businesses and voluntary associations. The adoption of formal structure can alter the character and goals of a movement. In the second half of this chapter, we will consider the resource mobilization perspective set forth by

Zald, Ash, and others, which applies formal organization theories and hypotheses to the study of social movements.

Poland's Solidarity movement utilized demonstrations, rallies, and strikes to press its demands upon the socialist government of Poland. Solidarity adopted a number of formal structures to take these actions. The movement's growing strength and increasing demands set a collision course with the government of Poland, and although government response shattered the formal structure of Solidarity, it still remains a force to be contended with in Polish society.

Poland's Solidarity Movement

"Walesa is here! Walesa is here!" Cheers were raised as Lech Walesa, a short, stocky man with reddish-brown hair and a thick handle-bar mustache, slipped over the fence and into the Lenin Shipyard at Gdansk, Poland. It was the middle of August 1980, and workers had called a peaceful strike to demand pay raises and improved working conditions. The strike looked as if it were about to collapse until Walesa made his appearance. The workers knew and respected Lech Walesa, the electrician who had been fired eight months earlier for trying to organize a trade union. He had also been one of the leaders during the violent Lenin Shipyard strike of 1970.

Immediately, Walesa and others set about organizing for a protracted strike. They set up the Inter-Plant Strike Committee (MKS) to co-ordinate strikes in other areas of Poland and held meetings to clarify and agree upon worker demands. They also set up patrols to prevent the sabotage of shipyard equipment.

This was not the first time that Polish workers had tried to force concessions from their government. After World War II, Poland was brought under Russian control, and in terms of its structure, Poland's government was a carbon copy of the Soviet system. The Polish Communist party was run by the Soviets, a Russian general acted as Polish minister of defense and commander in chief of the Polish Army, and Soviet officers held other high offices in Poland's armed forces and government.

In June of 1956, riots occurred in the western city of Poznan. Demands were made for better living conditions and increased economic and political freedoms. Rioting and strikes soon spread to other areas, and a new communist government was established in October. It was headed by Wladyslaw Gomulka, a Polish nationalist who had once been kicked out of the Communist party and imprisoned for "right-wing" activities. Soviet officials were removed from their military and government posts and from Poland's Communist party. Economic planning was decentralized, and workers' councils were established to increase productivity.

Though Russians were not returned to Polish offices, the economic reforms brought about by the Poznan rioting eroded quickly, in part because Polish industries and agriculture were in great need of modernization. Rioting broke out again in 1970, the most bitter at the Lenin Shipyard. Workers sabotaged machinery and destroyed the Communist party head-

quarters, and many were killed as security police restored order. The Workers' Defense Committee (KOR) was formed to obtain the release of those arrested. Gomulka resigned and was succeeded by Edward Gierek. Gierek established the modernization of the Polish economy as the government's first priority. Wages were raised, supplies of consumer goods were increased, and about $20 billion were borrowed from Western sources to finance the modernization of industry.

Poor planning and the oil crisis of the 1970s contributed to the failure of these efforts. The supply of consumer goods soon fell far short of demand, new factories were poorly designed and managed, and severe inflation and a thriving black market undermined economic reforms. Finally, on July 2, 1980, the announcement of price hikes of 60 percent for some cuts of meat touched off strikes and rioting (Schaufele 1981).

Walesa presented the shipyard workers' demands to government negotiators in mid-August (see box, pp. 308–309). During negotiations, nearly all forms of censorship were laid aside, foreign journalists operated freely, and strikers across Poland were able to use telephones and telex. On August 31, the signing of the Gdansk Accords was televised throughout Poland.

The strikers won nearly all of their original demands. The accords assured government acceptance of free trade unions, independent of the Communist party, as well as the right to strike. Other concessions included reduced censorship and union access to government broadcasting facilities. Gierek resigned as first secretary of Poland's Communist party for health reasons, and Stanislaw Kania replaced him.

Within weeks nearly 10 million workers had joined numerous local unions under the popular title of Solidarity. During the same time, nearly a million people resigned from Poland's Communist party. Economic conditions in

The Demands of the Polish Workers

Demands of the striking work-teams at workplaces and businesses represented by the Inter-Factory Strike Committee:

The Inter-Factory Strike Committee represents both work-teams and institutions whose functioning is socially indispensable. This committee's goal is the carrying-on of negotiations to fulfill the expectations of the striking work-teams.

One of the five conditions of beginning negotiations is the unblocking of all telephones.

The demands of the striking work-teams represented by the Inter-Factory Strike Committee are as follows:

1. Acceptance of free trade unions independent of the party and employers in accordance with Convention No. 87 of the International Labor Organization ratified by the Polish People's Republic, concerning the freedom of the unions.
2. Guarantee of the right to strike and the security of the strikers and persons aiding them.
3. Compliance with the guarantee in the Constitution of the Polish People's Republic of freedom of speech, the press, and publication, and likewise the nonrepression of independent publishers, and the making available of the mass media to representatives of all faiths.
4. (a) A returning of their former rights to: people dismissed from work after the 1970 and 1976 strikes; students expelled from school for their convictions.
   (b) The freeing of all political prisoners (among them, Edmund Zadrozynski, Jan Kozlowski, and Marek Kozlowski).
   (c) An end to repression for one's convictions.
5. Making information available in the mass media about the formation of the Inter-Factory Strike Committee, and the publication of its demands.
6. The undertaking of actions aimed at bringing the country out of its crisis situation by the following means:
   (a) The making public of complete information about the social-economic situation.
   (b) Enabling all milieus and social classes to take part in discussions of the reform program.

Poland continued to deteriorate, while Solidarity pushed for more concessions. Walesa became a voice for moderation but still managed to win guarantees of a five-day work week on January 31, 1981. Nine days later, Kania was replaced by General Wojciech Jaruzelski.

Jaruzelski promised to honor the Gdansk Accords but requested that Solidarity, in turn, provide three months of labor peace to sort out the economy. Walesa also urged moderation, but wildcat strikes continued throughout the summer, and local unions began to demand the resignation of several communist officials. Walesa came under increasingly frequent attacks from other Solidarity (KOR) leaders for being too moderate. Finally, on December 12, despite the efforts of Walesa, Solidarity called for both a national referendum on the future of the communist government and a reexamination of Poland's military alliance with the Soviet Union. To paraphrase one commentator, this would be nearly the same thing as the AFL–CIO closing most of our factories and refusing to call workers back to their jobs until the president and congress resigned and the United States dropped out of NATO (Strybel 1981). That evening, Jaruzelski declared martial law in Poland. Thousands of Solidarity leaders and members were arrested within a few hours.

Walesa was jailed for nearly ten months before being released on November 14, 1982. In the meantime, the Gdansk Accords were set aside and Solidarity was outlawed. Numerous

7. All workers taking part in the strike are to be compensated for the period of the strike with rest leave paid for by the fund of the Central Council of Unions.

8. The base pay for each worker is to be raised by 2,000 zlotys/month as compensation for the recent rise in prices.

9. Automatic increase in pay is to be guaranteed, concomitant with the increase in prices and the fall in real income.

10. The internal market is to be fully supplied with food products, and only surpluses are to be exported.

11. "Commercial" prices are to be lowered, as is sale for hard currency in the so-called internal export.

12. The principle of the selection of management personnel on the basis of qualifications and not of party membership is to be introduced. Privileges of the SB (secret police), MO (regular police), and party apparatus are to be eliminated by equalizing family subsidies, abolishing special stores, etc.

13. Food coupons are to be introduced for meat and meat products (during the period of getting the market situation under control).

14. Retirement age for women is to be reduced to 50, and for men to 55, or 30 years employment in the Polish People's Republic for women, and 35 for men, regardless of age.

15. Old-age pensions and annuities are to be brought into line with what has actually been paid in.

16. The working conditions of the health service are to be improved to insure full medical care for workers.

17. A reasonable number of places in day-care centers and kindergartens is to be assured for the children of working mothers.

18. Paid maternity leave for three years is to be introduced for the purpose of child-raising.

19. The period of waiting for apartments is to be shortened.

20. The commuters' allowance is to be raised from 40 to 100 zlotys, with a supplement benefit for separation.

21. All Saturdays are to be nonworkdays. Workers in the four-brigade system or round-the-clock jobs are to be compensated for the loss of free Saturdays with increased leave or with other paid time off work.

INTER-FACTORY STRIKE COMMITTEE
Gdansk, August 22, 1980
Free Printshop of the Gdynia Shipyards

---

strikes and demonstrations occurred across Poland and were quelled by security police. During the summer of 1983, martial law was officially lifted, but many of the restrictions, such as censorship, remain in effect under the new government. Poland's economy still falters. Solidarity continues to be active as an underground organization, and the Gdansk Accords have not been forgotten.

The SBI Perspective and Social Movements

Nearly every social movement involves demonstrations. In the 1940s, auto workers used the sit-down strike. In the 1960s, the civil rights movement used the sit-in to desegregate lunch counters and restaurants, the "freedom ride" to desegregate interstate bus facilities, and "freedom marches" for voting rights. The National Indian Youth Council used fish-ins to press for Indian fishing rights in the Northwest. Truckers used their rigs to block the streets of Washington, D.C., during the gas shortages of the 1970s, and hundreds of farmers drove their tractors to Washington to protest federal farm programs. On any given day in the United States, there are local demonstrations against everything from unpopular officials to environmental threats.

The 1960s and 1970s witnessed several "occupation" demonstrations. Students on hundreds of campuses across the United States took over and held university administration buildings in protest of campus rules and the Vietnam War. In 1972 the American Indian Movement occupied offices of the Bureau of Indian Affairs in Washington, D.C. Out of this confrontation grew the seventy-day occupation of Wounded Knee, South Dakota. Both occupations were in protest of government mistreatment of American Indians. Finally, in the last few years, there have been numerous encampments near military bases in the United States, Germany, and England to protest the increased deployment of nuclear weapons.

Not all demonstrations are organized to protest something. Every election year we witness numerous demonstrations organized by advance workers to promote political candidates. We have also seen large religious rallies organized by the Unification Church, Billy Graham, and the Moral Majority. Most of us have participated in rallies before and after athletic events.

The Role of Demonstrations and Rallies in Social Movements

The Unification Church spent about $15 million organizing demonstrations and rallies between 1972 and 1976. The largest rallies were held at Carnegie Hall (1973), Madison Square Garden (1974), Yankee Stadium (1976), and the Washington Monument (1976). The Unification Church considered each of these a great success that added to the size of the movement and the morale of the members (Lofland 1979).

Lofland (1979) points out that organizing these demonstrations actually greatly altered the priorities of the Unification Church. The number of new recruits that joined because of the rallies was small compared to movement expectations. Though membership morale may have increased during part of this period, morale sagged toward the end because of ex-

haustion. Finally, the demonstrations and rallies produced a backlash of social criticism in the form of negative media coverage, local and federal investigations, and lawsuits by parents of converts.

The demonstrations and rallies carried out by Solidarity were probably a source of enthusiasm for its members and many other Polish workers. In the United States, these rallies and demonstrations were receiving glowing press coverage even while the president and many other commentators were denouncing strikes by American workers such as the air traffic controllers (PATCO). Still, some commentators realized that the growing numbers of demonstrations and rallies by Solidarity were making it increasingly difficult for the Polish government to reach some sort of face-saving accommodation with Solidarity. At least Walesa realized this in the months before the military government was imposed.

What is the role of demonstrations and rallies in the growth of social movements? Clearly, they represent more than theatrics and attention seeking, although these functions are clearly served.

Demonstrations are often the first public manifestation of a social movement. On February 1, 1960, for example, four black students from A&T College in Greensboro, North Carolina, sat down at a previously whites-only lunch counter at Woolworth's. This sit-in demonstration was a complete surprise to the white power structure of the city. Within two weeks, sit-ins had occurred in fifteen other North Carolina cities. In most instances, demonstrators were harassed, verbally and physically assaulted, and arrested. The emerging civil rights movement, however, received nationwide recognition (Zinn 1964).

Demonstrations can be used to test laws. In 1961, after the Interstate Commerce Commission ruled against segregated seating on interstate buses and segregated waiting rooms and lunch counters in bus terminals, a number of freedom rides were carried out to test this ruling (Peck 1962). In many instances, demonstrators were arrested on charges of trespass, disturbing the peace, and interfering with arrest. After numerous demonstrations, segregation ceased to be openly enforced, and in many instances, it disappeared altogether.

Demonstrations and rallies can also pressure authorities to take a movement's aims into account. Those arrested at demonstrations can swamp local jail and court facilities (Peck 1962). This is particularly true when demonstrators demand court hearings, appeal their convictions, and elect to serve jail sentences rather than pleading guilty, paying their fines, and going home.

Demonstrations and rallies can show movement strength. Civil rights organizations such as the Southern Christian Leadership Conference (SCLC), the Congress of Racial Equality (CORE), and the Student Nonviolent Coordinating Committee (SNCC) were first seen as small and weak organizations. But after mounting hundreds of demonstrations throughout the nation, they became recognized as a potent force for change in the area of civil rights (Zinn 1964).

Demonstrations and rallies can also create member commitment within social movements (Alinsky 1972). Participating in demonstrations gives members an opportunity to do more than give lip service to the goals of the movement. Taking part in a demonstration represents a public act of commitment both for the participants and for those who know the participants. Students who took part in civil rights and antiwar demonstrations frequently spoke of their actions as showing serious commitment to these ideals (Belfrage 1965). Often, these students had to defend their actions to worried and angry parents and concerned friends. For some, participation in the demonstrations and rallies contributed to a breakdown of social ties with those who opposed the aims of these movements. Conversely, the shared experiences involved in preparing for and carrying out demonstrations can clearly strengthen social ties among participants.

During extended periods of conflict, the attainment of movement aims can seem a very remote possibility. Leaders can promise victory in the distant future, but they need immediate accomplishments to maintain member interest and commitment (Lipsky 1968). Demonstrations and rallies can give focus and closure to movement activities. Thus a movement that is generally opposed to "godlessness" obtains much clearer focus when members picket and demonstrate against local adult bookstores or massage parlors. Planning for and carrying through with demonstrations creates intensive interaction among members and leaders. Alinsky (1972) notes that demonstrations and rallies often involve activities that are exciting or entertaining for the membership. Finally, because it is often unclear just what constitutes a successful demonstration, leaders have considerable freedom in declaring whether or not a demonstration was a success. A successful demonstration provides closure for a social movement: it is a battle won in the long war!

In short, demonstrations and rallies are an important and usually necessary component of social movements. To understand demonstrations, therefore, is to gain some understanding of social movements. McPhail (1983) reviews explanations and studies of participation in the demonstrations and rallies that are part of major social movements in the United States and Canada. He also expands the analysis of assembling processes to include the short- and long-range assembling involved in demonstrations and rallies.

Participation in Demonstrations and Rallies

Studies of participation in demonstrations and rallies can be roughly divided into two groups. First, some studies try to find out what kinds of people participate in demonstrations. These studies examine individual attributes, such as the socioeconomic status or attitudes of participants, and they sometimes compare the attributes of participants and nonparticipants. Other studies try to discover the kinds of social relationships that lead people to participate in demonstrations and rallies. These studies examine group and social network membership and participation. McPhail (1983) has reviewed both the attribute and social network studies.

Participant and Nonparticipant Attributes. There are two general attribute explanations of participation in demonstrations and social movements. One view is that participants usually have low socioeconomic status (SES), because low-SES people are more likely than others to feel deprived or discontented and have little access to established channels for the expression of their interests or grievances. The other view is that people of higher SES are more likely to participate in demonstrations and social movements, because they are more likely than others to feel politically effective, sensing that they can alter their situation by direct action.

McPhail (1983) reviewed studies that compare the socioeconomic attributes and attitudes of participants and nonparticipants in religious rallies and civil rights, antiwar, and campus demonstrations. Several moderate associations are reported between SES and attitudes toward civil rights, antiwar, and campus demonstrations. In general, low SES is associated with conservative or negative attitudes toward these activities. However, the relationship between SES and actual participation in demonstrations is less clear. Nearly all SES and participation associations are statistically insignificant or weak. Only two (of twenty) measures of SES variables are moderately associated with participation in civil rights demonstrations. These relationships suggest support for the high-SES explanation. Finally, one

study of a religious rally (Clelland et al., 1974) found that participants were slightly better educated, had higher incomes and occupational prestige, attended church more frequently, and expressed more conservative religious beliefs than others in the town in which the rally occurred.

Group and Network Membership. Some discussions of social movements suggest that participants tend to be social isolates. People with comparatively few social ties to family and community are likely to feel insecure and lonely. For them, participation in social movements provides a sense of belonging (Hoffer 1951; Catton 1957). Other discussions suggest that participants in social movements are drawn from those who are relatively well integrated into social life. People are drawn to social movements by way of social ties to family, friends, voluntary associations, and community (Morris 1981).

McPhail's survey indicates clear support for the social integration explanation of social movement participation. Extensive participation in black churches, colleges, and ministerial and civil rights organizations is clearly associated with subsequent participation in the black southern student sit-in movement of the 1960s (Zinn 1964; Morris 1981). Similarly, student participation in campus demonstrations of various types occurs by way of social ties to other students based on friendship patterns, residential proximity, and major area of study (Woelfel et al., 1974; Heirich 1971; Gales 1966). Similar support for the social integration explanation is reported for participation in the women's movement (Freeman 1975) and Pentecostal religious movements (Gerlach and Hine 1970).

Mobilization for Demonstrations and Rallies

Demonstrations and rallies consist of or are preceded by short- and long-range *assembling processes* in which spectators and members of the social movement are brought together. Movement leaders often select the locations and timing of demonstrations with the thought of producing large numbers of spectators. The mobilization of participants usually involves more elaborate and long-range efforts.

Spectators.   At many demonstrations, spectators may actually outnumber participants. The gathering of onlookers at the sight of a demonstration is similar to the short-range assembling that occurs at the scenes of accidents and fires. The sight of demonstrators sitting down, marching, or carrying signs and banners provides short-range visual cues that something is happening, while the chants and singing of demonstrators provide short-range audible cues that something is happening. Finally, demonstrators may block highways, bridges, streets, or sidewalks, thereby creating a gathering of captive onlookers. Spectator involvement is frequently limited to cheering or jeering, but occasionally spectators may either join or attack the demonstrators (Peck 1962). Controlling the spectators at the scene of a demonstration may create greater problems for the police than controlling the demonstrators does.

Spectators may converge over larger areas when demonstrations and rallies are given advanced publicity and are scheduled at convenient times, such as lunch hours. Work associates who normally eat lunch together may take their lunches to the rally. On university campuses, noon, late afternoon, and evening rallies tend to be accompanied by larger spectator crowds than rallies scheduled during prime class time—mornings and early afternoons.

Participants.   While the gathering of spectators at demonstrations typically follows along the lines of short-range assembling processes, the mobilization of participants in demonstrations—the active core—typically involves long-range assembling processes. Participants

may know of the demonstration weeks and even months in advance, and they usually converge over greater distances than spectators. Acts of political defiance, such as sit-ins, occupation of buildings, and blocking entrances to hazardous waste dumps, are usually planned in advance. When arrest seems likely, prior arrangements are usually made for bail money and legal counsel (Peck 1962). Finally, participants in demonstrations are usually at the scene much longer than any group of spectators. This is particularly the case for encampment or occupation demonstrations (Burnette and Koster 1974).

McPhail (1983) discusses ways in which organizers of demonstrations and rallies produce long-range assembling. One method of disseminating assembling instructions is known as *block recruiting*, in which organizers address long-range assembling instructions to known audiences and interest groups. Audiences include subscribers to special-interest magazines and newsletters, while interest groups include professional and trade associations, employees of public and private enterprises, political parties, and the thousands of other voluntary associations across the United States. The mailing addresses and telephone listings of these audiences and interest groups provide convenient and effective channels for spreading assembling instructions. In addition, these instructions can be repeated and augmented through informal networks of friends and acquaintances.

Assembling instructions can be included in announcements at group meetings prior to the demonstration. A show of hands or a sign-up list can be used to solicit public agreements to participate. People make additional commitments as they volunteer to provide rides or sign up for chartered transportation. Meetings also provide an opportunity to utilize friendship ties to urge participation.

Subsequent assembling instructions are directed toward likely participants by way of press releases, mail and telephone announcements, handbills, and posters. Finally, word-of-mouth assembling instructions provided by friends, family members, work associates, and neighbors are essential in producing long-range assembling for demonstrations. McPhail (1983) suggests that word-of-mouth is the most prevalant means by which people learn of pending demonstrations and rallies.

Long-range assembling instructions usually include the time and place of the demonstration, as well as a suggestion, invitation, or demand to attend. In addition, these assembling instructions usually specify likely demonstration activities, such as a march, picket, sit-in, celebration, or religious revival. Assembling instructions usually also include a justification for the demonstration and planned activities. McPhail (1983) refers to these justifications as "meta instructions."

Meta instructions include statements of strategy, values, and ideologies. People are urged to attend demonstrations because participation is in their group or self-interest (appeal to strategy) or because it shows commitment to certain values and ideology. Meta instructions include simple requests for large crowds to show support for a political candidate; they also include appeals to people to "bear Christian witness" by attending an antiwar demonstration. Meta instructions can effectively override competing instructions for activities that could preclude presence at a demonstration. Appeals to group or self-interest, values, and ideologies are a way to override such everyday concerns as shopping, visiting friends, or changing the oil in the car.

Availability to Carry Out Instructions. Thoughtful demonstration scheduling can further lessen the problem of competing demands and alternate activities. For the nine-to-five worker, noon-hour, evening, and weekend rallies are most accessible and most likely free of competing demands. Further, competing demands during these time slots can often be rescheduled to accommodate demonstration attendance. For senior citizens, unemployed union members, and housewives, morning and early afternoon rallies are also accessible. Some organizers can create availability for groups of people. For example, public agencies can give their employees extended lunch hours to participate in rallies that support an agency policy or incumbent officials. Teachers can dismiss classes for the afternoon so that students can celebrate important school victories or greet public officials or celebrities (Bruno and Greenfield 1971).

Access to Demonstration Site.   Attendance at demonstrations and rallies is made more likely when participants' access to the demonstration sites is increased. Organizers accomplish this by mobilizing a fleet of private automobiles or by chartering buses, trains, or airplanes. While these arrangements obviously increase accessibility to the demonstration site, they can serve other uses as well. Those who agree to provide rides for others and those who sign up in advance for charters are entering a firm and public commitment to be at the demonstration. Further, organizers are likely to contact these people several times prior to the demonstration with additional assembling instructions, such as when and where to meet, times of departure, and routes of travel.

Summary

A number of studies have tried to answer the question: Who participates in social movements? Findings suggest that there is no clear "participation-prone" personality, although people are selectively drawn into social movements on the basis of their ties to organizations and groups such as friends and family.

Finally, the assembling model provides insight into how people are mobilized for demonstrations and rallies. Organizers choose times and locations that are likely to produce large numbers of spectators. Participants are mobilized through long-range assembling instructions and meta-instructions. Frequent repetition of these instructions, the provision of transportation, and considerations of availability are necessary to override competing demands.

The Resource Mobilization Perspective and Social Movements

The mass hysteria, emergent norm, and value-added perspectives all share a common assumption regarding social movements, namely, that social movements tend to occur during times of social stress. This long and widely held view has been referred to as the "breakdown" tradition of social movements (Tilly 1975). Much discussion and research regarding social movements has been aimed, therefore, at identifying stressful conditions in society that give rise to social movements.

Many sociologists have been critical of the breakdown explanation of social movements. One objection has been that no one has been able to specify just "how much" stress is necessary to produce social movements. Another objection concerns empirical studies, such as those done by Gurr (1969) and Feierabend and colleagues (1969), which try to determine relationships between measures of social movement activity, particularly violent activity, and measures of system strain. Such studies, while very extensive, have failed to show clear relationships between measures of social movement activity and measures of deteriorating social conditions (Snyder and Tilly 1972).

Because of these problems, Meyer Zald and Roberta Ash (1964) set forth a new approach to social movements. Their work, and that of others who followed their lead, has come to be known as the *resource mobilization (RM)* approach to social movements. Resource mobili-

zation departs substantially from the central concern of the breakdown tradition, namely, identifying the kinds and levels of social strain that produce social movements. The RM approach assumes that there will almost always be sufficient strain, or breakdown, in society to produce social movement activity. The central concern in the resource mobilization approach is gaining understanding of how social movements accumulate resources, how they acquire members, and how they maintain member commitment.

Resource Mobilization: Definitions

At this point we must consider some definitions that are central to the resource mobilization (RM) perspective.

Social Movements. The RM perspective defines a *social movement* as the opinions and beliefs that indicate preferences for changing statuses, roles, and relationships among groups within the society. Opinions and beliefs may also indicate preferences for changing the distribution of rewards within the society (McCarthy and Zald 1977). A *countermovement* is the opinions and beliefs that arise in opposition to those of a social movement. Identified in this fashion, social movements and countermovements represent little more than noticeable shifts in people's views about their society.

Social Movement Organizations. Shifts of view, or social movements, become of consequence largely through social movement organizations. A *social movement organization (SMO)* is a complex and often formal organization that attempts to implement the goals of the social movement or countermovement. As such, the SMO represents the outward organizational manifestation of a social movement. An example of a social movement organization would be the Student Nonviolent Coordinating Committee (SNCC), which was organized in the 1960s to implement the goal of increased civil rights for blacks.

The RM definitions of social movements and social movement organizations represent a clear distinction that is not made in other discussions of social movements. In Smelser's value-added model, beliefs are essential in differentiating value-oriented from norm-oriented social movements. The RM approach generally keeps the "belief" components separate from and secondary to the organizational components of social movements. According to the RM perspective, the important differences and similarities among such diverse groups as civil rights organizations, paramilitary units, and environmental protest groups are their organizational goals, structures, and tactics rather than their ideologies, beliefs, and values.

Social Movement Industries. A social movement may foster a number of movement organizations that pursue nearly the same goals and use similar tactics. These groups compete for a limited amount of material resources and the same pool of potential members. In some instances, these SMOs may cooperate to mount large-scale demonstrations, boycotts, or lobbying campaigns. A cluster of similarly oriented and interrelated SMOs is referred to as a *social movement industry (SMI)*. One example of an SMI consisted of the Southern Christian Leadership Conference, the Congress of Racial Equality, and the Student Nonviolent Coordinating Committee. These civil rights organizations pursued similar goals and employed similar tactics during the 1960s. Further, they competed for donations and membership among segments of the population sympathetic to the cause of civil rights. Today, we see similar SMIs in the areas of environmental concern and religious fundamentalism.

The Social Movement Sector. The largest unit of analysis in the RM framework is the *social movement sector (SMS)*, which refers to

the large conglomeration of all social movement organizations within the society. In the United States, this includes all the diverse groups promoting causes ranging from environmentalism to religious revival. It includes groups favoring or opposing abortion, gun control, legalized marijuana, school prayer, and nuclear arms control. According to the RM perspective, some societies can support larger social movement sectors than others. The size of the SMS is dependent on the amount of discretionary income and time available within the society. Societies in which people can contribute considerable money and time to their favorite causes will have larger social movement sectors than societies in which people have fewer of these resources.

Resource Mobilization: Basic Processes

Fundamental to the RM approach to social movements is the assumption that social movement organizations can be understood in terms of formal systems, or the "institutionalization and goal displacement model of organizational transformation" (Zald and Ash 1966). What this means is that SMOs become increasingly formalized as they develop. The style of leadership, for example, comes to depend less on personal charisma and more on administrative skills. Social movement organization goals gradually shift from promoting social change to promoting the interests of the organization. In the end, fully developed SMOs function much like the formal organizations found in business and government. This suggests that SMOs develop along the life cycle described by Blumer.

According to the RM perspective, the transformation of SMOs during their life cycle can best be understood in terms of the classic theories of bureaucracy and organizational change developed by Max Weber and Robert Michels. General theories of collective behavior, such as

Smelser's value-added model, fail to address issues such as movement institutionalization, strategy, and the many resources that movements must control if they are to succeed (Barkan 1979).

The formal systems approach stresses the importance of formalized, *legal-rational* structures of authority within bureaucratic organizations. Initially, most SMOs are based on *charismatic* rather than on legal-rational authority. Typically, charismatic leaders create the rules under which they serve, and they have the power to alter these rules whenever they see fit. Often, charismatic leaders have no definite term of office—they are leaders for life—and the loss of a charismatic leader usually throws an organization into turmoil. As an SMO continues to operate, the authority structure tends to evolve in a complex and formal way. Rules that define the limits of authority proliferate and become more rational. Over time, then, systems of legal-rational authority emerge within SMOs, operating in much the same way as they do in bureaucracies. With legal-rational authority, leaders within the SMO become more or less interchangeable. Members of SMOs and bureaucracies see the authority structure as a way of "moving up" in the organization, thereby increasing member commitment.

As in bureaucracies, member commitment and productivity within an evolved SMO are maintained through the predictable reward structure of the organization. Some SMOs offer members salaries and room and board, while others may offer less tangible rewards, such as travel, achievement awards, and personal prestige. People take considerable time away from other concerns because the movement organization offers compensating material incentives.

Member Commitment.   Other theories suggest that member commitment to the movement and movement organization results from the strength of members' personal commitment to the goals and ideals of the movement. To the degree that leaders can maintain member enthusiasm and keep the movement organization faithful to the movement goals and ideals, members will remain with the organization. Movement organizations tend to split apart either because of attempts to change goals or because of inconsistencies between ideals and actions.

The RM perspective offers quite a different view of member commitment. The RM perspective suggests that member commitment is largely due to the movement organization's incentive structure; members remain committed to an SMO because they are rewarded for doing so. Rewards include *material incentives*, such as money and goods, *solidary incentives*, such as prestige, respect, and friendship, and *purposive incentives*, or the fulfillment of movement values. Some SMOs offer sufficient material and solidary incentives to maintain member commitment; in most SMOs, however, purposive incentives predominate. In practice, purposive incentives are usually manifested through quantitative achievements, such as successful demonstrations, fundraisers, and membership drives. Thus the achievement of material rewards is essential for both member commitment and organizational success. As long as the movement can provide tangible benefits, members will remain enthusiastic. Movement organizations falter or break up when they can no longer "bring home the bacon" for members.

Leadership.   The RM perpsective emphasizes the routinization of leadership within movement organizations. As SMOs grow, leadership becomes more like that of bureaucratic organizations. Leaders usually manage to get paid for their services: they may receive salaries and other perks or they may secretly or openly appropriate organizational resources. Movement organization leaders may become interchangeable; they may move from one organization to another or hold interlocking offices. The RM perspective notes that it is possible to pursue careers within social movement industries and sectors. Social movement–related careers may closely resemble those in business and government; in fact, they may even lead to positions in business and government.

Competition and Cooperation among Movement Organizations. Within social movement industries and sectors, movement organizations operate in much the same way as private businesses, corporations, and government agencies do within their respective industries and sectors. Most often, SMOs compete for scarce resources, such as money and membership, although they occasionally cooperate to maintain mutually advantageous positions in these markets.

Social movement industries are composed of inclusive and exclusive movement organizations. Inclusive organizations require a pledge of general support (and often money), without specific duties. Joining an inclusive organization seldom involves more than signing a registration form and mailing in a check. Inclusive SMOs require little activity from their members once they join: members can openly belong to other organizations and groups, required meetings are rare, and members needn't adhere to any particular lifestyle. Many environmental action groups are of this sort.

The exclusive organization is likely to hold new recruits in a long "novitiate" period, requiring them to submit to organizational discipline and orders. The exclusive organization requires that a certain amount of energy and time be spent in movement affairs, and it may demand a particular lifestyle from its members. Religious cults such as the Moonies fall within the exclusive organization category.

It would seem that organizations within a movement industry would cooperate with one another because they seek similar goals. But the RM perspective notes that a low level of interorganizational cooperation seems to be the rule. This is because SMOs are in direct competition for the same resources of individual and institutional support. Individual support includes votes, contributions, dues, and donations of goods and services, while institutional support includes political favors and grants from government and private agencies. Movement organizers often rely on unemployment compensation for subsistence, and student activists often live off their parents (Zald and McCarthy 1980). Under conditions of increased resource scarcity, fewer movements are likely to form, and conflict between existing movements is likely to occur.

Competition among inclusive organizations is likely to be civil and of low intensity. Because they require greater personal commitment from their members, competition among exclusive movement organizations is likely to be more intense and characterized by conflict, which can range from scathing public denunciations to sabotage and open violence.

According to the RM perspective, cooperation can occur for various reasons. Cooperation is likely when external threats confront a number of SMOs in an industry. Government broadsides against "environmental fanatics" are likely to bring forth a united reply from environmental groups. Inclusive groups find it easier to take cooperative stances than exclusive groups.

Cooperation is also likely when it is sure to produce immediate and tangible benefits. Movement organizations are likely to cooperate to press for passage of a mutually desired piece of legislation. In some instances, organizations may actually merge to win a coalition grant. Thus, small union locals merge to obtain greater financial and organizational support from national labor organizations.

Finally, cooperation is likely among organizations that have overlapping membership and leadership. This type of cooperation was observed among the SNCC, CORE, and SCLC civil rights groups in the 1960s.

Resource Mobilization: Praise and Criticism

The resource mobilization perspective is currently characterized as the "leading edge" of social movement theory and research (Zurcher and Snow 1981). It has clearly replaced the value-added perspective as the most popular paradigm for the study of social movements.

The RM perspective has shifted the analysis of social movements away from the longstanding concern with conditions of social breakdown and the characteristics and dispositions of individual participants. This earlier tradition has yielded few explanations of social movements that have withstood the probings of critics. Resource mobilization investigations now focus on the structure and operation of movement organizations.

Milgram and Toch (1969) once characterized Smelser's value-added model as a convenient means of organizing a large body of data. Much the same can be said of the RM perspective. Further, the RM perspective encourages us to examine the day-to-day processes that are part of social movement organizations. It also encourages us to examine, in greater detail than before, the interaction that occurs among social movement organizations during social movements. The RM approach was the first to emphasize that competition and conflict among social movement organizations can be more intense and consequential than the struggles of these organizations against organizations and agents of the established order. Perhaps internal dissension and group rivalry have destroyed more social movements than oppression by authorities has.

Social Movement Organization: Problems of Definition.   Some critics have noted that the definition of social movement organiza-

tions eliminates from consideration groups that have not achieved organization status but are nonetheless important to the development of movements. The RM perspective considers groups to be SMOs when they have "several levels of membership, lists of members, and a written document describing the structure of the organization" (Zald and McCarthy 1980; Gamson 1975). This characterization clearly ignores the early stages in the development of movement organizations, prior to their acquiring several levels of membership, lists of members, and bylaws. Until groups achieve this level of organization, they are outside the RM domain.

Further, some groups may well be active in social movements for extended periods while remaining comparatively undifferentiated. This includes local grassroots groups that are sufficiently small and sufficiently like-minded that levels of membership, a list of members, and bylaws are not needed. Many of the small, rural black churches that offered support to or participated in civil rights marches would fall within this category. This would also describe the structure of "affinity groups" and "cells" within revolutionary groups.

A social movement organization is defined as an organized group that identifies its goals as "changing some elements of the social structure and/or reward distribution of a society" (Zald and McCarthy 1980). How much change must a group seek to qualify as an SMO? It is unclear whether an organization can, from the RM perspective, become so well established that it ceases to be a movement organization. The RM perspective has identified many highly structured or long-established organizations as movement organizations. For instance, the National Association for the Advancement of Colored People (NAACP), the American Civil Liberties Union (ACLU), the National Organization for Women (NOW), the American Federation of Teachers (AFT), the National Education Association (NEA), and the United

FIGURE 15.1   *Social Movement Organizations*

Is this a social movement organization? The resource mobilization perspective uses theories of formal organizations to analyze social movements. Social movement organizations are patterned along bureaucratic lines, and members derive tangible benefits through participation in them. While the resource mobilization perspective offers some useful insights into social movements, one wonders if this small group constitutes a formal organization. Are tangible benefits being obtained by members during their midwinter demonstration? (Photo by Grant Bogue.)

Farm Workers Organization have all been identified as social movement organizations (Zald and McCarthy 1980).

Are groups such as those identified above sufficiently serious about changing social institutions to warrant being called social movement organizations? When members of these organizations also hold positions on government advisory commissions and corporate boards of directors or actively campaign for major-party candidates, their commitment to social change seems suspect.

If, indeed, organizations such as the American Federation of Teachers and the NAACP are to be considered social movement organizations, then it seems that virtually any established group could be classified as a social movement organization. For example, the Phillips Petroleum Corporation could be considered a movement organization when it spends millions of dollars to air commercials describing its latest efforts at environmental protection. The cost of this campaign likely exceeds the entire annual operating budget of most environmental activist groups. Further, Phillips's message is likely to reach far more people than any media campaign undertaken by environmentalists.

Sources of Organization. According to the RM perspective, SMOs develop formalized structures to facilitate the pursuit of goals. In the classic tradition of Weber, however, formalized structure emerges to achieve goals requiring the performance of repetitive tasks or tasks requiring more or less continuous effort (Bendix 1962:381–390). Because movement organizations seldom find it necessary to perform repetitive or continuous tasks, it would seem that pressures to formalize their structure must arise from other sources. For instance, groups may simply take on structure for the sake of appearances or because it is required that they do so. Some student groups, for example, develop constitutions and bylaws simply to meet university requirements. Religious, environmental, and charitable organizations develop and expand structure to comply with federal rules for tax-exempt status. Unless these structures are monitored by outside agencies, they are often shams that are ignored in the day-to-day activity of these groups. At the very least, these structures do not operate in the ways that they do in formal organizations that handle repetitive or continuous tasks.

Formal organization of a bureaucratic nature is often imposed on a group as a result of cultural expectations. In the United States, people impose formal structure on every conceivable voluntary association and special-interest group. In short, we tend to overorganize social life. Many of these structures seem to arise without any apparent reason other than "that's the way things are done." Presidents, vice-presidents, recording secretaries, and publicity officers are elected, and standard operating procedures and bylaws are adopted. Many times this tradition is more of a hindrance to effective action than it is a help. Nonetheless, when people prepare to take collective action typified by social movements, their first efforts tend to be organizational.

Forms of Organizational Administration. From the standpoint of the RM perspective, the formal structure of movement organizations operates largely along the lines of bureaucratic administration. Central to the bureaucratic form of administration is the use of legal-rational authority that separates the office from the office holder. Also central to the bureaucratic administration is formal training as a prerequisite of office and periodic review of performance. Though it is clear that many social movements utilize formal administration, the administration is often only a parody of, or bears no resemblance to, bureaucratic administration.

Administration within structured social movements often approximates what Weber termed *avocational* and *honorific* administration rather than the bureaucratic form. Both forms of administration operate in ways quite different from bureaucratic administration. In avocational administration, for instance, leadership and positions of influence fall to those who have the time and money to devote to these activities rather than to those who have had formal training or have talents in administrative skills. Many people in leadership and active core positions in social movements hold their positions by virtue of having time (or having made time) and material resources that allow them to participate more intensely than the rank and file. Their positions depend not so much on training, leadership ability, or administrative skills as on their being able to devote more time to movement activity than others.

In honorific administration, position is bestowed on the basis of favor and personal loyalty to the leader rather than on formal training, administrative skills, or even job performance. Jim Jones used an honorific style of administration within the People's Temple. He handed out positions of authority to his favorites and took them away from those he found personally offensive or overly assertive. Jones kept incriminating statements and documents on all his lieutenants in order to assure their personal loyalty.

Avocational and honorific styles of administration are fundamentally different from bureaucratic administration. Neither style clearly differentiates between the office and the office holder, as in the case of bureaucratic administration. In avocational and honorific administration, the nature and powers of the office are usually set by the office holder. In these forms of administration, there is seldom an orderly transfer of power. Transfer of power is characterized by conflict within the group, defections, factionalization, and purges.

In avocational and honorific systems, there are few direct checks on the well-entrenched leader's power. Movement goals and tactical decisions for attaining them are likely to be set by the leader, however eccentric, rather than by the interplay of social movement industry forces and the needs of members, as suggested by the RM perpsective.

In many structured social movements, power and influence go to those who can devote the most time and resources to movement activities. Jim Jones utilized powerful organizational techniques within the People's Temple. Avocational and honorific control operate quite differently from the bureaucratic means of organizational control considered within the RM perspective.

Organizational theory, which the RM perspective applies to social movements, has been developed largely with respect to bureaucratic forms of organization. Much organization that exists in social movements clearly operates along the lines of avocational and honorific administration. We know relatively little about these forms of administration. Rather than using theories of bureaucratic organization to understand social movements, we should examine social movements in order to better understand avocational and honorific forms of administration.

Personal Commitment. The RM perspective explains personal commitment to social movement organizations in terms of the movement's reward structure. People remain loyal and active because of immediate and real material incentives offered by the social movement. According to the RM perspective, a major task of movement leadership is to provide a structure of incentives that will attract and hold members. This view derives from the rational incentive explanation of behavior within bureaucratic organizations.

Some have argued that the RM perspective exaggerates the role of self-interest in social movement participation (Zurcher and Snow 1981; Perrow 1979). Statements of the RM perspective often use examples that cast movement participants and organizations in a self-interested and insincere light. For example, students protest the economic exploitation of migrant workers while their parents or federal loans pay their bills for their college education. Leaders and organizers live off unemployment compensation and member dues. Faculty and chaplains of tax-supported universities shirk their contractual duties while working with protest groups. Ralph Nader sued General Motors and used the proceeds to finance his enterprises (Zald and McCarthy 1980).

The RM perspective largely ignores the role of interpersonal loyalties and obligations (Zurcher and Snow 1981; Perrow 1979). These relationships function more openly in avocational and honorific systems of administration than in bureaucratic systems. Further, it has been shown repeatedly that friends, family, acquaintances, and neighbors play an important role in involving people in collective behavior events of all kinds (cf. McPhail and Wohlstein 1983). Many people become involved in social movements by way of shared activities with family members or friends. On the other hand, Lofland (1977) points out how some movement involvement is intensified by tactics that sever members' ties to their families and conventional groups. Finally, Jim Jones maintained control over members of the People's Temple through a combination of intense personal ties and interaction, misinformation, blackmail, threats, ritual chastisement, and isolation of the group in the dense jungles of Guyana.

In some instances, people flock to movement organizations that offer little or no material incentives for members. This was the case after the Three Mile Island nuclear accident (Barkan 1979). People sought out antinuclear groups to get information and to voice their grievances. This sudden peaking in interest created organizational dilemmas for these groups. People may temporarily utilize existing groups to express and resolve their grievances rather than to secure immediate tangible benefits.

Theories of Social Movements: A Discussion

The two most widely used theories of social movements in the last twenty years have been Smelser's value-added theory and the resource mobilization theory of Zald and Ash. Each has guided the thinking and research of a generation of scholars. Each theory sets forth in a different direction, and yet both encounter the dilemma of circularity.

The value-added theory views social movements and all other forms of collective behavior as responses to strain within a social system. According to this view, strain can result from conflict or from inconsistencies between values and norms. Strain can be generated by any deprivation, real or threatened and absolute or relative (Smelser 1962:245). Strain can

also result from inadequate knowledge. This view becomes circular because by these definitions, almost any event can be taken as evidence of structural strain.

The resource mobilization perspective substitutes rational incentives for structural strains. People are supposed to participate in movement organizations because it is clearly rewarding for them to do so. Movement organizations relate to other movement organizations primarily through efforts to maximize their own resources or market position within social movement industries. Within the RM framework, the rewards are usually tangible resources, such as money, votes, members, and weapons.

Rational, collective goal attainment strategies are possible only when movement goals are well defined, consensual, and relatively stable (Zurcher and Snow 1981). This is seldom the case. The goals of a movement organization are frequently unclear, and many movements have multiple goals (Gambrell 1980). Quite often, leadership and the membership see movement goals quite differently. The RM interpretation that a particular type of movement activity is rational and goal oriented often seems quite forced. There is the danger of confirming the rational incentive hypothesis on the basis of after-the-fact identification of resources, goals, and achievements.

In order to resolve the above problem, some have suggested expanding the definition of rewards to include nonmaterial incentives. Rewards would come to include political liberties, prestige, status, sanctification, atonement for sins, personal growth, and personal gratification. Viewed in this fashion, however, rewards and incentives are as broadly defined as structural strain. That is, virtually any outcome of a social movement could be identified as the "reward" that inspired it. At this point, the explanation of participation in terms of rewards and incentives becomes circular.

The above discussion is not intended to lead to the conclusion that the concepts of social strain and material incentives are totally useless in explaining social movements and the reasons that people participate in them. Granted, some disorganized societies seem to be "movement prone." At times, social movement organizations do compete for donations and members, and some movement organizations do use a portion of their resources to entice greater member participation. Still, these represent only a small portion of the problems we confront in the study of social movements.

We encounter the circularity dilemma when we broaden the concepts of structural strain and material incentives to encompass all or a very large portion of social movement phenomena. Perhaps the only way to avoid circularity is to restrict the use of these concepts to situations in which they apply in a clear and straightforward fashion. This would include only those instances in which most of the people involved clearly and similarly identify the problems facing them. Further, these people must be preparing to take action that, if successful, will obviously alter the situation in a manner beneficial to them. Such restrictions, however, would reduce the focus of these theories to very few social movements.

Although the RM perspective offers some valuable insights into social movement dynamics, it draws attention away from the nonbureaucratic aspects of social movements. It also poses the dilemma of identifying some long-established organizations, such as the American Federation of Teachers, as "typical" movement organizations. Though some structured social movements do utilize bureaucratic means of formal organization, many others use avocational or honorific means. We know relatively little about the characteristics of these other forms of administration.

It is beyond the scope of this discussion to outline a new general theory of social movements. For the time being, at least, we must be satisfied with midrange theories that attempt to account for portions of social movement phenomena. However, we can increase our knowledge of social movements through renewed attempts to carefully observe them.

In reading Mooney's (1896) description of the Ghost Dance, for example, one is overwhelmed by the study's attention to detail. Much of the description was obtained through firsthand observation and conversations with the people involved in the events of the Ghost Dance. Mooney spent nearly two years and traveled thousands of miles in collecting data on the Ghost Dance itself and the Indian culture from which it emerged.

When we read the discussions of nativistic and messianic movements found in collective behavior texts, it is obvious that much of what is contained in Mooney's study has been overlooked or generalized away. Not only does collective behavior need more studies like Mooney's, we need to more fully utilize the material contained in existing descriptions of social movements.

A Postscript

Your introduction to collective behavior, the most diverse field in sociology, is concluded. Those of us who work in the field thrive on this diversity of subject matter and on the wealth of competing theories. Although we have discovered much about collective behavior in the past twenty-five years, there is much yet to be explored. I hope some of you will join us in that exploration.

◆ BIBLIOGRAPHY ◆

Alinsky, Saul D.
   1972   *Rules for Radicals*. New York: Vintage Books.
Allport, Gordon W., and Postman, Leo J.
   1965   *The Psychology of Rumor*. New York: Holt, Rinehart & Winston.
Angle, Paul M.
   1975   *Bloody Williamson*. New York: Alfred A. Knopf.
Arnold, Kenneth, and Palmer, Ray
   1952   *The Coming of the Flying Saucers*. Amherst, WI: Amherst Press.
Asch, Solomon E.
   1958   "Effects of Group Pressure upon the Modification and Direction of Judgments," in Eleanore E. Maccoby, Theodore Newcomb, and Eugene Hartly (eds.), *Readings in Social Psychology*. 3d ed. New York: Holt, Rinehart & Winston, pp. 174–183.
Aveni, Adrian
   1977   "The Not-So-Lonely Crowd: Friendship Groups in Collective Behavior," *Sociometry* 40:96–99.
Bailey, Jane, and McPhail, Clark
   1979   "The Assembling Process: A Replication and Procedure for Further Study," paper presented at the annual meeting of the Midwest Sociological Association, Minneapolis, Minnesota.
Barkan, Steven E.
   1979   "Strategic, Tactical and Organizational Dilemmas of the Protest Movement against Nuclear Power," *Social Problems* 27 (1):19–37.
Barton, Allan H.
   1969   *Communities in Disaster: A Sociological Analysis of Collective Stress Situations*. Garden City, New York: Doubleday.
Beal, Merrill D.
   1963   *I Will Fight No More Forever: Chief Joseph and the Nez Percé War*. Seattle: University of Washington Press.
Belfrage, Sally
   1965   *Freedom Summer*. New York: Viking Press.

Bell, Daniel, and Held, Virginia
   1969   "The Community Revolution," *The Public Interest* 16 (Summer):142–177.
Bendix, Rinehard
   1962   *Max Weber: An Intellectual Portrait*. New York: Doubleday.
Berk, Richard A., and Aldrich, Howard E.
   1972   "Patterns of Vandalism during Civil Disorders as an Indicator of Selection of Targets," *American Sociological Review* 37:535–547.
Best, Richard L.
   1977   *Reconstruction of a Tragedy: The Beverly Hills Supper Club Fire*. Boston: National Fire Protection Association.
Black, Paul W.
   1912   "Lynchings in Iowa," *Iowa Journal of History and Politics* 10:151–254.
Blanchard, Eric D.
   1968   "The Poor People and the 'White Press,'" *Columbia Journalism Review* 7:61–65.
Blumer, Herbert
   1937   "Collective Behavior," in Robert Park (ed.), *Principles of Sociology*. New York: Barnes & Noble.
   1939   "Collective Behavior," in Robert Park (ed.), *Principles of Sociology*. 2d ed. New York: Barnes & Noble, pp. 221–279.
   1946   "Collective Behavior," in A. M. Lee (ed.), *New Outline of the Principles of Sociology*. New York: Barnes & Noble, pp. 170–222.
   1957   "Collective Behavior," in J. B. Gittler (ed.), *Review of Sociology: Analysis of a Decade*. New York: Wiley, pp. 127–158.
   [1934] 1969   "Outline of Collective Behavior," in Robert R. Evans (ed.), *Readings in Collective Behavior*. Chicago: Rand McNally, pp. 65–88.
   1972   "Outline of Collective Behavior," in Robert R. Evans (ed.), *Readings in Collective Behavior*. 2d ed. Chicago: Rand McNally, pp. 22–45.
Broom, Leonard, and Selznick, Phillip
   1968   *Sociology: A Text with Adapted Readings*. 4th ed. New York: Harper & Row.

Brown, Dee
1971   *Bury My Heart at Wounded Knee.* New York: Holt, Rinehart & Winston.
Brown, Earl
1944   *Why Race Riots?* New York: AMS Press.
Brown, Roger W.
1954   "Mass Phenomena," in Gardner Lindzey (ed.), *Handbook of Social Psychology* (vol.2). New York: Free Press, pp. 833–876.
Bruning, James L.
1964   "Leadership in Disaster," *Psychology* 1:19–23.
Bruno, Jerry, and Greenfield, Jeff
1971   *The Advance Man.* New York: Bantam Books.
Bryan, John L.
(1983) *An Examination and Analysis of the Dynamics of the Human Behavior in the MGM Grand Hotel Fire.* (Rev. ed.). Boston: National Fire Protection Association.
Buckner, H. Taylor
1965   "The Flying Saucerians: An Open Door Cult," in Marcello Truzzi (ed.), *Sociology and Everyday Life.* Englewood Cliffs, NJ: Prentice-Hall, pp. 223–230.
Buckwalter, Doyle W., and Legler, J. Ivan
1983   "Antelope and Rajneeshpuram, Oregon—Clash of Cultures: A Case Study," *Urbanism Past and Present* 16 (8):1–13.
Bullock, Paul
1969   *Watts: The Aftermath.* New York: Grove Press.
Burnette, Robert, and Koster, John
1974   *The Road to Wounded Knee.* New York: Bantam Books.
Bush, John C.
1979   *Disaster Response: A Handbook for Church Action.* Scottsdale, PA: Herald Press.
Cahill, Tim
1979   "Into the Valley of the Shadow of Death," *Rolling Stone,* January 25.
California Governor's Commission on the Los Angeles Riots
1965   *Violence in the City—An End or Beginning? A Report.* Los Angeles: City of Los Angeles.
Cantril, Hadley
1940   *The Invasion from Mars.* New York: Harper & Row.
1941   *The Psychology of Social Movements.* New York: John Wiley.
1966   *The Invasion from Mars: A Study in the Psychology of Panic.* New York: Harper & Row.

Catton, William R., Jr.
1957   "What Kinds of People Does a Religious Cult Attract?" *American Sociological Review* 22:563.
Clelland, Donald A.; Hood, Thomas C.; Lipskey, C. M.; and Wimberley, Ronald
1974   "In the Company of the Converted: Characteristics of a Billy Graham Crusade Audience," *Sociological Analysis* 35:45–56.
Cohen, Jerry, and Murphy, William S.
1966   *Burn, Baby, Burn! The Los Angeles Race Riots, August, 1965.* New York: Dutton.
Coleman, Terry
1972   *Going to America.* New York: Pantheon Books.
Conot, Robert
1967   *Rivers of Blood, Years of Darkness.* New York: Bantam Books.
Couch, Carl J.
1968   "Collective Behavior: An Examination of Some Stereotypes," *Social Problems* 15:310–322.
1970   "Dimensions of Association in Collective Behavior Episodes," *Sociometry* 33:457–471.
Cranshaw, Ralph
1963   "Reactions to Disaster," *Archives of General Psychiatry* 1:157–162.
Dacy, Douglas C., and Kunreuther, Howard
1969   *The Economics of Natural Disaster.* New York: Free Press.
Danzig, Elliott R.; Thayer, Paul W.; and Galanter, Lila R.
1958   *The Effects of a Threatening Rumor on a Disaster-Stricken Community.* Pub. no. 517. Washington, D.C.: National Academy of Sciences, National Research Council.
Davies, James C.
1969   "The J-curve of Rising and Declining Satisfaction as a Cause of Some Great Revolutions and a Contained Rebellion," in H. D. Graham and T. R. Gurr (eds.), *Violence in America.* New York: Bantam Books, pp. 690–731.
Demerath, Nicholas J., and Wallace, Anthony F. C.
1957   "Human Adaptation to Disaster," *Human Organization* 16:1–2.
Douglas, Jack D.
1967   *The Social Meanings of Suicide.* Princeton, NJ: Princeton University Press.
Drabek, Thomas E.
1969   "Social Processes in Disaster: Family Evacuation," *Social Problems* 16:336–349.

Drabek, Thomas E., and Haas, J. Eugene
1969 "How Police Confront Disaster," *Transaction* 6:33–38.

Drabek, Thomas E., and Quarantelli, Enrico L.
1967 "Scapegoat, Villains, and Disasters," *Transaction* 4:12–17.

Dynes, Russell R.
1970 *Organized Behavior in Disaster*. Lexington, MA: Heath.
1975 "The Comparative Study of Disaster: A Social Organization Approach," *Mass Emergencies* 1:21–32.
1978 "Interorganizational Relations in Communities under Stress," in Enrico L. Quarantelli (ed.), *Disasters: Theory and Research*. Beverly Hills, CA: Sage, pp. 49–65.

Erickson, Kai T.
1976 *Everything in Its Path: Destruction of Community in the Buffalo Creek Flood*. New York: Simon & Schuster.

Eszterhas, Joe, and Roberts, Michael D.
(1970) *Thirteen Seconds: Confrontation at Kent State*. New York: Dodd, Mead.

Evans, Robert R., and Miller, Jerry L. L.
1975 "Barely an End in Sight," in Robert R. Evans (ed.), *Readings in Collective Behavior*. 2d. ed. Chicago: Rand McNally, pp. 401–415.

Fagan, Brian M.
1976 "Introduction," in Brian M. Fagan (ed.), *Avenues to Antiquity: Readings from Scientific American*. San Francisco: W. H. Freeman, pp. 1–8.

Feierabend, Ivo K.; Feierabend, Rosalind L.; and Nesvold, B.
1969 "Social Change and Political Violence: Cross-National Patterns," in Hugh D. Graham and Ted R. Gurr (eds.), *Violence in America*. New York: Bantam Books, pp. 632–688.

Form, William
1958 *Community in Disaster*. New York: Harper & Row.

Franke, Richard H., and Kaul, James D.
1978 "The Hawthorne Experiments: First Statistical Interpretation," *American Sociological Review* 43:623–643.

Freeman, Jo
1975 *The Politics of Women's Liberation*. New York: McKay.

Freud, Sigmund
[1921] 1945 *Group Psychology and the Analysis of the Ego*. London: Hogarth.

Fritz, Charles E.
1961 "Disaster," in Robert K. Merton and Robert A. Nisbet (eds.), *Contemporary Social Problems*. New York: Harcourt Brace Jovanovich, pp. 651–694.

Fritz, Charles E., and Marks, Eli S.
1954 "The NORC Studies of Human Behavior in Disaster," *Journal of Social Issues* 10:26–41.

Fritz, Charles E., and Mathewson, J. H.
1957 *Convergence Behavior in Disasters*. National Research Council Disaster Study no. 9. Washington D.C.: National Academy of Sciences.

Fritz, Charles E.; Rayner, Jeannette F.; and Guskin, Samuel L.
1958 *Behavior in an Emergency Shelter: A Field Study of 800 Persons Stranded in a Highway Restaurant during a Heavy Snowstorm*. National Academy of Sciences, National Research Council. Washington D.C.: National Academy of Sciences.

Gales, Kathleen
1966 "A Campus Revolution," *British Journal of Sociology* 17:1–19.

Gambrell, Richard
1980 "Issue Dynamics in Student Movements," *Social Forces* (March): 187–202.

Gamson, William A.
1974 "Violence and Political Power: The Meek Don't Make It," *Psychology Today* (July): 35ff.
1975 *The Strategy of Social Protest*. Homewood, IL: Dorsey Press.

Gamson, William A.; Fireman, Bruce; and Rytina, Stephen
1982 *Encounters with Unjust Authority*. Homewood, IL: Dorsey Press.

Garrett, W. E.
1980 "Thailand: Refuge from Terror," *National Geographic* (May):633–642.

Gerlach, Luther P., and Hine, Virginia H.
1970 *People, Power, Change: Movements of Social Transformation*. Indianapolis, IN: Bobbs-Merrill.

Goffman, Erving
1974 *Frame Analysis*. Cambridge, MA: Harvard University Press.

Gregg, Richard B.
1966 *The Power of Nonviolence*. New York: Schocken Books.

Grimshaw, Allan D.
1960 "Urban Racial Violence in the United States: Changing Ecological Considerations," *The*

American Journal of Sociology (September): 109–119.

1968   "Three Views of Urban Violence: Civil Disturbance, Racial Revolt, Class Assault," *The American Behavioral Scientist* (March–April): 2–7.

Guillen, Abraham
1973   *Philosophy of the Urban Guerrilla, The Revolutionary Writings of Abraham Guillen*, Donald C. Hodges (trans.). New York: William Morrow.

Gurr, Ted R.
1969   "A Comparative Study of Civil Strife," in H. D. Graham and T. R. Gurr (eds.), *Violence in America*. New York: Bantam Books, pp. 572–626.

Gutschenritter, Martin J.
1977   "Operation CB/ID: Crime Prevention's Answer to CB Radio Thefts," *Police Chief* (April):62.

Haas, J. Eugene, and Drabek, Thomas E.
1973   *Complex Organizations: A Sociological Perspective*. New York: Macmillan.

Heirich, Max
1971   *The Spiral of Conflict: Berkeley, 1964*. New York: Columbia University Press.

Hitler, Adolph
1943   *Mein Kampf*. Boston: Houghton Mifflin.

Hobsbaum, Eric J.
1959   *Social Bandits and Primitive Rebels*. New York: Free Press.

Hoffner, Eric
1951   *The True Believer: Thoughts on the Nature of Mass Movements*. New York: Harper & Row.

Houseman, John
1948   "The Men from Mars," *Harper's* (December):74–82.

Hundley, James R., Jr.
1968   "The Dynamics of Recent Ghetto Riots," *Detroit Journal of Urban Law* 45:627–639.

Hunter, Floyd
1963   *Community Power Structure, A Study of Decision Makers*. Garden City, New York: Doubleday.

Hynek, James Allen
1972   *The UFO Experience: A Scientific Enquiry*. New York: Ballantine Books.

Jacobs, David M.
1975   *The UFO Controversy in America*. Bloomington: Indiana University Press.

1980   "The Debunkers," in Curtis G. Fuller (ed.), *Proceedings of the First International UFO Congress*. New York: Warner Books, pp. 123–138.

Jacobson, D. J.
1948   *The Affairs of Dame Rumor*. New York: Holt, Rinehart & Winston.

Jahoda, Gloria
1975   *The Trail of Tears*. New York: Holt, Rinehart & Winston.

Janowitz, Morris
1968   *Social Control of Escalated Riots*. Chicago: University of Chicago Press.

Johnson, Donald M.
1945   "The Phantom Anesthetist of Mattoon: A Field Study of Mass Hysteria," *Journal of Abnormal and Social Psychology* 40:175–186.

Jones, Rhys
1971   "The Demography of Hunters and Farmers in Tasmania," in Derek J. Mulvaney and Jack Golson (eds.), *Aboriginal Man and Environment in Australia*. Canberra: Australian National University Press.

Keerdoja, Eileen P., and Sethi, Patricia J.
1980   "CB Couldn't Keep on Truckin'," *Newsweek* (July 21):12.

Kelner, Joseph, and Munves, James
1980   *The Kent State Coverup*. New York: Harper & Row.

Kemp, William
1971   "Energy Flow in a Hunting Society," *Scientific American* 225(3):104–115.

Kerckhoff, Alan C., and Back, Kurt W.
1968   *The June Bug: A Study of Hysterical Contagion*. New York: Appleton-Century-Crofts.

Kerckhoff, Alan C.; Back, Kurt W.; and Miller, Norman
1965   "Sociometric Patterns in Hysterical Contagion," *Sociometry* 28:2–15. Also in Robert R. Evans (ed.), *Readings in Collective Behavior*, 1975. 2d ed. Chicago: Rand McNally College Publishing Co.

Killian, Lewis M.
1952   "The Significance of Multi-Group Membership in Disaster," *American Journal of Sociology* 57(4):309–314.

1954   "Some Accomplishments and Some Needs in Disaster Study," *Journal of Social Issues* 10:66–72.

Kinston, Warren, and Rosser, Rachel
1974   "Disaster: Effects on Mental and Phys-

ical States," *Journal of Psychosomatic Research* 18(6):437–456.

Klapp, Orrin E.
1972   *Currents of Unrest: An Introduction to Collective Behavior*. New York: Holt, Rinehart & Winston.

Klein, Lloyd, and Luxenburg-Ingle, Joan
1980a   "Smokey and the Beaver: Police and Highway Rest Area Prostitutes," paper presented at the 32d meeting of the American Society of Criminology, San Francisco.
1980b   "Those CB Hookers are Giving Prostitution a Bad Name!" Paper presented at the annual meeting of the Association for Humanist Sociology, Louisville, Kentucky.

Knoph, Terry A.
1969a   "Sniping—A New Pattern of Violence?" *Transaction* 6:22–29.
1969b   *Youth Patrols: An Experiment in Community Participation*. Brandeis University: The Lemberg Center for the Study of Violence.
1975   "Rumor Controls: A Reappraisal," *Phylon* 36:23–31.

Kohl, Larry
1981   "Encampments of the Dispossessed," *National Geographic* (June):757–775.

Kurjack, Edward B.
1971   "Prehistoric Lowland Mayan Community and Social Organization: A Case Study at Dzibilchaltun, Yucatan, Mexico," Ph.D. diss., Ohio State University.

Lang, Kurt, and Lang, Gladys E.
1961   *Collective Dynamics*. New York: Thomas Y. Crowell.

LaPierre, Richard T., and Farnsworth, Paul R.
1949   *Social Psychology*. New York: McGraw-Hill.

Latané, Bib, and Darley, John
1968   "Group Inhibition of Bystander Intervention in Emergencies," *Journal of Personality and Social Psychology* 8(4):377–383.

Lawson, Alvin H.
1980   "Hypnosis of Imaginary UFO 'Abductees,'" in Curtis G. Fuller (ed.), *Proceedings of the First International UFO Congress*. New York: Warner Books, pp. 195–239.

LeBon, Gustave
[1895]   1960   *The Crowd*. New York: Viking Press.

Lee, Alfred M., and Humphrey, Norman D.
1968   *Race Riot (Detroit 1943)*. New York: Octagon Books.

Lenski, Gerhard, and Lenski, Jean
1978   *Human Societies: An Introduction to Macrosociology*. New York: McGraw-Hill.

Levine, David Allan
1976   *Internal Combustion: The Races in Detroit 1915–1926*. Westport, CN: Greenwood Press.

Levine, Gene N., and Modell, John
1965   "American Public Opinion and the Fallout-Shelter Issue," *Public Opinion Quarterly* 29:270–279.

Lewis, Jerry M.
1972   "A Study of the Kent State Incident Using Smelser's Theory of Collective Behavior," *Sociological Inquiry* 42:87–96.
1982   "Crowd Control at English Football Matches," *Sociological Focus* 15:417–423.

Lieberson, Stanley, and Silverman, Arnold R.
1965   "The Precipitants and Underlying Conditions of Race Riots," *American Sociological Review* 30:887–898.

Lipsky, Michael
1968   "Protest as a Political Resource," *American Political Science Review* 62: 1144–1158.

Lofland, John
1966   *Doomsday Cult: A Study of Conversion, Proselytization, and Maintenance of Faith*. Englewood Cliffs, NJ: Prentice-Hall.
1977   *Doomsday Cult: A Study of Conversion, Proselytization, and Maintenance of Faith*. 2d ed. Englewood Cliffs, NJ: Prentice-Hall.
1979   "White-Hot Mobilization: Strategies of a Millenarian Movement," in Mayer N. Zald and John D. McCarthy (eds.), *The Dynamics of Social Movements: Resource Mobilization, Social Control, and Tactics*. Cambridge, MA: Winthrop, 221–228. Also in James L. Wood and Maurice Jackson (eds.), *Social Movements: Development, Participation, and Dynamics*, 1982. Belmont, CA: Wadsworth.
1981   "Collective Behavior: The Elementary Forms," in Morris Rosenberg and Ralph H. Turner (eds.), *Social Psychology: Sociological Perspectives*. New York: Basic Books, pp. 441–446.

Lohman, Joseph D.
1947   *The Police and Minority Groups*. Chicago: Chicago Park District.

McCarthy, John D., and Zald, Mayer N.
1973   *The Trend of Social Movements in America: Professionalism and Resource Mobilization.* Morristown, NJ: General Learning Press.

Mackay, Charles
1932   *Extraordinary Popular Delusions and the Madness of Crowds.* Boston: L. C. Page.

McLuckie, Benjamin F.
1970   "A Study of Functional Response to Stress in Three Societies," Ph.D. diss., Ohio State University.

McPhail, Clark
1971   "Civil Disorder Participation: A Critical Examination of Recent Research," *American Sociological Review* 36:1058–1073.
1978   "Toward a Theory of Collective Behavior," paper presented at the Symposium on Symbolic Interaction, University of South Carolina at Columbia, March 17.
1983   "On the Origins of Gatherings, Demonstrations, and Riots," paper presented at the annual meeting of the Midwest Sociological Society, Kansas City, Missouri.

McPhail, Clark, and Miller, David L.
1973   "The Assembling Process: A Theoretical and Empirical Examination," *American Sociological Review* 38:721–735.

McPhail, Clark, and Wohlstein, Ronald T.
1983   "Individual and Collective Behaviors within Gatherings, Demonstrations, and Riots," *American Review of Sociology* 9:579–600.

Maddocks, Melvin
1978   *The Great Liners.* Alexandria, VA: Time-Life Books.

Marighella, Carlos
1970   "Minimanual of the Urban Guerrilla," *Tricontinental Bimonthly* (January–February): 16–56.

Martin, Morgan
1964   "The True Face of Disaster," *Medical Times* (February).

Marx, Gary
1970   "Issueless Riots," in M. Wolfgang and J. F. Short (eds.), *Collective Violence Annals of American Academy of Political and Social Science.* Philadelphia: American Academy of Political Science, pp. 21–33.
1974   "Thoughts on a Neglected Category of Social Movement Participant: The Agent Provocateur and the Informant," *American Journal of Sociology* 80(2):402–442.

1980   "Conceptual Problems in the Field of Collective Behavior," in Hubert M. Blalock, Jr. (ed.), *Sociological Theory and Research: A Critical Appraisal.* New York: Free Press.

Masotti, Louis A., and Corsi, Jerome R.
1969   *Shootout in Cleveland.* New York: Bantam Books.

Medalia, Nahum Z., and Larsen, Otto N.
1958   "Diffusion and Belief in a Collective Delusion: The Seattle Windshield Pitting Epidemic," *American Sociological Review* 23:221–232.

Menzel, Donald H., and Boyd, Lyle G.
1963   *The World of Flying Saucers: A Scientific Examination of a Major Myth of the Space Age.* New York: Doubleday.

Merton, Robert K.
1960   "The Ambivalences of LeBon's *The Crowd*," introduction to the Compass edition of *The Crowd.* New York: Viking Press.

Meyersohn, Rolf, and Katz, Elihiu
1957   "Notes on a Natural History of Fads," *American Journal of Sociology* 62:594–601.

Mileti, Dennis S.; Drabek, Thomas E.; and Haas, J. Eugene
1975   *Human Systems in Extreme Environments: A Sociological Perspective.* Monograph no. 21, Institute of Behavioral Science, The University of Colorado.

Milgram, Stanley; Bickman, Leonard; and Berkowitz, Lawrence
1969   "Note on the Drawing Power of Crowds of Different Size," *Journal of Personality and Social Psychology* 13:79–82.

Milgram, Stanley, and Toch, Hans
1969   "Collective Behavior and Social Movements," in Gardner Lindzey and Elliot Aronson (eds.), *Handbook of Social Psychology* (vol. 4). 2d ed. Reading, MA: Addison-Wesley, pp. 507–579.

Miller, David L.
1975   "Class Attendance: An Empirical Examination of Periodic Assembling," Ph.D. diss., University of Illinois at Urbana–Champaign.
1979   "Assembling in the Company of Others," paper presented at the annual meetings of the Midwest Sociological Society, Milwaukee, Wisconsin.

Miller, David L.; Mietus, Kenneth J.; and Mathers, Richard A.
1978   "A Critical Examination of the Social Contagion Image of Collective Behavior: The Case of the Enfield Monster," *Sociological Quarterly* 19:129–140.

Mintz, Alexander
  1951   "Nonadaptive Group Behavior," *The Journal of Abnormal and Social Psychology* 46:150–159.
Momboisse, Raymond M.
  1967   *Riots, Revolts and Insurrections.* Springfield, IL: Thomas.
Mooney, James
  1896   *The Ghost-Dance Religion and the Sioux Outbreak of 1890.* Fourteenth Annual Report of the Bureau of Ethnography to the Secretary of the Smithsonian Institution, 1892–1893, J. W. Powell, Director. Washington, D.C.: Government Printing Office.
Morris, Aldon
  1981   "Black Southern Sit-In Movement: An Analysis of Internal Organization," *American Sociological Review* 46:744–767.
Moss, Peter D., and McEvedy, Colin
  1967   "Mass Hysteria," *Scientific American* 216:58.
Mostert, Noel
  1974   *Supership.* New York: Knopf.
Myers, Robert C.
  1948   "Anti-Communist Mob Action: A Case Study," *Public Opinion Quarterly* 12:57–67.
National Advisory Commission on Civil Disorders
  1968   Report. Washington D.C.: U.S. Government Printing Office.
National Opinion Research Center
  1954   *Human Relations in Disaster Situations.* Chicago: National Opinion Research Center.
Nkrumah, Kwame
  1969   *Handbook of Revolutionary Warfare.* New York: International Publishers.
Oberschall, Anthony
  1968   "The Los Angeles Riot of August 1965," *Social Problems* 15:322–341.
Park, Robert E.
  1924   *Introduction to the Science of Sociology.* Chicago: University of Chicago Press.
Peck, James
  1962   *Freedom Ride.* New York: Simon & Schuster.
Penrose, L. S.
  1952   *On the Objective Study of Crowd Behavior.* London: H. K. Lewis.
Perrow, Charles
  1979   The Sixties Observed, in Mayer Zald and John D. McCarthy (eds.), *The Dynamics of Social Movements.* Cambridge, MA: Winthrop Publishers, pp. 192–211.

Perry, Joseph, and Pugh, M. D.
  1978   *Collective Behavior: Response to Social Stress.* St. Paul, MN: West Publishing.
Perry, Ronald, and Lindell, Michael K.
  1978   "The Psychological Consequences of Natural Disaster: A Review of Research on American Communities," *Mass Emergencies* (September):105–115.
Perry, S. E.; Silbert, E.; and Bloch, D. A.
  1953   "*The Child and His Family in Disasters.*" Pub. no. 394. Washington, D.C.: National Academy of Sciences, National Research Council.
Peterson, Richard E., and Bilorusky, John
  1971   *May 1970: The Aftermath of Cambodia and Kent State.* Berkeley, CA: The Carnegie Commission on Higher Education.
Piven, Frances F., and Cloward, Richard A.
  1979   *Poor People's Movements: Why They Succeed, How They Fail.* New York: Vintage Books.
Platt, Anthony M.
  1969   *The Child Savers.* Chicago: University of Chicago Press.
Pruden, Durward
  1936   "A Sociological Study of a Texas Lynching," *Studies in Sociology* 1 (1):1–8. Also in Bobbs-Merrill *Reprint Series in the Social Sciences S-479.*
Quarantelli, Enrico L.
  1957   "The Behavior of Panic Participants," *Sociology and Social Research* 41:187–194.
  1970   "Emergency Accommodation Groups: Beyond Current Collective Behavior Typologies," in Tamotsu Shibutani (ed.), *Human Nature and Collective Behavior: Papers in Honor of Herbert Blumer.* Englewood Cliffs, NJ: Prentice-Hall, pp. 111–123.
Quarantelli, Enrico L., and Dynes, Russell R.
  1968   "Looting in Civil Disorders: An Index of Social Change," *American Behavioral Scientist* 5:7–10.
  1969   "Dissensus and Consensus in Community Emergencies: Patterns of Looting and Property Norms," *Il Politico* 34:276–291.
Quarantelli, Enrico L., and Hundley, James R., Jr.
  1969   "A Test of Some Propositions about Crowd Formation and Behavior," in Robert R. Evans (ed.), *Readings in Collective Behavior.* Chicago: Rand McNally, pp. 538–554.
  1975   "A Test of Some Propositions about Crowd Formation and Behavior," in Robert R.

Evans (ed.), *Readings in Collective Behavior*. Chicago: Rand McNally, pp. 370–387.

Rappaport, Roy A.
1971   "The Flow of Energy in an Agricultural Society," *Scientific American* 225(3):116–132.

Rose, Jerry D.
1982   *Outbreaks: The Sociology of Collective Behavior*. New York: Free Press.

Rosen, Richard D.
1979   *Psychobabble*, New York: Avon Books.

Rosengren, Karl E.; Arvidson, Peter; and Sturesson, Dahn
1975   "The Barsebak Panic: A Radio Program as a Negative Summary Event," *Acta Sociological* 57:309–314. Also in Meredith D. Pugh (ed.), *Collective Behavior: A Source Book*, 1980. St. Paul, MN: West Publishing.

Rosenthal, A. M.
1964   *Thirty-Eight Witnesses*. New York: McGraw-Hill.

Rosnow, Ralph L., and Fine, Gary A.
1976   *Rumor and Gossip: The Social Psychology of Hearsay*. New York: Elsevier.

Ross, James L.
1970   "The Salvation Army: Emergency Operations," *American Behavioral Scientist* 13:404–414.

Roth, Robert
1970   "Cross-Cultural Perspectives on Disaster Response," *American Behavioral Scientist* 13:440–451.

Rudé, George
1959   *The Crowd in the French Revolution*. Oxford, England: Clarendon Press.
1964   *The Crowd in History, 1730–1848*. New York: John Wiley.

Sachs, Margaret
1980   *The UFO Encyclopedia*. New York: G. P. Putnam's.

Sanders, William T., and Marino, Joseph
1970   *New World Prehistory: Archaeology of the American Indian*. Englewood Cliffs, NJ: Prentice-Hall.

Sann, Paul
1967   *Fads, Follies, and Delusions of the American People*. New York: Crown.

Sapir, Edward
1937   "Fashion," in *Encyclopedia of the Social Sciences* (vol. 3). New York: Macmillan, pp. 139–144.

Schaefer, Richard T.
1979   *Racial and Ethnic Groups*. Boston: Little, Brown.
1983   *Sociology*. New York: McGraw-Hill.

Schaufele, William E., Jr.
1981   *Polish Paradox: Communism and National Renewal*. Headline Series 256. New York: Foreign Policy Association.

Schrier, Arnold
1958   *Ireland and the American Emigration, 1850–1900*. Minneapolis: University of Minnesota Press.

Sharp, Lauriston
1952   "Steel Axes for Stone Age Australians," in Edward H. Spicer (ed.), *Human Problems in Technological Change*. New York: Russell Sage Foundation, pp. 69–90.

Shibutani, Tamotsu
1966   *Improvised News: A Sociological Study of Rumor*. Indianapolis, IN: Bobbs-Merrill.

Silber, Earl; Perry, Stewart E.; and Bloch, Donald A.
1957   "Patterns of Parent-Child Interaction in Disaster," *Psychiatry* 21(2):159–167.

Simmel, George
1904   "Fashion," *International Quarterly* 10:541–558. Also in *American Journal of Sociology* 62, 1957.

Singer, Benjamin; Osborn, Richard W.; and Geschwender, James
1970   *Black Rioters*. Lexington, MA: D.C. Heath.

Smelser, Neil
1962   *Theory of Collective Behavior*. New York: Free Press.

Smith, Cecil W.
1962   *The Great Hunger*. New York: Harper & Row.

Snyder, David
1979   "Collective Violence Processes: Implications for Disaggregated Theory and Research," in Louis Kriesberg (ed.), *Research in Social Movements, Conflicts and Change: A Research Annual* (vol. 2). Greenwich, CT: JAI Press, pp. 35–61.

Snyder, David, and Tilly, Charles
1972   "Hardship and Collective Violence in France," *American Sociological Review* 37:520–532.

Spilerman, Seymour
1970   "The Causes of Racial Disturbances: A

Comparison of Alternate Explanations," *American Sociological Review* (August):627–649.

1971 "The Causes of Racial Disturbances: Tests of an Explanation," *American Sociological Review* 36 (June):427–442.

1976 "Structural Characteristics of Cities and the Severity of Racial Disorders," *American Sociological Review* 41:771–793.

Stalin, Joseph

1953 *The Russian Social-Democratic Party and Its Immediate Tasks.* Moscow: Foreign Languages Publishing House.

Stewart, James R.

1977 "Cattle Mutilations: An Episode of Collective Delusion," *The Zetetic* 1:55–66.

1980 "Collective Delusion: A Comparison of Believers and Skeptics," paper presented at the annual meeting of the Midwest Sociological Society, Milwaukee, Wisconsin.

1984 "On the Nature of Mass Hysteria," paper presented at the annual meeting of the Midwest Sociological Society, Chicago.

Stewart, Robert L.

1969 "Toward a Behavioristic Behavioral Science." Department of Sociology, University of South Carolina. Mimeographed.

Stone, Charles P.

1969 "The Lessons of Detroit, Summer 1967," in Robin Higham (ed.), *Bayonets in the Streets: The Use of Troops in Civil Disturbances.* Lawrence: University Press of Kansas, pp. 185–203.

Strasel, H. C., and Larkin, Paul G.

1968 *Rioters in Washington: A Study of People and Employment.* Falls Church, VA: Software Systems.

Strauss, Anselm L.

1944 "The Literature on Panic," *Journal of Abnormal and Social Psychology* 39:317–328.

Strybel, Robert

1981 "Report from Warsaw," *PolAmerica Magazine* 4:8–27.

Tarde, Gabriel

1903 *The Laws of Imitation.* New York: Holt, Rinehart & Winston.

Taylor, James B.; Zurcher, Louis A.; and Key, William H.

1970 *Tornado: A Community Response to Disaster.* Seattle: University of Washington Press.

Thomlinson, T.M.

1968 "The Development of a Riot Ideology among Urban Negroes," *American Behavioral Scientist* 2:27–31.

Tilly, Charles

1969 "Collective Violence in European Perspective," in Hugh D. Graham and Ted R. Gurr (eds.), *The History of Violence in America: Historical and Comparative Perspectives.* New York: Praeger, pp. 4–44.

1975 "Revolutions and Collective Violence," in Fred Greenstein and Nelson Polsby (eds.), *Handbook of Political Science* (vol. 3). Reading, MA: Addison Wesley, pp. 483–555.

Traugott, Mark

1978 "Reconceiving Social Movements," *Social Problems* 26:38–49.

Tumin, Melvin M., and Feldman, Arnold S.

1955 "The Miracle at Sabana Grande," *Public Opinion Quarterly* 19:124–139.

Turner, Ralph H., and Killian, Lewis M.

1957 *Collective Behavior.* Englewood Cliffs, NJ: Prentice-Hall.

1972 *Collective Behavior.* 2d ed. Englewood Cliffs, NJ: Prentice-Hall.

Turner, Ralph H., and Surace, Samuel J.

1956 "Zoot-Suiters and Mexicans: Symbols in Crowd Behavior," *American Journal of Sociology* 62:14–20.

Vacca, Roberto

1974 *The Coming Dark Age.* Garden City, NY: Anchor Press/Doubleday.

Veblen, Thorstein

1912 *The Theory of the Leisure Class: An Economic Study of Institutions.* New York: Macmillan.

Velfort, Helene R., and Lee, George

1943 "The Cocoanut Grove Fire: A Study of Scapegoating," *Journal of Abnormal and Social Psychology* 38:138–154.

Walker, Henry Pickering

1966 *The Wagonmasters: High Plains Freighting from the Earliest Days of the Santa Fe Trail to 1880.* Norman: University of Oklahoma Press.

Wallace, Anthony F.C.

1957 "Mazeway Disintegration: The Individual Perception of Sociocultural Disorganization," *Human Organization* 16:23–27.

Warheit, George J.
  1970   "Fire Departments: Organizations during Major Community Emergencies," *American
  Behavioral Scientist* 13:362–368.
Wenger, Dennis E.
  1978   "Community Response to Disaster:
  Functional and Structural Alterations," in Enrico
  L. Quarantelli (ed.), *Disaster: Theory and Re-
  search*. Beverly Hills, CA: Sage, pp. 17–49.
Westrum, Ron
  1978   "Social Intelligence about Anomalies:
  The Case of Meteorites," *Social Studies of Science* 8:461–493.
Wheeler, Ladd; Deci, E. L.; Reis, H. T.; and Zuck-
  erman, M.
  1978   *Interpersonal Influence*. 2d ed. Boston:
  Allyn & Bacon.
Williams, Higbee
  1962   "Mobs and Riots," *American Jurispru-
  dence* 54:499–548.
Winfrey, Carey
  1979   "Why 900 Died in Guyana," *New York
  Times Magazine* , February 25.
Woelfel, Joseph; Woelfel, John; Gillham, James;
  and McPhail, Thomas
  1974   "Political Radicalization as a Communication Process," *Communications Research*
  1:243:–263.
Wohlstein, Ronald T.
  1977   " Filming Collective Behavior and the
  Problem of Foreshortened Perspective: A Cor-
  rective Method," *Studies in the Anthropology of
  Visual Communication* 4:81–85.
  1982   "Riot Participation: Some Proposals
  for Future Study," paper presented at the Midwest Sociological Society, Kansas City, Missouri.
Wood, James L., and Jackson, Maurice
  1982   *Social Movements: Development, Participation and Dynamics*. Belmont, CA: Wadsworth.
Wormington, H. M.
  1957   *Ancient Man in North America*. 4th ed.
  Denver Museum of Natural History, Popular Series no. 4.
Wright, James D.; Rossi, Peter H.; Wright, Sonia
  R.; and Weber-Burdin, Eleanor
  1979   *After the Clean-Up: Long Range Effects
  of Natural Disasters*. Beverly Hills, CA: Sage.
Zald, Mayer N., and Ash, Roberta
  1964   "Social Movement Organization: Growth,
  Decay, and Change," *Social Forces* 44:327–341.

Zald, Mayer, and McCarthy, John D.
  1980   "Social Movement Industries: Competition and Cooperation among Movement Organizations," in Lewis Kriesberg (ed.), *Research in
  Social Movements, Conflicts and Change* (vol.
  3). Greenwich, CT: JAI Press, pp. 1–20.
Zinn, Howard
  1964   *SNCC: The New Abolitionists*. Boston: Beacon Press.
Zurcher, Louis A.
  1968   "Social-Psychological Functions of
  Ephemeral Roles: A Disaster Work Crew," *Human Organization* 27:281–297. Also in Meredith
  Pugh (ed.), *Collective Behavior: A Source Book*,
  1980. St. Paul, MN: West Publishing.
Zurcher, Louis A., and Snow, David
  1981   "Collective Behavior: Social Movements," in Ralph Turner and Morris Rosenberg
  (eds.), *Social Psychology*. New York: Basic
  Books, pp. 450–482.

NAME INDEX

◆ SUBJECT INDEX ◆